KT-223-517

DICTIONARY OF THIRD WORLD TERMS

Kofi Buenor Hadjor is Professor of African Studies at the University of California, Santa Barbara. He has had first-hand experience of Third World politics as a press aide in the Publicity Secretariat of Kwame Nkrumah's government. He also represented Ghana on the permanent secretariat of the Cairo-based Afro-Asian Peoples' Solidarity Organization and was UNESCO communications adviser to the government of Tanzania. He created and, for a long time, edited the influential international quarterly *Third World Book Review*; he was editor of *New African*, a leading news magazine on Africa; and has been Director of the Tanzania School of Journalism. His most recent publications include *On Transforming Africa: Discourse with Africa's Leaders* (1987), *Kwame Nkrumah and Ghana: The Dilemma of Post-Colonial Power* (1988) and *Africa in an Era of Crisis* (1989). He has also edited *On the Brink: Nuclear Proliferation and the Third World* (with Peter Worsley, 1987) and *New Perspectives in North–South Dialogue: Essays in Honour of Olaf Palme* (1988).

KOFI BUENOR HADJOR

DICTIONARY OF
THIRD WORLD TERMS

PENGUIN BOOKS

To my daughter and friend, Dede Malika
To Kyrah Malika Daniels and Najda Ife Robinson
To Elizabeth Robinson and Claudine Michel

PENGUIN BOOKS

Published by the Penguin Group
Penguin Books Ltd, 27 Wrights Lane, London W8 5TZ, England
Penguin Books USA Inc., 375 Hudson Street, New York, New York 10014, USA
Penguin Books Australia Ltd, Ringwood, Victoria, Australia
Penguin Books Canada Ltd, 10 Alcorn Avenue, Toronto, Ontario, Canada M4V 3B2
Penguin Books (NZ) Ltd, 182–190 Wairau Road, Auckland 10, New Zealand

Penguin Books Ltd, Registered Offices: Harmondsworth, Middlesex, England

First published by I. B. Tauris & Co., in association with Penguin Books Ltd, 1992
Published, with additional entries, in Penguin Books 1993
3 5 7 9 10 8 6 4 2

Printed in England by Clays Ltd, St Ives plc

To the memory of Elizabeth R. Harris,
mother of Jeanne Levy-Hinte,
for her kindness to me

Introduction

For centuries prior to the great upheaval of the Second World War it was the countries of Europe and those established by European immigrants which monopolized the starring roles on the historical stage. Other countries appeared in small supporting roles as causes of European rivalry or areas of European conquest. The most significant change in the nature of world history since 1945 has been the emergence of the countries which had been eclipsed by Europe onto the centre of the stage to assume important and often determining roles.

In the latter half of the century now approaching its close most major social and political upheavals have taken place in what has been variously known as the 'East', the 'South', the 'Colonial World' and the 'Third World'. The independence of India, the Chinese revolution, the Korean War, the Cuban revolution, the Vietnam War, the Palestine question, South Africa and the Gulf War are some of the events which have dominated post-war international relations.

Not surprisingly, before 1945 little attention was given to the study of the history or social and economic reality of the Third World. Africa, Asia, Latin America and the Middle East were regarded, even by many of their inhabitants, as peripheral to world affairs. What they had in common was no more than their shared exclusion from a central role in history. Books about these continents tended to be by authors with esoteric interests and tended to concentrate on the strange and exotic. This was one of the ways in which the nature of what was normal, developed and European was defined. In the universities anthropologists wrote their monographs for an audience composed mainly of colonial administrators.

After the Second World War all this was turned upside down. A war which originated among the traditionally strong European powers had the ironic result of shaking the nineteenth-century colonial system to its foundations. Mass movements demanded independence and liberation and threatened the control of the leading colonial powers. Major problems invite and necessitate study and this upsurge of revolt unleashed an avalanche of study and writing on hitherto ignored areas of the world.

To begin with, very little of this study could be termed objective. It was undertaken with more explicit political ends in the context of a world dominated by the bipolar conflict between the USSR and the USA and their respective allies in the 'East' and the 'West'. The new breed of specialists on questions related to the Third World responded in grand measure to the ideological exigencies of the Cold War between the superpowers. 'Theories' about development often on examination turned out to be no more than apologetics for one social system or another and to have no roots in the reality of the Third World or of history.

Not all writing on the Third World was of this kind, and over the years a substantial body of important analytical and theoretical writing by scholars and writers in the developed countries and from the Third World itself has demanded attention and has influenced thinking. At the same time the study of the Third World has become a subject in its own right. While tens of thousands of books claim authority on Third World issues, universities all over the world offer a huge range of courses on the Third World and support research and study institutes on the Third World.

It is natural that out of this vast volume of new literature and study has developed a new vocabulary – indeed various new vocabularies – and the aim of this book is to make a critical evaluation of this vocabulary. It is neither a dictionary nor a reference book of a traditional kind. There are already a large number of such reference books available on the Third World, many of which are useful or even indispensable. Many of them, however, assume exactly what we aim to question here: the meaning of the vocabulary which we use in discussing the Third World. To take meanings for granted, to fail to explore them critically, is to restrict the analytical power of study. That is why our objective in this book is not simply to define but to assess critically both definitions and usages.

In hardly any field of study are words straightforward technical terms capable of uncomplicated, unambiguous definitions. This fact is particularly true of the study of the Third World, both because it is a relatively new field of study and because it is a field into which numerous ideological, political and social conflicts enter. The vocabulary of Third World studies is therefore more liable than most to be imbued with problems. Words may express a particular experience or attitude or cultural norm or viewpoint; or they may involve a prejudgement of the questions to which they correspond.

The problems are many: one is a very high degree of imprecision of terms, not surprising in an area of study which is so new and where writers and scholars are searching for terms adequate to the reality. It is disappointing, none the less, that few people who use these terms are aware of their imprecise and provisional nature and most use them in an uncritical manner. Another general problem arises from the fact that such a vast amount of the study of the Third World takes place in the developed countries of the North. The North's dominance of the cultural and intellectual life of the world, springing from its economic and political dominance, means that many words used to describe and analyse the Third World contain and reflect the assumptions of external observers, often imbued with a sense of the superiority of their own societies, sometimes ethnocentric and in the extreme cases racist.

The vocabulary of the Third World is therefore a battlefield of conflicting meanings. This dictionary is not the work of a war correspondent but of a participant in the battle, attempting to fight for clarity and analytical power from the standpoint of the Third World and its people.

We have been unable even to enter this battlefield without beginning to use a term whose history and present are problematic and conflictive. So, before anything else, to indicate the nature and direction of the work as a whole let us pause and explore the meaning of the term 'Third World' itself.

The Third World

The French economist and demographer Alfred Sauvy must take the credit for first using the term 'Third World' in an article published in 1952. But the concept which the term expresses is not the invention of a single intellectual but rather the reflection of the reality of the continents which have been excluded from power in the world. The term has come to embody the idea that this very exclusion has generated a set of common characteristics in the historical experience of the peoples of Africa, Asia, Latin America and the Middle East. What drew attention to these common characteristics was not one individual's observation but rather a set of common reactions by the peoples of many Third World countries to their position in the world – reactions of unrest, struggle and resistance to their opposition. The attraction of the term has partly been due to its seeming avoidance of the static and often negative connotations of other terms used to encapsulate the same areas of the world.

Before the term 'Third World' appeared, a very different vocabulary held the field. Words like 'backward', 'underdeveloped', 'uncivilized', 'primitive', even 'barbarian' or 'savage', abounded and expressed both the traditions of Western superiority, whether it be in a racist or paternalist version. Such terms stress the inferiority of what is being described and at the same time suggest an objective for the improvement of such societies: to be 'advanced', 'developed', 'civilized' – in other words to emulate the countries of the West.

The term 'Third World' does not carry these connotations. The emphasis of Alfred Sauvy when he coined the term was on the exclusion and aspiration of the Third World. His article concludes with the words: 'the Third World has, like the Third Estate, been ignored and despised and it too wants to be something.'[1] Sauvy saw the Third World (Tiers Monde) as a modern parallel to the Third Estate (Tiers État) of the French Revolution – the class of commoners. In this way Sauvy's term carries not only the connotation of exclusion from power but also, especially from a French writer, the idea of revolutionary potential. Sauvy's idea of the meaning of the 'third' of the Third World was, however, different from the 'third' of the Third Estate. The latter was third in a social hierarchy in which the second (the clergy) was subordinate to the first (the aristocracy). For Sauvy the third meant less 'number three in a hierarchy' but rather 'excluded from its proper role in the world by two other worlds' – namely, the East and West whose conflict monopolized the spotlight of history. It was this concept of the Third World as an excluded world which meant that the First World and the Second World have not become popular concepts in the same way as the Third World. The third in a hierarchy of three or more does not mean the same as the third which is different from both of two others.

It is mostly in relation to this sense of 'third' – as excluded and aspiring to a role in history independent of the superpowers and the conflicts between them – that there has been some overlap between the 'Third World' and other terms such as 'non-aligned' or 'tricontinental'.

There is another notion of third to which the term 'Third World' has also often given rise, and which perhaps can also be found in Sauvy's article, in which third means something other than 'each one' of, rather than 'both' of, the other two. In this sense the 'Third World' has been interpreted as the setting for a third social and economic system different from the capitalism and the socialism of the first and second worlds.

Not all concepts of the Third World have defined the first two in the same way. One of the most influential adoptions of the term was by Mao Zedong, whose definition of the 'first' and 'second' worlds was different from the ones mentioned so far. In Mao's analysis the first world represents the superpowers which dominate international relations (the USA and the USSR), the second world consists of the subalterns of these two powers (the smaller developed countries mostly of Western and Eastern Europe, the members of NATO and the Warsaw Pact), and the Third World, as in other analyses, consists of all the poor and powerless countries,[2] including, of course, China. For Mao, the theory of the differentiation of the three worlds is at the same time a critique of the hegemony of the superpowers. Maoist political analysis depicts superpower domination as the key threat to China and the rest of the Third World. It is for this reason that the preamble to the 1975 constitution of the People's Republic of China states that 'China will never be a superpower'.

Perhaps something should be said not only about the nature of the meanings attached to 'third' but also those attached to 'world'. The importance of the word has been to draw attention to the vast extent of the areas which form part of the Third World. They are, it suggests, at least as much a world as the countries which dominate world history, containing as they do around three-quarters of the world's population and including two countries each of which have populations the size of the total world population at the beginning of the twentieth century, and several with a population greater than that of the world as a whole at the start of the nineteenth century.

It also can suggest that the Third World is a world of ideas and culture as well as of functioning economic, political and social systems. In short, if it is a 'world' then it should be able to exist and function on its own independently of the other worlds which dominate it.

Some of these connotations were hidden in the term when it was first used and only emerged with more explicitness later. They help to explain, however, why after the initial resistance, the term acquired such popularity – it seems to be compatible with a positive outlook on the Third World which does not presuppose that the answer to all its problems is to become exactly like the first or second worlds.

This much can be seen with hindsight. The initial resistance to the term, however, was very strong. Four years after Sauvy's coining of the phrase a group of left-wing French intellectuals took it up and founded a renowned journal with the title *Tiers Monde*, but it was to be at least another decade before use of the term became widespread. It filtered from its French origins into other sections of the left in the West, but its more widespread use was hampered by strong 'official' opposition in both West and East.

Western writers were wary of a term which was used almost exclusively by writers of the left and which seemed to contain connotations of a disinherited world with potential for forging its own future. If the old terminology of explicit superiority or ethnocentrism was gradually being abandoned because the new world climate made it increasingly embarrassing, the new terminology which replaced it emphasized not dispossession and independence but poverty, unreadiness and backwardness. A metaphor of age crept in. The ex-colonial countries were 'young' or 'emerging', which by implication needed to grow up under the tutelage of more mature adults and might also be expected to be for a time irresponsible. So Third World protests could be explained away: they were irresponsible youthful exuberance rather than a revolt against dispossession. That many of the 'young' nations had a much longer national history than some of the 'mature' nations of the West was forgotten; young nations had no history or their history could be regarded as irrelevant to their modern condition since they were starting out again.

Alongside the metaphor of age sprung up another variety of terminology which stressed economic, political and social backwardness. The nations of the Third World were undeveloped or had traditional societies, and so by implication they needed to be developed and modernized. Such words seemed to carry the rider (often explicitly theorized) that under- or undevelopment was an original state, akin in the poor countries to the situation of the richer countries centuries earlier; and that the way out was to pursue the policies which brought the richer countries of the West out of their backwardness. This terminology later changed, as the countries of the Third World gained more influence, into more euphemistic forms like 'less-developed' or 'developing' or 'low-income'. (▶ euphemisms, ▶ modernization, ▶ stages of economic growth, ▶ underdevelopment.)

In this way the youth or undevelopment of the poor countries provided a kind of apologia on the causes of underdevelopment. This seemed to rule out the idea that the Third World had in many ways been systematically prevented from developing by the already developed countries and that its poverty and underdevelopment might be the dark side of the same coin which had made some countries rich and powerful.

So in the West, in official and conservative circles at least, the new term made little headway at first and it is not hard to find strong ideological reasons why. Yet in the East also, the so-called second world, the term met with a great deal of resistance. The USSR, and most of the official communist parties under its influence, rejected the term mainly because it seemed to imply that there might be an alternative to capitalism other than that provided by the official Soviet-led communist movement. A Soviet writer summed up the view by saying that the term was illegitimate because in reality the countries concerned 'frequently side with one or the other of the two main social systems even though they are not part of the same system'.[3]

It was not only Soviet-line communists who rejected the term but also others who regarded themselves as orthodox Marxists. Their argument was either that the term 'Third World' seemed to offer a non-socialist alternative to capitalism or that it disguised the fact that the under-developed countries were by and large an integral part of the capitalist world economic system.

In addition to Marxists, many influential thinkers in the Third World rejected the term for similar reasons. One such was Kwame Nkrumah who objected to the use of the term 'Third World' because of its popular identification with non-alignment. According to Nkrumah, the 'very mention of the "Third World" suggests some kind of passivity, a non-participation, an opting out of the conflict between the worlds of capitalism and socialism'.[4] Nkrumah argues that there is no middle way between socialism and capitalism and to suggest a third road invites only passivity. According to Nkrumah, the oppressed nations are objectively on the side of socialism. From his point of view there are only two worlds: 'the revolutionary world and the counter-revolutionary world – the socialist world tending towards communism and the capitalist world with its extensions of imperialism, colonialism and neo-colonialism'.[5] In other words Nkrumah, from a standpoint in the Third World, adopted a position very similar to that of the orthodox communists. It seems to us, however, that there is a difference betwen Nkrumah's formal conclusion (rejecting the use of the 'Third World') and the implicit content of his views.

This, then, was the situation towards the end of the 1960s: the Third World was a term used mostly by a small number of Western left-wing, but not orthodox Marxist, intellectuals; and then in the space of a decade and a half the term became all but universal in West and East and in the Third World itself, and to a great extent it also broke ideological barriers even though the old terminology still prevails in the official publications of international organizations. What was the cause and meaning of this sudden change of fortune for the term 'Third World'?

The main one was surely the emergence of a growing consciousness among the peoples of different Third World countries themselves that they shared significant common problems and experiences in relation to other countries. This common consciousness was partly aroused by identification with a number of political and military struggles (most particularly Vietnam) against the imperialism of the big, largely Western, powers. But it was also affected by less dramatic confrontations such as those which took place at major international conferences in which the poorer countries increasingly acted together to obtain some redress for what was considered an unjust world economic order (▶ NIEO, ▶ Group of 77). Because 'Third World' became not only acceptable, but increasingly the chosen terminology in the Third World itself, it was adopted by all those who wished to show solidarity with, or simply not excessively to offend, the Third World.

The term 'Third World' is useful, of course, only if it captures something which all its supposed components have in common and which transcends their obvious differences. These differences, therefore, and the fact that in many respects they have continued to grow, have been used by some commentators and analysts to question the validity of the Third World concept.

Such evident differences between countries are still used to call into question the original validity of the concept. Nigel Harris, for instance, in his book *The End of the Third World*, suggests that 'newly industrializing countries and the majority of the low-income countries had as little in common with each other as each had with the more developed countries'. He concludes by arguing that the 'very poor – like the very rich – existed everywhere, in all "worlds", and the responsibility for sustaining or changing poverty lay not with different worlds but with one world of reality'.[6] According to this approach, there is only one world and the term 'Third World' simply mystifies the fact that all nations are part of a single system. Such a critique, therefore, though it uses the well-known economic differences of more recent origin between different countries, is essentially one which could have been made at any time during the debate.

What is left of official communist movements after the developments of the late 1980s has often adopted the terminology of the Third World but continued to stress differences within it between socialist-oriented and other countries. Concessions on vocabulary do not always imply any acceptance of the concepts which originated that vocabulary.

Recently we have entered, according to some viewpoints, a period which might be described as 'post-Third World'. Some writers, without exactly rejecting the validity of the term, have argued that it has at least partly lost its relevance because of the profound differences in the recent experiences of Africa, Asia, Latin America and the Middle East. It is an emphasis on these differences, especially the economic ones, which has led to the invention of terms like the 'least developed countries' as distinct from the 'developing countries' which, in less official parlance, has been translated as the 'Fourth World' as opposed to the 'Third World'. The differentiation into third and fourth worlds is justified by a distinction between the experiences of countries such as the so-called newly industrializing countries (▶ NICs) which have had high levels of growth in output and exports plus a marked degree of industrialization and, at the other extreme, many of the countries of Africa which have experienced decades of decline in their national income and lurch from crisis to crisis. Since there is such an enormous difference in economic circumstances and record how, it is asked, can such countries all be placed in the same category?

It is in attempting to answer that question that we can decide whether or not the terminology and conceptualization of the Third World has been and continues to be valid. For no one can assert that the countries which have been held to compose the Third World do not exhibit tremendous differences – historically, politically, culturally and economically. The question is: do they also have enough in common historically, politically, culturally or economically to include them in a common analytical category which contrasts them qualitatively with other countries? In order to understand the world is it useful and important to draw this particular line between groups of countries?

It seems to us that the answer is still very clearly in the affirmative: that the concept of the Third World, while it does not for one moment answer

7

all relevant questions, is a concept of fundamental importance for understanding the world as a whole. One way in which we can try to demonstrate that is by dismissing the various arguments against the use of the concept.

The main arguments used against the concept are two: that it postulates a non-existent third road to development which is neither capitalist nor socialist; and that it postulates a non-existent unity within a group of countries which in fact are very diverse.

To the first objection there are logically two possible replies: that such a third way does exist or that the concept does not necessarily suggest that. Our argument is not that there exists really or potentially some third social system, neither capitalist nor socialist, which is or will be the social system of the Third World. It is rather that the countries of the Third World, be they capitalist or socialist, share a set of historically determined socio-economic characteristics which mean that both capitalism and socialism have different characteristics in a Third World country than in a developed country. A capitalist Third World country is qualitatively different from a developed capitalist country due to its inferior exploited situation within the world capitalist division of labour. A Third World country attempting to pursue a non-capitalist path will, for the same reason, encounter problems which would not arise in a developed country attempting to do the same; and these problems result from the heritage of capitalist and colonial exploitation.

There is also another response to this argument which has been gaining ground in debates about the Third World: that development in Third World countries need not and should not assume the same characteristics as development has assumed in both capitalist and socialist developed countries. While not necessarily sharing all versions of this argument, it seems to us to have the merit of allowing an element of choice to the Third World in the definition of its social and economic objectives. It therefore makes some sense to think of a third road which is not an alternative to capitalism and socialism in the abstract but which may be regarded as an alternative to actually existing capitalism and socialism.

As to the second main argument against the use of the term, it would be absurd not to recognize that there are very wide differences between Third World countries with regard to just about any social or economic indicator (▶human development, ▶indicators, ▶NICs, ▶purchasing power parity). It is also necessary to recognize that in many ways the polarization between countries is increasing. We believe, however, that despite all these differences there is a real qualitative divide between the countries of the Third World and the developed countries and that the root of this qualitative divide is the difference in their national historical experience of the modern era of capitalist development and industrialization. The idea of the Third World is closely connected with the rejection of the notion that all countries are qualitatively equal and are ranged along a linear axis between undeveloped and developed, and so 'development' is the same process for all. This was the original contention of thinking about development in both capitalist and socialist circles. Subsequently, however, an increasing body of writing, perhaps especially from what has been called the school of ▶ dependency theory, originating to a great extent within the Third World itself, has undermined this idea. It has substituted the much more powerful idea that the underdevelopment of today is not an original state but is something which has been created both as a by-product and as a condition of development. The process has been, therefore, one of systematic polarization; and the Third World is that part of the world which has been on the negative side of that polarization. Dependency theorists have often employed a difference between metropolis and periphery to capture this difference. But, except in rather academic circles, the terminology has not gained much popular usage. The Third World has often been used instead within analyses which are essentially based on dependency theory. The influence of this theory therefore has indirectly helped to popularize the term 'Third World'.

At the empirical level it is possible to identify many manifestations of the continued importance of that qualitative, historical gulf: the structure of economies, the form and degree of participation in world markets, and in political power in the world (▶ agrarian question, ▶ exports). The basic difference, however, is not a descriptive empirical, quantitative one which can be grasped with a few facts. Percentages and averages can convey something of the difference but perhaps a more powerful idea of it can be gained simply by sensitive observation: anyone who has walked in the streets of Cairo, Lusaka, Bombay, São Paulo or Kuala Lumpur will surely be struck by the presence of something similar. This often intangible similarity cannot be reduced merely to poverty. Poor European cities like Palermo or Lisbon are very different from their Third World counterparts. What distinguishes what you see in Cairo from what you see in Lisbon is their history. The social and economic landscape of the Third World in all its aspects is conditioned by the cumulative effect of colonization, imperialism and Western domination. What one cannot fail to see is a society distorted by the imprint of protracted foreign domination. Even countries such as Cuba, Nicaragua, Vietnam or Laos which have opted for a radical break with the past are haunted by the same historical legacy, which is the basic reason why we distinguish between the Third World and the rest of the globe.

It is our contention that this gulf is real and that, therefore, the terminology of the Third World remains valid and analytically powerful. This does not imply that other divisions and other gulfs between countries, some of which may even cut across the Third World and developed country divide, are not also real and important. But we do insist that the divide which produced the idea of the Third World is qualitatively fundamental and justifies this analytical grouping of the countries of the world.

After the late 1960s there was a growing disillusion with optimistic perspectives for the development of poor countries, as well as the growing realization (helped by the Vietnam War) of the political/military hostility between developed and poor countries. These changes in ideas contributed to a growing influence of the critical, historical view of underdevelopment and so reinforced the use of the term 'Third World' which, the old objections notwithstanding, became almost universal. The universalization of the term, however, does not by any means imply universalization of the thinking which underlies it. The term 'Third World' was introduced as part of a substantive and not merely a terminological battle. Its widespread use today is evidence of the power of that substantive argument. It is important, therefore, to realize that the Third World is not merely a shorthand way of saying Africa, Asia, Latin America and the Middle East, but is a term which implies an analysis of the world.

It is not a term which should be understood in a primarily geographical sense as referring to continents and countries; it refers to the experience and formation of the societies and peoples which inhabit these countries. For this reason it seems entirely appropriate that the term has acquired very common usage in progressive American movements when referring to citizens and inhabitants of the USA whose ethnic and national origin is geographically in the Third World. So the very large non-white populations of the USA whose origins, often very distant, are in Africa or Latin America or Asia are increasingly referred to as Third World people. Such usage has not significantly spread to Europe, but it seems appropriate in some ways that it should since it refers to a shared experience of people inside the developed countries which arises from the historical formation of their countries of origin. In this way the term may come increasingly to have an ethnic as well as a national and a historical dimension.

While many have accepted the term without accepting the thinking behind it, others have shared the thinking while never accepting the term. It is now possible to see that a number of those who objected to the term when its use was first proposed did so on grounds which with hindsight look very like the same arguments we have used for accepting it. What Nkrumah called the 'oppressed' peoples, for instance, are the same as the countries of the Third World, even though he rejected the term.

What ultimately remains important is not the terminology but the analysis. However, this dictionary bears the title *Dictionary of Third World Terms* because we believe that the term 'Third World' still best encapsulates a particular way of analysing the world. It is a way which helps us see that the existence of a generalized crisis of agriculture or of political legitimacy in virtually all African countries, or the existence of civil war and conflict in places as far apart and dissimilar as Fiji, Sri Lanka and Lebanon are not coincidences but rather manifestations of a common historical legacy which makes all these countries part of a single entity – the Third World. To say that is not, of course, to analyse each of these phenomena; the use of the term is not a substitute for the specific analysis of specific societies, but it does suggest a starting point for the examination of all the variants of social and political development. We cannot change the history which has produced the Third World; but we cannot change the Third World without some awareness of this history. That is the strength of the term.

We do not contend that the term 'Third World' is very precise or that it by itself conveys much meaning. The importance of using it as the primary term to refer to all the countries comprised by the concept is that it symbolizes a particular form of analysis, one not symbolized by any of the other terms in use. The actually existing alternatives at present are:

(1) to use no term at all for the countries of Africa, Asia, Latin America, the Caribbean and the Middle East; this signifies that they do not have anything significant in common;

(2) to use rather cold, clinical, technical terms like 'low income countries', 'countries of low human development', 'developing countries', 'less developed countries'; these terms have been chosen by international and official agencies as largely euphemistic terms which carry little more than a descriptive, statistical meaning;

(3) to use the terminology of North–South which has also gained considerable popularity, partly because of its use by the ▶ Brandt Report, which we shall certainly use from time to time as a shorthand for 'Third World', but which contains the danger of converting a social, economic and political division into a geographical one;

(4) to use the terms 'centre' (or 'metropolis') and 'periphery', which do carry considerable analytical force but which are burdened with a rather inaccessible academic flavour;

(5) to speak of the Third World, which, for all its ambiguities and problems, suggests that the countries included have something in common; this arises particularly out of a historical analysis stressing their colonial experience and their separation from power in the modern world, which is in widespread use among peoples of those countries themselves, and which contains the positive ideas that they are a 'world', a vast and living social organism.

We argue that the choice is clear and hence the title of this dictionary.

The scope of this work

The controversy over the term 'Third World' is symptomatic of the more general conflict of meanings and prescriptions. The aim of this book is to bring to the surface the conflicting assumptions behind many of the key terms relating to the Third World. Through critically exploring their origins and meaning it is hoped that their relevance, or lack of it, will become evident to the reader.

Until now we have emphasized the need for a survey of Third World-related terms which is critical rather than apologetic, but there is an equally important and in some ways logically prior justification for a dictionary which discusses Third World-related terms: it is the tendency for existing critical texts of this kind on the vocabulary of society, culture and the social sciences generally to restrict themselves to the consideration of Western experience. For example, a very widely used dictionary of Marxism published in the early 1980s[7] contains a pitifully small amount of serious consideration of Third World-related questions which have been discussed by Marxism, or of reference to contributions to Marxism from the Third World. Such ethnocentric bias is not at all unusual in the literature and redressing the balance is long overdue.

As part of the task of redressing the balance this work attempts to treat its subjects from the point of view of Third World problems, Third World perceptions and Third World figures, those who make history and those who analyse it. As much as possible we have attempted to see questions with a perspective where the location of the observer is in the Third World.

The dictionary is not designed as a factual work of reference like an almanac, but many questions cannot be analysed without reference to factual information and it is evident that a work such as this requires a strong informational base. Biographical data on key figures in Third World history and politics, outlines of movements, parties and institutions, and information on economic and social reality are needed to help view the world from a Third World viewpoint. For the same reason there are a number of entries relating to the formative events in recent Third World history such as the war in Lebanon, the Nicaraguan revolution and the struggle against apartheid in South Africa. Such events are not only important in their own right but are also a major part of the social and historical context within which ideas and concepts have developed.

Any dictionary has to be selective and here we have tried to select entries which create a balance between the critical discussion of concepts and the presentation of factual material. The selection of the factual material has been informed by the same spirit as the dictionary itself: an attempt to see reality from a Third World viewpoint. Those facts relating to the Third World which seem important to the developed countries and those which seem important to the Third World will not always coincide.

The entries are all presented in straightforward alphabetical order. The form of the entries, however, varies according to what seems the best way of treating each term. Factual and technical terms, for example, are discussed relatively briefly in a definitional manner. More controversial words and concepts require a more discursive, critical treatment and are dealt with in the form of small essays. The relative amount of space given to the discussion of each term more or less reflects our view of their influence in or relevance for the Third World.

The user of the dictionary can consult it, entry by entry, or take a number of possible itineraries which, by means of cross-references, the entries suggest. One of these could, for instance, start with the ▶ colonial situation and pass through ▶ colonization, ▶ decolonization, ▶ imperialism, ▶ neo-colonialism, ▶ liberation. A development itinerary could begin with ▶ development and pass through ▶ underdevelopment, ▶ dependency theory, ▶ stages of economic growth, ▶ euphemisms, ▶ indicators, ▶ human development. Another might be more specifically related to international economics and start from ▶ balance of payments, taking in ▶ exports, ▶ terms of trade, ▶ export-led growth, ▶ NICs, ▶ OPEC, ▶ petrodollars, ▶ ISI and perhaps extending into ▶ MNCs, ▶ aid, ▶ debt crisis, ▶ IMF, ▶ World Bank. The measurement of development is discussed in ▶ indicators, ▶ GDP, ▶ purchasing power parity, ▶ human development. An itinerary related to the state might start from ▶ post-colonial state and include ▶ Bonapartism, ▶ military government plus some of the political leaders and parties which receive an entry. A very different itinerary would start with ▶ religion and take in ▶ Islam, ▶ liberation theology, ▶ Rastafarianism. Such itineraries will often be indicated by cross-references; they are no more than suggestions; they will intersect and overlap; and the reader will create other ones reflecting a particular interest and a particular creative way of exploring the book. Lists of further reading, organized according to the title of the entries, have been added to enable readers to delve deeper into the questions which we explore here.

We make no claim to complete objectivity or definitiveness in these choices. The views of readers will differ about the relative importance of entries, and even more about their content. Such differences are inevitable and are positive in so far as they represent the reader's entering into the critical debates. That is the purpose of this work.

Further reading

P. Worsley, *The Third World: a vital new force in international affairs,* London 1964.

P. Worsley, *The Three Worlds: culture and world development,* London 1984.

Notes

1. Alfred Sauvy, 'Trois mondes, une planète', cited in V. Laroste, *Unité et diversité du tiers monde*, Paris 1980, p. 14.
2. See *People's Daily*, 1 Nov. 1977.
3. D.S. Papp, *Soviet Perceptions of the Developing World in the 1980s*, Lexington, Mass. 1985, p. 2.
4. K. Nkrumah, 'The Myth of the Third World', *The Struggle Continues*, London 1981, p. 74.
5. Ibid., p. 76.
6. Nigel Harris, *The End of the Third World*, Harmondsworth 1986, p. 144.
7. T. Bottomore, with Lawrence Harris and Ralph Milliband, *A Dictionary of Marxist Thought*, Oxford 1983. Even Raymond Williams, a leading expert on culture with tremendous knowledge of world affairs, did not recognize the need to address the newly added vocabulary with a Third World connotation in his reputable book *Keywords* (London 1985).

Select bibliography

Suggestions for further reading appear at the end of a number of entries in the dictionary. These suggestions are chosen either because they relate to the arguments taken up in the dictionary entries or because they give more information. For reasons of space the lists have been restricted to books in English. Where a reference exists in the text of an entry it has usually not been included again as further reading. The suggestions do not include either reports of international organizations or sources of statistics. There are a number of sources of international statistical and other information which are easily available and can be useful. They include:

World Bank, *World Development Report*, annual
United Nations Development Programme, *Human Development Report*, annual
World Resources Institute, *World Resources*, annual
Amnesty International, *Report*, annual

In addition, there are numerous journals devoted to analysing events in the Third World and many of them will include many articles on the entries covered in the dictionary. Among the best known are:

Economic Development and Cultural Change
Journal of Concerned Asian Scholars
Journal of Development Studies
Journal of Latin American Studies
Journal of Modern African Studies
Journal of Peasant Studies
Latin American Perspectives
Monthly Review
Race and Class
Review of African Political Economy
Third Word Quarterly
World Development

A

ACP countries

African, Caribbean and Pacific countries. These are the 69 countries that have signed the ▶ Lomé Convention and its renewals with the European Community.

African, Caribbean and Pacific countries ▶ ACP countries

African National Congress ▶ ANC

African Socialism

The notion of African Socialism flourished in the early 1960s, when nationalist leaders throughout the continent espoused some variant of this ideology. The wide-ranging support that the ideology enjoyed was revealed in December 1962 at a special 'Colloquium on Policies of Development and African Approaches to Socialism' in Dakar. This colloquium, convened by President Léopold Senghor of Senegal, attracted a wide range of African leaders, politicians and trade unionists.

The Dakar coloquium clearly revealed, however, that there was no real consensus as to what was meant by the term 'African Socialism'.[1] Instead, it became clear that the term meant all things to all men. As Mamadou Dia, the former prime minister of Senegal, noted: 'It is becoming good form, in the developing countries, to call oneself a socialist and the word attracts, day by day, more of a mystical overtone affording specialists in social psychology a limitless field for study.'[2]

Back in the early 1960s even right-wing advocates of capitalism felt the need to describe their worldview as socialist. Félix Houphouët-Boigny, the leader of the Ivory Coast, and Tom Mboya, a senior government figure in Kenya, both on the right wing of the political spectrum, assumed the mantle of African Socialism. Mboya's writings on the subject reveal the lack of substance behind the term. According to Mboya, 'the adoption of the policy of African Socialism is not merely an attempt to be different from everyone. It is not based on any inward-looking policies but on sound, meaningful and positive attitudes that can best promote the spirit and atmosphere within which the urgent task of economic reconstruction can take place.'[3]

Mboya's argument reveals why African Socialism became so fashionable with Africa's leaders. Faced with the daunting tasks of nation-building and economic development, many African leaders looked for ideological support. Socialism became an ideal instrument for winning popular backing for the policies promoted by the new African governments. Socialism was thus cynically manipulated in an attempt to win legitimacy for the new governments of Africa. As Modibo Keita warned:

> We will not allow ourselves to be caught by the magic of words. Most of the states speak of African Socialism – even Senghor speaks of African Socialism.
> If we are not careful the word socialist will be emptied of its meaning and bourgeois systems of the most reactionary kind will be able to camouflage themselves under the sign of socialism.[4]

In most cases, the ideology of African Socialism had an entirely rhetorical character. There was little attempt to elaborate this ideology into a coherent system of thought. Certain individuals, like President Kaunda of Zambia, attempted to evolve a more coherent worldview, but Kaunda's philosophy of Humanism brought together inconsistent elements of capitalist, populist and socialist views into one eclectic framework which could have very little meaning in terms of practical action.

It was among a few more radical and consistent exponents of African Socialism, including Modibo Keita and Julius Nyerere, that this ideology acquired a degree of coherence. Both of them emphasized the egalitarian strand in socialist thought.

Nyerere's is the most developed version of African Socialism. His starting point is an assumption that Africans are naturally oriented towards socialism. Through reinterpreting history, Nyerere develops the myth that traditional African societies were organized along lines that were essentially socialist. Nyerere claims that in traditional society 'everybody was a worker'. Even those who possessed wealth and prestige were workers at one time or another. Thus, the elder, who enjoyed a degree of wealth without working, had in fact laboured during his youth.

Nyerere also suggests that in traditional society there could be no class of parasitic exploiters, since everybody was obliged to work. He writes: 'Capitalist exploitation was impossible. Loitering was an unthinkable disgrace.'[5] He cites the well-known Swahili proberb, 'Treat your guest as your guest for two days; on the third day give him a hoe', to illustrate what he considers to be the old ethic of traditional socialism.

Nyerere's interpretation of history, however, is too fanciful to provide the foundation for a modern ideology. The harmonious portrayal of African tradition does not stand up to the scrutiny of historical investigation. Traditional African society was no less conflict-ridden than any other rural society. In any case, cooperation for survival was not a voluntary act but a relation imposed by material circumstances. To be sure, a degree of egalitarianism did prevail in traditional Africa, but this egalitarianism was a product of the relative absence of sufficient surplus for accumulating private wealth.

In any case, whatever may have happened in pre-colonial Africa has little relevance for the contemporary period. African society has, in the meantime, been transformed beyond recognition by colonialism. As a result, a social hierarchy composed of antagonistic classes prevails throughout the continent. Under such circumstances it is not possible to recreate traditional norms and forms of organization. According to Nyerere, the foundation of African Socialism is the extended family. If that is so, African Socialism can have little meaning for today. The cooperation that may exist within the family cannot be reproduced at the level of society. Families now exist at different levels of the social hierarchy. They are now part of a class structure and exist in a relation of competition with other families.

The irrelevance of historic myths is perceived even by those who advocate this point of view. Not even Nyerere suggests that Africans go back to the past and adopt the forms of social organization of pre-colonial times. Consequently, even the egalitarian version of African Socialism has no practical consequence. That is why it is not surprising to find that African Socialism for Nyerere is primarily an attitude of mind. It is primarily an ethic, a vision of the world, rather than a guide to action.

As an ethic, it is difficult to disagree with African Socialism. Many of its tenets – equality, liberty, compassion and justice – are values which are above controversy. The difficulty lies with transforming the ethic into a perspective which can practically shape reality. A philosophy which is merely an attitude of the mind is simply a form of wishful thinking. Thus, African Socialism becomes at best an inclination to do good rather than a force for changing society.

From today's perspective it is evident that the widespread adoption of African Socialism had little to do with logic or conviction and much to do with pragmatism and opportunism. Many of the new nationalist leaders simply lacked a coherent perspective; they needed to legitimize their rule ideologically and a variant of socialism appeared to have the greatest appeal. The free market philosophy of capitalism made little sense in post-colonial societies where state regulation of the economy was a long-standing practice. Nor could the leaders of Africa expect to win popular support for the perpetuation of capitalist inequalities. An egalitarian ethic dressed up as African Socialism became the appropriate solution to the crisis of ideology experienced by the leaders of the new states. Through its reference to the traditional past, African Socialism was used to justify state-regulated neo-colonial economies as a form of organization rooted in the continent's history.

The disintegration of African Socialism is strikingly illustrated through the career of one man, Kwame ▶ Nkrumah. In the late 1950s and in the 1960s, Nkrumah put forward Consciencism, his own variant of African Socialism. Although Nkrumah did not go as far as Nyerere in presenting an idealized conflict-free African past, he tended in that direction. Not surprisingly, he shared Nyerere's view that socialism was an attitude of mind. Nkrumah called Consciencism a personal philosophy and expected that lofty morals would triumph over evil through changing attitudes.[6]

Eventually, Nkrumah had to confront the reality of class conflict, exploitation and neo-colonialism. After his overthrow by a Western-inspired coup, Nkrumah was forced to rethink his views. He came to understand the irrelevance of African Socialism and other abstract philosophies. His experience showed that social change could only be realized through the class struggle. Towards the end of his life, Nkrumah's writings show a clear appreciation of a practically oriented strategy of social change based on the class struggle: that is, an appreciation of real socialism.

Today, African Socialism has little appeal. It is widely seen as empty rhetoric which is cynically manipulated. The collapse of this ideology is now often used to discredit socialism itself. It is necessary to counter this tendency by pointing out that the collapse of African Socialism has nothing to do with the failure of socialism as such. African Socialism has never been more than a form of propaganda – its collapse should make it possible, for those so inclined, to promote real socialism.

Further reading

M. Babu, *African Socialism or Socialist Africa?*, London 1981.

Notes

1. For a review of the event see W.H. Friedland and C.G. Rosberg (eds), *African Socialism*, Princeton, NJ 1966.
2. See *West Africa*, 29 Dec. 1962, p. 1449.
3. T. Mboya, *The Africa Bureau Anniversary Address*, London 1963, pp. 7–8.
4. Cited in A. Mohiddin, *African Socialism in Two Countries*, London 1981, p. 15.
5. J. Nyerere, *Ujamaa: the basis of African Socialism*, Dar es Salaam 1962, p. 3.
6. See K. Nkrumah, *Consciencism: philosophy and ideology for decolonization*, London 1965.

Afwaj al-Mugawama al-Lubnaniyya ▶ AMAL

agrarian question

The agrarian question relates to the structure of production and social relations in agriculture. It is concerned with how the agrarian sector carries out its role of producing food and raw materials, and how it provides a living for the rural population. It is important to acknowledge that agricultural systems in the Third World differ greatly from each other. There are, for instance, enormous differences between huge plantations in the Caribbean, the coexisting latifundia and minifundia in South America, the cash-crop and labour migration systems of West Africa and the small farms of peasants dependent on usurers in parts of South and South-East Asia. There is the world of difference between a country such as Brazil where 20 per cent of landholders (those with more than 50 hectares each) own 86 per cent of the land and the much more egalitarian land-holding system in South Korea, for instance, where no individual holding exceeds 5 hectares. There is an enormous difference between the intensive agriculture of Asia where it is estimated that 83 per cent of the possibly cultivable land is already in use, and Africa where only 22 per cent of the possibly usable land is in use. There is a vast gap between the yields produced by a farm using new varieties of seeds (▶ green revolution), fertilizers, irrigation and machines, and a farm with none of these advantages.

With such variety it is natural to wonder if any generalizations can be made about the agrarian question and how it manifests itself in the Third World. Detailed factual knowledge of the agrarian sector in different countries can only be obtained from the vast amount of specialized writing on the subject. Often, however, such studies conceal as well as reveal because they are naturally concerned with specificities. Common characteristics which apply to the whole or large parts of the Third World may be missed. There are, however, important recurrent themes which can be said to constitute the core of the agrarian question in the Third World. Behind the many concrete and specific manifestations are more abstract general features.

Because agriculture is the traditional activity of most of humanity before the industrial era, it is common to think of the Third World agrarian sector as traditional, unchanged and primitive. The first of the generalizations which we can make is that this preconception is totally false. Agriculture in all parts of the Third World takes its present form because of the impact of centuries of contact with the capitalist world market and the colonial experience. Those experiences undermined and ultimately destroyed traditional, stable subsistence agriculture which was adapted to the needs of the local community. Agriculture under the impact of colonialism and the world market had to supply new needs in addition to fulfilling its traditional role of supplying the local community with food.

The common impact of these processes has been the growth of inequality and the almost universal failure of the agrarian sector to provide all the population with land, food and employment. Hence the characteristic growth of landlessness, hunger or even ▶ famine and chronic unemployment or underemployment in the countryside.

The speed with which insertion in the market and colonialism created such problems varied very greatly and so the extent of the problems still varies today. Some examples will show just how widespread they are: landlessness and extreme rural poverty are endemic throughout Latin America even though many of the countries appear relatively high in the indices of development; in India, Bangladesh and Pakistan numerous studies have estimated that as many as one-third of the rural population typically have no land, and so have a desperately fragile hold on the means of livelihood; in Africa famine seems to be becoming more common with the spread of commercial agriculture and the worst-stricken countries have continued to export food to more profitable markets in times of famine; while the overall extent of world hunger is very hard to estimate, nearly all global studies suggest that at least 40 per cent of the population of the Third World suffer from hunger.

19

Unlike in, say, Europe, subsistence agriculture was not succeeded by a general agricultural revolution. As a result, the Third World peasant has often had the worst of both worlds. He enjoyed neither the benefits of subsistence farming, nor the advantages of the agrarian revolution that characterized European capitalist development and from which some parts of the peasantry gained. The process of integration into the world market did not lead to the progressive *transformation* of production relations. It merely led to the *reorientation* of production activity towards the world market. As a result, many features of the pre-capitalist agrarian systems survived alongside market-oriented plantation and cash-cropping activities.

Productivity in food production failed to increase and so agriculture failed in its primary task of feeding the population. Nor could agriculture become, as it became in Western Europe and the USA, part of a growing economy in a symbiotic relation with industry (a supplier of industrial raw materials and a market for industrial products) because the industrial sector was also held back.

Without an agrarian revolution, integration into the world market represented dislocation but not progress. The retention of pre-capitalist forms of social organization meant that agrarian development would be circumscribed, ensuring the emergence of a long-term crisis on the land. It also meant that the development of agriculture was essentially linked to the cycle of price fluctuation and demand on the world market. The historic expression of this pattern was the highly uneven nature of agrarian development: a few areas of cash-cropping were surrounded by a sea of low productivity agriculture. The consequences for the development of the peasantry are well documented. Market relations and the cash nexus destroyed the option of subsistence. Peasants were forced to produce for the market or sell their capacity to labour. With the passing of time, pressure on the land expressed itself in soil erosion, landlessness and the polarization of land holdings.

The above is a kind of stylized history of the impact of colonialism and the world economy on the agriculture of a Third World country. It is not a precise description of any one country. It is a kind of theme on which each country is a variation, but what is remarkable is that, despite national differences, so many strands of this theme are identifiable throughout the Third World.

Once the imperialist-affected agrarian structures were established, they were to prove remarkably resistant to change. During the past three decades, there have been countless attempts made to tackle the problem of agrarian relations (▶ land reform). The failure of almost all these attempts has puzzled many. The stock explanation given is that the reform policies were not implemented wholeheartedly or rationally. That, of course, does not take us very far. We have to explain why, even in the few cases where they exist on paper, serious agrarian reform policies are so seldom implemented.

The answer, we believe, is devastatingly simple. The existing structures of agriculture may well be irrational from the point of view of society as a whole. Nevertheless, a privileged minority of landlords and capitalist farmers actually benefit from the perpetuation of the status quo. This is particularly evident in the case of Latin America, where, historically, landlords developed a mututally beneficial relationship with foreign capital. For the big landlords, the externally oriented agrarian system means profits, stability and privilege.

Even in societies where the growth of the landlord class is relatively restricted, e.g. West Africa, capitalist cash-crop farmers have fought attempts to alter the structure of land tenure. Since the rural élite plays an important role in maintaining law and order and stability, they can always use their political power to thwart attempts to reform agriculture. Hence, the agrarian problem is ultimately a political one. Existing political systems are very often synonymous with a balance of power which protects the élite in the countryside. There can be no change in agrarian relations without destroying the political power of this rural élite. It is this power that helps preserve the agrarian system established in the colonial era.

Since most Third World governments are closely linked with the rural élites, they have no interest in challenging the existing relations of power. That is why their agrarian reform policies soon reveal themselves as not worth the paper they are printed on.

The solution to the agrarian problem lies not so much in the sphere of agriculture as in the field of politics. Political change leading to a social revolution is the precondition for bringing about the agrarian revolution that the Third World so desperately needs. Such a revolution means the destruction of the power of the rural élite so that the imperialist-imposed agrarian system can be replaced by one directed towards the needs of Third World societies.

A further aspect of the agrarian question concerns the situation of women. In various parts of the Third World the problems of the agrarian sector are especially the problems of women. In many countries, especially in Africa, men have tended to migrate to the cities on a larger scale than women. Women, therefore, are left behind in the agricultural sector where they are obliged to assume the work previously done by men as well as their own traditional work. In African agriculture women traditionally assume a very large proportion of agricultural tasks, but in places where men have traditionally undertaken the tasks of clearing new land and other agricultural investments their absence leads to a decline in productivity and an increase in the difficulties of the women who are obliged to live off the land. The easier migration of men has led also in some cases to women being disproportionate victims of famine because their traditional role in caring for children gives them much less freedom to migrate. Women suffer also from exclusion, in the great majority of cases, from legal title to land, and there are almost no agrarian reform programmes which have redistributed land to women.

Further reading

S. Baraclough (ed.), *Agrarian Structure in Latin America*, Lexington, Mass. 1973.
K. Griffin, *The Political Economy of Agrarian Change*, London 1974.
D. Grigg, *The World Food Problem 1950–1980*, Oxford 1985.

A. de Janvry, *The Agrarian Question and Reformism in Latin America*, Baltimore, Md. 1981.

J.W. Mellor and D.M. Desai, *Agricultural Change and Rural Povety: variations on a theme by Dharm Naraln*, Delhi 1986.

agribusiness

Over the last thirty years, agriculture has become increasingly industrialized within the regions of the North. Food is less and less exclusively associated with farming or agrarian activities. The industrialization of agriculture means mechanization, irrigation, manufactured fertilizers and pesticides and plant-breeding, and alongside these technologies an expanded use of fossil fuel energy in food production.

These technologies involve major economies of scale, and lead to crop specialization and, often, monoculture. Fish, meat and egg production are organized as huge factory operations. Large multinationals such as Unilever, Nestlé and Nabisco have emerged, which integrate farming activities with food processing and wholesale and retail operations. Agricultural imports are supplied by multinational companies. This is agribusiness, which has emerged in the prosperous regions of the North and has grown in influence inside the Third World.

The main impetus behind the growth of agribusiness in the Third World has been the general failure of ▶ land reform and other attempts to develop national agriculture. The widespread failure of land reform had become evident by the late 1960s. Many Third World governments abandoned any attempt to find a national solution to the problem of agriculture and looked to Western capital, technology and expertise instead. Many international agencies such as the World Bank were only too pleased to promote agribusiness since they recognized that this was potentially a profitable sphere of foreign investment.

An object lesson in the problems associated with agribusiness took place in Iran in the 1970s. The former shah became a leading advocate of agribusiness. After the failure of his land reform package, the so-called White Revolution, he invited Western experts and companies to grow food in Iran. In 1974, US$250 million were allocated to developing the Moghan Plain. A plan was drawn up by Hawaiian Agronomics, a US company, according to which the Shahsavan tribe, consisting of 40,000 pastoralists, were to be moved off their traditional grazing grounds to make way for the project. Hawaiian Agronomics argued that the pastoralists would benefit later once the project was more fully established.

Reporting on the Moghan project, the London *Financial Times* commented on 10 July 1979:

> Some officials brush aside the involvement of the Shahsavan as almost irrelevant . . . . If that feeling prevailed then the Shahsavan would have had a rough deal in being moved off their age-long pastures in the Moghan. It would also make nonsense of the efforts

22

> the project management is now making through the head of the tribe to explain to the people the benefits they stand to gain.

Predictably the Shahsavan became the casualties of agribusiness. They lost valuable pasture land and the project turned into an expensive white elephant producing luxury food for the Tehran élite.

Disillusion with much industrialization in the Third World in the 1960s and 1970s led to a renewed awareness of the importance of agriculture. Agribusiness has, however, shown itself to be a kind of agricultural development which does not reduce the problems produced by industrial investments; it repeats them. The technology and methods it uses are often ill-suited to Third World conditions. It is highly intensive in capital and relies on a small core of labourers. It has a tendency to create unemployment rather than to absorb any of the millions of rural dwellers who are underemployed. Agribusiness is often designed to take advantage of cheap land. Taking advantage of poverty in the Third World, agribusiness directs its efforts towards providing the North with luxury items. In South-East Asia, for instance, agribusiness provides Japan with poultry, pork, seafood and a variety of fruit and vegetables.

The production of export crops has no direct relationship to the agricultural needs of the domestic economy. Often a crisis-ridden agricultural sector exists in parallel with a prosperous agribusiness sector. For example, during the famine in Senegal in 1974, the country was sending green beans, melons, tomatoes and strawberries to Europe. Similarly, during the 1984 famine in Ethiopia, coffee, meat, sugar, fruits and vegetables were exported abroad. Agribusiness has proved to have very one-sided benefits. It benefits the multinational agribusiness companies and parts of the Third World élite at the expense of the poor majority. Instead of solving Third World agricultural problems it has become the means through which agrarian resources are deployed for the benefit of the North.

Further reading

R. Burbach and P. Flynn, *Agribusiness in the Americas*, New York 1980.
B. Dinham and C. Hines, *Agribusiness in Africa*, London 1983.
S. George, *The Way the Other Half Dies*, Harmondsworth, 1977.
M. Mackintosh, *Gender, Class and Rural Transition: agribusiness and the food crisis in Senegal*, London 1990.

aid

The term 'aid' is highly mystifying, as it is used to describe a wide range of capital transfers from the West to the Third World. In its loosest sense aid means the transfer of resources from the industrial nations to the developing world. It is still a matter of debate as to which forms of resource transfer are entitled to be called aid. There is a common consensus among development experts that simple commercial transactions ought not to be termed aid. It is held that the term 'aid' is applicable if the following three criteria apply:

(1) The recipient project should be one that is developmental or charitable and not military.
(2) The donor's objective should be non-commercial.
(3) The terms of the transfer should have a concessional or grant element.

According to the Development Assistance Committee (▶ DAC) of the Organization for Economic Cooperation and Development (▶ OECD), only grants and loans whose interest rates are below current market rates can be labelled as what it calls official development assistance (ODA). In practice, it is very difficult to distinguish between aid and ordinary commercial transactions. Aid packages are open to abuse. No doubt funds and loans designed for general developmental purposes are in fact used for military purchases. US and French development assistance has always had a high military component. *Bilateral aid*, in particular, is seldom free of commercial considerations. It is often explicitly tied – that is, the proceeds must be spent on goods produced in the donor country. A dollar's worth of tied aid is worth much less in real terms than a dollar available to be spent anywhere – otherwise it would not be necessary to tie it to the donor's non-competitive goods. Lastly, concessionary loans, even if interest-free, are often directed towards projects based on the socio-economic approach of the donor country. Such an approach is rarely based on disinterested motives and to a considerable extent is linked to the national commercial interest of the donor country.

The history of aid helps put this phenomenon into perspective. The term came into common usage in the post-1945 period. Until the Second World War, investments in Third World countries were not referred to as aid. After 1945, however, the growth of the anti-colonial movement made the imperialist powers sensitive to the charge of exploitation. It was at this stage that investments in the colonial infrastructure came to be designated as aid. Investments in transport, communication and industry were now advanced in the form of aid grants by the metropolitan powers. Aid was seen by the colonial powers as an investment stake for the future. Financing future stability and ensuring a smooth transfer of power was the purpose of aid. Through aid it was hoped to minimize the disruptive effects of decolonization and to retain influence over the ex-colony. This practice continued into recent times. The independence of Zimbabwe was underwritten by British 'aid'. A significant portion of the aid package was earmarked for helping the government buy out white farmers and to pay the salaries and pensions of European civil servants. The aid of West European countries still goes almost exclusively to their ex-colonies.

After 1945, aid emerged as a significant component of international diplomacy. The rivalry between the USSR and the USA and the growth of what the West considers subversive movements gave impetus to the growth of aid. The USA has consistently used aid to reward its loyal friends and to mobilize support against radical forces. One of the most ambitious programmes of aid, the Alliance for Progress, launched by US President Kennedy, was a direct response to the threat posed by the Cuban revolution to American interests in Latin America. At the Punta del Este conference of Latin American governments in Uruguay in 1961, US representatives made it clear that money had to be spent in order to counter communist propaganda. Since Punta del Este, US aid has always been inseparable from big power diplomacy. When governments adopt radical policies, the flow of aid dries up. Thus, Allende's Chile was confronted with an aid blockade. Immediately after the 1973 military coup which overthrew Allende, aid started flowing in. Algeria, Jamaica, Peru and Nicaragua had the same experience. Even relatively modest acts of defiance can cause a disruption of aid. The Zimbabwean government's criticism of Washington's support of apartheid in 1986 swiftly provoked a reduction of US aid. Third World countries that are central for Western geo-political interests are often the main beneficiaries of aid. Israel and Egypt, the most important US allies in the Middle East, are also among the largest recipients of aid.

Since the recession of the 1970s, aid has been overshadowed by commercial rivalry on the world market. Competition for the export market has led Western rivals to use aid packages increasingly as incentives to purchase their goods. Such bilateral aid is designed to sell goods rather than to assist the development of the recipient country. According to most sources, more than half of bilateral aid is tied. Tied aid eliminates choice and forces the Third World to pay for goods way above the market prices. According to Hayter and Watson, 'on average, the prices of goods financed by aid exceed the world market prices by 25 to 30 per cent'.[1] Bilateral aid which forces Third World countries to buy goods from donor nations at high prices has more the character of a pragmatic commercial transaction than real development assistance. It is for this reason that many Third World governments prefer *multilateral aid* to bilateral aid.

Multilateral aid from institutions with an international membership such as the ▶ World Bank, the African Development Bank or the Inter-American Development Bank provides around a quarter of ODA. One of the main appeals of multilateral aid is that the recipient country has more leeway in the deployment of funds than with bilateral aid. The main drawback of multilateral aid is the issue of *conditionality*. International agencies led by the World Bank and the International Monetary Fund (▶ IMF) lay down conditions for the use of aid facilities or for loan rescheduling. Through the use of conditionality, multilateral aid is often circumscribed by externally imposed policies. The conditions that are demanded of recipient countries are austerity, reduction in government expenditure and the devaluation of currency. During the years 1977–83, a significant number of Third World countries such as Egypt, Jamaica, Sudan, Turkey and Zaïre were forced to accept IMF-imposed conditions.

The case of Zaïre shows the drastic character of conditionality. The 1976 stabilization programme of the IMF was designed to reduce pressures and permit a revival in economic activity through the following measures: a 42 per cent devaluation of the local currency, a reduction of real wages in the urban sector, an unspecified reduction in government expenditure and the liberalization of trade relations. In recent years, the imposition of monetarist economics on Third World countries by international agencies has become the norm (▶ monetarism). A recent review of IMF activities notes the continuing pursuit of monetarism with what it calls 'the increased emphasis on the need for a growth-oriented approach aimed at enhanced economic efficiency and competitiveness'.[2] This orientation towards competitiveness and the liberalization of trade has also been accepted by the UN-related agencies. The African Priority Programme for Economic Activity adopted at the UN session on Africa in 1986 explicitly linked its package of financial assistance to the introduction of monetarist policies. Since its passage, a lot has been heard about the virtues of monetarism in Africa and little about practical assistance. Thus it can be argued that the emphasis on conditionality behind multilateral aid indicates that the Western powers which control the multilateral agencies are more interested in dictating economic policy to the Third World than helping the cause of development.

It is difficult to distinguish between the aid policies of the different donor nations. The USSR's aid is all too often motivated by geo-political considerations and a large component of its assistance is military hardware. Of the Western nations, only the Scandinavian countries and the Netherlands have made any genuine attempts to provide development-oriented aid.

The donors are becoming increasingly sparing even with the dubious and at best ambiguous generosity represented by aid. In 1988 total development aid from the DAC countries amounted to US$48,000 million. That represents US$12 per head of the population of the recipient countries (varying between US$279 for Israel to US$0.60 for Iraq); it was 0.36 per cent of the national product of the donor countries (down from 0.48 per cent in 1965; varying between 0.21 per cent for the USA and 1.1 per cent in the case of Norway). The end of the Cold War is tending to reduce both Western and Soviet aid programmes; the decline in oil prices in the 1980s strangled the aid programme of the Organization of Petroleum Exporting Countries (OPEC) almost at birth: it dropped from nearly US$6000 million in 1976 to just over US$2000 million in 1988. In general this declining trickle of contaminated resources flowing to the Third World is heavily counterbalanced by other flows in the opposite direction (▶ debt crisis).

It should be mentioned that the extremity of the economic crisis in Africa during the 1980s led to the continent's countries becoming increasingly dependent on aid. At the end of the decade over 40 per cent of all development aid went to Africa compared with under 30 per cent at the start of the 1980s. In 1988, 19 African countries received aid equal to more than 10 per cent of their gross national product; and for six countries (Mozambique, Chad, Tanzania, Malawi, Somalia and Lesotho) aid amounted in that year to more than a quarter of their gross national product (GNP). This, of course, gave donors an even greater stranglehold on African governments (▶ neo-colonialism); it did not mark a new era of international generosity.

The term 'aid' is confusing. It suggests a meaning that is at variance with its reality. What is designated as aid ought to be called soft loans or state or multi-state sponsored investment. It is seldom appropriate to portray this form of aid as having anything to do with development assistance. Its intent is to consolidate Western influence in the Third World. Any benefits that may accrue to the recipient nation are incidental to its main purposes.

Further reading

K. Borgan and K. Corbett, *The Destruction of a Continent: Africa and international aid*, New York 1982.

R. Cassen and associates, *Does Aid Work?*, Oxford 1986.

T. Hayter and C. Watson, *Aid: rhetoric and reality*, London 1985.

J.R. Parkinson (ed.), *Poverty and Aid*, Oxford 1983.

Notes

1. T. Hayter and C. Watson, *Aid: rhetoric and reality*, London 1985, p. 15.
2. *IMF Survey*, 30 Sept. 1986.

AIFLD, American Institute of Free Labour Development

This subsidiary organization of the US trade union federation, the American Federation of Labour and Congress of Industrial Organizations (AFL–CIO), is dedicated to spreading the federation's policies in the Latin American labour movement. The AIFLD was founded in 1962, partly in response to the effects of the Cuban revolution, since when it claims to have helped to 'educate' half a million Latin American trade unionists. Education in large part consists of struggling against 'communist' tendencies in Latin American unions.

The AIFLD is almost entirely financed by the US government, but, unlike government departments, it does not have to give a public account of its activities. For this reason, it has often been used by the State Department and the Central Intelligence Agency (CIA) as a specially flexible, secret arm of US policies. It has played a role in the US opposition to progressive governments in Brazil under Goulart, in the Dominican Republic under Bosch, in Nicaragua in the early years of the Sandinista government and in many other places. It has also consistently tried to improve the image of US businesses in Latin America and up to 1980 had major executives of American multinational corporations on its board of directors.

The AIFLD has sophisticated its policies since its early days and was even known to criticize aspects of President Reagan's foreign policies. Its basic anti-communist line, however, has not changed. It claims to be 'non-political'.

Further reading

R. Radosh, *American Labor and United States Foreign Policy*, New York 1969.

Algerian liberation movement ▶ FLN

Allende Gossens, Salvador (1908–73)

Salvador Allende Gossens was president of Chile, 1970–3. Born into an anti-clerical family, as a student leader he took part in demonstrations against the Ibanez dictatorship in 1931 and was imprisoned. After qualifying as a doctor, he worked for the public health service and in 1933 helped found the Socialist Party of Chile (PSC). He was elected to the Chamber of Deputies in 1937, and became Minister of Health in the 1938–41 Popular Front government. As secretary-general of the PSC from 1943 he moved the party closer to the Chilean Communist Party. He was a senator for over twenty years and the left's presidential candidate unsuccessfully in 1952, 1958 and 1964 and successfully in 1970. He formed a Popular Unity government of socialists, communists, radicals and the Catholic left, and became generally recognized as the first Marxist leader to come to power in democratic elections. The West was bitterly hostile and he was forced to act to curb his supporters among the masses. In September 1973 he was killed in a right-wing military coup led by General Augusto Pinochet.

The three dramatic years of the Popular Unity regime under Allende were and still are the subject of tremendous debate. For some the lesson of Chile is that the government tried to go too far too fast; they say it should have modified its programme, compromised with its enemies and controlled its more radical supporters. Others say that its mistake was the opposite: it compromised too much and should have radicalized its programme and so mobilized greater and more unambiguous support.

The factors which constricted the Allende regime were extremely obvious. Aside from the hostility of the US government and destabilization plots by the American multinational corporation ITT, Chile had a well-established and organized bourgeoisie and an army whose officers were strongly identified with the right. Allende had won the election with less than 40 per cent of the votes in a three-way fight with two candidates from the right-wing parties which controlled the legislature throughout the Popular Unity period. The government attempted many tactical compromises and manoeuvres to escape from this strait-jacket including, ironically, replacing the army commander with General Pinochet who was considered more loyal and democratic, but who later led the coup and maintained a 16-year-long bloody dictatorship.

Should they have compromised more? It is impossible in retrospect to know what would have happened, but an obvious possibility is that the mass of Popular Unity supporters would have tried to continue the revolution without the government. Though, as a result, the forces behind the coup might have felt even more threatened the mass movement might have been able to resist them more effectively than it did. No one can predict the result of such a hypothetical struggle. In any case it is very doubtful that more compromise would have calmed the forces who made the coup; they always gave the impression that whatever olive branch they were offered by the government it was not enough.

Many have put the blame for the failure of the Allende government on the fact that it controlled so little of the power of the state. It held the presidency and cabinet, but controlled neither the legislature and the judiciary, nor the police and the military. Our view is that, while an ability to penetrate to more organs of the state could not have failed to make some difference to what happened in detail, the real problem was not how much of the state they controlled but the inevitable nature of that state, which cannot simply be controlled by the wishes of the politicians (▶ post-colonial state).

Others argue that the problems with the Popular Unity was that it was not revolutionary and refused to mobilize its popular base. Not only did it create illusions about the democratic nature of the armed forces but, to please the armed forces, it cooperated in the disarming of the masses. True as that may be, it does not solve the tactical questions: even if it is true that only full social revolution will make real lasting social gains possible, there is still the question of exactly how and exactly when. Besides, the criticism that Allende was not revolutionary enough reduces the question once again to the subjective ideas of a leader. Allende was not a revolutionary in the sense that his critics mean: not because he made a subjective mistake but because his whole lifetime of political activity was dedicated to a particular political project, which he certainly regarded as revolutionary but which aimed to achieve major social change without the violent confrontation of classes. That position was determined by Allende's social background and political formation; it was not simply a subjective mistake. Allende did what he did because he represented a certain social project; it seems pointless to criticize him for not being someone else with a different social formation.

Where Allende certainly cannot be criticized is in his consistency, rare in political leaders, in support of this project. He maintained a long and arduous political struggle and he died heroically defending himself against the insurgent army. This is why his name has rightly come to symbolize the struggle for social and political progress, and against imperialism and reaction in Latin America and even elsewhere in the Third World.

Further reading

N. Davis, *The Last Two Years of Salvador Allende*, Ithaca, NY and London 1985.

AMAL, Afwaj al-Mugawama al-Lubnaniyya (Lebanese Resistance Battalions)

'Amal' is Arabic for hope. Formed in Lebanon, 1975, as a non-sectarian militia-cum-social welfare organization, AMAL initially had about 20 per cent Christian membership but soon became exclusively identified with the Shia community and deeply involved in the Lebanese civil war, although it distances itself from the Islamic fundamentalism promoted by

▶ Hizbullah. Its founder, Musa Sadr, born in 1927 in Qom (Iran), trained as a mullah alongside Ayatullah Khomeini, later the leader of the 1979 revolution in Iran. In 1960 he moved to Lebanon to work with the Shi'ite community, which under the French-bequeathed communal constitution, was dominated by the Sunni Muslims (▶ Islam). Musa Sadr secured official recognition for the Shi'ite faith and formed the Higher Shi'ite Islamic Council, which became the focus for Shi'ite protests against landlords in southern Lebanon.

In August 1978 he disappeared and his followers claim he was killed by Colonel Gadhafi while on a visit to Libya, which the latter denies. Musa Sadr's followers now regard him as a martyr and he has not been replaced as leader of AMAL, although since 1980 a French-trained lawyer, Nabih Berri, has been 'deputy' leader. This symbolizes the takeover of what was an organization of the poor dispossessed rural peasantry and their urban kin in the Beirut slums by the new business and professional class that has emerged among the Shias since the early 1970s, many bringing wealth from West Africa where they had prospered in business under colonial rule. Berri was born in Sierra Leone, but studied at the Arab University in Beirut and was a student leader.

As the Lebanese civil war began in early 1975, AMAL was supported and trained by the Palestine Liberation Organization (▶ PLO) but in January 1976 Musa Sadr called for Syrian intervention. This lost him support among Shias which he only began to recover with the Israeli invasion in 1978.

The success of the 1979 Iranian revolution boosted AMAL and it was drawn into fighting the PLO in Lebanon in 1980. The 1982 Israeli invasion finally split AMAL, as the Israelis successfully pressured the southern Lebanese Shias to act against the Palestinians and help put down local anti-Israeli communist guerrillas, while the Shias in Beirut, in alliance with the Syrians, helped defend the city against the Israelis. AMAL rebuilt its strength to some 10,000 fighters and in July 1983, armed by Syria, attacked the Maronites and their allies among the Western forces intervening in Lebanon and confronted the ▶ Druze in the Chouf mountains (▶ Progressive Socialist Party). After the withdrawal of US troops in February 1984, a Shi'ite-dominated coalition government took power in Beirut. After that, AMAL lost credibility by behaving increasingly as a private army rather than a liberation movement, and has been used by Syria to eradicate the Palestinian presence in Lebanon, participating in the sieges and starving of the Palestinian camps around Beirut in 1985–7. The AMAL 'deputy' leader Nabih Berri became a member of the pro-Syrian government set up under Omar Karamé in 1990.

Amazon Pact

This pact was initiated by Brazil and signed in 1978. The signatories included all the countries in the Amazon river basin – Bolivia, Brazil, Colombia, Ecuador, Guyana, Peru, Surinam and Venezuela. Its purpose was to develop the resources of the Amazon basin, restrict the activities of non-Amazonian countries, settle territorial disputes and promote joint research and other projects. As with virtually all projects of ▶ integration in the Third World, especially in Latin America, it fell victim to the crisis of the 1980s which obliged individual countries to abandon efforts towards regional integration in favour of national stabilization programmes and integration into the world market ▶ debt crisis, ▶ IMF.

American Institute of Free Labour Development ▶ AIFLD

ANC, African National Congress

Originally named the South African Native National Congress, the ANC was formed in January 1912 in Bloemfontein to protest at the discriminatory provisions of the 1910 Act of Union by which South Africa achieved dominion status. Its founders were products of mission schools and its declared tactics constitutional and peaceful. Peaceful lobbying had made little impact before 1939. The ANC supported the government's war effort and participated in the 'Native Representative Councils' it set up to head off unrest. This led to friction between the ANC leadership and younger radicals like Oliver Tambo and Walter Sisulu who set up the Congress Youth League in 1944, seeking a more militant approach and reaching out to the masses with the aim of achieving first national freedom and ultimately socialism.

After 1948, the white Afrikaner-based Nationalist Party government introduced the system of ▶ apartheid. The ANC responded with mass protests and passive resistance from 1949, and in 1952 the old leadership was ousted and Nelson ▶ Mandela elected to the ANC's national executive. In that year it launched a mass disobedience Defiance Campaign against apartheid legislation after the government had rejected its offer to cooperate as equals; membership rose rapidly to 100,000. One thousand five hundred people were arrested and violence flared between blacks and police in several towns; in East London, 6 whites and 50 blacks were killed in firebomb attacks on government buildings and churches. The ANC recoiled from the violence and denounced it. Subsequent peaceful protests failed to halt the further elimination of black rights.

ANC radicals forged links with the South African Communist Party and in 1955 the ANC adopted elements of its strategy in the Freedom Charter setting out the goals of national independence and black majority rule, but not including socialism. On the basis of this charter it expanded its base by forming the Congress Alliance which united the South African Indian Congress, the white Congress of Democrats and the South African Coloured People's Organization, later joined by the South African Congress of Trade Unions.

In 1959, a section of the ANC rejected this cooperation with whites and split off to form the Pan-Africanist Congress (▶ PAC) which in 1960 launched a peaceful anti-pass law campaign. The police replied by shooting dead 67 unarmed blacks at Sharpeville in March. The government declared a state of emergency and banned the ANC and PAC, arresting ANC leaders who failed to flee the country or go underground. The government refused appeals for national negotiations and in 1961 the ANC was driven to adopt a strategy of violence, forming an armed wing, known in Xhosa as the Umkhonto we Sizwe (Spear of the Nation), which launched a series of acts of economic sabotage lasting into 1963. The government responded by arresting ANC underground leaders, including Nelson Mandela who was tried and jailed for life; in jail he became a focus and symbol for anti-apartheid activists.

The crackdown hit the ANC hard, and it did not recover until the mid-1970s when the ▶ Soweto uprising of June 1976 and the subsequent repression led many youths to flock to ANC training camps in Tanzania, and newly independent Angola and Mozambique. It renewed the armed campaign in 1978, destroying the SASOL oil-from-coal plant in 1980. Government repression simply won it more support.

During the 1980s, the ANC received financial support from many countries including Scandinavia and the USSR. Umkhonto we Sizwe was estimated at one point to have 1000 fighters inside South Africa and 8–10,000 in training camps outside the country. Oliver Tambo became its president in 1967, and it was based in Lusaka. Joe Slovo was the only white man on the 19-member executive and was also chief of staff of Umkhonto we Sizwe until March 1987, when he was replaced by Chris Hani.

However, the ANC played a limited direct role in the renewed conflict in South Africa in the 1980s, and rather devoted its energies to trying to get diplomatic pressure put on South Africa. Indeed, some of the tactics of the young township fighters, such as 'necklacing' with burning car tyres, embarrassed the official ANC leadership in exile. In 1987 ANC leaders held talks with leading white South African businessmen on the basis of the Freedom Charter, which it still adheres to despite pressures in the new powerful, black trade union movement for a more socialist emphasis.

At the close of the 1980s a new rise of popular resistance to apartheid and the spread of political organization (for instance ▶ UDF) put the racist system in crisis. The replacement of President Botha by President de Klerk in 1989 was the occasion for a dramatic shift of policy by the National Party regime. After secret negotiations Nelson Mandela was finally released from jail in February 1990 and the ANC legalized. Mandela assumed its vice-presidency (the official President Olivèr Tambo being still in exile and in poor health), but in effect became overnight the national ANC leader.

The ANC began to change its policies to match the new situation. Presenting itself increasingly as the alternative government it has campaigned for the immediate end to apartheid and the institution of a one-person one-vote constitution. During 1990 it publicly renounced the armed struggle and has shown itself prepared to negotiate a solution with the National Party.

In many ways in this latest phase the ANC has gone back to where it came from in the years before apartheid – a broad-based nationalist organization committed to a liberal capitalist and non-racial state in South Africa. It maintains some commitment to socialism but its specific socialist economic policies have been considerably softened.

The ANC continues to have the virtual monopoly of representation of the black South African population abroad. Within the country legalization has strengthened its influence but it still has to contend with rivalries from many other political organizations including the PAC and most dramatically with the Zulu-based organization Inkatha. Led by Chief Mangosuthu Buthelezi, Inkatha supporters have continually clashed with ANC supporters in bloody battles in spite of an agreed truce between the organizations' leaderships.

As apartheid crumbles, the ANC is clearly the country's leading political organization but its policies and leadership are bound to encounter a great deal of resistance in the struggle for liberation in South Africa.

In 1991, although the National Party-controlled police continued to attack ANC supporters, the process of negotiation between the two parties proceeded and an increasing coincidence of constitutional plans began to emerge. The ANC dropped its earlier insistence on a constituent assembly and opted instead for a multi-party conference at least to establish the principles of a new constitution. It also began to give more importance to the protection of minority communities in the future South Africa. It began to look as if major constitutional change in South Africa could be negotiated between the ANC and the National Party, although many sources of tension between the two parties remained and at times threatened to end the process of negotiation.

Further reading

T. Lodge, *Black Politics in South Africa since 1945*, London 1983.

Andean Pact

On 16 August 1966 the heads of state of Bolivia, Chile, Colombia, Ecuador, Peru and Venezuela signed the Declaration on Economic Cooperation and Mutual Assistance in Bogotá, the capital of Colombia. Economic cooperation was taken further when, on 16 May 1969, a pact agreeing to establish the Andean Common Market was concluded at Cartagena on the Colombian coast.

Venezuela was not a signatory to the 1969 agreement. It joined the Andean Pact on 10 February 1973. Chile left the pact on 30 October 1976.

As a common market the Andean Pact constitutes an agreement between the signatory nations to trade within the area free of all restrictions in terms of tariffs and quotas while maintaining a regime of controls with respect to other countries. It also provides a mechanism for aiding member countries with balance of payments problems through the Andean Rescue Fund.

The Andean Pact was one of the most ambitious of the many
▶ integration projects initiated in Latin America in the years before the

▶ debt crisis. It modelled itself in part on the European Economic Community. A council of ministers, an Andean court and Andean parliament were set up and in 1985 an effort was even begun to establish a regional, convertible currency, the Andean peso.

The Andean Pact, despite its advanced institutional development, made little impact on the economies of the member states. Integration was hampered by problems of communication, the similar nature of the member economies and a lack of commitment by political leaders. Even so, during the 1970s inter-Andean trade grew rapidly (by 22 per cent a year).

In common with other integration plans it could not maintain its impetus in the face of the crisis of the 1980s. In their effort to escape from the debt crisis all the member states pursued their individual policies, and were forced into a closer relationship with the world market at the expense of regional integration. The value of inter-Andean trade fell and was cut in half between 1981 and 1986, though it began to pick up again in the closing years of the 1980s. At present, however, the governments of the member states do not give priority to regional integration as a solution to the economic crisis.

Partly in response to President Bush's plan for a continental free trade area, the pact countries tried, in 1991, to give it a new lease of life, signing a new agreement to institute a full free trade area by 1992 (with certain exceptions, such as automobiles, to last until 1995); they also renewed the plan for an Andean parliament and a strengthened Andean Court of Justice. This should not be confused with the original intention of the pact which was based on a much more interventionist concept of integration which would strengthen the Andean economies against the forces of the world market and of foreign capital.

anglophone ▶ francophone

Angolan liberation movement

The first Angolan liberation organization was the Movimento Popular de Libertação de Angola (MPLA, Popular Movement for the Liberation of Angola), formed in December 1956. Its chief founders were Mario Coelho Pinto de Andrade, Antonio Agostinho ▶ Neto, both Angolan, and Amilcar ▶ Cabral, from Guinea-Bissau (▶▶ PAIGC). In Paris in 1957, these three formed the Movimento Anti-Colonista of Africans from all the Portuguese colonies. The MPLA was predominantly mestizo and urban based in Luanda and Benguela. The Portuguese cracked down on it in 1959–60. Its first military action was an attack on a Luanda prison in February 1961.

Neto, who emerged as the eventual leader, was born in 1922, the son of a Methodist preacher. After working in Luanda, he won a scholarship to study medicine in Portugal, graduating in 1958. He returned to Angola and opened a practice. He was imprisoned for his political activity and eventually fled to Kinshasa, where he was elected to lead the MPLA at its first congress, and then to Brazzaville.

The Frente Nacional de Libertação de Angola (FNLA, National Front for the Liberation of Angola) was formed in March 1962 by a merger of the União das Populaçoes de Angola (UPA, Union of Angolan Peoples), a predominantly Kongo grouping, and the Partido Democratico Angolana (PDA, Angolan Democratic Party), a Zambo grouping. The UPA was founded in 1957 in northern Angola; its leader was Holden Roberto, who sought to make it a nationwide organization. Roberto was born in San Salvador in 1923 and was educated by Methodists in colonial Leopoldville. He remained in Zaïre working as a clerk in government and the private sector. In 1958 he travelled to Ghana and in 1959 to the United Nations to address the General Assembly on behalf of Angola. In March 1961 the UPA launched a Kongo peasant uprising and by the time the FNLA was formed it had secured rudimentary self-rule over much of northern Angola. In 1963 Roberto won recognition of the FNLA as the 'official' Angolan liberation movement from the Organization of African Unity, but subsequently the FNLA began to accept funds from the Central Intelligence Agency (CIA) to counter the Soviet-sponsored MPLA.

A split in the FNLA in December 1964 led to the formation of the União Nacional para a Independência Total de Angola (UNITA, National Union for the Total Independence of Angola) in Lusaka, Zambia in March 1966 by Jonas Malheiros Savimbi. Savimbi was born in 1934 in Mexico and won a scholarship to study at the University of Lisbon, subsequently continuing at Lausanne, Switzerland. He joined the UPA, became secretary-general and helped form the FNLA, but he broke with Roberto in 1964 and took most of the FNLA's Ovimbo supporters with him.

UNITA's first attack was on the Benguela railway, Zambia's lifeline, and President Kaunda expelled Savimbi and UNITA from Zambia. He eventually returned to Angola in 1968, but UNITA remained the smallest of the three organizations, receiving only modest amounts of arms from outside, from Beijing.

Following the Portuguese decision to decolonize, the MPLA and FNLA set up offices in Luanda in October–November 1974 and worked in the transitional government with the Portuguese; UNITA joined in January 1975. Tensions between the three organizations rose as settlers fled to Portugal and independence approached. UNITA sought support from South Africa. In July 1975 the MPLA drove the FNLA out of Luanda and civil war broke out. In October 1975 South Africa invaded; the CIA supplied mercenaries to the FNLA which reached the northern outskirts of Luanda in November while UNITA–South African forces neared from the south. The MPLA called for help from the USSR and Cuba which quickly airlifted troops in; by March 1976 the MPLA had won the war. The FNLA had all but disappeared, after the Clark Amendment in the USA cut off all covert CIA aid and UNITA was confined to the south, with South African aid. When the Clark Amendment was repealed in August 1985, UNITA was the beneficiary of the renewed flow of CIA funds.

UNITA grew with South African and US support, but has been largely restricted to its Ovamboland region with only occasional incursions outside, despite repeated South African sweeps and invasions. In January 1986 Savimbi was received at the White House and was promised Stinger surface-to-air missiles.

The MPLA used the occasion of the South African invasion in 1975–6 to crush its left opposition, tame the trade unions and then declare itself a Marxist-Leninist vanguard party as the MPLA–PT (Partido de Trabalho, Workers' Party). Neto died in 1979 and was replaced by José Eduardo dos Santos. Born in 1942, dos Santos joined the MPLA youth wing and fought with the guerrillas before going to study petroleum engineering in the USSR. He was foreign minister, 1974–8. A moderate, he signed the Lusaka Agreement with South Africa in 1984 which banned ▶ SWAPO from using Angolan–Namibian border areas as rear bases. He appealed to South Africa for talks and restored relations with Portugal.

An agreement in 1988 led to the withdrawal of both South African and Cuban troops from Angolan territory over the next two years. The fight between government troops and UNITA, however, continued. In 1989 the MPLA government agreed to negotiate a settlement to the war with UNITA. Negotiations were hosted by the Zaïrean President Joseph Mobutu; after ceasefire agreements broke down, further talks were hosted by Portugal in 1991, resulting in an agreement to end the war and call multi-party elections in 1992.

apartheid (Afrikaans = separation)

The series of laws ratifying oppression of the South African black majority was introduced by the Afrikaner-led National Party which came to power in 1948. Extreme segregation and oppression already existed in South Africa and had been maintained by previous white governments and by legislation, such as the Land Acts of 1913 and 1936 which restricted land available for black farming to 13 per cent of the country, and the pass laws which restricted the black population's freedom of movement. The apartheid laws, however, introduced a grotesque systematization of this pre-existing racial discrimination. The laws of apartheid included: the Population Registration Act, which registered all individuals by racial group; the Mixed Amenities Act, which codified racial segregation in public facilities; the Group Areas Act to segregate urban suburbs; the Immorality Act, which illegalized white–black marriages and sexual relations; and the establishment of the so-called ▶ Bantustans.

The apartheid system has given rise to successive waves of resistance from the black population of South Africa (▶ ANC, ▶ AZAPO, ▶ black consciousness, Nelson ▶ Mandela, ▶ PAC, ▶ Soweto, ▶ UDF). It has also been the focus of numerous international anti-apartheid activities including a campaign for economic ▶ sanctions against South Africa, which have been implemented in a very marginal and ineffective way.

The rapid political developments in South Africa from 1989 seem to have made the apartheid system unsustainable. After growing African resistance even the Nationalist Party government under President de Klerk announced in 1991 its intention to abolish all the laws which had supported apartheid and the party declared the whole policy to have been a political mistake. Whether this renunciation does anything to prolong the life of the all-white party as a governing élite is questionable but there is no doubt that apartheid as a legal system is dying. The struggle to eliminate racial discrimination in South Africa is, however, in its infancy.

Further reading

M. Murray (ed.), *South African Capitalism and Black Political Opposition*, Cambridge, Mass. 1983.
R. Price and C.G. Rosberg, *The Apartheid Regime*, Berkeley, Calif. 1980.

appropriate technology

Appropriate technology is the technology which is appropriate to the development needs of the Third World. The term is now commonly used to denote what is still sometimes referred to as 'intermediate technology'. The latter term was often rejected because it seems to suggest that the Third World should have less than the best technology.

The idea that there is a technology appropriate for the needs of the Third World which is, therefore, different to the technology in use in developed countries has various roots. One argument for it is based on an apparently simple economic deduction: the Third World has large amounts of labour and is short of capital; the industrialized countries have the opposite. Hence, while a capital-intensive technology is economically efficient in the industrialized countries a more labour-intensive technology will be more economically efficient in a Third World country. While that argument may have some validity, it ignores some factors. For some forms of production, there really may not be a range of different technologies to choose from: while there are relatively labour-intensive ways of making clothes or of building roads there is no labour-intensive way of refining petroleum. Even where a choice exists in theory it may not be operative because the demands of the world market or competition from imports impose a kind of standardization which comes only from the use of a capital-intensive method of production.

There is a further argument for the use of labour-intensive technology: in practice, industrial investments in the Third World often create very little local employment. The result is the coexistence of technologically advanced factories with widespread unemployment and poverty. Appropriate technology is also, therefore, seen as employment-creating technology.

Other arguments for appropriate technology are more intangible but just as important. One of the original proposals came from the economist Fritz Schumacher in his widely read book *Small is Beautiful* (1973). Schumacher's argument is for a small-scale technology which creates work units which are more tolerable than the great mass-producing factories associated with capital-intensive technology. Clearly this has some connection with the position of ▶ Gandhi in favour of maintaining and developing small-scale activities. Others, taking off from this position, attach importance to using a technology which produces less disruptive and unbearable forms of social upheaval and change than those which characterized the industrial countries and are common in the Third World.

Recently, arguments for appropriate technology in the Third World have increasingly overlapped with those for an alternative technology based on ecological concerns. This stresses the dangers of using carbon-based energy generation and the excessive use of scarce resources.

The debate on appropriate technology is still in its infancy but, although many issues are unresolved, it has introduced important questions into the discussion of development. It exposes the gap which may exist between a technology which is rational in a profit-oriented economy and one which is desirable from the point of view of the lives of those who have to work with it. If the Third World can find a way to development which does not involve the hardships suffered by peasants and workers in the industrialized countries, that would be a positive step; but strong words of caution are necessary. Some arguments for technology are positive but others can sometimes be conservative and reactionary. For some it is an argument for tolerable change; for others it can be an argument against change at all. The ecological argument for alternative technology can be used as an argument against any industrialization in the Third World when ecological problems are primarily the responsibility of the industrialized nations (▶ environment).

However convincing the argument may appear in theory, the practice may be different. It is not always true that small-scale labour intensive technology is more tolerable than other technologies, and in many cases technologies with the supposed appropriateness simply do not exist. This may not be accidental since the technology in existence reflects past research and development, which reflects the needs of those who have financed the research and development; and these are the industrialized countries. With different research priorities it is quite possible that technologies would arise which are much more appropriate for the Third World (for example, cheaper solar energy technology). In a world where technological research, like every other aspect of the economy, is dominated by the industrialized countries this will not happen unless the Third World makes it happen. Here, therefore, is another argument in favour of North–South cooperation.

Technology is not separate from other aspects of economic life. The type of technology in use therefore depends on the type of economic system. Many inappropriate features of technology in the Third World are determined by the fact that it is a subordinate part of the world capitalist market. It will be difficult to make the choice of a more appropriate technology rational without at the same time breaking out of the power of the world market.

Further reading

M.R. Bhagavan, *Technological Advance in the Third World: struggles and policies*, London 1990.

R.K. Diwan and D. Livingston, *Alternative Development Strategies and Appropriate Technology*, New York 1979.

F. Stewart, *Technology and Underdevelopment*, London 1977.

Aprismo

The radical programme of the Alianza Popular Revolucionaria Americana (APRA, American Popular Revolutionary Alliance), the main party in Peru founded by Víctor Raúl Haya de la Torre (1895–1979) in 1924, called for land reform, the nationalization of industry, opposition to US imperialism and the political unity of Latin America. As a student leader, Haya de la Torre took part in the 1919 student–worker riots and was exiled to Mexico in 1923. Influenced by the Indigenismo movement there, he founded APRA as a pro-Indian and mestizo organization. APRA was banned until the 1940s, by which time it was the largest party in Peru. It was banned again between 1948 and 1956. By then it had modified its radicalism; it dropped its pan-Latin Americanism and changed its name to the Partido Aprista Peruano (PAP, Peruvian Aprista Party) in 1956. Haya de la Torre narrowly failed to win the 1962 presidential election. In 1968 the army took power led by the radical General Juan Velasco Alvarado who was influenced by the ideas of the Peruvian socialist and indigenist José Carlos ▶ Mariátegui (▶▶ Sendero Luminoso). APRA supported Velasco and won support in the Church. Conflicts developed between the leadership and radical elements. Velasco was overthrown by more conservative officers in 1975. In 1982 Alan García Pérez became APRA's secretary-general. He won the Peruvian presidency for APRA and APRA dominated both houses of congress. In power from 1985 to 1990, it pursued reactionary policies but engaged in confrontations with the International Monetary Fund and refused to pay Peru's debts in full.

Aprismo has considerably influenced parties in other Latin American countries, notably Venezuela, Costa Rica, the Dominican Republic and Mexico (▶ PRI). The failures of the García government, however, left the party disastrously discredited in its country of origin and its showing in the 1990 presidential elections was derisory.

Arab nationalism

Modern concepts of the Arab nation became important from the first decade of the twentieth century, especially among Arab intellectuals in Syria. At that period, Arab nationalism developed in reaction to the Turkish domination of the Ottoman Empire. At the same time other more specific nationalisms emerged in Egypt, Algeria and Tunisia which were reactions to British and French colonial rule in those areas.

It was in the 1940s and 1950s that these nationalisms were fused in the minds of intellectuals and in the projects of significant politicians into a broader concept of a nation which would include all the Arab world. The two key developments in this direction were the birth of the ▶ Ba'th Party and the coming to power of Gamal Abdel ▶ Nasser. Both these projects for Arab unity were based on the concept of a modern secular state, though they often included in practice some subsidiary element of ▶ Islam. In the form of mass support for the figure of Nasser, Arab nationalism at this point became in many Arab countries a genuinely popular demand. Though less important figures, such as Muammar ▶ Gadhafi, have tried to keep it alive, identification with the Palestinian

39

conflict with Israel has fuelled it, and the US-led war against Iraq provided it with a new boost, the project of an Arab nation none the less passed its peak with the demise of Nasser. More recently the Islamic element has had more prominence and the Arab element less in projects for greater unification of the Arab world.

Further reading

A. Abdel-Malek (ed.), *Contemporary Arab Political Thought*, London 1983.
S. Amin, *The Arab Nation*, London 1978.
A. Hourani, *A History of the Arab Peoples*, London 1991.
B. Tibi, *Arab Nationalism: a critical enquiry*, London 1981.

ASEAN, Association of South-East Asian Nations

This organization was established in 1967 at a meeting in Bangkok, Thailand, between the foreign ministers of Indonesia, Malaysia, the Philippines, Singapore and Thailand. Papua New Guinea was also present as an observer. The organization's aims were not closely defined, referring in general terms to economic, cultural and social progress in the South-East Asian region.

Currently, ASEAN has a standing committee with headquarters in Singapore which meets monthly. It also has a number of specialized committees devoted to policy development in particular areas, as follows:

City and country	Committee
Bangkok, Thailand	Navigation
Jakarta, Indonesia	Food
	Tourism
	Science and technology
Kuala Lumpur, Malaysia	Communications and telecommunications
	Mass media
	Finance
Manila, the Philippines	Trade and industry
Singapore	Civil aviation

The first full-scale summit of the member nations was held in 1976. On 7 March 1980 ASEAN signed a cooperation agreement with the European Community. In July 1981 ASEAN sponsored a regional United Nations conference on Kampuchea demanding the withdrawal of Vietnamese troops from that country.

The ASEAN nations have established a certain basis of cooperation and consultation but little integration, either political or economic. At the economic level they have been characterized more by competition than cooperation. In 1991, however, Singapore, Malaysia and Indonesia established a joint 'industrial triangle' – a new region of industrial development crossing the frontiers of the three countries, largely designed to link Singapore's surplus capital with Indonesia's and Malaysia's surplus labour. At present, while such specific economic projects may spread to the rest of the region, there is little sign that ASEAN will move towards more thoroughgoing economic integration.

Association of South-East Asian Nations ▶ ASEAN

ayatullah (Arabic = giving divine signs)
In the Shi'ite Muslim sect, an ayatullah is the name of a scholar who interprets the rules of the Koran for the faithful. In 1979 Ayatullah Khomeini led the Iranian insurrection against the Shah of Iran and established the Islamic Republic of Iran.

Azanian People's Organization ▶ AZAPO

AZAPO, Azanian People's Organization
Azania is the Greek form of the Persian Zanj-bar, meaning land of the Zanj, which was used to describe the east coast of Africa from the first century AD. Azania is the name ▶ black consciousness supporters now use for South Africa.

AZAPO was formed on 1 May 1978 to carry on the black consciousness tradition in South Africa after Steve Biko's murder and the subsequent repression of his movement. AZAPO became prominent during the uprising of 1985, when it successfully disrupted US Senator Edward Kennedy's tour of South Africa. The group has since been involved in clashes with supporters of the United Democratic Front (▶ UDF). At the end of the 1980s it was estimated to have 86 branches and an estimated 110,000 members.

After Biko was killed, AZAPO moved away for a time from his emphasis on 'psychological oppression' and cultivated links with socialist organizations like the Trotskyist Cape Action League, in a front called the National Forum, founded in 1983. However, after clashes with the UDF it moved back towards extreme black separatism, sometimes with anti-Semitic overtones.

B

balance of payments

A country's balance of payments is a double entry account showing financial flows to and from other countries. The balance of payments (or more often simply 'balance') can also mean the net outcome of the inward and outward flow of payments, either as a whole or for part of the account. If the net balance is positive the country has a surplus and if negative a deficit.

Like any double entry account, the credit and debit items must balance. Any deficit or surplus on one part of the account can be balanced by a surplus or deficit on another, but a deficit or surplus on financial transactions as a whole will be balanced by a change in the country's reserves of foreign currencies or gold.

The standard presentation of the balance of payments account is under the three broad headings of current account, investment and other capital flows and official financing:

(1) *Current account.* The current account includes the financial flows resulting from trade in goods and services, earnings in the form of interest, profits and company dividends and transfers such as gifts or remittances from migrant workers.

Thus, within the current account there is a 'visible' trade account which is an account of the exports and imports of tangible goods. If these exports exceed imports this will be shown as a surplus on visible trade since more money is entering the country on export sales than is leaving the country to buy foreign goods. A broader presentation of the trade account will include trade 'invisibles' or services. This involves such things as shipping services, earnings from foreign tourists and the sale of banking and insurance activities overseas.

Taken together, these two items represent the goods and services trade account and from this a 'balance of trade' is computed – a surplus if earnings on exports are greater than payments for imports; a deficit in the case of the opposite.

Interest, profits and dividends involve flows of finance relating to existing investments. Past foreign investment and lending to private business and the government of one country would lead to a present outflow of such payments. Similarly, past overseas investment and lending by the government or private business would produce a present inflow of these payments. Again, a balance can be computed.

Next come so-called transfers (current payments and receipts not related to trade or investment). Some Third World countries are traditionally important sources of labour for advanced capitalist countries. This can result in sizeable transfers of wage earnings to workers' countries of origin. North African and Turkish labour in continental Europe are long-standing examples.

The growth of migrant labour in the oil-producing countries of the Persian Gulf in the 1970s and 1980s had a major effect on the balance of payments of a number of Asian countries. In the 1980s remittances by Pakistani and Bangladeshi migrants were very nearly as great as their countries' earnings from exports. Another item under transfers are 'gifts' which in the case of one country, Israel, amount to an important source of inflows.

All these various flows come under the heading of the current account. The 'current balance' constitutes the difference between earnings and payments on the current account and may be in surplus or deficit.

(2) *Investment and other capital flows*. This part of the balance of payments depicts capital as distinct from current financial flows. The government, business and individuals in one country may invest overseas. Investment may be in other government bonds, the portfolio of existing overseas companies or the establishment of new businesses abroad. The same country will also be subject to similar inward capital flows from foreign investors.

Though the export of capital represents an accumulation of foreign assets it constitutes a financial outflow. Similarly, an import of capital means foreigners increasing their ownership of a country's assets through the inflow of finance. If capital exports exceed imports it will appear as a deficit on the capital account.

(3) *Official financing*. There is nothing about the current or capital account which demands that the flows of money exactly balance each other. Indeed, an actual balance would be extremely unlikely since the current and capital accounts are the outcome of millions of individual decisions by consumers and investors.

An aggregate deficit on the current and capital account, however, is tantamount to an erosion of the financial means available to sustain external transactions at the existing level in the future. For instance, if the UK is in deficit it means that more sterling is flowing out of the country than foreigners require to finance their current or capital transactions with the UK. This would lead to downward pressure on the sterling exchange rate. The consequent erosion of the buying power of sterling would, thereby, threaten to disrupt the scale of external transactions at the existing level.

Official financing constitutes all those transactions by the government which are designed to accommodate the discrepancy in the current and capital account payments. This involves the use of the government's foreign currency reserves and gold. It also involves utilizing financial resources available through International Monetary Fund arrangements. If a country is in deficit it will use these reserves to buy back its own currency on the money markets, effectively balancing the inward and outward flows of its currency. If it is in surplus it will sell its own currency resulting in an increase in its reserves of foreign currency.

A reduction in foreign reserves to cover a deficit will appear with a plus sign (+) in the payments account though it represents a reduction of a country's foreign assets in the form of foreign currency reserves. This is because the deficit that exists before such official intervention is signified in the accounts as a minus sign (−). Similarly, an addition to external reserves due to a balance of payments surplus will appear in the account under a minus sign.

It is important to realize that official financing effects only a balance in the financial flows in and out of the country. It does not transform the actual situation of, say, a deficit in trade where the value of goods exported is less than those imported. This is important because foreign reserves held by the government are exhaustible. If such deficits persist, in the long run it reduces the level of reserves and increases the pressure for an actual change in the trade in goods through a mixture of raising exports and reducing imports.

Finally, it should be mentioned that official financing never exactly equals the observed deficit or surplus on the current and capital accounts. This is because there is also an item, usually incorporated in the capital account, known as the 'balancing item'. This arises from normal discrepancies in the flow of finance and recorded transactions of goods. It is standard commercial practice that goods are paid for at some date later than the delivery date. The recipient of goods will issue a bill of exchange amounting to a promise to pay in the future, e.g. three months' time. In a period where such due payments are heavy it will make financial transactions on trade appear greater than the actual transaction of goods in the same period. The balancing item also reflects goods transactions that are never officially recorded but whose financial corollary does appear.

In this context it is possible for the payments account to appear in deficit before consideration of the balancing item which could produce a surplus and, therefore, an addition to foreign reserves.

The balance of payments surplus and deficits of all the countries in the world (both the total, and each of the separate parts of the account) must equal zero; all the deficits must balance all the surpluses, though in practice due to errors in measurement there is always a difference in the published figures. Few countries are able to develop very large surpluses or deficits over long periods without these being corrected, but in the 1980s some significant surpluses and deficits developed in the world economy. In the trade account, the USA experienced a chronic large trade deficit. Two countries almost monopolized the corresponding trade surplus – Japan and West Germany – and correspondingly on the capital account the USA received large amounts of capital inflow (and therefore had a surplus) from West Germany and Japan (which therefore had a deficit).

The other major imbalance of recent years has involved the Third World more directly and emerges from the ▶ debt crisis. In general, it can be said that Third World countries face continual pressures which tend to produce a deficit on their current account; these arise both from high demand for imported consumer goods and from the need to import capital goods for development purposes. Third World countries tend to finance these deficits where possible through aid and foreign investment inflows, but financing is not always possible and balance of payments crises, high tariff protection (▶ protectionism), major devaluations of currencies and emergency measures are endemic features of economic life in Third World countries. Reducing a balance of payments deficit requires major cutbacks in consumption and investment and causes both immediate hardship and long-term economic damage.

Converting a deficit into a surplus obviously implies even greater hardship and damage. Yet this is precisely what a number of Third World countries have been obliged to do as a result of the debt crisis of the years since 1982. With no new inflows of capital or aid, fulfilling the obligation to service and repay the debt has meant that large debtor countries have had to produce a surplus on their balance of trade with which to make the payments. For Latin America and the Caribbean as a whole this surplus amounted to around US$25 billion a year during the latter part of the 1980s.

Because the prospects of expanding export earnings have been so bleak, this surplus had to be created almost entirely by reducing the level of imports, and that was done by cutting back government spending, by cutting incomes and by reducing investment. No one in the Third World countries concerned benefits from this and as usual the poor tend to pay a higher price while the debt gets paid.

At the same time, those in the Third World countries who have any wealth often respond to the economic crises provoked by debt repayment by converting their wealth into foreign exchange and exporting it. This in balance of payments terms is a negative item in the capital account, though it often does not get explicitly registered because it is clandestine. It also requires a further current account surplus item to balance it. The ironic and tragic result of these circumstances is that Third World countries which logically should have a deficit in their current account and a surplus in their capital account are in the opposite position. They are obliged to produce a surplus on their current account in order to transfer capital to the richer countries in the form of debt repayments to the Western banks and the transfer to safe havens of the wealth of the local élite (▶▶ capital flight).

balance of trade ▶ balance of payments, ▶ exports

banana republic

This term is used to characterize unstable political regimes usually run by arbitrarily imposed dictators in a close relation with foreign business interests. The term originates from the early part of the twentieth century. It emerged as a widely used description of the countries of Central America whose economies were almost entirely dominated by the banana plantations of US companies.

The instability of banana republics is the result of their subservience to foreign interests. At the turn of the twentieth century, the foreign domination of Central America assumed an extreme form. In Costa Rica, El Salvador and, particularly, Honduras and Guatemala, US banana companies virtually ran the country. One company, United Fruit of America, had a near-monopoly on banana production and controlled railway and port facilities. US interests owned the best land and established an enclave directed outwards towards the world economy. The railways which United Fruit built connected the plantations to the ports, leaving the rest of the country virtually without any system of transport. As a result, the rest of the country stagnated, its only role being to provide labour for the plantation enclaves.

To enforce their interests, the banana companies played a central role in the political affairs of the countries of Central America. It was the decisive influence of these companies on domestic politics that inspired the term 'banana republic'. US companies intervened in political rivalries, played one side against the other and promoted their own candidates to run the affairs of the state. On occasions, economic rivalry between different banana companies provided the impetus for local political conflict. Thus the intense competition between United Fruit and the Cuyaxel Fruit Company in Honduras sparked off a bitter civil war in 1923. Virtually every president in the region was elected with the blessing of the banana companies. Banana companies have played a leading role in organizing repression of popular worker and peasant revolts.

With the development of new sectors of the economy in the post-war period, the influence of US plantation owners has declined. Nevertheless, with the exception of Nicaragua and to some extent Costa Rica, Central American countries have continued to exhibit many of the characteristics of banana republics. US influence, now exercised through the state, is still decisive and shapes government policy in Central America. As Washington's hostile reactions to the Nicaraguan revolution and to Panama indicate, it considers Central America as its 'backyard', since the power of the governments and the local élites resides in their connection with the USA rather than in popular support. They lack authority and legitimacy. It is for this reason that most of Central America remains inherently unstable. Popular resistance is widespread and the survival of the regimes of Central American banana republics is directly dependent on the military forces of the USA.

Bandung Conference

Bandung is a city on the Indonesian island of Java which was the site of a conference of 29 African and Asian countries which issued a declaration in April 1955 calling for closer economic, cultural and diplomatic ties between the countries of the two continents. The conference was an important precursor to the foundation of the Movement of Non-Aligned Countries, which was launched in 1961 (▶ non-aligned movement). The leading participants were Jawaharlal ▶ Nehru, Kwame ▶ Nkrumah, Ahmed ▶ Sukarno, Gamal Abdel ▶ Nasser and President Tito of Yugoslavia. ▶▶ NIEO.

Bank for International Settlements ▶ BIS

Bantustan

This term refers to the land of the Bantu, designated for an African ethnic group, and was introduced by the 1913 Land Act of the South African government which gave whites (19 per cent of the population) 87 per cent of the country's territory, leaving the rest to blacks. This land was the poorest agriculturally and was scattered into isolated reservations. The Bantustans were renamed Homelands in 1968, since when a number of them have been declared 'independent' by the South African government. This 'independence' has been a mockery and none of the Bantustans have been internationally recognized. The independence plan, however, was a cornerstone of ▶ apartheid, being designed to create the myth that the Africans had their own lands in which they were 'free'.

barter ▶ counter-trade

basic needs

The idea of a proposed reorientation of development strategy was advocated especially by the International Labour Organization in the 1970s. The concept emerged out of disillusion with what some observers referred to as 'growth without development': the prevalence of reasonable or even high growth of national product combined with an increase in unmet human basic needs. The idea was that, instead of concentration on maximizing macroeconomic goals (especially growth of production), governments should identify specific unmet needs (nutrition, housing, water, health care, education) and encourage development projects which fulfil some of these. It was argued by some that this, by improving health and skills in the population as well as the distribution of income, would have a positive effect of overall growth in the long run – a kind of 'trickle-up' effect. The idea was launched at a bad moment – the eve of the ▶ debt crisis and the wave of ▶ neo-liberalism which swept the world during the 1980s and under which many basic needs programmes had to be cut in order to service the debt. Basic needs, argue the neo-liberals, should not be specially encouraged because they will 'trickle-down' from successful market-oriented growth in general.

The idea of the strategy is one of the components of the recent United Nations Development Programme idea of ▶ human development which has been produced by some of the same personnel and also coincides in a number of respects with the advocacy of using ▶ appropriate technology.

Further reading

D.P. Ghai, *The Basic-Needs Approach to Development: some issues regarding concepts and methodology*, Geneva: ILO 1977.

R. Sandbrook, *The Politics of Basic Needs*, London 1982.

F. Stewart, *Basic Needs in Developing Countries*, Baltimore, Md. 1985.

P. Streeten and others, *First Things First: meeting basic needs in the developing countries*, New York 1981.

Ba'th (Arabic = renaissance)

Ba'thism is a pan-Arab nationalist movement founded in Syria in 1953 with the slogan of 'One Arab nation from the Atlantic Ocean to the Arabian Gulf' and the goal of Arab unity, independence and socialism. It was founded by Akram Hourani, the leader of the Arab Socialist Party, and Michel Aflaq, a disillusioned communist and founder of the Arab Resurrection Party. Its programme appealed to intellectuals, junior army officers, white collar workers and middle class merchants from Syria to Iraq and Lebanon.

Syrian Ba'thism. Ba'thists welcomed the union of Syria and Egypt in the United Arab Republic (UAR) in 1958, but in 1961, as Nasser attempted to centralize all commercial and industrial activity under his control and abolish the Syrian regional council, the Ba'thists rebelled, dissolving the UAR and taking power in Syria, proposing a pan-Arab federation. In 1963 Hourani and Aflaq were pushed aside by radicals in the Syrian army who seized power and proclaimed a socialist republic but with Islam as the state religion, and in 1969 made the Ba'th the sole party in Syria. In 1970 General Hafez al-Asad took power, instituting a secular regime, and warred against the ▶ Muslim Brotherhood. In an attempt to limit the Lebanese civil war in 1975, he sent troops to Lebanon which crushed the left-wing and Palestinian forces there. In 1980 the split in Ba'thism was so wide that Syria supported Iran in its war with Ba'thist-ruled Iraq. Syria moved back into Beirut with the renewed Lebanese conflicts in the 1980s, backing ▶ AMAL and alternately manipulated and attacked the Palestinian factions (▶ PLO).

Iraqi Ba'thism. Ba'thism spread to Iraq following the army overthrow of the pro-British monarchy in 1958. Ba'thists opposed the moderate Karim Qassim government, and backed soldiers who overthrew him in 1963, but the new regime soon turned against the Ba'thists, who were persecuted until the installation of the regime of General Ahmad al-Bakr in 1968. The leader of the Ba'thists was Saddam Hussein who temporarily allied with the powerful Iraqi Communist Party, and the Ba'thists increasingly became the real power, shifting the country into a pro-Soviet position and finally removing al-Bakr in 1979. In September 1980, with the informal backing of the USA, he attacked Iran and began the

Iran–Iraq War. During the war Iraq kept good relations with both East and West. Like the Syrian Ba'thists, the Iraqis have shelved their original commitment to radical Arab independence, allowing the West and moderate Arabs to use them to prevent the spread of the Shi'ite revolt from Iran.

From long-term enmity and war by proxy, the two nations ruled by Ba'thism became direct enemies in war in 1990 and 1991 when Syria joined the US-led coalition which defeated Iraq after the latter's occupation of Kuwait in August 1990.

Further reading

M. Farouk-Sluglett and P. Sluglett, *Iraq since 1958: from revolution to dictatorship*, London 1990.

S. al-Khalil, *Republic of Fear*, London 1989.

E. Kienle, *Ba'th v. Ba'th: the conflict between Syria and Iraq, 1968–1989*, London 1990.

V. Randall (ed.), *Political Parties in the Third World*, London 1988.

Ben Bella, Ahmed (1916–)

The first president of independent Algeria was born in Marnia, Algeria, 25 December 1916. He joined the 14th regiment of Algerian sharpshooters in 1939 and served with distinction in Italy, where he won the Croix Militaire for valour. Back home again in 1945, he witnessed the Sétif massacres. He then joined the illegal Parti du Peuple Algérien (PPA, Party of the Algerian People), and later the Organisation Secrète (OS, Secret Organization). Ben Bella participated in an attack on the main general post office in Oran on 4 April 1949, but was captured and jailed by the French until 1952, when he managed to escape to Nasser's Cairo. However, in 1956 the French diverted to Algiers a Moroccan plane he was on en route for Tunis, and he was then imprisoned in France until 1962. On his return to Algeria, Ben Bella became first prime minister and then president of the new country. While in power, he supported many national liberation struggles around the world, particularly Arab ones. In 1965, he was overthrown by his former comrade Houari Boumedienne and imprisoned until 1979, when he was released by President Chadli Bendjedid and exiled. Ben Bella returned to Algeria in 1990. ▶▶ FLN.

Berlin Conference

Held on the initiative of the German Chancellor Otto von Bismarck, this conference (1884–5) was attended by the UK, Austria–Hungary, Belgium, Denmark, France, Spain, the Netherlands, Luxemburg, Germany, Norway, Portugal, Russia, Sweden, Turkey, the USA and Italy. It recognized the River Congo as an 'international' river (i.e. open to free trade), accepted the abolition of slavery (prompted by the shortage of labour on the West Coast of Africa) and carved up the remaining African territory which had not yet been divided among the European powers.

Biko, Steve ▶ black consciousness

BIS, Bank for International Settlements

Established in Basle, Switzerland, in 1930 to coordinate payments of war reparations, BIS since 1982 has become heavily involved in the international ▶ debt crisis, playing a prominent role in managing central bank bridging loans.

black consciousness

The programme of the Black People's Convention (BPC), a separatist organization founded in South Africa in 1972 but banned in 1977, black consciousness derived its programme from two sources – the pan-Africanist tradition of Robert Sobukwe (▶ PAC) and the US ▶ black power movement of the 1960s. Its leader was Steve Biko (1947–77), who was born in Kingwilliamstown, Natal. Biko studied medicine at the University of Natal Medical School until he helped found the South African Students Organization (SASO) in 1969. SASO went on to organize the Black People's Convention in 1972, whose slogan was 'Black Man – you are on your own'. Though several leading members of the Pan-Africanist Congress helped found the BPC, the movement was mostly inspired by the black power ideology from the USA. Biko was its honorary president. He attempted to use the method of dialectics to oppose the multi-racialism of the African National Congress (▶ ANC): 'Since the thesis is a White racism, there can only be one valid antithesis, i.e. a solid Black unity to counterbalance the scale.'

The BPC's aim was 'to unite and solidify the Black People of South Africa with a view to liberating and emancipating them from both psychological and physical oppression'. BPC supporters were mostly from black universities and seminaries. The BPC was banned in 1973, but it continued to work inside South Africa with SASO in organizing resistance. Unlike the ANC, it played a major role in the ▶ Soweto uprising of June 1976. Biko was arrested and murdered by the police in September 1977, when they drove him from Port Elizabeth to Pretoria in the back of a Land-Rover. The policeman in charge, Colonel Goosen, was later promoted. In the aftermath of Biko's death, the black consciousness movement was subjected to full-scale repression by the state. The black consciousness tradition is nowadays voiced through the Azanian People's Organization (▶ AZAPO), formed shortly after Biko's death.

black economy

Sometimes known as the underground economy, this term is used to describe economic activity which goes unrecorded in official statistics. In Western industrialized nations certain sectors of the economy are traditionally associated with a high incidence of 'casually' employed workers, i.e. workers whose employment goes unregistered. Hotels, restaurants and public bars are prime cases, as are areas where seasonal factors affect employment (agriculture, the tourist industry). Individuals registered as employed may also be active in the black economy. Some workers take on a second, casual, job. Among building workers, electricians and plumbers, work involving unrecorded financial transactions outside company hours and without an employer's knowledge, is widespread. Another example is work inside a family carried out with commercial aims. This may be the case with little retail outlets or small clothes-making concerns. Working mothers often employ child-minders on an informal basis and for a nominal sum. This too can be classified as work within the black economy.

In effect, any activity carried out involving some kind of financial transaction, but where such employment remains unregistered in official statistics for economic activity, can be considered part of the black economy.

In advanced capitalist countries the term 'black economy' has a moral stigma attached, given by a generally dominant liberal consensus. It is associated with tax avoidance, claiming state benefits while actually employed, the use of child labour, etc. This raises problems in using the term 'black economy' in relation to backward capitalist countries. Distinctive social and political factors often endow the whole economic structure with a more 'illegitimate' character. The most important is the questionable legitimacy of the central authorities in many Third World countries.

Where central government is relatively weak in relation to class and regional interests there exist plenty of opportunities for 'under-recording' commercial activity. This might be to escape taxes or legal rules on the employment of labour. Such practices are often widespread among both indigenous and foreign capitalist producers. A graphic, though for obvious reasons exceptional, example of the black economy in the Third World can be found in Colombia and Bolivia. Here the collective efforts of local businessmen, police and judges and Western middlemen ensure a massive under-recording of the production and export of cocaine. In effect, the weaker character of capitalism in the Third World, the harsh requirements of its survival, as well as its questionable hegemony, make the distinction between the black and the legitimate economy less relevant. ▶▶ informal sector.

black power

Black power was the slogan of black US radicals frustrated at the failure of Martin Luther King's civil rights movement and the 1964 Civil Rights Act to produce any meaningful change. From the assassination of

Malcolm X in 1965, the black power movement turned increasingly radical under the influence of Stokely Carmichael (now Kwame Touré) and the Black Panthers. They did not exclude violence in pursuit of their aim to overthrow the existing political and economic institutions as a prerequisite for the liberation of black Americans. The black power movement reached its height in 1968. More recently its best-known leaders have moved in various inconsistent directions.

Bonapartism

This concept was developed by Karl Marx in his book, *The Eighteenth Brumaire of Louis Bonaparte*, in analysing the coup d'état in France in 1851 by Louis Bonaparte (nephew of the Emperor Napoleon Bonaparte, who later ruled as Napoleon III from 1852 to 1870). Marx attempts to explain why the revolution of 1848 supported by the working people and the progressive sections of the French capitalist class ended in the establishment of the regime of Bonaparte which was not a government of the capitalist parties and which presented itself as being above class interests altogether. Marx gave the name Bonapartism to this situation which he characterized as a case where the capitalist class was too weak, its power too finely balanced with other classes, to rule in its own name. In such circumstances an individual or small group is able to gain political power claiming to act in the interests of the nation as a whole and to be above class interests but ultimately upholding the existing social order in which the capitalist class is dominant.

The concept of Bonapartism has considerable relevance for the Third World. In most Third World countries, especially the ex-colonies, the capitalist class is characteristically weak. It lacks economic independence and is often sustained through its relation with foreign interests. Its lack of independent economic power places a major restriction on its political power. Its lack of political confidence is illustrated by its reluctance to concede parliamentary democracy. In general, it is forced to exercise its rule more directly and coercively than is necessary in the more affluent Western states.

In general, the capitalist class has two options through which it can compensate for its lack of social power. It can govern through making itself the explicit instrument of foreign interests and hold down the popular masses through coercion, or it can attempt to win the support of the people through establishing a populist regime. In both cases the Bonapartist strategy of raising the government above classes is necessary.

Right-wing Bonapartism depends on a clique of military or authoritarian politicians to secure the interests of capital. Such a clique is tolerated by the indigenous bourgeoisie because only they can guarantee to maintain the conditions for its privileges. Many of the military dictatorships in the Third World play this role. Often, military governments are seen as the products of the interests of the military alone. In reality, military dictatorships are preserving capitalist social relations with the approval of the capitalist class. Such military regimes, e.g. that of Pinochet in Chile, are the only means through which the existing socio-economic structures can be maintained. In general, right-wing Bonapartist regimes require foreign assistance for their survival. In return, these regimes are prepared to give up their economies to foreign interests and are ready to serve as junior partners to imperialism. El Salvador, Chile and Indonesia are illustrations of right-wing Bonapartist regimes.

The class character of right-wing Bonapartist regimes is not difficult to discern. The craven subservience of Arap Moi in Kenya or of Pinochet in Chile to foreign capital is clear and open. It is the left-wing populist Bonapartist regimes that present more of a problem for analysis.

In certain situations, the Third World national bourgeoisie has a temporary opportunity to pursue its own independent interests. Under such circumstances, it adopts a strategy of economic nationalism to free itself from foreign domination. To realize this objective, the leadership of the bourgeoisie is prepared to adopt anti-imperialist rhetoric and may even mobilize the masses against foreign capital.

Since the nationalist bourgeoisie cannot mobilize the masses in defence of its own class interests, it is forced to broaden its appeal. Usually, it adopts a radical rhetoric and finds an individual leader who assumes the role of the Bonaparte. The Khomeini regime in Iran is an example of this approach. Other well-known leaders playing a similar role are Sukarno, Nasser and Perón. Left-wing Bonapartist leaders adopt an aggressively populist stance. Their radical rhetoric is directed primarily against foreign interests. At the same time, they adopt a more moderate course of action towards their domestic problems. Populist leaders tend to argue that class conflict is wrong since all the people should stick together. They elevate a mystical concept of the people and dismiss those who insist on the necessity for class as troublemakers.

Many Bonapartist leaders genuinely seek progressive changes. However, the conflict of interests between classes forces them to side with the existing social order. Marx's comments on this point are pertinent: 'Bonaparte would like to appear as the patriarchal benefactor of all classes, but he cannot give to one class without taking from another.'[1] Bonapartist leaders like Perón and Nasser usually begin by giving concessions to the masses in order to gain popular support. However, at a certain stage, the requirements of the capitalist system force these leaders to take back previous concessions and a shift to the right becomes the predictable outcome. This appears to be the universal pattern followed by radical Bonapartist leaders.

The rightward shift of populist Bonapartist regimes often represents a prelude to their demise. Such a shift leads to the loss of popular support, and without the backing of the masses, such regimes find it difficult to sustain their economic nationalist strategy, and at the same time they cease to be of any use to the economically privileged classes. Often, too, as in the case of ▶ Sukarno and Perón (▶ Peronism) they face foreign pressures which they are too isolated to resist. In such cases a military coup usually follows and the masses are contained by a more coercive and violent form of state rule; ineffective, degenerating left Bonapartism is replaced by ruthless and determined right Bonapartism.

The concept of Bonapartism is, therefore, a pertinent one for the understanding of Third World regimes. There is a danger, however, that in explaining the logic of Bonapartist regimes as a result of the weakness and dependence of the Third World bourgeoisie the conclusion will be reached that Bonapartism is the only possible form of Third World regime. This is clearly not so since other varieties of government exist in the Third World, sometimes on a long-term basis, as for instance in the parliamentary democracy of India. Bonapartism in Latin America suffers periodically from such a decline in prestige and popular hatred that the way is open for other forms of rule, unstable as they often are. Such has been the situation in South America during the second part of the 1980s when several military Bonapartist regimes were forced out of office in favour of a more democratic alternative (▶ Aprismo, ▶ military government).

Note

1. K. Marx, *The Eighteenth Brumaire of Louis Bonaparte*, London 1851, p. 177.

brain drain

The term 'brain drain' is given to the flow of trained and qualified people from one country to another. It was first used to refer to the flow from the Third World to the developed countries but has more recently been applied to the flow of scientists, for instance, from Europe to the USA. The flow from the Third World may be a mechanism making for economic polarization since resources invested in training and education by Third World countries are put to use in developed ones; the former pay and do not benefit while the latter benefit but do not pay. The brain drain reflects the fact that there exists in practice a relatively free world labour market in highly skilled labour and an extremely restricted one in unskilled labour. Surgeons and airline pilots can work in virtually whatever country they like while most construction workers and farm labourers have to stay at home. This fact, as well as leading to the brain drain, tends to maintain especially high salary differentials within Third World countries.

The brain drain, however, also reflects the fact that a neo-colonial training and higher education system in the Third World often produces skills which are more suited to be used in the context of developed countries rather than in activities which promote real development. And in any case many highly educated people who stay in Third World countries often fail, because of failures of development and economic policy, to find jobs which use their skills. In this respect the effects of the brain drain may be exaggerated since it is really only part of a larger problem.

Finally, on the other side of the coin, the brain drain is often part of a family survival strategy and leads to a return flow of remittances from the skilled worker abroad. Thus, it may harm development potential but assist short-term survival. ▶ migration.

Brandt Report

North–South: a programme for survival is the report of the Independent Commission on International Development Issues under the chairmanship of the West German politician Willy Brandt. Commonly known as the Brandt Report, it was published in 1980. Based on two years of work, the report sought to provide arguments for the renewal of the so-called ▶ North–South dialogue.

The Brandt Report provides an eloquent summary of the profound crisis facing the countries of the South. It places emphasis on the unequal position of the South in the international order. Moreover, the report confirms that the structures of the international system work against the interests of the South and reproduce the existing relations of inequality. Its recommendations are designed to alter the present international balance in favour of the South.

The report recommends an action programme of emergency and long-term measures to assist the impoverished regions of Africa and Asia. It argues for at least US$4 billion per year to deal with the pressing problem facing the poorest countries in the Third World. The report also advocates the establishment of a system of food security so that famine conditions can be effectively tackled. Allied to the provision of food aid is the suggestion that assistance be made available for the purposes of agrarian reform. The Brandt Report also urges international assistance for national population problems to tackle the problem of malnutrition. This emphasis is in line with its perspective that priority must be given to the poorest Third World countries and to the abolition of hunger. It states that 'the world must aim to abolish hunger and malnutrition by the end of the century through the elimination of economic inequalities'.[1]

The Brandt Report puts forward a series of proposals for reforming the existing international order. It proposes the establishment of a Common Fund for the purposes of stabilizing the price of commodities. It argues for the implementation of industrial adjustment policies with a view to removing protectionist barriers to the export of Third World manufactured goods. The report advocates the proclamation of an international code of conduct on the sharing of technology. It argues that transnational companies should encourage investment in mineral development in Third World countries and provide expertise and resources for that purpose.

The Brandt Report also tackles the existing monetary system and finance. It puts forward a case for the reform of the monetary system. It argues that the existing financial mechanisms are insufficient to meet the requirements of Third World development. Accordingly, it suggests that annual official development assistance should more than double. In addition, it calls for the rationalization of development finance and the provision of more funds through loans.

Finally, the Brandt Report favours greater participation in decision-making by the countries of the South. It argues for a new international order where the South is treated not as an irritating supplicant but as an active partner in a real dialogue.

Unfortunately, the proposals of the Brandt Report have the character of wishful thinking. It is easy to make recommendations but how are they to be carried out? It is unlikely that the North will voluntarily accept proposals which will reduce its power in response to moral appeals. The report understands that its appeals will be ignored by the North if they are couched in terms of fair play. Consequently, it seeks to address the self-interest of the North.

The report argues repeatedly that 'there are growing mutual interests between North and South'.[2] It is based on the notion that the North and the South have a common interest in the elimination of world poverty and so the reforms and generosity which it recommends are no more than enlightened self-interest for the North.

In a very abstract sense the report is right. In theory it would be possible for there to be a general expansion of the world economy from which everyone benefits and, in addition, both North and South in a very general sense have a common interest in preserving a healthy environment and preventing such results as the greenhouse effect or the destruction of the ozone layer and eliminating epidemic diseases. The problem with the theory of the common interest of humanity, however, is that it fails to see that there is no mechanism to ensure the rational pursuit of those common interests. Humanity is not organized into one unit capable of taking rational decisions about the common future of all. Humanity is divided into classes and nations who struggle with each other to keep or expand their share of what exists here and now, and this struggle very often prevents the long-term common interests of humanity from being acted upon. Indeed the pursuit of national or class interest may adversely affect the common fate of humanity.

So, notwithstanding common interests in the abstract, the reality is competition and conflict in the concrete. The Brandt Report says that the North needs markets in the South and so the development of the South is in the interests of the North. This is at best a half-truth. Some firms in the North would benefit from a larger market, but at the same time the South owes money to the banks of the North and so the banks' interests are that the debt be paid. For this reason they have imposed stabilization programmes on the South which reduce income and the demand for the exports of the North. To take another example, the North imposes high protection on many agricultural products which could be sold by the South, but the agricultural capitalists of the North refuse to allow more exports from the South, even though consumers in the North would benefit.

From these examples it appears that, in concrete terms, at best only sections of the population in the North have an interest in expanding incomes in the South. For this common interest to be translated into the political realm, however, means that fundamental social conflicts in the North (and, of course, in the South) must be tackled. The Brandt Report, however, betrays no glimmer of awareness of a world divided into warring classes with divergent interests, and that is not surprising since the commission was largely made up of slightly repentant capitalist politicians who want to disguise the fact that these social and national conflicts exist.

Their proposals for a voluntary redistribution of world power and wealth are thus abstract and utopian expressions of patrician goodwill which have no relevance to the possibilities of the real world and serve only to create illusions in the possible efficacy of a North–South dialogue.

Further reading

W. Brandt and others, *Common Crisis: North–South cooperation for world recovery*, London 1983.

W. Brandt and others, *North–South: a programme for survival*, London 1980.

Notes

1. W. Brandt and others, *North–South: a programme for survival*, London 1980, p. 271.
2. Ibid., p. 20.

Broederbond (Afrikaans = brotherhood)

This secret society of prominent Afrikaners was formed in 1918 to maintain the religion of the Dutch Reformed Church and white supremacy and to win state power. Today, the organization has been subordinated to the National Party.

Bumiputra (Malay = son of the soil)

It refers to those of ethnic Malay origin living in Malaysia, and implies that they alone are entitled to full citizenship of the country, excluding the Chinese and Indian communities. The Bumiputra ideology has enabled Malays to secure a privileged political position in the country and provided a basis on which the Malay ruling class could rally the mass of the Malay population behind it. Most Malays are Muslims, while Chinese and Indians are not, and since Islam is now the state religion, Bumiputra has acquired heavy religious as well as communal overtones. ▶ communalism.

C

Cabral, Amilcar Lopes (1924–73)

Combining his highly developed technical abilities with an unrivalled intellectual grasp of his subject, Cabral has been regarded as Africa's leading Marxist theoretician. A strong believer in the Marxian precept – 'The philosophers have interpreted the world, the point is to change it' – Cabral was not interested in intellectual enquiry unless it would give practical solutions to the problems facing the African nationalist movement in the 1950s and 1960s.

Cabral also proved to be a remarkable political leader: in 1956 he founded and became the leader of the African Party for the Independence and Union of the Peoples of Guinea and Cape Verde (PAI), which in 1960 was renamed the African Party for the Independence of Guinea and Cape Verde (▶ PAIGC).

Born on 12 September 1924, in Bafata, Guinea-Bissau, Cabral studied initially at the lycée on the island of San Vincente, and then at the Lisbon Institute of Agronomy where he graduated in 1952. As a student, he took an active part in the growing anti-fascist and anti-military movement in Portugal. Cabral's return to Guinea-Bissau in 1953 as an engineer agronomist was short-lived – within two years he was exiled for anti-colonial activity.

Transferring to work as an agronomist on the sugar plantations in Angola, Cabral worked with Agostinho ▶ Neto and other Angolan radicals to set up the Popular Movement for the Liberation of Angola (MPLA; ▶ Angolan liberation movement), which gave him the necessary organizational experience to start work setting up the PAIGC. His close association with the Angolans typified Cabral's approach to international issues – he was a firm believer in the decisive role of solidarity among progressive forces, and argued that all the achievements of progressive revolutionary thought should be taken into account in the course of the liberation struggle and adapted and applied to prevailing concrete conditions.

Initially, Cabral argued that the nationalist forces in Guinea-Bissau and Cape Verde should pursue the legal and traditional methods of political competition – demonstrations and strikes – but this strategy was changed after a number of strikers were brutally gunned down at Pijiguiti in 1959. Following that the PAIGC decided to start mobilizing the rural population and take up guerrilla warfare tactics, while continuing the political struggle in the towns.

The PAIGC moved the headquarters of its leadership to Conakry, while the military activists organized the guerrilla struggle within Guinea-Bissau. Widespread armed activity broke out in 1963, and the PAIGC was able to hold its first congress on liberated territory in 1964. At this point, on Cabral's and the activists' insistence that organs of popular power be established, that provision be made for health and education, and that more efficient economic organizations be set up in the liberated areas, the PAIGC was reorganized and made more democratic.

By 1973, the PAIGC controlled two-thirds of Guinea-Bissau and Cape Verde, but Cabral was showing increasing concern with the direction of the African nationalist movement. As he told the Third All-African Peoples' Congress in Cairo in 1963:

> In many cases the practice of the liberation struggle and the prospects for the future are not only devoid of a theoretical basis but more or less cut off from reality. Local experience and that of other countries, concerning the achievement of national independence, national unity and the basis for future progress, has been forgotten.

One of Cabral's biographers, Jock McCulloch, calls him an 'involuntary theorist'. When Cabral was asked if he was a Marxist, he replied: 'Judge what I do in politics. Labels don't concern us. The only issue is: "Are we doing well in the field?" ' Yet Cabral was not an empiricist unconcerned with theory – he was by general consent one of the best-read African nationalists, but always directed the objects of his enquiry towards political ends.

Cabral had little time for the theorists of ▶ Negritude as for him a uniform and unchanged pre-colonial African identity was as mythical as the idea of an entirely classless pre-colonial Africa. Cabral saw 'traditional' forms of stratification and hierarchy being used in the service of colonialism and domestic economic exploitation.

Arguing strongly that class was more important than ethnicity, Cabral made a comprehensive study of the interplay of the two factors in his society. He attached importance to social and cultural differences of pre-colonial origin, which are usually ignored by those who only look at political economy – differences between state and stateless societies, differences between pagan and Islamicized societies, differences between societies with different systems of land holding, inheritance and land use.

While he saw the necessity of drawing the peasantry into the liberation struggle, Cabral argued that they would need a revolutionary catalyst if they were to combine with the small urban working class to overthrow colonialism. This catalyst or 'ideal proletariat' was the petty bourgeoisie, the class that Cabral was born into. Recognizing the limitations of the petty bourgeoisie, many of whom worked for the colonial authorities in one way or another, Cabral argued that the nationalist and revolutionary elements of the class would break off, like himself, with the aim of fostering class unity among the peasantry and working class and fighting ethnic divisions.

In practice, the petty bourgeoisie proved too heterogeneous to give rise to a consistent political orientation. Neither was Cabral's hope that they would commit 'class suicide' and give up political power to the peasant and working class movement after national liberation realized. Indeed, Cabral's theory of the post-colonial state is the weakest pont in his analysis of Guinea-Bissau.

It was a double tragedy that Cabral did not live to see Guinea-Bissau and Cape Verde achieve national independence in 1974: it was a tragedy in personal terms and a tragedy for the movement to lose his valuable theoretical contributions at this crucial time. He was assassinated in January 1973 by gunmen alleged to have been in the pay of the Portuguese authorities.

Further reading

A. Cabral, *Revolution in Guiné: an African people's struggle*, London 1971.

A. Cabral, *Unity and Struggle*, London 1980.

P. Chabel, *Amilcar Cabral: revolutionary leadership and people's war*, Cambridge 1983.

B. Davidson, *The Liberation of Guiné*, Harmondsworth 1969.

capital flight

This term refers to the transfer by the economic élite of Third World countries of money capital to safe havens in developed countries. Capital flight requires that the wealth to be transferred be converted into foreign exchange. The foreign exchange which a country acquires through exporting, loans, aid or in any other way can be diverted in various ways to people who want to transfer money abroad: legal currency exchange or transfer, illegal currency, fake allocation of foreign exchange to purchase imports and so on. Some capital flight is only temporary because of such inducements as real interest rate differences, but some may be permanent and represent a way of preparing a subsequent exit from the country by the people transferring the capital. In a potential sense, capital flight often implies the loss of resources which could be nationally invested, though for such investment to occur would normally require more than stricter regulations against capital transfers.

Since much of it is secret and illegal, capital flight is almost impossible to estimate with accuracy and efforts to do so have produced very divergent results. Some widely quoted estimates for a number of Latin American countries have been made by the Bank for International Settlements (▶ BIS). BIS estimated that capital flight between 1978 and 1987 was a sizeable fraction of the countries' debts (see Table).

Table: Capital flight compared with debt to banks in US$ billion

Country	Capital flight (net change in foreign assets) 1978–87	Total debt to banks 1988
Argentina	31.4	35.1
Brazil	32.1	75.9
Colombia	4.1	6.9
Mexico	56.1	69.3
Venezuela	38.7	25.5

This comparison suggests that much of the borrowing done by the countries in the table (which has created the ▶ debt crisis) has in practice produced the foreign exchange which was necessary to allow the élite to ship their wealth out of the country. Thus the state has become a debtor while the rich have acquired equivalent credits. The countries as a whole are, thus, less in debt than appears to be the case. Yet the foreign assets of the rich are not accessible to pay off the liabilities of the state which they usually control. This fact may explain in part why so few governments seem to be attracted by the default option regarding their debt; the ability to borrow allows them to safeguard their wealth. So while the debt is a burden to the country, it is the counterpart of a benefit for the rich. The burden of paying the debt, therefore, by definition falls on those who have no wealth or who are not able to ship it out.

Caribbean Common Market ▶ CARICOM

CARICOM, Caribbean Common Market

This organization of Caribbean states to promote economic integration was formed in 1973 as a development out of the Caribbean Free Trade Area (CARIFTA) which was formed in 1966. Its members are all ex-British colonies: Antigua and Barbuda, Bahamas, Barbados, Belize, Dominica, Grenada, Guyana, Jamaica, Montserrat, St Christopher and Nevis, St Lucia, St Vincent, Trinidad and Tobago.

The aims of CARICOM were for a more thorough form of economic integration than simply the free trade area envisaged by CARIFTA. The aims, however, have not been achieved. Its members continue to compete with each other and the tendency for division rather than integration of Third World economies has been accentuated by the ▶ debt crisis which ties Third World countries more thoroughly to their creditors and has undermined efforts at Third World ▶ integration.

Even so, some efforts have been made to put flesh on the bones of the Nassau Consensus of 1984, in which the heads of state put emphasis on the need for long-term structural changes. CARICOM, however, is still a long way even from instituting internal free trade and a common external tariff.

Castro, Fidel (1927–   ) and Castroism

Fidel Castro Ruz was born in 1927 in Mayarí, Oriente Province, Cuba. He read law at Havana University and became active in politics, initially with the Ortodoxo Party, for which he stood in the 1952 elections until they were cancelled by the Batista coup. On 26 July 1953 he led an unsuccessful attack on the Moncada barracks in Santiago de Cuba; he was caught and imprisoned. During his trial he made his famous speech now known as 'History will absolve me'. He was amnestied and exiled in 1955.

In Mexico he met Ernesto 'Che' ► Guevara and in 1956 they formed the 26 July Movement. They led a small group of men who sailed in the *Granma* to Cuba, but most of the group were at once wiped out on the beach by Batista's troops; the rest moved to the Sierra Maestra and launched a guerrilla war against Batista.

The small group gained successes and growing prestige and became a model for the theory that revolution could be spread from small, rural guerrilla bases (► focismo). The programme of Castro's group was a broad nationalist, welfarist one. The Batista regime was undermined by wider discontents and actions, sometimes but not always coordinated with Castro's guerrillas. On 1 January 1959 Batista fled and Castro and his army made a dramatic entry into Havana.

Castro already had sufficient political weight to be head of the new government, which was a coalition with other non-communist anti-Batista forces. Castro still remained publicly non- and even anti-communist.

The USA attempted to isolate the new regime and in 1960 broke off diplomatic relations. In 1961 the CIA launched a disastrous invasion by right-wing émigrés at the Bay of Pigs (Playa Girón). This drove Castro closer to the USSR which provided crucial aid to Cuba. More moderate elements in the 26 July Movement were ousted and, following the Bay of Pigs, Castro's 26 July Movement joined up with the Popular Socialist Party (PSP), the old Cuban Communist Party, to form the Integrated Revolutionary Organizations (ORI). The PSP had criticized Castro when he was leading the guerrillas. Non-communist elements were purged, the ORI was proclaimed to be a Marxist-Leninist organization and no other parties were allowed. In 1962 the ORI became the United Party of the Cuban Socialist Revolution (PURSC), which in 1965 became the Cuban Communist Party (PCC) with Castro as secretary-general. In 1976 he became president of Cuba. US hostility was unrelenting and Cuba became isolated and heavily dependent on Soviet aid.

Castroism is hardly a distinctive political philosophy; it is a term which has been used to refer to various distinctive elements of the political ideas and actions of Castro. Since these have not always been consistent there is no authorized version of what is Castroism. To some it still refers to the strategy followed by Castro in fighting Batista and more or less coincides with focismo. To others it has more to do with the particular economic policies advocated by Castro, especially during the mid- and late 1960s when the declared Marxist-Leninist government was at its most distant from both the Soviet and Chinese governments. A distinctive element of his policy at this time was the stress on moral incentives as part of the rapid construction of a communist economy, minimizing the use of money and the market. Yet others see Castroism as referring to Cuba's extremely active foreign policy characterized from 1968 onwards by general support for and increasing alliance with the USSR, an extremely active role in the ► non-aligned movement, and radical foreign policy interventions marked by the dispatch of aid and military support to governments and movements which were regarded as sympathetic. Thus Cuban soldiers were sent to Ethiopia in 1975 (► Eritrean liberation movement) and to Angola in 1977 (► Angolan liberation movement).

Whether in such moves Cuba was acting independently or as the more flexible and radical arm of Soviet foreign policy has been debated. Whatever is the truth of that, relations with the USSR deteriorated from 1985 onwards. The more moderate Soviet regime under Mikhail Gorbachev criticized Castro: his foreign policies threatened its quest for rapprochement with the West, and the USSR was tiring of subsidizing his domestic policy and criticized him for his 'inefficient' management of the Cuban economy (somewhat ironical in view of the state of the Soviet economy).

As the rest of the socialist world was transformed in the years after Gorbachev's rise to power, Castro continued to resist and criticize the developments in Eastern Europe and elsewhere and to assert that Cuba would continue to fight for socialism alone if necessary. Aid from the USSR continued but at a declining rate and, with the continuation of the US embargo, Cuba's economic situation grew progressively more isolated and difficult. At the time of writing observers are divided between those who see Castro's days as numbered and those who see his regime as resilient and still popular.

Further reading

P. Bourne, *Castro: a biography of Fidel Castro*, Basingstoke 1987.
J. Stubbs, *Cuba: the test of time*, London 1989.

caudillo (Spanish = chieftain)

It was originally used to describe those leaders who organized private armies of gauchos or llaneros to vie for power with each other in the vacuum created by the withdrawal of the Spanish from their South American colonies, following the wars of independence in the 1820s and 1830s. Today, it is sometimes used in Third World politics to describe any personalist form of rule.

Central Intelligence Agency ▶ CIA

CIA, Central Intelligence Agency

The US Central Intelligence Agency was created by the American government in 1947. Taking on the role of dominant power in the capitalist world, preparing itself for continuing conflict with the USSR, and gathering its resources for controlling developments in the Third World, the US government saw a need for reorganization and consolidation of its intelligence gathering and covert action operations. In the subsequent decades, the CIA has been an important arm of US foreign policy. Its particular role in organizing the destabilization and the overthrow of governments which the USA deemed undesirable has made the CIA a leading symbol of US imperialism.

In 1953, for example, the CIA organized the overthrow of the Iranian government of Prime Minister Mohammed Mosaddeq. In 1951 Mosaddeq had nationalized the British-owned Anglo-Iranian Oil Company (the sole oil company operating in the country), and he had been able to withstand the British military threats and attempts at economic strangulation. However, in August 1953 the CIA organized and financed anti-Mosaddeq street demonstrations which precipitated a division in the army. After a brief conflict, in which the USA supplied guns and other equipment to the opposition, Mosaddeq was ousted. The Shah of Iran, who had had little authority during the Mosaddeq era, returned to power, and the US government and international oil companies had a friend in Iran for the next twenty-five years.

Similarly, in 1954, the CIA got rid of the Guatemalan government of Jacobo Arbenz. President Arbenz, who took office in 1951 after having been elected by a wide margin, attempted to institute a land reform as the centrepiece of his programme. As the reform was implemented, vast amounts of uncultivated land owned by the US United Fruit Company were expropriated. Spurred on by United Fruit, as well as by its fear of the broader political and economic agenda of the Guatemalan government, the US government had the CIA organize opposition to Arbenz. After lesser abortive attempts, the CIA (with some financial support from United Fruit) undertook a combined air and ground attack which drove Arbenz from power in June 1954. Right-wing military governments have ruled the country ever since.

Iran and Guatemala, two very successful cases, head the list of CIA covert operations in the Third World, and it is a long list. The Philippines, South Korea, Costa Rica, Syria, Indonesia, Haiti, Ecuador, the Congo, Brazil, Chile, Vietnam, Laos, Nicaragua, Cuba – these and many other countries find their place in the documented history of the CIA. As to the extent of the undocumented history, one is forced to speculate; such is the nature of clandestine operations.

As a major actor in implementing the US government's foreign policy from the Second World War to the present, the CIA has always cloaked its activities in a rhetoric of anti-communism. Each time it has moved to topple a government which in one way or another challenged US interests – the conservative nationalist Mosaddeq or the more progressive nationalist Arbenz, for example – the explanation has been that the actions were necessary to stop the spread of communism. (Even when a right-wing government has become a burden or embarrassment for the USA – such as Trujillo in the Dominican Republic or Diem in Vietnam – CIA actions have found rationalization in the allegation that, if that government were to remain in power, it would be subject to a communist take-over.)

CIA operations are certainly not confined to the Third World. Both Eastern and Western Europe have received considerable attention from the agency. Nor are its actions confined to military interventions. Much of the CIA's work is taken up with intelligence gathering and analysis, i.e.

with spying. Also, psychological warfare, economic destabilization, assassinations and sabotage (including the infamous infection of livestock in Cuba, a form of biological warfare) all complement the more spectacular military and paramilitary operations of the CIA.

Further reading

P. Agee, *Inside the Company: CIA diary*, Harmondsworth 1975.
W. Blum, *The CIA: a forgotten history*, London 1986.
S.C. Breckinridge, *The CIA and the US Intelligence System*, Boulder, Col. 1986.
E. Ray (ed.), *Dirty Work 2: the CIA in Africa*, London 1980.

clientelism

Western political scientists have shown considerable interest in patron–client relations in Third World societies. Drawing on the work carried out by anthropologists, Western political studies of the Third World have given clientelism a major role.

The institution of clientage is widespread throughout the Third World. It is one of the most prevalent forms of social relations that exists outside of family/kinship ties. According to most studies, clientelism comes into its own when kinship arrangements are unable to sustain the necessities of life. In such circumstances, when the survival of families is under threat, individuals are forced to step outside the existing system of kinship and establish relations with patrons. Such situations are found throughout Africa and Asia.

Patron–client relations are inherently unequal and presuppose a relation of domination. This relation can be reproduced through generations – which endows client people with the status of inferiority. The transfer of these traditional patron–client relations into the sphere of politics and the creation of new patron–client relations for the purpose of political mobilization is the main focus of interest of the political scientist.

F.G. Bailey's famous work, *Politics and Social Change: Orissa in 1959* (1963), has been one of the most influential studies of the subject. Bailey's work provides well-illustrated arguments about the relevance of clientage in local elections in the Indian state of Orissa. Bailey showed that party candidates related to the voters through an informal machine run by a chain of brokers or party bosses. The local party bosses were motivated by patronage – access to licences, contracts, government grants – and their position in the party machine provided them with their resources. In return the brokers could mobilize their clients to vote for the candidate concerned.

Some political scientists have drawn parallels between Third World patron–client links and US machine politics.[1] In drawing such comparisons, the aim of political scientists is to stress the individual character of political relations. Patron–client ties in the Third World and machine politics in the US are by nature non-ideological and non-class. Patrons and political machines are not interested in principles. Their sole concern is to gain access to resources through their links with political office.

The clientelist perspective does often appear to correspond to Third

World realities. To this day, local brokers in India can often deliver the votes of their clients in rural areas. Patronage and corruption are rife in Africa and Latin America and political relations sometimes have the character of a business transaction. Certainly, the more scholarly studies of clientelism such as those of Bailey provide useful insights into the politics of Third World societies.

Nevertheless, the perspective of clientelism is fundamentally flawed. It is often assumed that traditional forms of patron–client relations provide the underpinning of modern political mobilization. A recent study praises this approach on the grounds that it focuses 'the attention of political scientists on traditional social and political institutions'.[2] It can be argued that the continuity between traditional political institutions and contemporary politics is more apparent than real. Successful politicians are the products of the post-colonial capitalist system rather than of tradition. Local brokers can only survive if they too become linked to this system.

From our perspective, clientelism cannot be understood on its own. The individuated, non-ideological character of politics in certain Third World societies is very much the product of the inability of the capitalist class to act as a class. In many parts of the Third World direct access to the state is the precondition for the survival of individual capitalists. For the political élite the state is a business of which they are the insecure shareholders. Patronage is thus built into the institutions of the neo-colonial state. To secure their position, individual patrons require clients. A very modern institutionalization of corruption provides the mechanism through which political patrons are able to secure a base of support.

Clientelism can survive as long as the masses are excluded from political life. Its perpetuation is the monopolization of power by a small group of political patrons. Under conditions of scarce resources, political patrons will fight any attempt to democratize society. Behind the façade of the patron–client relation lies the usurpation of power by the neo-colonial political bosses. To understand the mechanics of this process readers should look at the discussion on the neo-colonial state (▶ post-colonial state).

Notes

1. See A. Weingrod, 'Patrons, patronage and political parties', *Comparative Studies in Society and History*, 10, July 1968.
2. See V. Randall and R. Theobald, *Political Change and Underdevelopment*, London 1985, p. 50.

Club of Paris

This international finance committee of 13 Western states has been meeting regularly in Paris since the 1950s for the purpose of negotiating financial agreements, moratoria or debt rescheduling with Third World countries which are indebted to the states of the 'club'. In general, this means especially African states since the majority of the debt of Latin

American states is to the banks; the 'club' does not directly concern itself with commercial debt (▶ debt crisis).

CMEA ▶ COMECON

COCOM, Coordinating Committee for East–West Trade Policy

Founded in January 1950, with its headquarters in Paris, COCOM is the West's institution which has regulated trade with Warsaw Pact countries, to ensure that they do not secure any military benefit from economic trading links. A similar organization – CHINCOM – deals with trade with China. The events of 1990 led to a loosening of COCOM restrictions.

Cold War

The term 'Cold War' is used to describe general hostility in relations between the West and the USSR beginning in 1947 and lasting at least until 1966 and to some degree beyond. It was first used by US banker Bernard Baruch in April 1947, and popularized the same year by Walter Lipmann in his book *Cold War*. After a detente, the period of renewed hostility between East and West after the USSR's December 1979 invasion of Afghanistan was called the Second Cold War. The period of Gorbachev's rule in the USSR is generally seen as the definitive end of the Cold War.

There is much speculation about what will be the consequences of the end of the Cold War for the Third World. Many argue that with the absence of superpower competition the Third World will become even more marginalized: that it will receive less investment, less trade and less aid since these things were sometimes the result of being able to 'play' the Cold War by allowing the superpowers to compete for favour in the Third World. It is added that Eastern Europe, because it is close to the vast West European market and is anyway more developed than the Third World, will offer a competing economic attraction and will employ resources which might otherwise have gone to the Third World. It is also argued that the USSR was able to offer aid to countries, such as Cuba and Nicaragua, which were spurned or attacked by the capitalist powers and so it did something to allow the possibility of radical developments in the Third World; the end of the Cold War has seen the USSR withdrawing from such commitments, both because of its own economic and political crisis and out of a desire not to transgress the wishes of the USA. This pessimistic assessment of the situation is usually based on the presumption that the end of the Cold War will leave the USA in supreme command of the whole world, able to do what it likes with less constraints than at any time since the few years after the end of the Second World War; the US victory over Iraq in 1991 is regarded as evidence of this uncontested dominance.

The details of the pessimistic view may be true but the problem with it is that it places too much emphasis on the idea that progress in the Third World depends only on the ability to attract help and interest from the more developed parts of the world. If the USA could be relied on to support reactionary Third World regimes and movements, the USSR and China were far from consistent in supporting progressive ones, as many Afghans, Kampucheans and Eritreans, among others, could attest. One of the positive effects of the end of the Cold War is that it could mean that what happens in the Third World is less of a by-product of the relations between the superpowers and more of a direct product of decisions taken in the Third World about issues which relate to its needs.

Further reading

F. Halliday, *The Making of the Second Cold War*, London 1983.

colonial situation

There is now a general consensus which recognizes the exploitation and oppressive character of colonialism in the Third World. What is less recognized is the far-reaching and fundamentally disruptive nature of colonial domination. The colonial situation was one that represented a thoroughgoing reorganization of Third World societies into a series of dependent satellites systematically subordinated to the metropolitan powers.

Through colonial domination the societies of the Third World were forced into a direct relationship with the world economy. Either directly or indirectly, the laws of the capitalist market were imposed on societies which were still primarily based on an economy of subsistence. This was an event of historic proportions: the very act of world market integration had the effect of destroying or dislocating the pre-colonial forms of social or economic organization.

Even societies such as those of Chad and Burma, which were of relatively marginal economic importance to imperialism, suffered from the process of disintegration. Why? Because the very process of establishing colonial domination implied a reorganization of the existing social structure. At the very least, the colonial regimes were interested in raising taxes for the purpose of running their administration. Taxation brought the money economy, the cash nexus and ultimately market relations. How could subsistence farmers pay tax? Soon everyone was forced into the money economy, even if only episodically – this was the beginning of the end of the subsistence economy.

Taxes could only be paid through directing farming towards exchange. In many cases the colonial authorities encouraged and sometimes forced peasants to grow particular cash crops for the metropolitan powers. Where cash-cropping took off, productive activity was redirected towards exchange. Soon everything was up for sale, even land. Cash-cropping encouraged individual enterprise at the expense of the communal farming systems of the pre-colonial era. This communal form of farming provided the basis for social organization including the extended family and system of cultural norms. The decline of the communal organization of production represented the first step towards the destruction of the social structure that was based on it.

Not all regions of the Third World were drawn directly into the world economy. In parts of Africa, the imperialists did not engage in economic activities. In such places, change was slow and disruption was less extensive. In regions like Central Africa, the colonial impact expressed itself in a slow corrosion of society. Its effects were indirect but still far-reaching. The colonial regime slowly destroyed the existing economies by holding up development through artificially conserving the rural societies.

The reorganization of societies in areas of economic interest to imperialism was swift and dramatic. The colonizing powers often expropriated the best and most fertile land, as in South Africa, Cuba, Latin America and the Philippines, but stealing land was not enough. The colonial powers also needed the indigenous people to work on their new estates. Through economic coercion and sometimes through forced labour, the colonial regime ensured that a new group of landless workers was available for their purposes.

In regions where the colonialists did not expropriate land, such as West Africa or India, they forced people to produce for the market. In this way they could obtain the food and raw materials which the metropolitan powers needed. Moreover, by controlling the sale and distribution of cash crops, the colonial regime was able to appropriate a significant share of the product of the labour of the cultivators.

The power to dominate was exercised ruthlessly. The colonial powers could use their possessions for whatever end they thought fit. Thus it allocated Cuba the role of sugar producer. It turned Malaysia into a producer of rubber, while Sri Lanka became a tea plantation. It did not matter whether these activities were organic to the previous development of the societies concerned. Many of the cash-crop economies of the contemporary Third World are the products of colonial economies. Sugar was brought to Cuba by the colonialists, as was cocoa to Ghana and cotton to Sudan.

Just as cash crops were forced onto Third World societies, so too was labour arbitrarily distributed. African slaves were brought to work on the plantations of Cuba and Guyana. Chinese and Indian workers were brought to South Africa. Tamils were taken to Sri Lanka and Chinese to Malaysia. Colonial people were uprooted and distributed throughout the Third World. This policy made economic sense for imperialism. It also made possible the politics of divide and rule. Through migration, different nationalities and ethnic groups were brought together. The colonial governments used every opportunity to encourage rivalry and tension between them. The recent conflicts in Fiji, Punjab and Malaysia are the legacy of this imperialist reorganization of the colonies.

Colonial disruption was devastating enough, but the colonial powers not only destroyed the old way of life; they also prevented the economic development of their fiefdoms. The role of the colonies was to complement the economic requirements of the metropolitan powers. The needs of domestic development were a matter of indifference to them. In many cases, imperialism directly discouraged internal economic development since they wanted to prevent the emergence of new competitors. Colonies were thus assigned the role of providing cheap raw materials and acting as markets for manufactured goods from the metropolitan powers.

The impact of colonialism had the cumulative effect of dislocation. The colonial situation was where the indigenous people lacked the economic resources to control even the most elementary aspects of their life. Foreign domination was not restricted to the sphere of economics. Economic bondage was complemented by the cultural and spiritual enslavement of the people. Western religion and culture were aggressively promoted.

In each region the colonial government set about establishing a group of indigenous collaborators. Local collaborators were rewarded with bribes and positions in the colonial apparatus. A small group of collaborators was educated in the colonial outlook and drawn behind imperialism. The beneficiaries of colonialism were placed in strategic positions to influence the rest of society. When the growth of national resistance became too powerful to ignore, these collaborators were trained to look after the interests of imperialism in the post-colonial era.

The colonial situation is not simply of historic significance. The reorganization of colonial societies around the interests of imperialism had a major influence on all aspects of social and economic life. It meant a loss of control over economic affairs, education and cultural life. This reorganization has ensured that political independence has a qualified character. As long as the structures of the colonial era remain unaltered, independence means little more than a change of personnel. Those who have tried even with formal independence to destroy the colonial legacy have found the task difficult. In many cases they have been forced to confront military intervention from abroad. Nicaragua, Cuba and Vietnam show that imperialist powers are loathe to give up the colonial structures they have created.

colonialism ▶ imperialism

colonization

Colonial expansion into the Third World by industrial powers in the last quarter of the nineteenth century has had an enduring impact on the societies of Africa, Latin America, Asia and the Middle East.

It is important to situate colonial expansion as a key component of capitalist development. Thus, from our perspective, colonialism was not an accidental episode but the inevitable consequence of capitalist accumulation in nineteenth-century Europe and the USA and later on Japan. Capital expansion and the search for profits are indissolubly linked. By the mid-nineteenth century, it had become clear that profitable production on an expanding scale gave rise to profound rivalries between capitalist enterprises, both inside the nation-state and internationally. It was the largest and most effective producers that were the most productive. This process of expansion led to the concentration and centralization of capital and more and more the competitive battle was fought beyond national boundaries.

By the last quarter of the nineteenth century, capitalist competition had become truly international, eventually leading to struggles for the division of world markets. Each industrialized nation began to organize its resources with a view to establishing a sphere of influence in the world economy. The drive to win colonial possessions was a direct consequence of this process.

The new conquest policies of the imperialist powers were fuelled by three important forces. First, there was increased competiton for markets. The domestic market of the imperialist nations was saturated and the further expansion of industry required winning markets abroad. Second, there was intense competition for the control of sources of raw materials. Access to cheap raw material sources was seen as essential for industrial expansion. Third, there was vigorous competition to win spheres of influence for capital investment. Expansion required new areas where capital could be invested productively. These three motives of new markets, sources of raw materials and spheres for capital investment were the driving forces behind the colonization of the Third World.

The question that needs to be posed is: Why did the internationalization of capital necessarily resolve itself in colonization? In the first half of the nineteenth century, for example, the UK, the most powerful imperialist power, emphasized the virtues of free trade. As late as 1852, Disraeli, the future prime minister, spoke of getting rid of the colonies. Yet within a couple of decades, the imperialist attitude towards the establishment of colonies had fundamentally changed.

The shift towards colonialism was the result of the emergence of a handful of imperialist powers that were in direct competition with each other. As long as the UK was a world power, in a class of its own, the policy of 'peaceful conquest' of markets was viable. With Germany, France and the USA breathing down its neck, the UK had to change its approach.

Another imperial factor at work which stimulated the colonial scramble was the growth in capital export. The export of capital implies a different attitude to colonialism to that implicit in the export of goods. The export of goods or trade in commodities generally implies a simple transaction and a single payment. Although world trade usually follows an established pattern, it involves a series of one-off transactions. With capital exports matters are entirely different. Capital exports are usually long-term investments and the question that arises is how this investment can best be safeguarded.

Soon, the answer to this question became self-evident. For the imperialists, the best way of defending their investments was by establishing control over production and the economy. This recognition was but a first step to the final conclusion that control over the economy required also political domination. A colonial state protecting imperialist interests was the most obvious way of defending long-term investment, but the colonial system had other advantages. It protected the colonizing power from competition from other imperialist powers. A British colony could exclude, for example, French capitalists and ensure that markets and sources of raw materials were its monopoly.

It was the very process of capital accumulation which could only continue on an international scale that unleashed a veritable scramble for colonial possessions. During the period 1875–1914, virtually the whole of the Third World became enslaved. The UK led the way. During this period the UK annexed almost half of Africa. It established new colonies in Asia and the Pacific. France followed the UK into Africa and established colonies in the western and northern parts of the continent. It also conquered colonies in Asia – Vietnam and Laos became French possessions. Germany also established possessions in Africa. Little Belgium built up a huge empire in the Congo, and the USA began to take over the possessions of Spain, such as Cuba, Puerto Rico and the Philippines. The USA also sought to strengthen its grip over Latin America through its agents in the ruling class and through the liberal deployment of gunboat diplomacy.

Colonial expansion transformed the Third World. The new colonies were integrated into the world economy and gradually the existing forms of economic organization were destroyed. Economic life was redirected towards servicing the interests of the imperialist powers. The Third World was not only plundered – it was relegated to the role of providing the resources and labour required by the colonial countries. Colonial transformation implied social and economic deformation. The internal needs of the Third World were of no concern to the colonizers. The only question was: What contributions could the colonies make to the economic development of the metropolitan powers?

It is necessary to emphasize that the development of capitalism could not have been continued without colonialism. Pre-imperialist forms of colonialism were always external to the economic life of the colonizers. Colonies provided plunder or a place to settle excess population. Imperialist colonization is always different. The metropolitan economy depends on profits from abroad and on the minerals and other raw materials from its colonies. Without its colonies, the UK, for example, would soon have become a third-rate power.

For the imperialists, the colonies were a major benefit. For the people of the Third World colonization implied enslavement and impoverishment. The disruption of life was so profound that to this day the former colonies have not been able to repair the damage. In many cases the colonial social and economic structures have had such devastating consequences that post-colonial societies still remain in bondage to their former conquerors (▶ colonial situation, ▶ neo-colonialism).

The Table gives the names of the colonial powers and the dates of annexation of most of the countries in the Third World which were subject to colonization. The date of colonization does not always give an accurate idea of the timing of colonization since there were many differences between the formal annexation of an area and its actual incorporation into the empire concerned. In many cases territories

Table: Five centuries of colonization of the Third World

Country	Colonial power	From	To
Algeria	France	1830	1962
Angola	Portugal	1482	1975
Argentina	Spain	1536	1816
Bahamas	Spain	1492	
	UK	1729	1973
Bahrain	UK	1867	1961
Bangladesh (India)	UK	1698	1947
Barbados	Spain	1509	
	UK	1627	1966
Belize	UK	1662	1981
Benin	France	1892	1960
Bermuda	UK	1612	
Bhutan	UK	1865	1949
Bolivia	Spain	1538	1825
Botswana (Bechuanaland)	UK	1885	1966
Brazil	Portugal	1500	1822
Brunei	UK	1888	1984
Burundi	Germany	1885	
	Belgium*	1916	1962
Cameroon	Germany	1884	
	UK*	1916	1961
	France*	1916	1960
Canary Islands	Spain	1498	
Cape Verde	Portugal	1600	1975
Central African Republic	France	1879	1960
Chad	France	1897	1960
Chile	Spain	1540	1818
Colombia	Spain	1525	1819
Congo	France	1839	1960
Costa Rica	Spain	1509	1821
Cuba	Spain	1512	
	USA	1898	1902

Table: *continued*

Country	Colonial power	From	To
Cyprus	UK	1878	1960
Djibouti	France	1862	1977
Dominica	UK	1763	1978
Dominican Republic	Spain	1493	1821
East Timor	Portugal (Indonesia)	1859 1975	
Ecuador	Spain	1524	1822
Egypt	France UK	1798 1882	1801 1922
El Salvador	Spain	1525	1821
Equatorial Guinea	Portugal Spain	1472 1778	1968
Eritrea	Italy	1890	1941
Ethiopia	Italy	1935	1941
Falkland Islands/Malvinas	UK	1832	
Fiji	UK	1874	1970
'French' Guiana	France	1664	
Gabon	France	1839	1960
Gambia	UK	1664	1965
Ghana (Gold Coast)	Netherlands UK	1637 1874	1957
Goa	Portugal	1498	1961
Grenada	France UK	1650 1783	1962
Guadeloupe	France	1635	
Guam	Spain USA	1565 1898	
Guatemala	Spain	1523	1821
Guinea	France	1949	1958
Guinea-Bissau	Portugal	1558	1973
Guyana	Netherlands UK	1581 1814	1966

Table: *continued*

Country	Colonial power	From	To
Haiti	Spain	1493	
	France	1660	1804
Honduras	Spain	1525	1821
Hong Kong	UK	1860	
India	UK	1773	1947
Indonesia	Netherlands	1602	1950
Iraq	UK	1920	1932
Ivory Coast	France	1843	1960
Jamaica	Spain	1509	
	UK	1655	1962
Jordan	UK	1920	1946
Kampuchea	France	1863	1954
Kenya	UK	1885	1963
Korea	Japan	1905	1945
Kuwait	UK	1899	1961
Laos	France	1893	1949
Lebanon	France	1920	1945
Lesotho (Basutoland)	UK	1867	1966
Libya	Italy	1912	1951
Macao	Portugal	1557	
Madagascar	France	1885	1960
Malawi (Nyasaland)	UK	1891	1964
Malaysia (Malaya)	Portugal	1511	1641
	UK	1795	1957
Maldive Islands	Netherlands	1609	
	UK	1796	1965
Mali	France	1898	1960
Malta	France	1798	
	UK	1800	1964
Manchuria	Japan	1932	1945
Martinique	France	1635	

Table: *continued*

Country	Colonial power	From	To
Mauritania	France	1903	1960
Mauritius	Netherlands	1598	
	France	1715	
	UK	1810	1968
Mexico	Spain	1521	1821
Morocco	Spain	1912	1956
	France	1912	1956
Mozambique	Portugal	1505	1975
Myanmar (Burma)	UK	1826	1948
Namibia (South West Africa)	Germany	1884	
	South Africa*	1915	1990
Nepal	UK	1792	1950
New Caledonia	France	1853	
New Guinea	UK	1914	1975
Nicaragua	Spain	1523	1821
Niger	France	18??	1960
Nigeria	UK	1861	1960
Oman	UK	1820	1972
Pakistan (India)	UK	1877	1947
Palestine	UK	1920	1947
Panama	Spain	1513	1821
	USA (Canal Zone)	1903	
Papua	Germany	1884	
	UK	1914	1975
Paraguay	Spain	1537	1811
Peru	Spain	1531	1824
Philippines	Spain	1564	
	USA	1898	1946
Puerto Rico	Spain	1509	
	USA	1898	
Qatar	UK	1916	1971
Rwanda	Germany	1897	
	Belgium*	1916	1962

Table: *continued*

Country	Colonial power	From	To
Sahara	Spain (Morocco)	1884 1956	
St Lucia	UK	1814	1979
Samoa	Germany New Zealand*	1884 1914	1962
Senegal	UK France	1783 1809	1960
Seychelles	France UK	1768 1794	1976
Sierra Leone	UK	1787	1961
Singapore	UK	1824	1959
Somalia (British)	UK	1884	1960
Somalia (Italian)	Italy	1889	1960
South Africa	UK	179?	1910
Sri Lanka (Ceylon)	UK	1796	1948
Sudan	UK	1899	1956
Surinam	Netherlands	1621	1975
Swaziland	UK	1902	1968
Syria	France	1920	1944
Taiwan (Formosa)	Japan	1895	1945
Tanzania (Tanganyika)	Germany UK	1885 1918	1961
Tanzania (Zanzibar)	UK	1890	1963
Tobago	Spain France UK	1498 1783 1814	1962
Togo	Germany France*	1884 1914	1960
Tonga	UK	1887	1970
Trinidad	Spain UK	1498 1797	1962
Tunisia	France	1881	1956

Table: *continued*

Country	Colonial power	From	To
Uganda	UK	1885	1963
United Arab Emirates	UK	1820	1971
Upper Volta	France	1896	1960
Uruguay	Spain	1726	1811
	Portugal	1816	1822
Vanuatu	France	1886	1980
Venezuela	Spain	1500	1821
Vietnam	France	1883	1954
West Irian	Netherlands	1828	1962
Yemen, South (Aden)	UK	1839	1967
Zaïre (Belgian Congo)	Belgium	1885	1960
Zambia (Northern Rhodesia)	UK	1891	1964
Zimbabwe (Southern Rhodesia)	UK	1890	1980

* League of Nations Trust.

were captured, exchanged and traded between the colonial powers in such a complicated way that the history cannot be summarized in the table. The table therefore is a rough guide and should be supplemented in specific cases by more detailed historical reading.

Further reading

V.G. Kiernan, *European Empires from Conquest to Collapse 1815–1960*, London 1982.

COMECON, Council for Mutual Economic Assistance
(Also known as CMEA)

The council was founded in January 1949 by Albania, Bulgaria, Czechoslovakia, East Germany, Hungary, Poland, Romania and the USSR, to develop economic relations between the participating countries. Albania withdrew in 1962, and Mongolia was admitted to membership the same year. Cuba and Vietnam were admitted in 1972.

Yugoslavia, Finland, Angola, Ethiopia, Iraq, North Korea, Laos and Mexico have signed cooperation agreements with COMECON.

The political disintegration of the Soviet bloc since 1985 led to a very rapid decline in the significance of COMECON. The European COMECON members have been looking to increase their economic involvement with the West and the idea of planning regional trade and economic activity has fallen into complete disuse. At the beginning of 1991 COMECON began to price all trade between member states in US dollars, thus eliminating its basis as a separate trading bloc. It was accordingly disbanded in June 1991.

The Third World members of COMECON, such as Cuba, Vietnam and North Korea, were never more than marginally integrated and the decline of the council has probably had little real effect on them. However it was part of a process in which what economic help they were receiving from COMECON or its members had virtually dried up, leaving them more than ever with the two alternatives of integration into the world capitalist market or self-sufficiency.

Further reading

M. Kaser, *Comecon: integration problems of the planned economies*, London 1967.

commodities ▶ exports

communalism

One of the most striking features of African and Asian societies is the prevalence of conflict between ethnic groups and communities. The division of society along communal/ethnic lines is evident from India to Nigeria through to Sri Lanka. These conflicts, referred to as communalism, are often regarded as the typical defining feature of Third World politics. The main conclusion drawn by writers on communalism is that the main divisions of society are those of tribe/community/culture/nationality rather than of class. Those who uphold a communalist thesis may be characterized as pluralist as opposed to class theorists.

There are many variants of the pluralist school. What unites all pluralists is that they take tribal, ethnic or communal divisions as given rather than something that has to be explained through analyzing history. According to Clifford Geertz, communalism is the product of political independence. He argues that the imminence of independence provokes particular communities to assert their identity so that they can obtain a share of resources available through the independent state.[1]

Geertz, like most advocates of the communalist point of view, believes that the new nationalism of the independent state is generally weaker than the older sub-nationalism of the different communities. Consequently, communalism is identified as an institution steeped in tradition which has stronger roots in the past then the newer nationalism. The equation of communalism with tradition is the first principle of the pluralist school. The second main assumption of the pluralists is that the existence of a multi-cultural society itself gives rise to communalism. Let us explore these assumptions one by one.

The equation of tradition with communalism does not stand up to the scrutiny of history. Many of the most communally minded groups, such as the Ibo of Nigeria, the Asante of Ghana, the Sinhalese of Sri Lanka or the Malays of Malaysia, had no real national consciousness in pre-colonial times. For example, the Ibo of Nigeria lacked any centralized authority and any conception of a national identity. According to one writer, 'in pre-colonial Malay society, a Malay "national" identity did not exist'.[2] Yet, today, Malaysia is dominated by communal conflict. So what has happened between pre-colonial times and today?

It is through the establishment of colonial territories that different ethnic groups were brought together into one political system. In many situations colonialism imported whole communities from abroad, such as Chinese people into Malaysia, Indians into Kenya or Tamils into Sri Lanka. In this process the traditional political systems were destroyed or transformed to suit the purpose of the colonial regime. Tradition can have very little to do with the subsequent conflict between communities but, does the existence of a multi-cultural society inevitably lead to communalism? The growth of communalism cannot be reduced to the existence of different communities. Nor does a communal identity necessarily lead to conflict with other ethnic groups.

During the colonial era, the strategy of the state was to foster local or regional forms of identification. National movements were discouraged and local leaders were rewarded with status and authority. The separation of different ethnic groups was fundamental to colonial policy. Segregation was extended into the occupational structure. Certain groups were chosen as privileged and the policy of divide and rule was followed with great consistency. Consequently, the distribution of resources and power was institutionalized on a communal foundation.

The profoundly communal institutions of colonialism became the tragic legacy bestowed to post-colonial governments. It was a legacy eagerly grasped by the new ruling classes which, lacking economic power, had to find other ways of consolidating their position. The solution they all found was communalism. By mobilizing the community the ruling class could strengthen its claims to power through excluding competitors from other ethnic groups. Capitalist competition for resources thus assumed the form of a conflict between communities.

Communalism has become the mainstay of the ruling classes. It is an extremely effective weapon for destroying popular resistance. Thus, when a multi-cultural Labour Party threatened the established politicians in Fiji in 1987, an army coup was organized, ostensibly to defend the Fijian community against the Indians. The communal riots that followed obscured the real meaning of the coup, which was the destruction of a popular movement for change. Communalism in Fiji as elsewhere does not replace class antagonism. Rather, communalism provides a means for holding class antagonisms in check.

Notes

1. See C. Geertz, 'The integrative revolution: primordial sentiments and civil politics in the new states', in C. Geertz (ed.), *Old Societies and New States*, New York 1963.
2. Hua Wu Yin, *Class and Communalism in Malaysia*, London 1983, p. 10.

community development

The term covers projects initiated by, or with the participation of, the inhabitants of a locality, which are intended to benefit them collectively. The projects may concern education, social welfare, health, infrastructure such as roads, wells or irrigation, farming, manufacture or commerce.

The concept was widely used by the British, French and Belgian colonial administrations in Africa and Asia after the Second World War in rural areas. In British Africa, for instance, departments of community development were created with community development officers to staff them. After independence, community development was seen as a means of mobilizing rural people for mass literacy and educational campaigns, e.g. the movement for self-reliance in Tanzania or the Harambee movement in Kenya.

The Indian case was very important. ▶ Nehru, encouraged by foreign advisers, thought that community development would provide a way of restoring true democracy to India's villages.

In the 1960s the term 'community development' came to be applied to projects in deprived urban neighbourhoods in mid-1960s USA and late 1960s UK. Over time, the emphasis of community development shifted from a concentration on the social pathology of the community to finding inexpensive methods to solve visible local poverty and unemployment, usually through self-help schemes.

comprador (Portuguese = purchaser)

The term was originally used in China and India to denote a local merchant performing the function of a middleman between foreign producers and the local market. Particularly by Marxists and dependency theorists it has been used to describe those local bourgeois that owed their privileged position to foreign monopolies, and consequently developed an interest in the preservation of the colonial set-up. Such people are referred to as a comprador bourgeoisie, meaning a bourgeoisie which has no independence (▶ dependency theory).

conditionality ▶ aid, ▶ debt crisis, ▶ IMF

confessionalism

This is the principle of dividing all aspects of government and political representation into fixed proportions based on religious sectarian divisions in the population. It was applied particularly to the situation in Lebanon up to the 1975 civil war, and had been introduced by the French colonial power. All government posts were divided among the various religious groups according to the 1932 census. This ratified the Christian domination of the country, and placed the Muslims and Druze into a permanent minority in government, though by the 1970s they formed a majority of the population.

Contadora Group

This loose temporary grouping comprised Colombia, Mexico, Panama and Venezuela, whose foreign ministers met on the Panamanian island resort of Contadora in January 1983 to seek peaceful settlements of the regional conflicts in Central America, particularly those of the USA and its allies with the El Salvador guerrillas and with the Sandinista government in Nicaragua.

The Contadora collaboration formed a step towards the creation of the 'Cartagena Group', now known as the Group of Eight, a consulting group of three of the Contadora nations (minus Panama) plus five other 'democratic' nations of Latin America (Ecuador, Peru, Brazil, Uruguay and Argentina). The Group has discussed economic more than diplomatic and military questions and has aimed to coordinate international policies.

Contras

This abbreviation of the Spanish 'contrarevolucionarias' (counter-revolutionaries) is used to describe a range of guerrilla groups opposed to Nicaragua's radical regime of the Frente Sandinista de Liberación Nacional (FSLN, Sandinista National Liberation Front) from 1982 to 1990 (▶ Sandinistas).

The aftermath of the 1979 overthrow of the Somoza regime of the dictator Anastasio Somoza Debayle in the Sandinista-led popular revolution threw up a multiplicity of opposition groups – first from the forces of Somoza's notorious and numerous National Guard; later from the political forces which had accepted or even welcomed the overthrow of Somoza and then, usually from a conservative standpoint, fallen out with the Sandinistas, social groups disenchanted with Sandinista rule, such as the Miskito Indians of the Atlantic Coast, many of whom fled to Honduras, and finally even from discontented sections of the Sandinistas themselves. There were, therefore, to some extent disagreements of a social, political and ideological kind between and within the numerous Contra groupings. Their tendency to split and fuse, however, reflects in general their absence of a real social base and their prodigious opportunistic manoeuvring in order to get a part of the available handouts from the Central Intelligence Agency (▶ CIA) which were the material basis of the groups' existence.

The history of the Contra groups is labyrinthine and dozens of groups were formed at one time or another, some with names as unlikely as the Jeanne Kirkpatrick Task Force. The main ones were:

(1) Fuerzas Democráticas Nicaragüenses (FDN, Nicaraguan Democratic

Forces), formed in 1981 by an alliance of anti-Somocistas with ex-National Guardsmen. At its peak it had 10,000 members and was one of the two largest Contra groups. It was the chief recipient of CIA aid. Its leaders were Adolfo Calero Portocarrero (who had founded the Nicaraguan Democratic Conservative Party in Nicaragua), Enrique Bermudez (assassinated in Nicaragua in 1988) and Indalecio Rodriguez. In 1983 Calero was named 'president-in-exile' and in 1987 visited the UK as a guest of the right-wing Committee for a Free Britain. When the FDN's offer of a ceasefire in return for elections supervised by the Organization of American States was rejected in 1983, it formed a provisional government inside Nicaragua. The CIA pressured it to merge with ARDE (see below); they formed a front and in September 1984 their alliance was launched as the Unidad Nicaragüense para la Reconciliación (UNIR, Nicaraguan Unity for Reconciliation), with the additional support of the MISURA, a Miskito Indian group.

(2) Unión Nicaragüense de la Oposición (UNO, Nicaraguan Opposition Union), the second attempt at a Contra coalition of the FDN, the ARDE and the Coordinadora Democrática Nicaragüense (CDN, Nicaraguan Democratic Coordination), an alliance of exiled conservative and social democratic politicians. It was founded in June 1985 in El Salvador to campaign for the CDN's peace proposals. In late 1987, when the Sandinistas accepted the peace plan of the Costa Rican President Oscar Arias, the UNO held negotiations with Sandinista representatives: the UNO raised the stakes, calling for the Sandinistas to dissolve local defence committees, break up state farms, end food rationing, etc. The negotiations broke down.

(3) Alianza Revolucionaria Democrática (ARDE, Democratic Revolutionary Alliance), the largest of the non-Somocista Contra groups. It was formed in September 1982 in Costa Rica by the Frente Revolucionario Sandinista (FRS, Sandinista Revolutionary Front) led by disgruntled ex-Sandinista commander Edén Pastora, the Movimiento Democrático Nicaragüense (MDN, Nicaraguan Democratic Movement) an anti-Somocista and anti-revolutionary group led by Alfonso Robelo Callejas, the MISURASATA (see below) and others. It aimed to support 'democratic revolution' without the 'totalitarianism of the Sandinistas'. Its leaders were Alfonso Robelo Callejas, Fernando Chamorro Rappaccioli and Adolfo 'Pop' Chamorro. Its first military commander, Edén Pastora, resigned in 1984 when ARDE allied with Somocista Contras in the UNIR. When its December 1982 call for all Cuban military personnel to be expelled was rejected, it began guerrilla operations from Costa Rica, but in April 1984 Costa Rica closed down its San José office. In July 1984 it allied with the FDN on the basis of the CDN's demands and both joined the UNIR. In June 1985 it joined the UNO alliance.

(4) Bloque Opositora del Sur (BOS, Southern Opposition Bloc), formed in 1985, led by Edén Pastora, José Dávila Membereno and Afredo César Aguirre, and opposed to the UNO coalition on the grounds that the CIA discriminated in favour of the Somocista organizations within it.

(5) MISURASATA, the original Miskito Indian group formed in 1982 by Brooklyn Rivera to resist alleged Sandinista oppression of the Miskito peoples. It joined the ARDE in 1982. Rivera's military campaign against

Managua was largely unsuccessful, but he was more successful in organizing a mass migration of Miskito Indians to Honduras between 1982 and 1984. In October 1984 he opened talks with the Sandinistas, and the movement split, the opponents of negotiations led by Joaquín Jessy remaining in the ARDE; the talks with the FSLN broke down in May 1985 but, soon after, the FSLN declared a unilateral ceasefire. Many Indians subsequently returned from Honduras, responding to the Sandinistas' promises and self-criticism and disillusioned with the Contras.

The adoption of the Contras by the Reagan administration as the vanguard of its 'freedom fighters' against communism was crucial to their existence and to their ability to harass the Sandinista regime and attack the Nicaraguan people. Reagan's Contra war represented the major tactic of imperialism in the epoch after its military defeat in Vietnam; less able to intervene directly, it became patron to all the anti-revolutionary forces of Nicaragua.

After around 1984 the Sandinistas were involved in a major war against the Contras, acting mainly from Honduras, though occasionally from Costa Rica. The costs of this war were immense – in the 30,000 or more Nicaraguan lives lost, in the severe disruption of the economy and of all concrete reforms in the country, and in the political loss of orientation which it created.

From 1987 the Sandinsta government was involved in several attempts to resolve the Contra war by diplomatic means but all failed owing to US opposition. None the less, the intensity of the war was partly reduced through a series of ceasefires. By this time the Sandinista army had effectively defeated the Contras at the military level.

Only after the defeat of the Sandinistas in the 1990 elections was an agreement reached between the new government of Violetta Barrios de Chamorro and the Contras for their disarmament and reincorporation into Nicaraguan society (with promises of money and land to the Contra soldiers). With great delays this agreement was finally implemented in 1991, though it failed to pacify Nicaragua. The Bush administration ended support for the Contras but was reluctant to transfer it even to the new pro-US administration. Occasional Contra attacks continued into 1991.

Coordinating Committee for East–West Trade Policy ▶ COCOM

Council for Mutual Economic Assistance ▶ COMECON

counter-trade

This term is used in economics to classify a variety of means by which goods are traded on the world market. At first sight it seems to embody a very simple idea – that two producers directly exchange their goods with each other rather than the more standard practice of goods being exchanged for money. Virtually every commentator on the subject declares, however, that counter-trade practices are highly complex. Indeed, much academic effort is being expended at the moment trying to decide what can and what cannot be designated as counter-trading practice. What is certain is that counter-trading is a highly specialized and highly contentious facet of the trading system which until the 1980s was a very marginal part of the world economy.

It is useful to give a basic explanatory outline of the jargon of counter-trade:

(1) *Barter*. This is a situation where one company in country A sells goods to another in country B and in payment for these goods receives goods of another kind from the latter. This is a simple idea to grasp, but essential to an understanding of the more complex forms. Just because goods flow from country A to country B and, subsequently, vice-versa, does not necessarily embody any counter-trading practice. The essential point is that in counter-trade the second movement is an a priori condition and obligation that facilitates the initial movement, but 'pure' barter agreements are extremely rare.

(2) *Counter-purchase*. This may also be referred to as 'indirect compensation' or 'parallel contract'. Counter-purchase is the bread and butter of counter-trade practice today. It differs from barter in a number of ways. First, it does not necessarily involve a movement of goods of equivalent value. The actual terms are entirely dependent upon the agreement reached between the two contracting parties. Thus, the proportion of the imports that the company in B pays for in the form of goods may vary in theory anywhere between 1 per cent and 100 per cent – though almost invariably in practice it is over 10 per cent. Second, a counter-purchase agreement does involve the movement of money. When the company in A exports its goods under the agreement, B does pay the agreed price in money. Often, the contractual agreement involves the money being held with a mutually agreed financial body, with stipulations designed to prevent either defrauding the other. For instance A, having exported goods and obtained financial payment, might then renege and refuse to buy the goods it originally agreed to buy. However, the requirement that B lodge a sum of money with A's bank or some other agreed institution prevents B from obtaining goods from A and, subsequently, refusing to fulfil its part of the contract. Third, unlike barter, the goods that are returned as payment for the exports of A do not necessarily constitute goods which are useful in A's production. In other words, A must subsequently resell these goods, either itself or through a third party. Here, of course, is the importance of strict arrangements concerning the money involved in the transaction since this factor can give A an added incentive to renege on the obligation to buy. Fourth, as a result of all these factors we can see that the money involved does not act as a means of effecting the exchange of the goods. Rather, its complete movement simply expresses the fact that the counter-purchase contract has been fully fulfilled.

(3) *Advance purchase*. This is a variation on counter-purchase. Again, it

involves a contractual arrangement for A to accept payment for its exports in goods. However, it involves A receiving the payment in goods before it delivers the exports. A then sells these goods and places the money in an account, again one agreed as suitable to both A and B. Under the arrangement A can then reclaim the money from the account as it makes the deliveries of its exports to B. If we conceive B as a Third World country with difficulties in acquiring foreign exchange we can see the rationale in such an agreement. Effectively, B is able to obtain essential goods for its own production process that are not available domestically. Advance purchase is a possible means by which a company in a country B can get around the restrictions on access to foreign exchange.

(4) *Escrow account.* This term is given to the financial account that is used in the course of counter-purchase and advance counter-purchase agreements. Its distinctive character is that it exists as a holding account which is terminated once the terms of the contract have been fulfilled. It can exist for a number of years since the terms of an agreement may involve the delivery of goods over an extended time-span, in which case the money will be drawn out of the account in line with the deliveries.

(5) *Clearing.* Clearing arrangements can come into operation when the terms of a counter-purchase agreement are extended into what are often called 'framework agreements' or 'product exchanges'. These most commonly involve the company in B importing intermediate goods such as iron and steel and chemicals. Again, this is likely to be the case if B is a Third World country, where such manufacturing capability may not have been developed. The other factor making an agreement of this nature possible is that these are goods that have to be continually imported at regular intervals to carry on production. Such an agreement will be longer term involving higher volumes of trade and, most significantly, non-specific in the products which can be claimed as payment for the exports: the exporter may be able to choose from a variety of agreed products. For this reason, the operation of framework agreements is often done through the central government of the importing country. The clearing arrangement is an account whose balance moves with the movement of the goods and, thus, indicates the mutual obligations of the partners in the agreement at any one time. It should be noted that the central role that governments play today in management of the economy means that their role in counter-purchase and clearing arrangements is widespread. Nevertheless, this remains an extremely grey area of counter-trade practices as most governments prefer to operate on very much an ad hoc basis, dictated by the state of world trade. So, though the practices are virtually universal today, only a few governments have incorporated them into any mandatory legal code. These include Indonesia, Yugoslavia, Australia and New Zealand. In the case of Australia, all imports by the government and public bodies must contain a 30 per cent counter-purchase clause.

(6) *Switch.* Switch dealing is a function of the operation of clearing accounts. It involves the imbalances in these accounts becoming an exchangeable commodity. The basic principle we can illustrate by a

simple three-way example. B might engage in a normal commercial transaction with A, yet could face difficulties in raising the hard currency with which to pay. However, if it has a favourable clearing account balance with C, with which it operates a counter-purchase arrangement, then the possibility of selling this goods-credit exists, using the hard currency obtained to pay A. In effect, through the mediation of a switch-dealer the claim to goods from C circulates as an asset to be bought and sold. It takes little imagination to see that this can become a very complex business when scores of countries each have a number of counter-purchase deals operating at any one time.

(7) *Buy-back*. Some forms of counter-trade relate to the export of capital goods. A buy-back deal involves the payment for imports of machinery and plant in the form of the subsequent production of goods from this capital equipment. If we consider the relationship between an advanced capitalist country and a Third World country then a number of factors can motivate such a deal. For the Third World country these can be industrial development without incurring massive debts, improving its competitive position and access to new technology. For the exporting company the advantages can be stable sources of raw materials at cheap prices or the ability to steal a march on its rivals. Though buy-back accounts for only a small proportion of counter-trade activity, it is one of the fastest-growing areas.

(8) *Offset*. This form of counter-trade mainly involves the export of military hardware and aerospace equipment. Invariably embodied in such contracts, given the very high levels of finance involved, is an obligation on the part of the exporting country to invest capital in the recipient country. These investments offset the cost of the import. Usually, this is in the form of plant and equipment for the production of components related to such goods, and training in their use. Again the terms of such an agreement can determine which potential supplier actually gets the contract in these highly lucrative but also competitive markets.

(9) *Disagio* (Portuguese = discount). This term essentially reflects the highly important role that middlemen and financial institutions play in such deals. Their complexity requires highly specialized knowledge of the law and trends in the commodity markets. Companies can make big losses if tied to counter-purchase deals when commodity market prices are highly volatile. The disagio is essentially the price charged by such institutions for the function of managing counter-purchase deals.

(10) *Evidence account*. Competition between different firms for contracts to set up points of production in other countries can involve an obligation to export a certain proportion of the production – imposed by the country offering the contract.

Those Third World countries with a developed resource base have been able to take advantage of counter-trade through gaining access to technology without having to spend hard currency reserves. Counter-trade, at least in the form of barter, provides an attractive alternative for even poor countries who want to get around the obstacles of the Western-dominated world economy. Barter among the countries of the Third

World has considerable potential for reducing dependence on the world economy. Since counter-trade has the potential for disrupting the existing patterns of trade it has been strongly opposed by Western economists and politicians. According to former US Secretary of State George Shultz: 'Barter is a communist way of dealing, and the US government will not get into it.' This hostility is shared by such international institutions as the General Agreement on Tariffs and Trade (▶ GATT) and the International Monetary Fund (▶ IMF).

Though counter-trade as such represents little real danger to the existing international order, it has considerable scope for strengthening trade and economic relations within the Third World. For that reason it ought to be a part of any comprehensive development strategy.

Creole

A Creole is a person of Spanish ancestry born in the Americas, to be distinguished from a peninsular, a person born in the Iberian peninsula. The Creoles were the main social force behind the nineteenth-century Latin American wars of independence from Spain. It later came to refer to any person of European descent born in the Americas, but specifically those who still held to the languages and customs of their ancestors. In the USA, it usually refers to people of French descent.

Creole language

This is the hybrid language spoken in Haiti, an amalgam of French maritime dialects and West African grammar. It is spoken by 90 per cent of the Haitian people but was only recognized as the official language of the country in 1969. School lessons, however, are still delivered in French, the language of the élite class in Haiti. Black intellectuals have tried to establish Creole as the language of black culture.

Cuban missile crisis

The week-long confrontation between the USSR under Nikita Khrushchev and the USA of President Kennedy over the installation of Soviet nuclear missiles in Cuba took place in October 1962. The USSR put the missiles in Cuba to forestall another invasion like the abortive Bay of Pigs raid by US-backed Cuban exiles the previous April. Kennedy initiated a blockade of Cuba to stop the delivery of missiles. On 28 October the USSR agreed to withdraw the missiles when Kennedy guaranteed that there would be no more invasion attempts. Both sides claimed a victory.

The event is a misnomer in the sense that the missiles sites were in Cuba but when the crunch came, Cuba was totally marginalized from the situation. It was a US–USSR missile crisis. This fact led to the Cuban government distancing itself from the USSR in the subsequent years until Fidel ▶ Castro, under pressure from his economic dependency, lined up a little bitterly behind Brezhnev's invasion of Czechoslovakia.

The crisis teaches a particularly important lesson about the role of the

Third World in the period of the ▶ Cold War. A Third World country acquired significance in the world political order not because of its own needs but because of the competition between the superpowers.

Further reading

E. Abel, *The Missiles of October: the story of the Cuban missile crisis*, London 1969.

Cultural Revolution

The term was first used by Lenin at the 1918 Third Congress of Soviets in Moscow to describe a radical transformation of attitudes and the cultural development of the masses in its broadest sense.

It was also used by Chairman ▶ Mao Zedong to describe the massive purge of the Chinese bureaucracy by Red Guards which he launched between August 1966 and April 1969. An estimated 4.5 million were purged. The term 'Great Proletarian Cultural Revolution' was first used in the *Army Daily* of 18 April 1966. Red Guards were militant unarmed youth groups consisting of secondary and post-secondary school students. The first Red Guard contingent was formed at a school attached to Tsinghua University in May 1966. In August 1966 one million Red Guards paraded before Mao in Beijing. A considerable 'personality cult' was built up around Mao during the Cultural Revolution when Red Guards were called upon to be 'boundlessly loyal to Chairman Mao'. Mao delegated control of the Red Guards to Lin Biao (Lin Piao), who used the People's Liberation Army for local coordination of the campaign.

Membership of the Red Guards was restricted to children of industrial workers, poor peasants and revolutionary cadres and martyrs. The Red Guards were modelled on the first Chinese Red Army units founded in 1927. Their role was to eliminate 'the old bourgeois remnants in Chinese culture and administration'. By 1969, there were 'several million' Red Guard units.

The Red Guards were used not only against party bureaucrats but also to suppress large urban political movements such as the general strike in Shanghai in January 1967. After this the campaign became increasingly violent and increasingly directed against the leading 'capitalist roaders' in the national leadership, in particular Liu Shaoqi (Liu Shao-chi). Mao began to turn the campaign against the Red Guards themselves, by using the army against them and by re-establishing the central bureaucracy. The Red Guards were to be helped to continue their studies and, in 1968–9, a large number were sent into the countryside as part of the May 1968 rustication drive. Ostensibly aimed at developing the agrarian sector, this campaign had the result of preventing the emergence of a large urban-educated stratum in the cities that could challenge the party leadership for power. By the late 1970s, when the campaign officially ended, up to 15 million secondary graduates had been resettled.

The Cultural Revolution was too complicated a social upheaval to be simply summarized. What its leaders intended was by no means what always happened. If the immediate purpose was to restore Mao's waning power inside the top bureaucracy, it also represented a continuation of themes which had concerned Mao when he unleashed the ▶ Great Leap Forward a decade earlier – a hostility to the cities and an effort to find an unconventional development process which did not proceed through traditional urbanization and concentrated industrialization. In this aim, however, like the Great Leap Forward, it both failed and caused much human and economic destruction, and reaction against it restored the power of the factions of the bureaucracy which had been most attacked.

Further reading

S. Leys, *The Chairman's New Clothes: Mao and the Cultural Revolution*, London 1977.

S. Schram (ed.), *Authority, Participation and Cultural Change in China: essays by a European study group*, Cambridge 1973.

D

DAC, Development Assistance Committee

This committee of the Organization for Economic Cooperation and Development (▶ OECD) is a forum of the principal aid donors which meets periodically in Paris to consult on all aspects of assistance policies, bilateral and multilateral aid programmes and the amount and nature of their contributions (▶▶ aid).

debt crisis

The term refers to the situation existing since 1982 in which the Third World has been burdened with an amount of debt which clearly cannot be paid and which has produced and threatened major financial, economic and social upheavals. Most of the existing Third World debt was accumulated between 1973 and 1982, though the total continues to rise year by year. In 1970 the Third World's total debt was about US$100 billion; in 1982 it had risen to US$850 billion and by 1990 it stood at US$1300 billion.

The debt rose in the 1970s partly because Third World countries needed to borrow to finance the sharp increase in the price of oil imports which took place in 1973/4. This cause is, however, often much exaggerated. It rose more because the international banks were, as a result of the oil price increase, awash with ▶ petrodollars and were obliged to lend them fast or lose profitability; and their customary borrowers, investing firms in the developed countries, reduced their spending plans due to recession. It rose because the US government encouraged the banks to lend to Third World countries so as to maintain demand for American exports during the slump. It rose because ruling élites in Third World countries saw a way of using the debt to convert their wealth into liquid form and to ship it out of their own country (▶ capital flight), and it rose because the conditions of indebtedness did not look very burdensome. The banks had much to lend and so nominal interest rates were relatively low; and real interest rates were much lower because inflation was unusually high.

Once a large volume of debt had been accumulated the conditions of indebtedness suddenly changed for the worse. In great part due to the changes in US economic policy introduced by Reagan, nominal interest rates suddenly rose to finance the American deficit caused by the rise in military spending and the cut in taxes; inflation suddenly ended due to the use of restrictive monetary policy and so real interest rates rose even faster; and the prices of exported raw materials began to fall sharply. The burden of debt suddenly became intolerable and starting with Mexico in

August 1982 the indebted countries all indicated that they could not pay what was due and required some form of renegotiation of the debt.

The first fear was that the debt crisis would undermine the leading banks so much that there would be a monetary collapse. This did not happen and the banks have gradually adjusted their balance sheets so they are less vulnerable, though some of them continue to suffer the consequences of the crisis. Since the first moment of crisis a bewildering number of stopgap solutions to the inability of the debtors to pay have been introduced:

(1) numerous renegotiations and rescheduling of debts with just about all the debtor countries;
(2) unilateral moratoria on payments;
(3) the introduction of adjustment plans supervised and inspired by the International Monetary Fund (▶ IMF) so that more of the debt can be paid;
(4) various plans from that of Peru to pay no more than 10 per cent of export earnings to the US Brady plan to convert non-functioning debt into a lower amount of functioning debt.

Up to the present none of these measures has been sufficient to end the crisis and the debt continues to be an enormous burden. During the 1980s the economies of the leading debtor nations in Latin America were transformed so that they could pay the debt: demand was reduced so as to cut imports and allow maximum incentive to export so as to produce a trade surplus out of which to pay the debt. The result was that in the second half of the decade about 6 per cent of the continent's national income was transferred to the banks in payment of the debt. By the end of the decade, despite efforts to ease the burden, the IMF was obliged to admit there was a net transfer of resources from the Third World as a whole to the developed countries. As a result of the debt the poor are sending resources to the rich.

Within the poor countries it is not generally the richer part of the population which pays the debt. Sometimes it is quite the opposite: the élites have used the foreign exchange provided by debt to ship out their wealth in the form of capital flight. So it is the poor of the poor countries, by enduring a declining standard of living, who are sending resources to the rich countries (and usually to the rich of the rich countries).

There are various ways in which the present burden of the debt in Third World countries can be measured. The total value of the debt or the amount paid in debt service (interest plus principal repayments) can be compared either to the national product, to export earnings (out of which the debt has to be paid), or per head of the population. The relative total size of the debt measures the long-run burden to the economy assuming that the debt is paid; and the relative size of the debt service payments measures the current burden which can change from year to year with economic fluctuations and exact schedules of payments due.

Using these measures the most indebted countries in 1988 turn out to be the following:

(1) Total debt:
  (a) as a multiple of the national product: Nicaragua (4), Mozambique (4), Congo (2), South Yemen (2);
  (b) as a multiple of exports: Mozambique (43), Somalia (35), Nicaragua (34), South Yemen (26);
  (c) per head of the population: Iraq (US$4200), Gabon (US$2400), Panama (US$2350), Congo (US$2300).
(2) Debt service:
  (a) as a percentage of the national product: Jordan (20%), Jamaica (15%), Congo (13%), Malaysia (13%);
  (b) as a percentage of exports: Laos (142%), Algeria (76%), South Yemen (47%), Colombia (40%);
  (c) per head of the population: Oman (US$380), Malaysia (US$330), Venezuela (US$270), Algeria (US$260).

Brazil, Mexico, Argentina and Venezuela scarcely appear in the above estimates of the four countries with the highest burden yet they are normally known as the 'highly indebted countries'. This is because they are the countries with the highest amount of total debt and so have most importance for the financial stability of the banks. To call them the highly indebted countries is, therefore, to have a creditor-centric view of the debt crisis. None the less, precisely because they are of most interest to the creditor banks, the population of those countries has paid an enormous price in the last decade as a result of the debt crisis. No measure of the indebtedness of Brazil or Mexico is as dramatic as the fact, shown above, that Mozambique owed in debt the equivalent of 43 years of its current exports, or that Mozambique and Nicaragua both owed the equivalent of four years of their total production, or that Iraq owed per inhabitant the equivalent of fifteen years' income of the average African inhabitant.

The debt burden consists not only of the exact amount which is owed or which is paid; it has also the less quantifiable effect of producing an extra chain between the Third World and its creditors in the West – its governments, its banks and its international financial police forces.

The creditors are not always the same. In general, Latin America owes most of its debt to the banks while Africa owes most of its debt to governments and international organizations. In some ways this means that Latin America's debt dependence is more financial and Africa's more political, but in both cases the debt crisis has led to a huge reduction in the economic independence of Third World countries, ever more obliged to justify every detail of their behaviour to their creditors.

Nearly ten years since its inception the debt crisis remains. It is a major source of financial and political tension in the world and is not within sight of a solution. Radical solutions such as general pardoning of the debt (an act of the creditors) or general default (an act of the debtors and thus much more revolutionary in its import) exist but are as yet hardly mentioned.

Further reading

S. Bradford and B. Kucinski, *The Debt Squads: the US, the banks and Latin America*, London 1988.

S. Griffith-Jones and O. Sunkel, *Debt and Development Crises in Latin America: the end of an illusion*, Oxford 1986.

A. MacEwan, *Debt and Disorder: international economic instability and US imperial decline*, New York 1990.

C. Payer, *Lent and Lost: foreign credit and Third World development*, London 1991.

J. Ruddick, *The Dance of the Millions: Latin America and the debt crisis*, London 1988.

debt peonage

Debt peonage is a system of debt-incurred semi-slavery in Latin America in which the worker (peón) is required to provide his labour to pay off his debts to a creditor. Mainly involving Indians, the system was enforced by the state and the peón was tied to the local hacienda. Since the peón was rarely able to pay off his debt owing to interest charges, the debt was frequently transferred to his children. Peonage was in widespread use by the turn of the century in Guatemala, Ecuador, Bolivia, Peru and Mexico. It was declared illegal thoughout Latin America in the 1920s and 1930s but it still exists today in remote areas of Latin America.

decolonization

The process by which Europe's Third World colonies gained their political liberation, decolonization is a central theme of this book – its suddenness, its world importance and its incompleteness.

The decolonization of most of the Spanish and Portuguese American colonies came in the early nineteenth century even before much of Africa and Asia had been officially subjugated to colonial rule. The modern process of decolonization which followed the end of the Second World War was extraordinarily rapid. Between the independence of India and Pakistan in 1947 and that of Angola and Mozambique in 1974 the greater parts of Asia and Africa threw off colonial rule: around one hundred new independent nations came into being. The exact timing of the decolonization process for most of these countries is shown in the Table under ▶ colonization. This table also shows that there are some countries where the decolonization process has still not taken place since they remain colonies or have passed under the rule of Third World countries (▶ Eritrean liberation movement, ▶ FRETILIN, ▶ POLISARIO).

Decolonization resulted from a major political change inside the colonial powers and, by creating the Third World, changed the political structure of the world (▶ Introduction). None the less, decolonization has not produced true liberation (▶ colonial situation, ▶ liberation, ▶ neo-colonialism, ▶ post-colonial state).

dependency theory

Dependency theory evolved in response to the discussions in the 1960s on the causes of underdevelopment in the Third World. In the post-war period the main orthodoxy among Western academics was the view that lack of development in the Third World was due to internal obstacles (▶ development, ▶ modernization). Western social scientists argued that internal obstacles such as the absence of entrepreneurial spirit, the lack of pluralistic conventions, or the persistence of traditional social and cultural norms and institutions were responsible for the stagnation of the Third World. In response to this perspective, a group of scholars, many of them from the Third World, argued that underdevelopment was not internally generated. It was suggested that foreign domination – both political and economic – created a global structure which prevents the possibility of independent development of the Third World. Instead, at best a form of dependent development occurs subject to the dictates of powerful Western economies.

The term 'dependence' was used as a conscious counterpoint to 'independence'. The lack of real independence in terms of economic and political power placed Third World countries in a dependent relationship to the world economy. Dependency as a form of social subjugation meant that though Third World governments could make policy choices, these choices would be constrained by the overriding interests of foreign powers.

It was the work of writers around the US journal *Monthly Review* that provided the inspiration for the dependency theoreticians. The works of Paul Baran and Paul Sweezy emphasizing the distortions of Third World economies by Western imperialism were influential in providing an alternative model to the existing academic orthodoxy.[1] According to Baran, the economic development of the Third World was directly antithetical to the interests of capitalist countries and consequently the dominant powers reduced the poor nations to a state of underdevelopment. In the 1960s a number of writers elaborated the *Monthly Review* thesis in relation to the experience of Latin America. This is the origin of the dependency school of underdevelopment. The best-known advocate of the approach is André Gunder Frank.[2]

A number of Latin American theoreticians made significant contributions to the school of thought.[3] Others applied the theory to Africa.[4] 'Dependentismo' acquired considerable influence in Third World studies. This perspective inspired the analysis of the ▶ non-aligned movement and provided the intellectual argument for the demand for a New International Economic Order (▶ NIEO).

Theories of dependency provided a powerful antidote to the smug complacency of the Western assumptions about underdevelopment. As a critique of Western modernization theory the dependency school still retains considerable relevance. Frank's writings coherently dismiss the argument that underdevelopment is a natural state caused by internal forces and shows that it is the form of capitalist development of the West that is responsible for the underdevelopment of the Third World.

While dependency theories represent an advance over the Western modernization perspective, they tend to have only a limited capacity to explain the nature of underdevelopment. The main weakness of the dependency school is that it is static and descriptive. Frank's analysis tends to reduce itself to the timeless proposition that the Western metropolis dominates the Third World periphery. According to Frank, the world economy and, more specifically, the relations of trade established in the sixteenth century provide the foundations for contemporary underdevelopment. Leclau has powerfully argued that Frank's model is ahistorical and ignores the changing forces that shape the relation between the West and the Third World.[5]

The emphasis on dependency fails to explain why in certain periods the Third World stagnates while in some it experiences a measure of growth. Critics of dependency argue that the impact of the world economy on the Third World operates differently at different times. Through its sole emphasis on external factors, dependency theory becomes a mirror image of the Western modernization perspective. It ignores the internal dynamic of Third World countries and fails to explain why some have managed to grow despite internal obstacles. The most eloquent challenge to the dependency school is the existence of the so-called newly industrializing countries (▶ NICs) like South Korea and Taiwan which made considerable headway in terms of economic growth in the 1970s and 1980s. Dependency theorists have not been able to offer a convincing explanation of these 'exceptions'; and for many observers NICs are enough to invalidate the dependency approach. Bill Warren, in another influential work, has even gone to the opposite extreme from dependency and has argued that the imperialist world economy actually stimulates development in the Third World.[6]

Today, it is clear that a theory that simply counterposes 'external factors' to 'internal factors' can yield few insights. The currently widespread duel between those who stress the positive stimulus of the world economy for development against those who see in it only the chains that enslave the Third World, is much too general. Brazil may be dependent on the world economy and so is Chad – yet the economic evolution of these two countries shows little in the way of a common pattern.

At the same time, it would be wrong to reject the contribution of dependency theory to an understanding of the Third World. Dependency theory played a pioneering role in exposing the ethnocentric assumptions of modernization theory. It showed that the Third World could not be studied in isolation from the historical impact of colonization and economic domination. It drew attention to the continuous transfer of surplus from the Third World to the West – a transfer which significantly limited the scope for indigenous industrialization and development. Despite its severe limitations, dependency theory has helped advance an understanding of Third World conditions.

Further reading

M. Blomström and B. Hettne, *Development Theory in Transition: the dependency debate and beyond*, London 1984.

F.H. Cardoso and E. Faletto, *Dependency and Development in Latin America*, Berkeley, Calif. 1979.

A.G. Frank, *Capitalism and Underdevelopment in Latin America*, Harmondsworth 1979.

D. Seers (ed.), *Dependency Theory: a critical reassessment*, London 1981.

Notes

1. See P. Baran, *The Political Economy of Growth*, New York 1957.
2. See A.G. Frank, *Capitalism and Underdevelopment in Latin America: historical studies of Chile and Brazil*, Harmondsworth 1969.
3. See F.H. Cardoso, 'Dependency and development in Latin America', *New Left Review*, No. 74, 1972; F.H. Cardoso and E. Faletto, *Dependency and Development in Latin America*, Berkeley, Calif. 1979.
4. See W. Rodney, *How Europe Underdeveloped Africa*, London 1988.
5. See E. Laclau, 'Feudalism and capitalism in Latin America', *New Left Review*, No. 67, 1970.
6. See Bill Warren, *Imperialism: pioneer of capitalism*, London 1980.

desaparecidos (Spanish = those who have disappeared)

Desaparecidos is the name given to those 30,000 Argentinian political detainees who are still missing after being arrested between 1976 and 1982 by the military dictatorship. The term has also been used in Chile, Colombia, El Salvador and other Latin American countries. The demand for an account of the fate or whereabouts of the desaparecidos has been an important rallying cry against Latin American dictatorships.

desertification

The process of degradation of land to the state that it is unable to sustain vegetation is a process which exists in all parts of the world, though dry tropical soils are particularly vulnerable. There are major controversies about the causes and results of desertification. In particular, one widely held idea is that desertification is the result of traditional Third World peasant agriculture and nomadic pastoralism due to 'primitive' methods and population pressure (▶ environment, ▶ Malthusianism), and that this desertification in turn is a major cause of backwardness, hunger and famine. Popular as this theory is (especially in the West), it has little if any scientific backing. More land is put out of use by over-intensive mechanized agriculture and large-scale stock raising (both usually modern, capitalist enterprises) than by peasant agriculture.

While there may be areas where desertification contributes to hunger and famine, it is not a major cause in itself. Rather desertification is a symptom of those social and economic factors, like changing land use and land-holding patterns, which also help to cause hunger and famines. The evidence suggests that peasant agriculture and nomadic pastoralism prevent both desertification and ▶ famine. ▶▶ agrarian question.

Further reading

P. Harrison, *The Greening of Africa: breaking through in the battle for land and food*, London 1987.

J. Westoby, *Introduction to World Forestry*, Oxford 1989.

developing countries ▶ euphemisms

development

Theories of progressive change first emerge with the establishment of capitalist society. Development as the progressive evolution of society is a central theme in the writings of French evolutionary sociologists and British political economists of the late eighteenth and early nineteenth centuries. French evolutionists such as Turgot, Condorcet and Saint-Simon saw a general tendency towards continuous cultural and economic progress. The standpoint also characterizes the work of Adam Smith and Marx.

Precisely because the social theory of the nineteenth century was impregnated with the idea of progress the question of the causes of development as such was seldom studied. Development was assumed as the natural state of affairs and the only question was how far and how fast. It was not until the cyclical fluctuations of world capitalism led to slumps and depression that the optimistic perspective came to be questioned.

Development as a specific problem requiring major theoretical elaboration and institutional innovation arose in response to events in the Third World. Until the Second World War, the literature on the Third World was monopolized by anthropologists and explorers recounting their travels. Social and economic issues were rarely discussed and there was an ethnocentric assumption that the progressive evolution of society was not necessarily applicable to the non-Western world. After the Second World War, however, the view that Third World societies were resistant or indifferent to change could no longer be sustained.

From the point of view of the imperialist powers, the Second World War had an unsettling effect on the Third World. The anti-colonial movement grew in strength and throughout the colonies the demand was for political emancipation and economic advance. The intensity of the pressure for change in the Third World was evident from the revolution in China, insurrections in Vietnam and Malaya and mass protest in the colonies of Africa. This was an era of revolutions, nationalist mass movements and decolonization.

The attainment of independence in the Third World put the question of development firmly on the agenda. Economic stagnation and poverty could no longer be accepted as a 'natural' state of affairs. Among the newly established Third World governments there was a craving for economic growth. The West had to be sensitive to these pressures to prevent further instability. This was particularly the case during the escalation of Cold War tensions, as there was a real fear that discontented nationalist movements might get drawn into the Soviet orbit. In fact it was the threat of communist influence that stimulated Western academics to explore the problem of development in the Third World. Much of the early literature is marred by this narrow preoccupation with the dangers of communism. Gunnar Myrdal, in his well-known *Asian Drama*, was right in his complaint that 'a major source of bias in much economic research on poor countries is thus the endeavour to treat their individual problems from the point of view of the Western political and military interest in saving them from communism'.[1]

The overriding political motives that dominated the discussion of development problems in the 1950s gave it a superficial character. Development was equated with Western industrial capitalism. Development was seen as a process of change which would take a 'traditional' Third World country to the doorsteps of Western society. The underlying assumption of this modernization theory (i.e. the modernization of traditional societies) was that societies go through the same stages of development. In this framework the Third World simply represents a stage that the West passed through long ago. The experience of European industrialization was turned into a schema which would constitute a model for Third World development. The most famous proponent of this approach was Rostow, who used this schema as the prescription for Third World development (▶ stages of economic growth).

The equation of development with Western industrial capitalism explains little about the problem. It simply projects on the Third World the experience of the West and calls for its repetition. However, it is unlikely that the Third World can repeat the unique experience of nineteenth-century Europe. It is worth recalling that industrialization in Europe took place in a world that was fundamentally agrarian. New industries did not need to compete with those from abroad – they could grow through monopolizing trade in manufactured goods in both domestic and international markets. This option is not available to a Third World country industrializing in the contemporary era. It faces formidable competition on the international market and even its own domestic market is likely to be saturated with cheap foreign goods. Critics of modernization theory also contend that the Third World today is in fact a product of Western industrialization. European industrialization was intimately linked with colonial expansion. Colonial plunder provided resources for Western industrial growth, and the colonial markets were important in stimulating production. It is argued that European industrialization actually underdeveloped the Third World, even destroying already existing industries in places like India and China. Accordingly, rather than existing as traditional societies, the Third World itself is the product of European capitalist development[2] (▶ dependency theory). From this perspective the development of the Third World requires the elimination of the structures of dependency imposed upon it by a Western-dominated world system.

But what does development mean in a Third World context? There have been many attempts to treat development as a quantitative process – one that can be measured by a series of indices, such as growth figures, the number of telephones and the rate of literacy. It is important that development as a process of change is not reduced to a series of numbers. Development as a process of social transformation implies not just quantitative but qualitative change. Thus, in Europe, capitalist development did not simply mean economic growth but an all-pervasive change in social relations. It led to the establishment of new classes, changed the relation between town and country and stimulated the emergence of a new mental outlook. However one views European development it is clear that it did not mean more of what existed previously – it qualitatively changed every aspect of social life.

Pure quantitative growth in and of itself does not produce development. There are examples of Third World countries that have grown quantitatively without a major impact on everyday life. Oil-rich Middle Eastern countries like Saudi Arabia and Kuwait have very high per capita incomes. Yet this wealth has remained in the hands of the small élite and much of the country lives as before. Statistically, these countries look developed – closer inspection, however, shows a resistance to change.

There is no consensus on what constitutes development. The most conflicting policies are justified in the name of development. From our standpoint, development only makes sense in order to improve humanity's well-being. A general improvement in the lives of men and women requires that society be more and more capable of understanding, coexisting with and sometimes controlling the forces of nature. Improvements in agriculture and industry ensure that society ceases to be the victim of the elements and copes with changes in climate and other natural conditions.

Development, therefore, implies changes in technology and an increase in useful material resources. Without some such increase there can be no improvement in the quality of life which is the basic precondition for individual men and women to have more freedom to choose the way they live. In contrast, lack of development means that most people have insufficient material resources and are obliged to struggle even to survive.

Consequently, one of the central criteria of development is the level of the productivity of labour. The more resources that an individual can produce in a given amount of time, the more is available for consumption and investment. Development historically has coincided with a continual increase in the productivity of labour. Whereas at the dawn of history every human individual had to work hard for all the time available simply to guarantee survival and reproduction, today in a highly developed country like Japan two or three hours' work a day provides enough resources for this purpose. Another way of looking at productivity is this:

the shorter the time necessary to guarantee survival and reproduction, the more time available, in principle, for the pursuit of individual activities which go beyond survival and reproduction. In other words, there is time to pursue those things which constitute human self-expression.

A rise in labour productivity is, therefore, a necessary condition for development, seen as a shift from a life dominated by survival to one allowing self-expression, but it is not a sufficient one. The pursuit of rising labour productivity does not necessarily result in development. In Third World countries, such as India or Brazil, the promotion of some industrial activities has created sectors of the economy where labour is highly productive but productivity in the rest of the economy remains low, in particular because agriculture remains stagnant. A few industrial showpieces do not produce development; nor is the answer, as some orthodox economists argue, simply to increase the number of high productivity industries. The productivity gap between the Third World and the developed countries is much greater in the agricultural sector than in industry. The Third World, therefore, cannot develop without a rise in the productivity of the sector where most of the population work and on which they directly depend – agriculture. There is a world of difference between a transfer of workers to industry while agriculture is left to stagnate (which is what often happens in Third World countries) and a transfer in conditions where agriculture is increasing its productivity (which is what has happened in countries which have successfully developed). Rising agricultural productivity requires agrarian change which is much more general than just technological improvements; it also needs social change (▶ agrarian question, ▶ green revolution).

This conclusion is important because it shows that the production of more material resources which is part of development is not just a technical problem but also a social one. Development, or a general improvement in the quality of life, both depends on and stimulates social transformation.

Such social changes must involve a shift in the location of power in society and an end to privileges. These are not only obstacles to the growth of productivity; they also mean that, when productivity does grow without sufficient social change, its benefits are unequally distributed and do not generally improve the quality of life. Often high productivity workers do not benefit themselves from their high productivity.

This view of development means that it can have no simple indicators. It cannot be reduced to the level of material productivity but depends in part on how the potential benefits of that productivity are used and distributed. Nor can it be regarded as a merely economic phenomenon since its economic elements are impossible without social preconditions.

This view of development also suggests that it is a process and not a state. There are no totally developed countries. Development can continue indefinitely, but there are many countries, rich and poor, where there are many changes but little real development.

We do not mean to imply here that there is only one road to development or that it requires a particular social or political formula. Some development in the past has taken place under a variety of very different systems. To what extent those options remain open is discussed elsewhere in this book (e.g. ▶ dependency theory).

Further reading

H. Bernstein (ed.), *Underdevelopment and Development*, Harmondsworth 1973.

C. Furtado, *Development and Underdevelopment*, Berkeley, Calif. 1975.

G. Kay, *Development and Underdevelopment*, London 1975.

G. Kitching, *Development and Underdevelopment in Historical Perspective: populism, nationalism and industrialization*, London 1982.

J. Larrain, *Theories of Development*, Oxford 1989.

Notes

1. G. Myrdal, *Asian Drama*, Vol. I, Harmondsworth 1968, p. 13.
2. See the powerful arguments of A.G. Frank, 'Sociology of development and underdevelopment of sociology', in A.G. Frank, *Latin America: under-development of revolution*, New York 1969.

Development Assistance Committee ▶ DAC

dirigisme (from French *diriger* = to direct or guide; Spanish *dirigismo*)
The term is used for a directed economy with a high degree of government control. It is more or less the opposite of ▶ neo-liberalism. In particular, it is used to refer to left-wing regimes that reject foreign domination of the economy, and focus on generating local capital by state intervention, central planning and nationalization of key sectors of the economy. It is not to be confused with the more thoroughly state-controlled 'command' economies of the former Eastern bloc.

disinvestment

This describes the practice whereby capitalist concerns seek to divest themselves of investments outside their own nation. Given the un-developed character of industry in the Third World and the high level of foreign control over more developed sectors, a policy of disinvestment can have a significant destabilizing effect on these nations.

During the 1980s a good deal of disinvestment from Latin America took place. The ▶ debt crisis and the measures to deal with it led to a major reduction in domestic demand. Many foreign-owned companies found it unprofitable to continue their operations and withdrew investments by running down operations or by selling them locally.

domino theory

This theory refers to the US government's justification for intervening in Vietnam, even though the US had few interests or historical ties there. It was argued that if one country fell to the communists, neighbouring countries would also fall – like a line of dominoes.

drug traffic

The export of heroin and cocaine has been almost certainly the fastest-growing Third World trade in the last ten years or so. The industry has had a major social and economic impact in a number of Third World countries and it has been an increasingly important element in political relations between the West and the Third World.

There is no official version of the facts since in all countries the trade is illegal, but economists specializing on the theme have made the following rough estimates of the scale of operations: the total retail value of sales of illegal drugs (mostly of heroin and cocaine) in the USA (by far the largest consumer) and Europe combined was in 1988 around US$150 billion a year, the equivalent of 2 per cent of their gross domestic product; the amount received by the exporting countries in the Third World was around US$35 billion a year, making it about 35 per cent of all Third World exports of non-mineral primary products and its largest export commodity after oil (▶ exports); of the US$35 billion, perhaps US$10 billion was taken by the drug barons and lords and the rest distributed among all the other participants in the production process. The farmers growing coca leaf or opium poppies could not receive more than about one-fiftieth of the final retail value of their product.

The major sources of heroin are Pakistan and the area known as the 'golden triangle' on the borders of Thailand, Burma and Laos. The major sources of coca are Bolivia and Peru. The semi-processed paste is then processed into cocaine largely in Colombia and shipped to the USA. The impact of the narcotics industry in these countries is immense. In Bolivia the industry is estimated to give employment in total to 600,000 people. The value of production of coca leaf alone is about equal to the value of all other agricultural output, and the value of coca-related exports (leaves and paste) is estimated to be about equal to the value of all other legal exports. Even though the peasant growers of the coca leaf receive such a derisory share of the final retail value of the product, the growing of coca has become for them a relatively lucrative activity. The pattern of income received from cocaine and opium is the same as with other peasant-grown crops, but the immensely high value of the final product (due to the combination of its addictive qualities and the illegality of its supply) allows the small grower to be better rewarded in this case.

The large and complex chain of middlemen (longer for an illegal commodity than for most legal ones) undoubtedly reaches into very high levels of society both in the exporting and the consuming countries. The rewards are so great that it provides a powerful source of corruption and extortion in many parts of the public administration. A new class of exploiting gangsters have gained social power. As in the case of some other primary products, the conversion of land to produce coca leaf or opium poppies has had the effect of reducing the supply of food products and has disrupted the social life of the countryside in a destructive way.

The Reagan and Bush administrations have publicly declared 'war' on drugs. They have demanded of Colombia the extradition of arrested drug offenders. Bush invaded Panama on the pretext of arresting the then President Noriega for drug offences. The USA has sent military units and arms to Colombia, Bolivia and Peru to help physically eliminate the drug industry. At the same time the consumption continues to thrive inside the USA with, self-evidently, involvement of the 'respectable' strata of society. At the same time, structural adjustment programmes in drug-producing countries, supported by the US government and the International Monetary Fund (▶ IMF), have based themselves on the foreign exchange amassed as a result of drug exports. The drug trade is thus 'accepted' by the American administration with one hand (so that the banks can be paid) while being 'rejected' with the other (so that elections can be won). The drug war is ideologically useful to the US administration in that it provides a many-sided internal and external 'enemy' at a time when the Cold War is ending, but real conflicts of interest within the ruling strata of US society make it impossible for the USA to develop a consistent policy.

In the producing countries, the consequences of eliminating the industry would be economic catastrophe. All the governments concerned have proposed schemes to convert to the production of other products and to prosecute the processors and wholesalers, but to implement these policies in a decisive manner would require little short of a social revolution.

Druze

The Druze are a 300,000-strong Muslim community living mainly in Lebanon (in the Chouf mountains south of Beirut) and in southern Syria and northern Israel (in the occupied Golan Heights). They derive from a split from the Shi'ite/Isma'ili wing of ▶ Islam, and are followers of the Fatimid Caliph, Abu Ali Mansur al-Hahim (985–1021), whom the Druze believe was an incarnation of Allah. Orthodox Muslims hold that the Druze are therefore heretics, and over the centuries subjected them to persecution, because the orthodox believe that the Prophet Mohammed was the last of God's messengers.

The Druze succeeded in staving off Muslim attacks on them, and in the process built up a fierce military tradition. Consequently, Druze serve as commanders in a number of Middle Eastern armies, not least the Israeli army for which they are eligible for compulsory national service, unlike the Israeli Arabs.

dualism
(Also known as dual economy)

Dualism is the simultaneous coexistence within the same economy of two different levels of development with different technologies. The concept was originated by J.H. Boeke in his book *Economics and Economic Policy of Dual Societies* (1953). Boeke described the coexistence of modern and traditional sectors in a colonial economy. Today, dual economy is also applied to the world economy to describe the division between the prosperous North and the impoverished South.

E

Economic and Social Council ▶ ECOSOC

economic integration ▶ integration

ECOSOC, Economic and Social Council

This council coordinates the work of the specialized agencies of the United Nations.

Ejército de Liberación Nacional ▶ ELN

ELN, Ejército de Liberación Nacional (National Liberation Army)

A left-wing guerrilla group in action against governments in Colombia since the 1960s, the ELN was formed in 1965 by pro-Maoist leaders and joined in 1966 by a former priest, Father Camilo Torres Restrepo, who called on Catholics to join the revolution. Under its leader Nicolás Rodriguez Bautista, it became a Guevarist group (▶ Guevara and Guevarism) incluenced by Latin American liberation theology and advocating an egalitarian socialist society.

From the mid-1980s the various guerrilla groups in Colombia began one by one to negotiate ceasefire agreements with the central government (e.g. ▶ M-19). The ELN at this point, however, opted to continue and formed a common front with the Fuerzas Armadas Revolucionarias de Colombia (FARC, Revolutionary Armed Forces of Colombia), the guerrilla group of the Communist Party. This front is known as the Coordinadora Nacional Guerrillera Simón Bolívar (CNGSB, Simón Bolívar Guerrilla Coordination Committee). Finally, in mid-1991 the CNGSB also opened negotiations with the government and there seemed good reason to suppose that they would follow M-19 into legal political activities.

environment

The 1980s were the decade of the discovery of the environment. The question of the relationship between the social and economic life of humanity and its natural environment was discussed in a more scientific way than ever before. Major environmental crises were foreseen, and a worldwide environmental movement was established.

Neither the analysis nor the movement was homogeneous. Different theories, conclusions and actions reflected different concerns and interests. There were many in the Third World who were inclined to dismiss the environmental movement as a luxury for the middle classes of the rich countries and which had little relevance for countries that desperately needed to develop.

The attitude, however, is very wrong. Environmental questions are in many respects of immediate concern to the Third World and its development. First, the limited amount of new development which occurs in the Third World, as well as the maintenance of existing economic activities, may imply environmental contradictions. A little industrialization can produce a great deal of environmental damage, such as the pollution of air and water supplies and industrial accidents, and the continuance of existing agricultural practices may result in erosion of the soil, making it impossible for it to continue indefinitely. All economic activity has environmental consequences which may materially affect the people who work and live within its orbit. It is important, therefore, to seek ways in which any development which takes place in the Third World can be sustainable. This is part of a process of learning from the mistakes of predecessors. ▶ sustainable development.

The environment also concerns Third World development in other more indirect ways, both long and short term. One long-term problem may be the following: if the more alarmist arguments about the exhaustion of resources, the generation of contamination and the greenhouse effects are correct, it will almost certainly prove impossible to realize the ideal of applying the standard of life in the developed countries to the rest of the world. Canada, to give an extreme example, has a level of energy use of 9683 kg of coal equivalent per person per year. For Chad the figure is 12 kg. If the whole world strives to live like Canadians it may physically destroy itself in the process. In other words, the development of the world on the pattern of the existing developed countries may not be physically possible, and yet in a broad sense that is still the stated or unstated aim of all development policy.

How will this contradiction be overcome? One possibility is that the Third World will simply be prevented from developing. If this is not to be the outcome, what must happen? One line of reasoning, increasingly popular in the developed countries among concerned environmentalists, is that the Third World must look for less contaminating and wasteful ways to develop. This answer, however, is really beside the point in the short term because the industrialized countries will continue to pollute the world at the present dangerous rate. It is they which contribute over 80 per cent of the production of gases that contribute to the greenhouse effect. The redesigning of the human way of life so as to be less wasteful and destructive is, therefore, primarily a task for the countries which produce the destruction, and they show almost no signs at present of preparing to change.

Meanwhile, the Third World may be losing out in the debate. Concern with environmental pollution in the developed countries is shifting some especially polluting industries to the Third World where the pressures are less strong and where, in the situation following the ▶ debt crisis, countries compete desperately with each other to get new foreign investment so as to be able to service their debts. If that investment produces environmental problems, that is not the immediate concern.

In addition, there is a quite disproportionate amount of concern in the developed countries with activities in the Third World which might cause global environmental damage, especially the question of the tropical forests. Third World countries are blamed for the environmental crisis because they are destroying their forests. This ignores the fact that it is in the developed countries where most of the problem of contamination exists, that the forests are often destroyed by Western companies to supply Western demand for precious woods and that, if the Third World gets any money out of it, it is used to service the foreign debt.

The environmental debate is still one which is dominated by a Western perspective. It is just as important for the Third World but its terms need to be redefined so that the debate centres around the interest of the Third World for development and for a healthy environment, and not merely around the concerns most vocally expressed in the developed countries. This will require an enormous leap in international collective responsibility and action at a moment when ideologies of competition and non-interference by the state are in command.

Further reading

C. Caulfield, *In the Rainforest*, London 1985.

M.R. Redclift, *Development and the Environmental Crisis: red or green alternatives*, London 1984.

J. Westoby, *The Purpose of Forests: follies of development*, Oxford 1987.

Eritrean liberation movement

The movement fighting for the independence of Eritrea from Ethiopia is divided between the pro-Western Eritrean Liberation Front (ELF) and the more radical Eritrean People's Liberation Front (EPLF). After some success in the 1970s, the movement was isolated by shifting alliances in the region.

Eritrea, of which half the population is Muslim and half Christian, was colonized by the Italians who were driven out in 1941 by the British who governed it until 1952 when it was federated with Ethiopia, without the Eritreans being consulted. In 1962 the Eritrean assembly voted to dissolve itself and for Eritrea to fuse with Ethiopia. The United Nations endorsed this decision and has since refused to back the Eritreans' fight for self-determination; the Organization of African Unity (▶ OAU) has also refused to support the Eritreans in their struggle. The ELF was formed by some Muslim Eritreans in Cairo in 1961, backed by Egypt, to fight annexation by Ethiopia. It sought and secured help from the Arab states. In the late 1960s differences arose between radicals and moderates, with the radicals backed by the radical Arab states and the Palestine Liberation Organization (▶ PLO), and in 1974 there was a split leading to the formation of the EPLF under Mohammed al-Din Amin which has since become the leader in the struggle against Addis Ababa. The EPLF is evenly made up of Christians and Muslims, was close to the radical Arab regimes and received aid from the communist states.

The ELF and EPLF took advantage of the turmoil following the 1974 coup in Ethiopia to launch an attack on Asmara, Eritrea's leading city, in February 1975, and they almost succeeded. In the next two years they captured all but the biggest towns, and set up their own administration, but in 1977 the Ethiopian military government switched alliances from the USA to the USSR, and the radical Arab and communist states that had helped the Eritreans now helped Ethiopia. In 1978, after making peace with Somalia, Ethiopian forces struck back in Eritrea driving back the rebels in many areas. The EPLF was isolated, without allies. The conservative ELF blamed the radicals for its setbacks and there was fighting between the two groups in 1981. Ethiopia continued to fight the Eritreans, fearing any concessions to them would not help in its fight against the secessionist movements in Tigré, Oromo and the Ogaden.

In 1985 under pressure from Arab backers, in particular Saudi Arabia, a new front of Eritrean organizations was formed. This was the Eritrean Unified National Council and it excluded the EPLF. It was the EPLF, however, which in the same year stepped up the war against the Ethiopian government and has continued to play the leading military role. After many advances and reverses, and a series of negotiations arranged by ex-US President Jimmy Carter, the conflict continued into the 1990s.

During the first half of 1991 the EPLF, the Tigrayan liberation fighters and other groups opposed to the Ethiopian regime of Colonel Mengistu stepped up the level of military struggle and Mengistu, having lost his Soviet and Cuban support, crumbled, fleeing to Zimbabwe in May 1991. At this point the USA attempted to become the broker of Ethiopia's fortunes and convoked a peace conference in London. It appeared as if the EPLF's control of all Eritrean territory would enable it at least to guarantee a referendum on Eritrea's future.

Further reading

L. Cliffe and others (eds), *Behind the War in Eritrea*, Nottingham 1980.
H. Erlich, *The Struggle over Eritrea 1962–78*, Stanford, Calif. 1982.

ethnocentric

Ethnocentric literally means regarding one's own race as the most important. An ethnocentric bias has influenced Western views of the Third World. The assumption of Western superiority underlies both so-called serious texts and popular literature. Typical of an openly ethnocentric approach is this extract from a British geography textbook published in the 1950s:

> Today under the guidance of the Europeans, Africa is being steadily opened up. Roads and railways are being built and air routes are being extended. Doctors and scientists are seeking to improve the health of the Africans, who, on their part, are increasing in numbers; missionaries and teachers are educating the people; and traders and trading companies are extending their operations. The rights and the wrongs of 'the scramble for Africa' on the part of the European powers lie outside the field of geography, but the significant fact remains that the Europeans have brought civilisation to the peoples of tropical Africa, whose standard of living has, in most cases, been raised as a result of their contact with white peoples.[1]

For this author, 'civilisation' is the monopoly of 'white peoples' – Africa by definition is without civilization and the grateful beneficiary of European largesse. From this perspective European domination over the Third World is necessarily benevolent.

Ethnocentricity is not merely a narrow, ultimately false form of reference. Often in its direct unsubtle form it assumes a direct malevolent form of preaching Western superiority and Third World inferiority. An editorial in the British *Daily Express* on 2 June 1977 commented on the ► North–South dialogue in the following terms:

> What it all boils down to, whether the talk be about grants, soft loans, debt cancellations, or artificially maintained prices for the Third World, is that they want more of our money to go to them. Why? First, people like President Nyerere of Tanzania consider that they are exploited by the West, both now and in the colonial past, so that aid must be seen as a compensation for past wrongs. Secondly, the rich are held to have a general duty to help the poor.
>
> But the argument about exploitation does not really stand up to examination. If it were true, the Afro-Asian countries would have been worse off than they would otherwise be because of the activities in the West. Yet that is a manifestly absurd idea. On the contrary: it was Western capital that developed their economies in the colonial era, and socialist regimes since independence have often retarded progress. More: it is on the industrial markets of the West that they depend for their sale of goods and primary products. To put it bluntly, West 'exploitation' is a convenient excuse for Third World politicians to explain their own failures.

The *Daily Express* articulates in a crude manner the racism which is the logical conclusion of ethnocentrism. Unfortunately, such attitudes are not the monopoly of the popular press. Even academic analyses often suffer from similar prejudices. Take one example – the Western study of political development. Political development theory assumes the model of Western parliamentary democracy as the natural realization of human aspiration. According to two of the most influential figures in this discipline it is Anglo-American politics which 'most closely approximates the model of a modern political system'.[2] If the Western democratic system is the universal model then political development becomes the transition of Third World nations into an Anglo-American type society.

From the standpoint of political development theory it is inconceivable that the Third World could evolve modern institutions other than those which exist in the West. The possibility of modern institutions original to the Third World cannot be countenanced within this framework of analysis. It also follows that the standard of development is not organic to the experience of the Third World but is established a priori by Western academics. A Third World solution to its own political problems is thus precluded from the outset by this analysis.

Strictly speaking, despite its academic pretensions, such ethnocentrism has no intellectual base. Stripped of its rhetoric, it reduces to the view that the West knows best what is good for the Third World. It is thus a straightforward legitimation for Western domination.

Further reading

S. Amin, *Eurocentrism*, New York and London 1989.

Notes

1. J. Stembridge, *The World*, London 1956, pp. 347–8.
2. See G. Almond and J.S. Coleman, *The Politics of the Developing Areas*, Boston 1960, p. 533.

euphemisms

The decolonization of the Third World and the accession of its countries to membership of international organizations raised the question of what name was to be given to them collectively. Commonly used phrases like 'backward countries' or 'ex-colonies' or 'poor nations' naturally offended nationalist sentiment and seemed to contain both condescension and eurocentrism. The solution to these valid objections in official diplomatic circles, however, was not to look for terms which tried to summarize the real condition of the decolonized countries but to invent a new lexicon of diplomatic euphemisms. The most commonly used of these were 'developing countries' and 'less developed countries'. Everyone, they seemed to suggest, was either developing or else was partly developed; a travesty of the truth. More recently the *reductio ad absurdum* of such 'development-speak' is the term 'least developed'. Meanwhile, the terms 'underdeveloped' and 'Third World' are both ones which have acquired some critical analytical content and so have helped to unmask some of the reality of world poverty. This is enough to have made them virtually banned from use in official international publications and debates. ▶ Introduction, ▶ underdevelopment.

export-led growth

In development studies this is the obverse of import-substituting industrialization (▶ ISI). Rather than seeking to restrict imports it involves a Third World nation attempting to enhance its competitive position in world markets. In effect, industrial development is made dependent upon expanding exports.

Export-led growth is regarded as the 'pro-market' alternative and, as such, is favoured by neo-classical exponents of economic development. Countries such as South Korea, Taiwan, Singapore and Hong Kong, with a high dependence on overseas markets, are held up as proof of the superiority of free markets and full involvement in the world economy over state control as a condition of development.

In fact, this claim relies on a considerable ability to ignore facts – development in most of these countries has involved a tremendous amount of state intervention and control. Behind the seal of approval (▶ neo-liberalism) for these countries is an attempt to show that economic success is only possible from the pursuit of economic policies favoured by the West. The real 'virtue' of these countries has been their pro-Western political stance. ▶ NICs.

exports

All countries need to export in order to obtain foreign currency to buy imports of needed commodities which they cannot produce. Exports may also in some cases play a positive role in changing the whole economy of a country and being the vanguard of development (▶ export-led growth, ▶ NICs). In practice, however, exports may not be so healthy; they may preserve conservative and exploitative social and economic structures; they may divert resources to more development-oriented activities; they may not be spent on needed imports for development but on luxuries for the élite; and indeed they may not be spent on exports at all but used to service and repay debt or to provide foreign exchange to allow the élite to ship out their wealth. All of these questions are dealt with in other entries in this book (▶ capital flight, ▶ debt crisis, ▶ banana republic).

It is commonly believed that the Third World exports raw materials (primary commodities) in an unprocessed form and in exchange imports manufactured goods. This, for instance, is the starting point for the theory of the declining terms of trade (▶ terms of trade). This belief is both very false and very true, depending on how the figures are analysed.

Taking the exports of the Third World in total, we obtain a very different picture from the above-mentioned belief. Of total Third World exports more than half (60 per cent) is now of manufactured goods, 22 per cent is fuel, including petroleum, and only 17 per cent is other primary products, the exports which are most traditionally associated with the Third World; and while a great majority of the exports of the developed countries consists of manufactured goods, they also export nearly one-fifth of their total in the form of raw materials. This is more raw materials in terms of absolute value than are exported by the Third World. The figures are set out in Table 1.

111

Table 1: Composition of the exports of OECD and Third World countries, 1987

Category	OECD	Third World
Manufactured goods	1640 (62)	358 (14)
Fuels and minerals	141 (5)	133 (5)
Other primary products	243 (9)	103 (4)
Total	2024 (74)	594 (25)

Note: Figures are in US$ billion. Figures in parentheses are percentages of world total exports, excluding the USSR.

It is only quite recently that the Third World has become an exporter mainly of manufactured goods and it is entirely the result of the success of NICs in these markets. The four East Asian NICs, Hong Kong, Singapore, Taiwan and South Korea, between them account for half of the total manufactured exports of the Third World. Hence, if NICs are excluded as exceptions, the traditional picture of Third World exports remains largely true. Table 2 shows the proportion of primary products in the exports of 103 countries. From this it can be seen that there are 57 countries, all of them in the Third World, which have more than two-thirds of their exports in this form, and for many of these countries the great majority of exports are of one or two products.

Given that trade in manufactured goods has expanded much faster in recent decades than trade in primary products, many parts of the Third World have found themselves increasingly marginalized within the world trade system. So the share of world exports coming from Africa has fallen between 1970 and 1987 from 5 per cent to 2 per cent. For Latin America in the same period the share fell from 6 per cent to 4 per cent. Only the share of Asia has risen, largely because of the success of NICs.

There is an argument which has some validity that export-oriented development is damaging to the economy and that a more autarkic form of development will be less dependent. What has been happening in Africa and Latin America, however, is not a conscious retreat into autarkic development but a steady erosion of their markets without the internal transformation of the economy – in other words, the worst of both worlds.

Further reading

C. Edwards, *Fragmented World: competing perspective on trade money and crisis*, London 1985.

G. Helleiner, *International Trade and Economic Development*, Harmondsworth 1972.

Table 2: Primary products as a percentage of total exports, 103 countries

Country	%	Country	%
Uganda	100	Mali	70
South Yemen	100	Mexico	70
Libya	100	Guatemala	68
Liberia	99	Trinidad and Tobago	68
Oman	99	Central African Republic	67
Rwanda	99	Zimbabwe	64
Somalia	99	Malaysia	64
Mauritania	99	Costa Rica	64
Nigeria	99	Norway	62
Ethiopia	99	South Africa	61
Bolivia	98	Brazil	60
Algeria	98	Sri Lanka	59
Ghana	98	Mauritius	59
Niger	98	Thailand	58
Zambia	97	Uruguay	58
Ecuador	97	Morocco	53
Zaïre	94	Greece	49
Cameroon	94	Turkey	44
Papua New Guinea	94	Sierra Leone	44
Sudan	93	Netherlands	43
Ivory Coast	91	Jordan	41
Saudi Arabia	91	Denmark	40
Venezuela	91	Philippines	40
Chile	91	Tunisia	40
Nicaragua	90	India	38
Honduras	90	Haiti	37
Kuwait	89	China	36
Egypt	88	Canada	36
Burundi	88	Lebanon	35
Madagascar	88	Jamaica	34
Burkina Faso	88	Singapore	33
Panama	87	Nepal	33
Myanmar	87	Pakistan	32
Gabon	87	Ireland, Republic of	30
Malawi	84	Spain	27
Kenya	84	France	24
Tanzania	83	USA	24
United Arab Emirates	82	UK	24
Colombia	82	Belgium	21
Paraguay	81	Portugal	21
Congo	81	Finland	19
Togo	80	Sweden	16
Indonesia	79	Israel	13
Peru	78	Austria	13
Argentina	78	Italy	12
Australia	78	West Germany	10
Benin	78	Taiwan	9
El Salvador	77	South Korea	9
New Zealand	74	Hong Kong	8
Syria	72	Switzerland	7
Senegal	71	Japan	2
Dominican Republic	71	WORLD	25

F

Falashas (Originally Hebrew, but adapted by Amharic = exile)

The Falashas are the black Jews from Ethiopia. Operation Moses organized by Israel shipped most of them out of famine in 1985 from Ethiopia to Israel. The Mengistu regime in Ethiopia retreated from its embarrassing agreement with Israel, and prevented the transfer from being completed. Days after Mengistu's flight in May 1991, the USA intervened to oblige the collapsing remnants of his regime to allow the transfer of the remaining 14,000 Falashas to Israel. They were moved in a few hours in Israeli planes which were allowed to cross the air space of hostile Arab neighbours after more US secret pressures. One Israeli jumbo jet carried 1000 people, the largest number ever carried in a single plane. Thus did the Falashas unwittingly make aeronautic history. The Ethiopian regime, only days from its final collapse, still extracted a price of US$35 million for the Falasha refugees. Thus is the fate of historic peoples decided under the new international order!

Further reading

D. Kessler and T. Parfitt, *The Falashas: the Jews of Ethiopia*, London 1985.

Falklands/Malvinas

This group of islands off the east coast of Argentina was seized by the British in 1833, and used as a coaling station for ships on the Cape Horn route. A repossession effort by Argentina was repelled in 1982 at a cost of UK£2000 million and much loss of life.

famine

Famine means an acute situation in which people are unable to obtain enough to eat and die of starvation or its consequences. Major famines have occurred in most epochs of history. The modern drive towards ever higher labour productivity, green revolution, instant information, international organizations of cooperation and so on have completely failed to eliminate famine from the world. In fact, in the late twentieth century famines appear to be becoming more frequent and destructive. One of the boldest experiments ever in accelerating development and changing human society, the Chinese revolution, produced in 1961 what was probably the most destructive famine in history in which possibly 20 million people died of hunger. A famine in Ethiopia and parts of the Sahel regions of Africa in 1985 was followed in 1991 by the danger of another even more destructive famine in a number of African countries.

For a long time there was little debate about what was the cause of famines. Universally it was acknowledged to be a sudden deficiency in available food supplies. Recently, however, the work of the Indian economist A.K. Sen[1] has sparked off a major controversy on the subject. Sen, after exhaustive empirical research, has rejected food availability deficiency (FAD) as a convincing cause. Famines, he argues, have occurred where the overall food supply has declined very little, if at all, and sometimes they have not occurred even when food availability has declined. He concludes that famines are caused when a section of the population suddenly loses access to food ('entitlement') because it loses its land, its money income, its rights to the fruits of common property and so on, and famine occurs least, he argues, where the means of communication are most democratic and free to report the problem. Sen's general conclusion – that famine, therefore, has basically social and political roots – is a convincing one, even if some of the details seem more doubtful. For instance, the attention of the world's media to the prospect of famine in 1991 was met with general indifference in the quarters where action might have been taken. It is hard to avert the conclusion that some famines happen because those who have power in the world think it convenient that they should.

Further reading

D. Arnold, *Famine: social crisis and historical change*, Oxford 1988.
A.K. Sen, *Poverty and Famines: an essay on entitlement and deprivation*, Oxford 1982.

Note

1. See A.K. Sen, *Poverty and Famines: an essay on entitlement and deprivation*, Oxford 1982.

Fanon, Frantz (1925–61)

A central figure in post-war anti-colonial thought, Frantz Fanon was a major ideological influence on the Algerian National Liberation Front (▶FLN) and more widely in Africa's national liberation movements. Born in the French Antilles in 1925 and raised in Martinique, he moved to Algeria in 1951 and began to play an active political role.

Post-war intellectual and political life in France helped to shape Fanon's ideas. He went through secondary and university education in France during the period when the anti-colonial movement in South-East Asia and Africa was gathering momentum. After its catastrophic defeat at Dien Bien Phu the French colonial machine started to look much more vulnerable to the liberation movements.

Fanon trained as a doctor and psychiatrist, a background which often shows itself in acute analysis of the social, psychological and even physiological effects of racism. A highly original thinker, Fanon quickly attracted the attention of radical activists and writers in both Africa and Europe. France's Jean-Paul Sartre wrote the preface to Fanon's seminal work *The Wretched of the Earth*.

When the FLN, the guerrilla movement fighting for national independence from the French, launched its uprising, Fanon joined up. He was widely respected by his Algerian colleagues and carried out various political and diplomatic assignments for the Algerian provisional government after its formation in 1958. This was partly in recognition of his practical work in the movement, as well as of his outstanding contribution to the development of ideology in the African and Arab worlds.

Fanon was one of the first anti-colonial activists to argue that the colonial liberation movement must be linked to an indigenous-based anti-capitalist movement, and that a capitalist class should not be allowed to develop in the newly independent countries. At the same time, Fanon was not a direct propagandist for the socialist cause, and indeed was highly critical of those policies advocated in the name of ▶ African Socialism. Fanon's critique of socialism derived from its perceived 'foreignness'; this differentiated him from other African revolutionaries of the period who were more prepared to borrow and learn from the experience of the socialist movement in industrialized countries.

Instead, Fanon was insistent on an alliance of the dispossessed, a political movement which he believed could unify the peoples of the Third World. Instinctively, Fanon saw the barriers to such an alliance in the newly independent Third World countries where elaborate and undemocratic state machines were developing while their economies remained critically dependent on those of the former colonial power.

An implacable opponent of the one-party state, whether instituted for either socialist or capitalist ends, Fanon developed a prescription for instituting a democracy out of the political activity of the rural masses involved in the anti-colonial struggle.

It is the arguments put forward in *The Wretched of the Earth*, written and published in the last year of Fanon's life, which formed the basis for Fanon's attacks on the nationalist bourgeoisie and working class in colonial societies. Fanon argued that the native bourgeoisie coalesced into Africa's nationalist political parties, which began as patriotic and progressive forces but quickly deteriorated into tools for élite African hegemony.

Having asserted that power in the nationalist movement had to be wrested from the bourgeoisie, Fanon was sceptical about the role of the urban working class. From his experiences in the Algerian revolution, where the French working class played a highly reactionary role, Fanon argued that the African working class was equally untrustworthy. Relatively well paid and privileged, even under colonialism, the urban working class, he argued, would not seek any widespread social change – even after the end of colonial rule.

For Fanon the authentic revolutionary class in the Third World was the poor peasantry of 'the wretched of the earth'. They were loyal, dependent and dignified, the solid root from which the revolution would grow. After rebellion took root in the countryside, Fanon said it would spread quickly to the urban centres though the activities of the uprooted peasants, i.e. the urban lumpenproletariat of workers in the informal sector, the pimps, prostitutes and petty criminals.

While Fanon concurred with orthodox Marxism by defining class according to an individual's relation to the means of production, he argued that political behaviour is determined not by an objective measure of class but by perceived needs and scarcities, by the relative wealth of an individual, the size of the class he belongs to and the extent of this class's integration into the colonial system.

Fanon gave little practical guidance as to how his very specific theoretical conclusions should be used other than his belief that violence was necessary not only to defeat colonialism but also as a psychological purgative for the oppressed. Fanon wrote: 'Violence alone, violence committed by the people, violence organized and educated by its leaders, makes it possible for the masses to understand social truths and gives the key to them. It frees the native from his inferiority complex, and from his despair and inaction.'

Much of Fanon's thinking on class, race and violence derives from the Algerian struggle for independence, though there is an input from Fanon's training as a psychiatrist. Sadly, Fanon did not live to see peace restored to an independent Algeria. After serving as a representative for the Algerian liberation forces in Ghana, Fanon returned to Algeria where it was discovered he was suffering from leukaemia. Overstretched by his work commitments, Fanon did not receive treatment until it was too late. He was taken for treatment in late 1961 to Washington, DC where he died that year.

Further reading

F. Fanon, *Black Skin, White Masks*, London 1970.
F. Fanon, *Toward the African Revolution*, New York 1967.
F. Fanon, *The Wretched of the Earth*, London 1965.
R. Zahar, *Colonialism and Alienation: political thought of Frantz Fanon*, Benin 1974.

FAO, Food and Agriculture Organization

This agency of the United Nations was established in October 1945, with a secretariat in Rome. Its aims are to give international support to national programmes designed to increase the efficiency of agriculture, forestry and fisheries, and improve the conditions of people engaged in the relevant activities. It incorporates the World Food Programme (▶ WFP).

Farabundo Martí, Agustín (1893–1932)

The Salvadorian revolutionary activist was deported as a student at the University of El Salvador for insulting the party of the dictator Jorge Melendez, and thereafter was driven out of successive Central American countries for his radical political activities. In New York he worked briefly for a COMINTERN front organization. In 1928 he joined Augusto Sandino's struggle in Nicaragua against the US marines and the National Guard, but the two fell out over Sandino's refusal to endorse social revolution. Farabundo returned to El Salvador and was again deported. He went back once more to participate in and then lead the 1931 peasant uprising in which the newly formed Salvadorian Communist Party became engaged. The rebellion was drowned in blood: Farabundo was arrested and shot. The present guerrilla movement in El Salvador has named itself after him (▶ FDR–FMLN).

fascism (from Latin *fasces* = bundles)

Fascism was first used by Benito Mussolini in 1919 as the name for his Italian nationalist organization. It is now a widely abused term (meaning simply 'very reactionary') that is classically defined as the social force of despairing middle classes plunged into crisis, and manipulated by the establishment to attack working class organizations – in particular trade unions.

Further reading

N. Poulantzas, *Fascism and Dictatorship: the Third International and the problem of fascism*, London 1974.

FDR–FMLN, Frente Democrático Revolucionario—Frente Farabundo Martí de Liberación Nacional (Revolutionary Democratic Front—Farabundo Martí Front for National Liberation)

The FDR is the political wing of the FMLN, the guerrilla movement fighting the US-backed regime in El Salvador. The FDR was formed in 1980 to oppose the then military regime. Guillermo Manuel Ungo was elected its leader in 1981 and an armed struggle was launched, with Poder Popular Local (Local People's Power) being set up in liberated areas as an alternative government. The FDR–FMLN is made up of 20 groups ranging from Christian Democrats to the far left. Ungo is also leader of one of the groups, the Movimiento Nacional Revolucionario (MNR), and had been a member of the civilian–military government formed in 1979 but soon resigned protesting against its 'swing to the right'. The MNR is a member of the Socialist International. The FMLN boycotted the 1984 elections, but the FDR called on the new government of José Napoleón Duarte to negotiate for a ceasefire: talks continued on and off until October 1987 when the FMLN broke them off following the murder by death squads of human rights activist Herbert Anaya. Ungo then criticized the guerrillas publicly and called for renewed negotiations. In November 1987 Ungo and Reubén Zamora, the vice-president of the

FDR, returned openly to El Salvador to reopen talks with Duarte. While the FDR is social democratic, the FMLN guerrillas proclaim themselves Marxist-Leninist, and adhere to some brand of Guevarism (▶ Guevara and Guevarism): the FDR's room for manoeuvre has been limited by the FMLN's responses to brutal repression by right-wing death squads. Since Duarte's replacement by the ARENA Party President Cristiani in 1988, the alternation between rapidly abandoned negotiations and armed confrontations has continued. In 1991 an agreement was reached for the ending of the war and constitutional change and as part of a gesture of reconciliation Reubén Zamora became deputy president of the National Assembly.

Fedayin (Arabic = Muslim faithful)

This is the common name for Palestinian guerrillas (▶ PLO).

Fedayin-e Khalq, Sazman-e Cherika-ye Fedayin-e Khalq-e Iran
(Organization of the Iranian People's Self-sacrificing Guerrillas)

It was formed in 1971 under the leadership of Mustapha Mandani as a self-proclaimed Marxist-Leninist party rejecting the passivity of the pro-Soviet Tudeh Party, and believing that armed struggle could set off a mass uprising. The same year, the Fedayin was the first organization to embark on armed action against the Shah of Iran's government, with an attack on a police station, which had little military impact but won many recruits, mostly from the urban professional classes. It forged links with the Popular Front for the Liberation of Palestine (▶ PLO), sent members for guerrilla training in Lebanon and carried out attacks on police stations, banks, etc. During the 1970s, 180 members were executed and 10,000 jailed.

The Fedayin played an active part in the February 1979 uprising that brought Ayatullah Khomeini to power, but when he demanded they disarm, the Ayatullah branded them 'non-Muslims at war with Islam'. They believed in the Moscow two-stage theory of revolution, that the establishment of a democratic republic must precede the achievement of socialism in the Third World, and so called on Khomeini to proclaim a people's democratic republic. When the referendum of April 1979 asked only if Iran should become an Islamic republic the Fedayin boycotted it.

As Khomeini rejected its requests for popular participation in government, the Fedayin's ambivalence towards the regime deepened, some linking up with the Kurdish rebels. Eventually the organization split in June 1980, with the majority accepting Khomeini's rule and a minority going into active opposition. With the outbreak of the Iran–Iraq war, Khomeini moved against the Iranian left and during 1981 the Fedayin minority were effectively suppressed along with other left-wing groups (▶ Mujahedin); those who could fled to Kurdistan.

119

FLN, Front de Libération Nationale (National Liberation Front)

The Algerian FLN was formed in November 1954 to fight French colonialism and secure independence for Algeria and unity in North Africa. Since independence in 1962, it has been the governing party of Algeria.

Its origins lay in the Mouvement pour le Triomphe des Libertés Démocratiques (MTLD, Movement for the Triumph of Democratic Liberties) of Messali Hadj. Young militants split off to form the Organisation Spéciale (OS, Special Organization), the first group to use armed force against the French. In April 1954 several members formed the Comité Révolutionnaire d'Unité et d'Action (CRUA, Revolutionary Council for Liberty and Action), which formed the FLN in November 1954 and launched the Algerian war of independence. By 1956 it had nationwide support and established a government-in-exile in Tunis in 1958. The FLN's leader was Ahmed ▶ Ben Bella. The FLN's military leader was Houari Boumedienne (1927–78), who, after Arab–Islamic studies in Constantine and Cairo, worked with the FLN's military wing, the Armée de Libération Nationale (ALN, the National Liberation Army), becoming chief of staff in 1960. Ben Bella and Boumedienne led the FLN's political bureau at independence in 1962 and cracked down on radical elements, creating a one-party state.

Though the Algerian uprising helped make radical Third Worldism popular on the left internationally, the FLN never evolved a distinct ideology, its only lasting indirect contribution being the writings of the French West Indian Frantz ▶ Fanon, notably his *The Wretched of the Earth*.

In 1965 Boumedienne deposed Ben Bella and himself became president. In 1976 the FLN 'National Charter' was adopted pledging Algeria to 'Marxist-free socialism'. Islam was made the state religion. On Boumedienne's death in 1978 he was succeeded by Chadli Bendjedid, a former army colonel, under whose leadership Algeria moved increasingly into the Western camp.

In recent years, after being obliged to democratize the constitution, Chadli's government has faced increasing challenges from Islamic fundamentalists and other opposition forces.

Further reading

R. Tiemcani, *State and Revolution in Algeria*, London 1987.

focismo (from Spanish *foco* = focus or source)

Created by Ernesto 'Che' ▶ Guevara (▶▶ Castro and Castroism) and popularized by Régis Debray, the theory argues that anti-establishment attacks by a small band of guerrillas – a foco – can win peasants over to insurrection without any political preparation. Focismo rejects the orthodox Marxist emphasis on the working class, and the need to take account of objective conditions before launching an insurrection. Focismo also rejects the Maoist emphasis on the need for prior political work among the peasantry.

Food and Agriculture Organization ▶ FAO

foreign aid ▶ aid

foreign debt ▶ debt crisis

formal sector ▶ informal sector

Fourth World ▶ least developed countries

francophone (= French-speaking)

The term is normally used in reference to the former French colonies in the Third World, but also includes the province of Quebec in Canada (but not the Cajuns of the State of Louisiana in the USA). Anglophone and ▶ lusophone are the equivalent terms in the ex-British and ex-Portuguese colonies.

FRELIMO, Frente de Libertacão de Moçambique (Mozambique Liberation Front)

The movement which fought for and won independence for Mozambique from Portugal and is now the governing party was formed in Dar es Salaam, Tanzania, in 1962 uniting three existing exile groups. Its first president was Eduardo Chivambi Mondlane who was murdered by Portuguese agents in 1969 and succeeded by Samora Machel. In the early 1970s FRELIMO success pushed the Portuguese forces out of many provinces and in September 1974 FRELIMO formed a provisional government, following the Portuguese decision to decolonize. As independence came in June 1975, many Portuguese settlers fled. In 1977 FRELIMO declared itself to be a Marxist-Leninist vanguard party.

In 1976 Rhodesian intelligence created the Resistencia Nacional Moçambicana (RENAMO, Mozambique National Resistance) to oppose FRELIMO for its support of Zimbabwean liberation forces. Later South Africa took over support for RENAMO and launched several attacks on Mozambique. By 1984 this destabilization forced FRELIMO to the negotiating table with South Africa and led to the ▶ Nkomati Accord, by which each country agreed not to let itself be used as a base for terrorists operating against the other. For Mozambique this meant ending the activities of the African National Congress (▶ ANC), while South Africa simply continued to support RENAMO. Machel died in an air crash in 1986 and was succeeded by Joaquim Chissano.

Despite the Nkomati Accord, RENAMO has stepped up the war, which, combined with other factors, has led to a disastrous decline in the economy – one of the most serious in Africa. Despite general statements of willingness to negotiate by both sides no talks have materialized. In 1990 President Chissano renounced Marxism and announced major constitutional reforms including the end of the one-party state and free presidential elections in 1991. He has conceded that the RENAMO leader Dhlakama has the right to stand as a candidate. In 1991 FRELIMO entered into negotiation with RENAMO, though there seemed little prospect of a rapid solution to the war.

Further reading

A. Isaacman, *A Luta Continua: creating a new society in Mozambique*, Binghampton, NY 1978.

B. Munslow, *Mozambique: the revolution and its origins*, London 1983.

Frente de Libertacão de Moçambique ▶ FRELIMO

Frente Democrático Revolucionario—Frente Farabundo Martí de Liberación Nacional ▶ FDR–FMLN

Frente Popular para la Liberación de Sakiet el Hamra y Rio de Oro ▶ POLISARIO

Frente Revolucionario de Timor Leste Independente ▶ FRETILIN

Frente Sandinista de Liberación Nacional ▶ Sandinistas

FRETILIN, Frente Revolucionario de Timor Leste Independente
(Revolutionary Front for an Independent East Timor)

This liberation movement was formed in the Portuguese East Indies in April 1974, following the Portuguese revolution, to seek independence and resist annexation by Indonesia. It was set up in opposition to the pro-Portuguese party, the União Democrática Timorese (UDT, Timorese Democratic Union), and claimed 80,000 followers by the end of 1974. FRETILIN joined a coalition with the UDT in January 1975 following the arrival of a pro-independence Portuguese governor, but quit in May 1975. On 11 August 1975 the UDT attempted to eliminate FRETILIN before the Portuguese left, but many Timorese in the Portuguese army rallied to FRETILIN and the UDT failed: these soldiers formed the core of the Fuerzas Armadas de Libertação Nacional de Timor Leste (FALINTIL, East Timor National Liberation Armed Forces). When the Portuguese left precipitately at the end of August 1975, FRETILIN took power and called on the Portuguese to return to complete the decolonization process. As the Indonesian army began to make raids across the border, FRETILIN appealed for help from the United Nations and proclaimed the Democratic Republic of East Timor. Indonesian troops occupied the capital, Dili, soon after, apparently with the blessing of the USA and Australia. The UN General Assembly called on the Indonesians to withdraw but pro-Indonesian groups set up a provisional government.

In May 1976 a so-called people's assembly called for integration into Indonesia, which absorbed East Timor as its 27th province, Lora Sae, in July 1976, but Indonesian forces and their supporters held only the towns and FRETILIN organized liberation zones in the countryside. When Indonesia offered an amnesty in August 1977, FRETILIN was divided between those willing to negotiate and the rest, and Indonesia used the confusion to launch an all-out assault on FRETILIN's rural bases: by late 1978 the last open FRETILIN base had fallen. In December 1978 the President of FRETILIN, Nicolau Lobato, was killed in an Indonesian ambush. Throughout 1978 and 1979, the Indonesian air force carpet-bombed East Timor and concentration camps were set up for the peasants. A third of the population died between 1975 and 1979.

In 1981, as the influence of conservative elements was undermined by defeats, Kay Rala Xanana Gusmao was elected leader and FRETILIN moved to consolidate on a more radical basis with greater involvement of the peasants.

In 1982 the new Australian Labour Party government adopted a policy of self-determination for East Timor. Negotiations begun between Xanana and the Indonesians led to a ceasefire in March 1983, but it broke down in August. In 1984 FRETILIN set up the Revolutionary Council of National Resistance to broaden its base, while at the same time launching a peace plan calling for UN-supervised negotiations, but the call was never taken up, as Australia dropped its support for self-determination. Current estimates of FRETILIN's strength range from 400–500 (Indonesian authorities) to 6000 (FRETILIN). FRETILIN remains active with several thousand guerrilla fighters; and the regime continues to persecute and murder anyone suspected of sympathies with the organization.

Further reading

C. Budiardjo and Liem Soel Liong, *The War against East Timor*, London 1984.

Front de Libération Nationale ▶ FLN

front line states

The term first referred to five African states – Angola, Botswana, Mozambique, Tanzania and Zambia – which were regarded as being in the 'front line' of the fight to bring about an independent Zimbabwe. They began meeting together from 1976 and worked on the basis that the UK should maintain its responsibility for Rhodesia until elections could be held on the basis of one man, one vote, and that the two guerrilla groups, led by Robert Mugabe and Joshua Nkomo, should be supported

until then. In June 1980 a meeting of the Organization of African Unity
(▶ OAU) recognized Angola, Botswana, Mozambique, Zambia and
Zimbabwe as the front line states opposed to the ▶ apartheid regime of
South Africa.

FSLN ▶ Sandinistas

G

Gadhafi, (Colonel) Muammar (1942–)

The Libyan leader was born in a tent in Sirte, Libya, in 1942, to a nomad family. He became an admirer of Gamal Abdel ▶ Nasser while still at school. He was expelled from school in 1961 for agitating against King Idris. Imitating Nasser, he joined the British-run Libyan army and set up a Free Unitary Officers Movement. In 1969 he led a coup against Idris, establishing the Libyan Arab Republic and becoming chairman of the ruling Revolutionary Command Council (RCC). His plans for Arab unity got little support from the post-Nasser regime in Egypt or elsewhere. He turned to developing Libya, especially after the oil price rises of 1973. Gadhafi cut down his political and administrative tasks to write the three-volume *Green Book*, laying out an alternative to capitalism and communism called the 'Third International Theory'. He stressed state control over property and the importance of the family. In 1975 a system of people's congresses was set up to replace ministries, which were abolished, and in January 1976 a General People's Congress was given the powers the RCC had had. Gadhafi became general secretary of that congress, while armed militias were established.

In the late 1970s Gadhafi renewed efforts towards Arab unity and to fund Islamic opposition groups in other countries, from the Philippines to Chad, where he occupied the Aozou Strip. In the 1980s the West began to brand him a key supporter and financer of 'terrorism': in April 1986 US planes bombed Benghazi and Tripoli and in 1987 US aid crucially helped the Chadian leader Hissène Habré drive Gadhafi's forces out of Chad.

In 1991, however, Habré lost the backing of the USA, France and ironically also of President Saddam Hussein of Iraq, as they were all preoccupied with the Gulf War (on opposing sides). The leader of the uprising against Habré was former army chief-of-staff Idriss Deby, once an effective general against Libya, who had broken with Habré in 1988 and since then waged a war from Sudanese territory but increasingly with Libyan help. The new regime established close ties with Libya and Gadhafi appeared to be regaining influence after the setbacks of the 1980s.

Further reading

R. First, *Libya: the elusive revolution*, Harmondsworth 1974.

Gandhi, Mohandas Karamchand (1869–1948) and Gandhism

Mohandas Karamchand Gandhi – called Mahatma ('great soul') – was the outstanding leader of the national liberation movement in India and founder of the doctrine known as Gandhism. He was born on 2 October

1869 in the Gujarat principality of Porbandar. Gandhi was of the Bania caste and grew up in a family that strictly observed the Hindu religion, an upbringing which deeply influenced his worldview. His father was a minister in a number of principalities on the Kathiawar peninsula.

After studying law in England, Gandhi worked as an advocate in Bombay in 1891–3, but the seminal period in Gandhi's political development started with his move to South Africa where he worked as a legal consultant to a Gujarat trading company. Here Gandhi led the struggle against racial discrimination and oppression of the Indians and developed the philosophy and tactics of 'satyagraha' – the strategy of non-violent resistance to oppression.

The South African experience galvanized Gandhi into a life of political activism. On his return to India in 1915, he took a keen interest in the embryonic Indian National Congress (INC) which he joined in 1919. Gandhi rapidly developed into an effective orator and activist, travelling the country and gathering support for mass non-violent opposition to British colonialism.

It was Gandhi's ability to draw the masses into opposition to colonial rule that earned him the respect of his co-activists in the Indian National Congress. From the mid-1920s to 1947, Gandhi was the most influential activist in the INC while his philosophy of satyagraha was the dominant ideology of the organization. Under Gandhi's guidance the INC developed into a mass party enjoying the support of broad sections of the population in its opposition to colonialism.

As Gandhi's popularity grew among the Indian people, so did the colonial authorities' awareness of the threat which he posed and he was arrested and imprisoned on several occasions (1922–4, 1930–1 and 1942–4). Gandhi's most acrimonious brush with the colonial authorities was during the Second World War when he popularized the anti-colonial slogan 'Quit India' which infuriated the British establishment at the time.

Following the division of India into two separate states in 1947 – India and Pakistan – and the ensuing Hindu–Muslim pogroms, Gandhi tried to use his broad-based popularity to reconcile the battling factions. Gandhi was murdered by N. Hodse, a member of the Hindu nationalist organization Rashtriya Swayam Sevak Sangh, on 30 January 1948.

Apart from his crucial role in the struggle for India's national independence, Gandhi also bequeathed his tactics and philosophy of non-violent resistance to the world's political movements – it has been adopted by organizations as disparate as the African National Congress, the UK's Campaign for Nuclear Disarmament and the US civil rights movement with varying degrees of success.

The roots of Gandhism derive from the peasant traditions of Indian society – that is, the social ideal of 'sarvodaya' or the welfare of all and 'satyagraha', the method of achieving this through non-violent resistance. Gandhi's ideal of social justice was based on the 'golden age' of self-contained peasant communities. Gandhi contrasted this ideal society with the European machine civilization which he detested together with the market economy which he saw as destructive of the patriarchal village and the peasant artisan community.

Despite the seemingly utopian and archaic elements in this philosophy, Gandhi was able to use this vision of united self-sufficient communities to inspire broad sections of the Indian population in the anti-colonial struggle. These tactics and ideals involving enormous patience and protest, conservatism and spontaneous revolutionary feeling were accepted by the Indian peasantry brought up for centuries on a fatalistic religious worldview.

The fact that national independence in 1947 did not usher in sarvodaya led some peasants to question the value of the struggle and the Gandhist doctrine, while critics from the left argued that Gandhi had compromised too much with India's feudal landowning classes and its nascent urban bourgeoisie. In particular, they blamed Gandhism for the containment of the peasants' struggle for land reform.

While Gandhi's ardent calls for reconciliation between India's social classes served the purpose of creating a united national front against colonialism, he remained a strong believer in the peaceful resolution of differences between social groups which had demonstrably different economic interests. Consequently, Gandhi's name and philosophy have been used by those quite out of sympathy with his ideals – in particular by industrial and landowning interests – to deflect demands for greater economic and political democracy.

Notwithstanding these later developments, Gandhi remains the Indian leader best acquainted with the peasantry and their life in India's 500,000 villages. His effective campaign for the civil rights of India's 'untouchables' alone qualifies him for a major place in the country's history, but he will best be remembered for his intelligent and effective tactics in his country's struggle against colonialism. Currently, new thinking about the consequences of Western capitalist-style development is creating new interest in his social and economic doctrines (▶ appropriate technology, ▶ development).

Further reading

J. Bandyopadhyaya, *The Social and Political Thought of Gandhi*, Bombay 1969.

Garveyism

The movement is associated with Marcus Garvey (1887–1940), born in Jamaica, the man most linked to the founding of black nationalism in the USA. Following the First World War the black city ghettos of the USA provided fertile terrain for the growth of black nationalism, as integration and assimilation seemed to be going nowhere and racial opposition intensified, with numerous lynchings and race riots. Against this background Garvey launched his Universal Negro Improvement Association based in New York which spread rapidly all over the USA, with millions of supporters by the mid-1920s. It asserted black pride and argued that blacks should leave the USA and create a new homeland in Liberia. If blacks were united they would be a mighty race. By the late 1920s, when negotiations with Liberia collapsed, the movement was in disarray. Garvey was harassed by the US government and jailed on dubious charges. He died in London.

Garvey's vision of black pride and a united powerful race remained strong, and the realities of US life gave the rejection of integration a recurrent appeal. After 1945 new movements arose in the Garveyite tradition. The ▶ black power movement in the 1960s forcefully reasserted many of its sentiments, though it regarded Africa more as a symbol than as a haven. ▶▶ Rastafarianism.

Further reading

M. Garvey, *Philosophy and Opinions*, 3 vols, London 1967.

GATT, General Agreement on Tariffs and Trade

The agreement between member nations to apply non-discriminatory trade policies and to liberalize international trade emerged from a conference in Geneva in 1947; it was an extremely weakened version of a proposal to set up an International Trade Organization which had been vetoed by the USA, then the most powerful nation in world trade. From its 23 initial members GATT has expanded to include 98 full members, plus 29 which apply the GATT rules de facto. Together they account for over 85 per cent of world trade.

The main condition of GATT membership is that member countries shall not discriminate between each other but offer 'most favoured nation' status to all other GATT members. The great exception to this rule is the customs union or free trade area which is allowed to discriminate in favour of its component members.

The official philosophy of GATT is that of free trade: it promotes the liberalization of international trade through the lifting of tariff and non-tariff barriers. To this end it has organized a series of negotiating 'rounds' between the signatory states designed to reduce trade barriers. The most recent of these have been the Kennedy Round (1963–7), the Tokyo Round (1975–9) and the Uruguay Round (1986–92?). The past rounds have led to major reductions in trade barriers, though they have been followed in practice by the invention of new ones.

The present Uruguay Round aims to extend GATT to include trade in services and agriculture. The negotiations have been bitter and complex and in 1990 broke down completely, owing largely to disagreements between the USA and the European Community over the excessive protection of agriculture in the latter. There is a chance that the round will be resumed, though many believe that breakdown heralds a new wave of world protectionism like that of the 1930s.

GCC, GULF COOPERATION COUNCIL

The position of the Third World in GATT is weak. While the major nations profess to believe in free trade they in fact practice many forms of protectionism. The negotiating rounds tend to be struggles between them (at present between the USA, Europe and Japan) for a more favoured position in world trade. Third World countries have little independent voice but must judge which of the main countries it is convenient to line up behind in the hope of obtaining some indirect benefit. Hence in the Uruguay Round many agricultural-exporting Third World nations backed the US demand for a major reduction in European agricultural protectionism in the hope that this would allow them to expand their agricultural exports to the closed European market. Yet at the same time the USA used the negotiations to try to force through new rules on 'intellectual property' which would oblige Third World countries to start paying large royalties for the use of computer software.

Because of their weak bargaining power the Third World signatories of GATT are less able than the more powerful developed ones to violate its free trade rules in practice. As a result the free trade system of the world is a hypocritical one; the exceptions are legion and the rich and powerful nations get away with more exceptions than the poor and weak. The European Community preaches free trade to the Third World but jealously maintains its highly protectionist Common Agricultural Policy; the USA preaches free trade to the Third World while it introduces legislation which gives its government powers of massive 'retaliation' against countries indulging in 'unfair trade practices' against it. While it is a matter for debate whether the Third World would gain more from a free trade or a protectionist world, it is certain that it is descriminated against in the unequal, hypocritical free trade system which exists in practice.

Further reading

C. Raghavan, *Decolonization – GATT: the Uruguay Round and a new global economy*, London 1990.

Gaza Strip

The Palestinian border zone (capital: Gaza) is 40 km long and 10 km wide, and lies between Israel and the Egyptian Sinai Peninsula. The Gaza Strip has been occupied by Israeli troops since June 1967.

GCC, Gulf Cooperation Council

Officially called the Cooperation Council for the Arab States of the Gulf, it was formed on 25 May 1981 by six Persian Gulf states – Bahrain, Kuwait, Oman, Qatar, Saudi Arabia and the United Arab Emirates – with headquarters in Riyadh, Saudi Arabia. Its aims are to coordinate all economic, social, cultural and defence affairs. In November 1984 the

129

council agreed to create a rapid deployment force (▶ RDF), which fought as part of the US alliance in the Gulf War.

GDP, gross domestic product

The GDP is the most commonly used measure of the value of goods and services produced in a particular country. It is a measure of the total amount of productive economic activity. When divided by the population of the country, to give the GDP per capita, it is the most frequently used indicator of the relative level of development of a country compared to others. To assess its validity as an indicator of development, and to understand what it can tell us about the situation of Third World countries, we must discuss two kinds of problem related to the term: that of its definition in principle and that of its measurement in practice.

The GDP is intended to be a measure of the monetary value of all goods and services produced in a country during a given period of time (usually a year). This concept of a measure of total economic activity arose as part of the macroeconomic revolution of the 1930s, associated particularly with the work of the British economist John Maynard Keynes. To understand exactly what the GDP is we must contrast it with other terms. First, the GDP is 'gross' rather than 'net'. The difference between gross and net domestic product is that the second concept is obtained by subtracting from the first an estimate of the value of depreciation of the country's capital stock during the year. In other words, it is assumed that a part of what is produced cannot contribute to consumption or to new investments because it is needed to make good the deterioration in the capital stock, i.e. just to maintain the country's already existing productive capacity. The net figure is regarded, therefore, as a better measure of the production actually available to meet the needs of the society, but it is a more difficult value to estimate since it is difficult to calculate real depreciation of the capital stock in anything other than an arbitrary way. For this reason, it is more common to see figures for the GDP rather than the NDP.

The GDP also differs from another closely related concept, the gross national product. The two concepts are virtually the same except that GDP is a territorial concept (it measures value produced in a given country) and GNP is a national concept (it measures value produced by the factors of production of a given country, wherever they may operate). If there were no foreign investment and no labour migration, the two concepts would in practice be identical. The GNP is equal to the GDP plus or minus a figure known as 'net factor incomes from abroad', i.e. the income earned abroad by factors of production of the country whose product is being measured. This, at least, is the procedure recommended by the statisticians of the United Nations. Many countries (especially developed ones) include only 'net property income' and so exclude the earnings of migrant workers from the adjustment.

In the great majority of cases, the figures for GDP and GNP are very close but may significantly diverge when the country concerned experiences a very high level of foreign investment or of labour migration. The existence of foreign capital or of foreign labour migrants in countries will tend to make the GNP smaller than the GDP; conversely where a country has overseas investments, or when its citizens migrate to work elsewhere, the GNP will tend to be larger than the GDP.

Thus GNP is a better measure of the value of production available to produce income for the citizens of the country. Since foreigners' factor incomes, however, are sometimes hard to estimate, it is slightly more common to see comparative figures for GDP than for GNP, though both are relatively common.

A third concept, the national income, derives directly from the national product. The national income of a country is regarded as the income received by its citizens as a result of productive activities (i.e. their activities as owners of the factors of production, land, labour and capital) and is thus conceptually identical to the national product which is the value of goods and services which these factors of production produce. The value of the goods and services produced must be income for one or other of the factors of production. The national income, like the domestic or the national product, can be gross or net; without qualification, the term 'national income' is normally understood as meaning net national income, though in practice the usage of all the terms is very loose.

Numerous reservations have been made about the GDP and its related concepts. The main ones revolve around what is and what is not productive activity. The concept is a monetary one and so usually includes only those activities for which money is paid. Very occasionally it includes estimates of the monetary value of goods and services produced outside the monetary nexus. Housework, for instance, is systematically excluded in all countries, though in some an estimate is made of the value of self-consumed production (e.g. subsistence agriculture). Whether or not non-marketed goods are included can make a particularly large difference in Third World countries where many productive activities are of this kind. The exclusion of the product of unpaid labour has the effect of excluding a large proportion of the productive activities of women from measurement.

If this first kind of difficulty is about the exclusion from the definition of productive activity items which undoubtedly contribute to economic welfare, another criticism is that GDP includes many things which clearly do not contribute to economic welfare, because they may be harmful or may be regarded by many as of dubious value. So, for instance, the GDP includes the value of the production of goods which may contaminate the environment, but does not subtract anything representing the value of these 'bads', and the GDP also includes the value of the 'services' produced by secret police forces, prison guards and so on.

GDP is a monetary concept, but when it is measured in actual monetary values it cannot be used to make comparisons between one period and another (because prices change from year to year), nor for comparisons between one country and another (because they have different currencies). Hence GDP, once calculated for a given country for a given year, has to be processed to make it comparable with other years and other countries. To eliminate the effects of price changes the actual

GDP (the GDP at current prices) must be 'deflated' by an index of inflation, known as the GDP deflator to give the GDP at constant prices. Given that ▶ inflation is often extremely rapid in Third World countries, this can lead to major errors in the estimation of changes in the GDP from one year to another.

In order to compare the GDP of more than one country it is necessary to reduce figures in national currencies to a common currency, which is normally the US dollar. This is usually done by converting at the current exchange rate between the national currency and the dollar. While this is a simple procedure, it is full of problems. First, many Third World countries have different exchange rates and there are few rules as to which one to choose. Second, as even a casual traveller knows, exchange rates very often do not reflect the relative real purchasing power of different currencies. Here, therefore, are two more sources of possible error in the calculation of relative GDPs. (For a proposed solution to the second of these problems, ▶ purchasing power parity.)

A further problem arises from the fact that the GDP may be measured either at the prices of products as they emerge from the place of production (GDP at factor cost) or at the prices paid by the final purchasers of the products (GDP at market prices). The difference between the two results form the existence of indirect taxes and subsidies. In a country where these are important, and especially in cases where indirect taxes and subsidies do not balance each other out, there may be a significant difference between the GDP estimated in these two ways, though in practice the difference is not very important.

From all this it can be seen that the GDP (and equally GNP and national income) are subject to both conceptual and practical limitations. Despite these, the GDP per capita, converted at the current exchange rate, is the most widely used single indicator of the level of development and rate of economic growth of a country. It is not only a descriptive indicator but also has a functional role. The calculated level of a country's GDP or GNP per capita is used to assign it to a category of nation which may determine, for instance, its entitlement to receive loans on concessionary terms or to receive economic aid. It is also the figure which determines a country's level of dues to various international organizations. For these purposes it is obviously a deficient indicator. Yet its defenders would claim that, despite its recognized problems, it has the virtues of including many activities in one indicator, of being based on well-known and well-understood concepts, and of lacking a clear accepted alternative.

One of the basic conceptual problems of the GDP and related concepts is that they are based on an estimate of the level of economic activity and are then used (in their per capita versions) to indicate the level of economic welfare. There are many reasons why the two things may not coincide, but the most important is that GDP per capita is a simple national average which takes no account of the distribution of the fruits of the GDP. If GDP is high (or rises) and at the same time its distribution is unequal (or worsens), the welfare of the majority of the population will be low (or may become worse). The United Nations Development

Programme recently published a sample calculation which aims to adjust relative national GDP per capita by estimates of the level of inequality. The level of GDP per capita is deflated by a measure of inequality (using the most familiar measure of inequality, the Gini coefficient, as the measure) so that the value of the GDP of a country with high inequality is reduced more than the GDP of a country with low inequality. The result is given in the Table: for the countries sampled the order of GDP is reversed. Such methods would give a clearer indication of the welfare of the majority of the population but they remain in their infancy and are extremely controversial.

Table 1: The effect of adjusting income by distribution

Country	GDP per capita (US$) 1987	Gini coefficient of inequality	Distribution-adjusted GDP per capita (ppp$)
Panama	2240	0.57	1724
Brazil	2020	0.57	1852
Malaysia	1810	0.48	2001
Costa Rica	1610	0.42	2180

Note: in the first column of figures, the amounts are in US dollars; in the final column, in purchasing power parity dollars. In the middle column of figures, the higher the value is, the greater the level of inquality.
Source: United Nations Development Programme, *Human Development Report 1990*, New York 1990, p. 12.

For a listing of the calculated level of GDP per capita for the countries of the Third World see the Table under purchasing power parity, and for its relation with other indicators see the Table under indicators. ▶▶ human development, ▶▶ indicators, ▶▶ purchasing power parity.

General Agreement on Tariffs and Trade ▶ GATT

GNP ▶ GDP

Golan Heights

This mountainous region of Syria bordering Israel has been occupied by Israeli troops since June 1967.

Great Leap Forward

The Great Leap Forward was the ambitious social and economic transformation advocated and in part introduced by the Chinese Communist Party, following ▶ Mao Zedong, in 1958. It involved the rapid collectivization of agriculture and the formation of the People's Communes, and included a campaign to industrialize the countryside (often popularly summarized as 'backyard steelmills'). It was an almost unmitigated disaster in the short run. The initial very radical communalization of rural life, including the virtual abolition of the family, was rapidly abandoned due to fierce peasant opposition. The communes actually introduced were a very watered-down version of the original plans. The industrialization drive led to the setting up of inefficient plants and involved a vast waste of resources. Many of the experiments did not last long. The general disruption produced by such rapid change imposed from above was one of the contributory factors to the unprecedented famine of 1960–1 in which upwards of 20 million people died. The failure of the Great Leap Forward led to a period of more conservative retrenchment by the Chinese Communist Party leaders until the new offensive of the ▶ Cultural Revolution in 1966.

Further reading

W. Hinton, *Fanshen: a documentary of revolution in a Chinese village*, Brighton 1966.

N. Maxwell (ed.), *China's Road to Development*, Oxford 1979.

green revolution

The term 'green revolution' emerged in the literature of development studies some time in the mid-1960s. It suggested that new breakthroughs in agricultural technology could represent the solution to the agrarian problem of the Third World (▶ agrarian question). Technological innovations had led to the creation of new varieties of cereals, particularly rice and wheat. These new varieties were highly responsive to fertilizers and their use could lead to major increases in food production. A so-called miracle rice, which had a short stem and therefore would not topple over, was promoted as a solution to the food problem of the Asian sub-continent.

The term 'green revolution' had an implicit political and ideological content. This peaceful rational solution to the agrarian question through new technology was counterposed to the threat of a 'red revolution', which could now be averted. Thus the green revolution was seized on readily by development experts as the panacea they had been searching for. In reality the attraction of the green revolution lay in its potential for providing a technical solution to a social problem. The profound social upheaval of land reform could be evaded through technology.

The technology of the green revolution could indeed raise productivity in agriculture. However, the green revolution could not itself provide an alternative to land reform. The main restriction on the benefits of the green revolution is the cost of technology. The vast majority of Third World peasants cannot afford the new varieties of cereals, nor the fertilizers, pesticides and other inputs essential for cultivating them. Irrigation needed by the new strains of cereals is also a cost beyond the reach of most peasants.

The green revolution is heavily dependent on the products of ▶ agribusiness. Consequently, it can only benefit the larger, more prosperous farmers. Where the green revolution has been introduced it has led to the intensification of inequalities in the countryside. Prosperous landlords have used the technology to raise production and profits. Often, tenant farmers have been dispossessed and agicultural workers have been expelled from the land and replaced with machines. In Punjab the introduction of the green revolution led to a significant increase in both food production and landlessness.

It is also evident that the use of new technology in agriculture actually makes the Third World more dependent on the world economy. Imported inputs, in particular the energy-intensive inputs controlled by agribusiness, have constituted a major drain on the balance of payments position of some Third World countries.

The problems associated with the green revolution are strikingly illustrated by the case of Mexico. In the 1970s Mexico was held up as an example of a green revolution miracle. It is clear that, at least initially, the Mexican green revolution provided a major boost to agricultural production. However, there was a high price to be paid. The new technology strengthened the position of the large commercial farmers who could take advantage of the new opportunity for profit-making. Their success actually masked the reality of the situation. The areas untouched by the investments in revolutionary technology continued to stagnate and decline. According to Warnock, 'in the 1970s per capita production began to decline'.[1]

One ominous symptom of the green revolution in Mexico was the reorientation of agricultural production from subsistence to the more profitable sphere of cash-cropping. Consequently, the production of staple food crops such as rice and beans stagnated while export-oriented crops rose in importance. With this shift away from subsistence farming Mexico became more dependent on the import of cereals. Predictably, this led to the growth of a substantial trade deficit and helped increase Mexico's foreign debt.

Finally, the green revolution has proved to be a mixed blessing for the ▶ environment. The increased use of fertilizers and pesticides has created problems for the Third World environment. In Asia there has been a rise in water pollution from the chemicals used in the green revolution technology. According to surveys the production of fish in farm ponds has fallen in Indonesia, Malaysia and the Philippines. Pesticides in tropical areas have had a devastating effect on the ecological balance.

Experience has shown that the green revolution – in the sense of a technological miracle – is a fraud. New technology certainly has enormous potential to transform agriculture, but this technology can only improve matters in general if it is used in the context of a programme of land reform. Without land reform, the dictates of profit will ensure that technology benefits only the rich and that such benefits will be at the expense of the vast majority of Third World peasants and will not resolve the agrarian question.

Further reading

K. Griffin, *The Political Economy of Agrarian Change: an essay on the Green Revolution*, London 1974.

Note

1.   J.W. Warnock, *The Politics of Hunger*, London 1987, p. 16.

gross domestic product ▶ GDP

gross national product ▶ GDP

Group of 77

This caucusing group of Third World countries meets to coordinate policies prior to meetings of the UN General Assembly and other major agencies and conferences. It was formed by an original 77 countries in 1964 at the United Nations Conference on Trade and Development (▶ UNCTAD). Membership has risen to 127 countries, plus the Palestine Liberation Organization. In the period since the outbreak of the ▶ debt crisis and the wave of economic ▶ neo-liberalism which swept the world during the 1980s, the role of the Group of 77, along with most inter-Third World groupings, has dwindled to very little, but the demands for a new economic order with which it is identified maintain their relevance and the campaign for them can be expected to be renewed.

guerrilla war (from Spanish *guerrilla* = minor war)

The term 'guerrilla' came into use during the Peninsular Wars of 1808–14. It implies a small-scale war of attrition conducted by partisans or irregular troops against a conventional army of superior numbers and equipment. Guerrilla war, especially in the form of peasant rebellions, has a long tradition in the Third World, especially in Latin America. In the nineteenth century, the systematic guerrilla warfare of Mexican peasants defeated the French colonialists and in the twentieth century, the Zapatista guerrilleros succeeded in establishing a revolutionary regime. Other major guerrilla wars were conducted by the Prestes Column in Brazil in the 1920s and in Guatemala in the 1960s. In the post-war period, it was the success of Fidel Castro's guerrilla movement leading to the Cuban revolution of 1959 that led to the popularization of guerrillaism as a strategy for the anti-imperialist struggle. The subsequent success of large-scale guerrilla warfare in Vietnam showed that well-organized irregular detachments of committed freedom fighters were more than a match for even the most powerful nation's conventional forces. The importance of guerrilla warfare as an effective element in Third World resistance has been amply demonstrated by the experience of Cuba, Vietnam, Zimbabwe and El Salvador. The success of guerrilla armies has always been linked to their ability to win wider political support. However, during the 1960s a tendency to romanticize guerrilla warfare led to a celebration of armed action and an underestimation of the prior task of political mobilization. In Latin America, radical activists impatient with the slow progress of the anti-imperialist movement launched guerrilla-type activities as an alternative to political action. This approach was justified through foco theory (focismo), as elaborated by Ernesto 'Che' Guevara and popularized by Régis Debray.[1] ► Castro and Castroism, ► focismo, ► Guevara and Guevarism, ► Mao and Maoism.

The main weakness of focismo is that it treats a tactic – guerrilla warfare – as a philosophy. The disastrous consequences of Guevara's own heroic attempt to put focismo into practice in Bolivia provides the best argument against this outlook. The experiment was doomed from the start. Guevara's small guerrilla unit was ignorant of the local language and conditions. The conviction that a small group of organized guerrillas could, through their example, spark off a revolt proved to be naive. Guevara's guerrillas remained isolated and were not able to counteract the blows of the US-trained counter-insurgency forces of the Bolivian government.

Despite this experience, guerrillaism acquired considerable influence among Latin American activists. During the 1960s, there emerged groups of urban guerrillas in Venezuela, Guatemala, Brazil and Uruguay. Urban guerrillas sought to ameliorate conditions through armed action in cities. Their generalized failure was the result of a narrow political militaristic approach which substituted armed action for political mobilization.

In its proper context, it can be argued that guerrilla-based armed strategy has made a major contribution to modern military science. The importance of guerrilla warfare is shown by the new developments in the military strategy of the Western powers designed to counter what is seen as a major threat. Counter-insurgency technique, the so-called low-intensity warfare and the creation of rapid deployment forces (► RDF) are some of the recent innovations designed to minimize the risk of a protracted involvement in a war against guerrillas.[2] The need for a coherent response to guerrilla warfare was clearly explained by the US commander in Vietnam, General Westmorland:

> I believe that the prospect of many 'Vietnams' in the entire world presents a real danger for all freedom-loving peoples. That is why I consider the technique of insurgency warfare must be top of the list among our defences against the dangers we will have to face.[3]

That guerrilla warfare is 'top of the list' of General Westmorland's concern is a testimony to its effectiveness.

Further reading

R. Gott, *Guerrilla Movements in Latin America*, London 1970.

Notes

1. Ernesto 'Che' Guevara, *La guerra de guerrillas*, Havana 1960; and R. Debray, *Revolution in the Revolution: armed struggle and political struggle in Latin America*, Westport, Conn, 1967.
2. For an influential contribution on the subject see F. Kitson, *Low-intensity Operations: subversion, insurgency and counter-insurgency*, London 1971.
3. Cited in R. Faligst, *The Kitson Experiment*, London 1983, p. 9.

Guevara, Ernesto 'Che' (1928–67) and Guevarism

Guevarism refers to the ideas of Ernesto 'Che' Guevara. His theory of revolutionary guerrilla warfare is also known as ► focismo.

Guevara was born in Alta Gracia, Argentina in 1928, studied medicine and graduated as a doctor in 1953. He travelled extensively around Latin America, ending up in Guatemala in 1954 as a supporter of the left-wing Arbenz regime. After the US Central Intelligence Agency (► CIA) overthrew Arbenz, Che went to Mexico City where he met Fidel ► Castro in November 1955.

Guevara went to Cuba with Castro's guerrillas in 1956, and played a leading part in their armed struggle against the Batista dictatorship. After Batista had been ousted in 1959, Guevara became president of the Central Bank with wide powers relating to the organization of the economy. In this capacity he formed one pole in an important economic debate in Cuba covering such questions as the speed of industrialization and the possibility of abolishing money relations. His radical policies on these questions were later discredited as adventuristic.

Tired of grappling with the problems of building a new society in Cuba, Guevara resigned his government posts and disappeared in April 1965. He reappeared to take part in several liberation struggles around the globe, notably in the Congo. By 1967 he was in Bolivia, attempting to relaunch the Latin American revolution. He was cut down in a hail of bullets in a CIA ambush in Nancahuazu, Bolivia, on 8 October 1967.

The principles of Guevarism were outlined in Guevara's *Guerrilla Warfare* (1961) and also popularized by French left-winger Régis Debray,[1] who went on to become an adviser to the French socialist President François Mitterrand (►► Mao and Maoism, ►► Sendero Luminoso).

Guevara's ideas broke with the more passive traditions of the official Communist Parties in Latin America, by asserting that an armed struggle against the state was the central issue for revolutionaries. Guevarism enjoyed its heyday in Latin America from the late 1960s to the mid-1970s. However, with the eclipse of such movements as the ► Tupamaros and the Montoneros (► Peronism), its influence has declined. The idea of focusing on a peasant revolt seems less relevant in many Latin American countries, which have undergone a rapid process of industrialization and urbanization in recent years. Guevara himself, however, still personally inspires many Latin American revolutionaries, and several groups in

Bolivia bear his name. Recently the Colombian ▶ELN group has probably been the best-known Guevarist guerrilla group.

Note

1. R. Debray, *Revolution in the Revolution: armed struggle and political struggle in Latin America*, Westport, Conn. 1967.

Gulf Cooperation Council ▶ GCC

H

Hizbullah (Arabic = party of God)

Hizbullah is an Islamic fundamentalist group based among Lebanon's Shi'ite community. Its aim is the creation of an Iranian-style republic in southern Lebanon. Hizbullah was founded, financed, trained and armed by Iran's Islamic Revolutionary Guards from 1983. Based in the Beqaa valley, the 3000-strong group has won a reputation for being the most extreme anti-Western force in Lebanon, and is frequently blamed for the kidnapping of Western individuals in Beirut. Hizbullah has posed a challenge to the formally non-sectarian ▶ AMAL movement within the Shi'ite community. It has attracted support from former AMAL supporters demoralized by the latter's accommodation with Israel and by the campaign AMAL has waged against Palestinians on Syrian orders. Hizbullah's leader, Sheikh Fadlallah, was the target of a Central Intelligence Agency (▶ CIA) car-bomb set off in a Beirut suburb in March 1985. The bomb missed him, but killed 80 people and wounded 200 more.

Hizbullah is closely associated with the pro-Iranian groups holding a number of Western hostages whose fate is periodically used as a bargaining counter in international negotiations. In 1991 Fadlallah announced that, despite the improved relations of Iran with the West and with Syria in the aftermath of the Gulf War, the release of the hostages remained conditional on the release by Israel of the Shi'ite leader Sheikh Obeid and other Lebanese and Palestinian prisoners in Israeli jails.

human development

This concept has been developed by the United Nations Development Programme (UNDP), and means development which is geared towards satisfying ▶ basic needs rather than maximizing incomes. In 1990, in an effort to challenge the prevailing measures of development in terms of money income per capita, the UNDP issued the first of an annual series of *Reports on Human Development*. This report ranks countries according to an index of human development (HDI), which is a complicated average of three indicators: income per capita converted according to ▶ purchasing power parity, life expectancy and adult literacy.

This index produces considerable differences in the ranking of countries compared with the more traditional ranking according to the level of income per capita. The countries whose ranking changes most are listed in the Table. As can be seen from the table, the HDI favours countries which have had socialist regimes, plus the Latin American countries with a longer history of social programmes, and it demotes countries which have a high income (usually from oil) but have backward social spending programmes.

The HDI remains at the experimental stage and its authors aim to include more variables in the future. Like income per capita it does not

Table: Income per capita and human development compared

Country	HDI ranking compared with income per capita ranking
Sri Lanka	+ 45
China	+ 44
Vietnam	+ 40
Myanmar	+ 39
Laos	+ 38
Kampuchea	+ 37
Chile	+ 34
Costa Rica	+ 26
Cuba	+ 26
Jamaica	+ 25
Congo	− 26
Mauritania	− 32
Algeria	− 34
Kuwait	− 34
Libya	− 36
Angola	− 36
Saudi Arabia	− 43
Gabon	− 46
United Arab Emirates	− 50
Oman	− 56

Source: United Nations Development Programme, *Human Development Report 1990*, New York 1990.

take distribution into account, though there are plans for it to do so in the future. Whether it will come to replace income as the most commonly used indicator of development is doubtful; but its use is that it stimulates debate about what development is and how it can be measured. ► development, ► indicators.

Further reading

K. Griffin and J. Knight (eds), *Human Development and the International Development Strategy for the 1990s*, London 1989.

United Nations Development Programme, *World Development Report 1990*, London 1990.

hunger

Hunger is the condition of normally not having enough to eat in order to sustain life in the long run. It is, therefore, a form of slow death from underconsumption. Hunger exists in the Third World on a vast scale. The measurement of hunger is a contentious queston both from the point of view of what criterion to use and how to estimate the number of hungry people. The Food and Agriculture Organization has calculated that the number of people receiving less calories than necessary to maintain 1.2 times the basal metabolic rate in 1980 was 535 million, or 17 per cent of the population of the Third World.[1] Another widely quoted study for the year 1975 (which excludes China) estimates that the population receiving below the minimum amount of calories was as high as 1373 million or 71 per cent of the population.[2]

The absolute numbers of hungry people are growing and possibly the relative number also. The reason for this is not that insufficient food is being produced: world food production per capita has been rising by around 1 per cent a year for many decades.[3] The reason for hunger, therefore, is that a large part of the population is excluded from access to what is produced. That exclusion is a product of many things mentioned in other parts of this book – of ▶ imperialism, ▶ neo-colonialism and a discriminatory world economic system; and of the many sources of poverty and inequality in town and country in the Third World (▶ agrarian question, ▶ urbanization). While 20–70 per cent of the world's population go hungry, the developed countries produce an excess of food which they sometimes destroy as a matter of policy and sometimes store in order to maintain high prices. No person, faced with the task of devising even a half-way reasonable way of running the world, would have thought of this.

Further reading

R. Dumont and N. Cohen, *The Growth of Hunger: a new politics of agriculture*, London 1980.

S. George, *How the Other Half Dies: the real reasons for world hunger*, Harmondsworth 1977.

K. Griffin, *World Hunger and the World Economy*, London 1987.

Notes

1. Food and Agriculture Organization, *The State of Food and Agriculture 1981*, Rome 1982.
2. S. Reutlinger and H. Alderman, 'The prevalence of calorie deficient diets in developing countries', *World Development*, 8, 1980, pp. 399–411.
3. D. Grigg, *The World Food Problem 1959–1980*, Oxford 1985, Ch. 5.

IBRD ▶ World Bank

IDA ▶ World Bank

IFC ▶ World Bank

Ikhwan al-Muslimin ▶ Muslim Brotherhood

Imam (Arabic = guide)

From the Shi'ite wing of Islam, an Imam is one of the 12 infallibles who served as the legitimate rulers of the Muslim community after the death of the Prophet Mohammed. Shi'ites maintain that Ali, son-in-law of the Prophet, was the first true Imam. This is because Mohammed had no sons, but one daugher, Fatemah, whose husband was Ali. Shi'ites believe that all Imams descend from Ali's house.

It is common for every ruler of an Arab country to take the title Imam, and Ayatullah Khomeini also took the title – but only in the ordinary sense of the word, i.e. 'guide'. Part of the Shi'ite belief is that one day an Imam – in the special meaning of the word, 'one who has the divine right to rule' – will return, and this gives a messianic aspect to their sect.

IMF, International Monetary Fund

A United Nations Monetary and Financial Conference took place from 1 to 22 July 1944 at a health resort in Bretton Woods, New Hampshire, USA. It was attended by representatives of 45 states: Australia, Belgium, Bolivia, Brazil, Canada, Chile, China, Colombia, Costa Rica, Cuba, Czechoslovakia, Denmark, Dominican Republic, Ecuador, Egypt, Eire, El Salvador, Ethiopia, France, Greece, Guatemala, Haiti, Honduras, India, Iran, Iraq, Liberia, Luxemburg, Mexico, Netherlands, New Zealand, Nicaragua, Norway, Panama, Paraguay, Peru, Philippines, Poland, South Africa, UK, Uruguay, USA, USSR, Venezuela and Yugoslavia.

The declared aim of the Bretton Woods conference was to create and formalize a cooperative approach among nations to international monetary issues. This was regarded as important in the light of the experiences of the 1930s. The breakdown of the world monetary system had meant the collapse of international trade and a profound economic depression that ultimately helped to lead to the Second World War.

The main proposals at Bretton Woods came from the UK and the USA: the British representative John Maynard Keynes argued for an International Clearing Union (ICU). The most important aspect of this plan was a provision for an automatic redistribution of funds from countries experiencing current account surpluses to those with deficits. Keynes also proposed the creation of a new international currency called bancor to be backed by gold.

British representatives had an eye to the post-war situation when they came up with these plans. Given the ravaged state of European economies it was inevitable that there would be extensive reliance on US industrial goods to aid reconstruction. This meant that Europe would fall into deficit with the USA, a situation which itself threatened economic revival as European reserves of dollars were already very reduced. Behind the demand for the automatic redistribution of current account surpluses lay a mechanism for easing European revival.

Not surprisingly, the USA opposed Keynes' plan since it would have meant the provision of aid with few strings attached. In addition, the idea of an international currency was rejected since the USA owned more than 70 per cent of the world's official gold reserves. In other words, the US economy would have been obliged to assume the burden of highly permissive credit terms to the advantage of its competitors.

The IMF was the outcome of the Bretton Woods talks and the terms of its creation reflected the economic supremacy of the USA. In fact, the strong presence of Latin American countries at the talks was largely as a support group for US demands.

Over the forty years of its existence the IMF's role in the international monetary system has gone through important developments. These largely reflect more general changes in world economic conditions.

The years of boom (1945–70). The IMF formally came into existence on 27 December 1945 when 29 governments signed its articles of agreement devised at Bretton Woods. On 18 December 1946 the IMF announced an agreement by which the currencies of 32 member-states were tied at par values to gold and the US dollar. On 1 March 1947 the IMF announced that it was ready to commence currency trading.

Under these arrangements the price of gold was fixed at US$35 per ounce. However, gold could only perform to a very limited extent its traditional role as the medium through which international exchange was conducted.

As a result the dollar effectively took the place of gold as world money. Through this mechanism other currencies were held at a fixed rate against the dollar (more exactly, IMF member-states agreed to maintain their exchange rates within a 1 per cent range above or below the agreed parity with the dollar). This dollar regime was ensured by two conditions.

First, official holdings of US dollars abroad were made convertible to US gold on demand under IMF rules. In other words, international confidence in the US dollar was ensured by its being made 'as good as gold'. More importantly, the massive scale of international demand for goods in the immediate post-war period backed up the world status of the US dollar. European states attempting to revive their economies had little option but to seek dollars with which to buy US goods.

The strategic role of the US dollar was necessary for providing some stability to the conditions of more open international trade after the war. The dollar was more amenable to rapid expansion than gold. Nevertheless, it also provided US capitalism with particular economic advantages. US producers could obtain easy access to goods produced abroad. US imports could be expanded simply through the provision of more dollars since they were readily acceptable at the going rate elsewhere.

This could not be the case for weaker countries and least of all for Third World countries. Mexico, for instance, could not simply print pesos to buy imports. A rapidly growing supply of pesos in the money markets would soon threaten a collapse in its rate of exchange against the currencies, requiring domestic austerity to salvage its credibility.

In fact, the so-called dollar shortage in the world dictated the scope of economic policies even in Europe well into the 1950s. Despite signing the IMF articles of agreement, one of which demanded that restrictions on currency exchange after the war should be 'transitional', European nations maintained tight control over available dollars. The aim was to ensure that scarce dollars were used only for importing goods essential to economic revival. European currencies were not made freely convertible into dollars until after 1958.

In the case of the Third World the barrier to growth imposed by the international dollar regime bordered on the absolute. Their backward economies meant that there were limited opportunities to earn dollars in the first place. Further restrictions to development originated in the long-term decline in the price of primary products relative to manufactured goods. Third World trade in this period stagnated despite the rapid overall expansion of world trade.

Until the early 1970s, exchange rates fixed against the US dollar were seen as the cornerstone of stable and expanding world trade. To back up the system the IMF operated other mechanisms aimed at exchange rate stability.

The regime of fixed exchange rates did not mean that they were absolutely invariable. Individual countries could, subject to renegotiation under IMF auspices, change the exchange rate of their currency with the dollar (and therefore with all other currencies). It was in fact quite common for member-states to negotiate changes in currency exchange rates as part of a package to deal with a balance of payments deficit.

More important has been the IMF's role as a conduit through which international funds are provided to individual countries in order to aid solutions to balance of payments problems. Each member country is obliged to make a financial contribution to the fund. The size of each country's contribution is decided on the basis of measures of world economic standing: national income, monetary reserves and ratio of exports to national income. The original practice was that each should make one-quarter of its contribution in gold and the rest in its own currency.

The principle is that a member country with a balance of payments deficit can buy foreign currencies from the IMF with its own currency. This effectively means bolstering its foreign reserves and allowing the country more space to meet its external obligations. The aim of this is to reduce downward pressure on the deficit country's currency in the short term.

This short-term character of IMF support for member-state currencies was the distinctive aspect of its activities in this initial period. The IMF was not an unrestricted source of funds for problem countries. Its facilities were seen as making it easier for governments to institute domestic measures to provide a longer-term solution to a balance of payments problem.

This assumption that external deficits were essentially short-term and easily resolvable was based upon the prevailing conditions of rapid world (or at least Western) expansion involving an even more rapid growth of foreign trade. It was assumed that corrective measures could be achieved relatively easily with IMF facilities ensuring that they did not have undesirable international repercussions.

The terms of IMF facilities reflected this. Foreign currency was made available subject to an agreed package of domestic economic reforms. In addition, the fund recipient was expected to buy back its own currency given in exchange for others within a period of 3 to 5 years.

Special mechanisms for aiding Third World countries with longer-term balance of payments problems were limited in character. A 'compensatory financing facility' provides support for member-states suffering from financial losses due to falls in primary commodity prices.

In this initial period, therefore, the IMF's role was seen as relatively modest. External payments disequilibria were not regarded as structural but rather as temporary and easily solved. This, however, began to change as trends in the world economy took a turn for the worse.

The years of crisis (1970 onwards). Two factors were central in provoking change at the IMF in the 1970s. First, worldwide economic recession required greater use of credit as a prop to the capitalist order. Second, the fixed exchange rate system came under increasing pressure amid growing evidence of weaknesses in the US economy relative to that of its competitors.

Growing international pressure on the US dollar encouraged the IMF to seek new ways of carrying out its traditional functions. A meeting of the IMF General Assembly in September 1967 in Rio de Janeiro agreed in principle to the creation of a new international currency referred to as special drawing rights (SDRs). To facilitate the creation of SDRs the member-states of the IMF ratified the first amendment to its articles of agreement on 28 January 1969. The IMF formally established an account in SDRs on 1 January 1970. The SDR account established at the IMF in 1970 amounted to an equivalent of US$31 billion.

A country in balance of payments difficulties can go to the IMF and appeal for additional foreign currency, which it can then add to its reserves. Through IMF mediation the country whose currency has been disbursed in this way is obliged to accept SDRs from the IMF account instead of the currency of the deficit country.

In effect, SDRs are a new means by which a deficit country is given additional scope to deal with balance of payments problems. Again, SDRs are not an inexhaustible source of foreign currency for a deficit country. The amount that can be drawn on by a given member-state is determined by its level of contributions to the IMF. Also, the statutory obligation of a surplus country to accept SDRs is limited to a level twice that of its own special drawing rights at the IMF. Above that level it is not obliged to concur with SDR arrangements.

In its first three years of operation (1970–2) a total of US$9 billion in SDRs were used. However, its aim of ensuring exchange rate stability into the future was soon overtaken by events.

International speculation against the dollar in the wake of growing US balance of payments deficits destroyed the system of fixed exchange rates. In December 1971 a meeting at the Smithsonian Institution in Washington, DC agreed to a devaluation of the dollar by nearly 10 per cent against other major currencies. It also involved widening the parameters of currency variation from 1 per cent to 2.5 per cent above or below the new exchange rate against the dollar.

This attempt to maintain stable exchange rates finally ended in 1973 when all the major industrial nations converted to a system of floating exchange rates by which currencies were allowed to find their own position in the market.

The collapse of the Bretton Woods system of fixed exchange rates had an important impact on the IMF. In narrow terms it meant changes in, for instance, valuing SDRs as units of account. In July 1974 SDRs were pegged to a basket of 16 major currencies, the weighting system broadly reflecting the importance of the respective currencies in international exchange. The aim was to provide greater stability to SDRs by reducing the impact on their value of variations in the value of the dollar. In September 1980 the basket was reduced to five currencies: the US dollar, the German mark, the French franc, the Japanese yen and the pound sterling.

More importantly, the 1970s saw concern for currency stability and solving trade imbalances recede. The focus of international money management shifted to raising the level of credit in the world economy to generate economic revival after the 1974–5 recession. This reflected increasing concern for deeper structural problems at the heart of the world economy in place of a perception of problems as essentially short-term.

As part of this change the IMF established a Committee on Reform of the International Monetary System and Related Issues in 1972. The outcome was another series of changes in the IMF's articles of agreement. These changes were approved by the IMF's Board of Governors in April 1976 and came into force on 1 April 1978.

The changes involved the acceptance of greater flexibility in dealing with exchange rate arrangements. This effectively meant the IMF formally accepting the new international norm of freely floating markets. It also involved an aim to reduce further the role of gold in the international monetary system. This merely meant accepting another already established reality: that the last vestiges of gold's role in controlling international monetary expansion had been terminated. It also aimed at increasing the use of SDRs in the monetary system.

In fact, despite these measures, it was the private banking system of the advanced capitalist nations that took centre stage in the expansion of international credit in the 1970s. An important aspect of this was the flow of capital to the Third World. By providing a stimulus to demand in world markets this flow contributed to economic revival in the 1970s.

However, as the main, specifically international institution concerned with financial management the IMF has been at the centre of deliberations over Third World capital borrowing. Its role has been particularly central since 1982 when the accumulation of debt in the Third World became a ▶ debt crisis.

It is usually presumed that the IMF has been responsible for sustaining international financial cooperation in the post-war period. In reality the existence of the IMF largely formalized cooperation whose basis lay elsewhere. It was the uncontested supremacy of US capitalism in the world that facilitated stability in international financial relations. With the erosion of this position the Bretton Woods arrangements collapsed and the IMF could do nothing. This simply reflects the fact that the IMF has in effect been a rubber stamp for the desires of the US administration.

Economic trends since the early 1970s have ensured that the IMF plays quite a marginal role in relation to financial arrangements among the major capitalist powers. The financial policies of the USA under President Reagan are clear evidence that, in the case of the major powers, national considerations easily override notions of international responsibility.

In fact, it is only in the case of the Third World that the IMF's cooperative traditions have been sustained into the 1980s. In relation to this issue the IMF has represented cooperation between Western governments over coercing the Third World into paying back debt. Indeed, the IMF's role in this context is extremly important. Private banks with investments in the Third World generally have little pull when it comes to forcing governments to pay back 'sovereign debt'. The IMF has been the means through which Western governments have imposed austerity measures on the Third World in an effort to save their own banking systems.

The IMF's austerity measures, often called stabilization or structural adjustment programmes, are in their broad outlines the same for all countries to which they are applied, though they may differ in detail. Normally they comprise the following formula:

(1) The reduction of any government deficit by cutting subsidies and, if necessary, other programmes;

148

(2) The reduction or elimination of restrictions on imports and exports (i.e. moves in the direction of free trade);

(3) The elimination of restrictions on the import of foreign capital and the introduction of policies to encourage it;

(4) The devaluation of the exchange rate to a competitive level in order to encourage exports and reduce imports without the use of tariffs and other controls.

The IMF often makes the adoption of debt rescheduling programmes conditional on the introduction of such measures – a position known as conditionality. Through its powerful advocacy of such programmes in Third World countries the IMF has become the major institution responsible for the revival of ▶ neo-liberalism in the world economy. It claims that this form of stabilization will lead to healthy long-term recovery and growth in economies which have become dangerously distorted. There is no doubt, however, that the programmes have caused severe recessions in the short term and, as a result, much economic suffering. Many doubt that the IMF's long run will ever arrive.

Further reading

D. Ghai (ed.), *The IMF and the South: the social impact of crisis and adjustment*, London 1991.

T. Killick (ed.), *Adjustment and Financing in the Developing World: the role of the IMF*, Washington, DC 1982.

P, Körner, G. Maass, T. Siebold and R. Tetziaff, *The IMF and the Debt Crisis: a guide to the Third World's dilemma*, London 1985.

C. Payer, *The Debt Trap: the IMF and the Third World*, Harmondsworth 1974.

imperialism

In 1901 the *United States Investor*, a Boston-based weekly, argued the case for imperialism on the grounds that 'the whole civilised world has become equipped with an excessive machinery of production'. The editor argued that capital could find 'profitable employment' in the 'tropical countries' and suggested that this was an 'economic necessity'. The case for imperialist domination of the Third World was spelled out with care and precision:

> It is not necessary that the older civilised countries should build up manufacturing rivals in the undeveloped countries. They will undoubtedly do this to some extent but the logical path to be pursued is that of the development of the natural riches of the tropical countries. These countries are now peopled by races incapable on their own initiative of extracting its full riches from their own soil . . . . What is involved . . . (for the present) is not a revolution in the habits and capacities of the peoples of the tropics, but only their equipment with the best means of rendering their territory productive. This will be attained in some cases by the mere stimulus of government and direction by men of the temperate zones; but it will

149

be attained also by the application of modern machinery and methods of culture to the agricultural and mineral resources of the undeveloped countries.[1]

The compulsion for capitalism to expand and to dominate other parts of the world was well understood by big business. It was Lenin who provided the first systematic theory of imperialism and thereby helped explain why the West required the Third World for its survival.

Lenin's theory of imperialism. According to Lenin, when the domestic solutions to the problem of capital accumulation are insufficient, capital reaches its imperialist phase. Capital accumulates to such an extent that it cannot all find profitable use in the main capitalist countries and must, therefore, look abroad for profitable outlets. The economic function of imperialism can be seen as a system of measures that capital assumes to counter the effects of the crisis of accumulation and profit at home. The three driving forces behind the imperialist expansion that Lenin identifies are the search for: new spheres of investment, new markets and new sources of raw materials.

Cheap raw materials and energy are obvious ways of reducing costs of production (the cost of constant capital in Marx's terminology). A regular cheap supply of raw materials is important for, as productivity increases, the value of raw materials comes to form a growing proportion of the value of commodities as a whole and thus has a growing impact on the rate of profit. Foreign trade allows capitalists to overcome the barriers of the national market and capital exports allow the capitalist to secure a higher rate of return than that available at home. Overseas investment opens up new sources of labour and markets, and allows access to raw materials. It also often allows the capitalist to secure more favourable conditions for production than are available at home.

Lenin's theory of imperialism grew directly from Marx's idea that capitalism, like all social systems, would experience two phases: the first historically progressive and the second retrogressive. Once capital reaches its highest point on the basis of its own laws, further development has a regressive character. As Marx put it: 'As soon as this point is reached, the further development appears as decay, and the new development begins from a new basis.'[2] The tendency towards decay becomes most manifest in countries where capitalism is most mature. Thus the barriers to capital accumulation become more and more overwhelming, forcing capitalists to redirect investment abroad.

Historically, the UK was the first country to experience capitalist stagnation. Between 1870 and 1913 its share of world production fell from 32 per cent to 16 per cent.[3] During the same period, a tremendous outflow of capital from the UK indicated that the capitalist class could no longer systematically develop the forces of production at home. Thus it ignored new developments in technology and found itself displaced as world leader in industries like iron and steel, machine-building and chemicals. This was not due to lack of capital – it was due to the barriers to expanding existing capital investments on a profitable basis. As a result

British capital was exported abroad. The scale of capital investment is illustrated during the years 1910–13, when more than three-quarters of the capital raised by public issues was for overseas account.[4]

It was precisely with the UK in mind that Lenin defined the 'economic essence of imperialism' as 'capitalism in transition, or, more precisely, as moribund capitalism'.[5] The UK's decline had by the beginning of the twentieth century become a major topic for debate.

The British capitalist class acquired an increasingly parasitic character. The typical capitalist was no longer running productive industry but was a financier of overseas productions on a merchant basis. The UK had become a rentier state.

Today, the parasitic character of British capitalism is even more advanced than during Lenin's time. The British establishment is decreasingly committed to developing production at home – instead it is increasingly committed to living off its overseas earnings. Instead of investing in the UK, *The Economist* advised its readers on 4 June 1983 that 'foreign investment is probably the most prudent use of the North Sea's wealth. Inflows of interest and dividends will not match the foreign exchange benefits of oil, but they should last a lot longer!' While the British establishment lives off its dividends, industry is falling apart. Most people are no longer employed in manufacturing industry, and in 1983, for the first time since the Industrial Revolution, the UK's trade balance in manufacturerd goods fell into deficit.

Lenin characterized the imperialist epoch as one of stagnation and decay, but, as with every social process, this did not have the character of an absolute law but that of a tendency of development. Indeed, Lenin argues that stagnation coexists with economic growth. He writes:

> more and more prominently there emerges, as one of the tendencies of imperialism, the creation of the 'rentier state', the usurer state, in which the bourgeoisie to an ever increasing degree lives on the proceeds of capital exports and by 'clipping coupons'. It would be a mistake to believe that this tendency to decay precludes the rapid growth of capitalism.[6]

In other words imperialism cannot be reduced to decay; rather it presents capitalist decay alongside capitalist growth. Both of these tendencies find an expression in the movement of capital. Lenin explains:

> In the epoch of imperialism, certain branches of industry, certain strata of the bourgeoisie and certain countries betray, to a greater or lesser degree, now one and now another of these tendencies. On the whole, capitalism is growing far more rapidly than before; but this growth is not only becoming more and more uneven in general, its unevenness also manifests itself, in particular, in the decay of the countries which are richest in capital (Britain).[7]

The same forces that lead to stagnation and decay also unleash within the bourgeoisies of the imperialist nations fierce and aggressive tendencies.

The restoration of profitability through the struggle for world market domination provides the framework for imperialist expansion and conflict. To compensate for domestic stagnation the capitalist class depends more and more on tribute that flows back from abroad. Parasitism becomes the prerequisite for prolonging the life of capitalism.

The imperialist era. As capitalist accumulation comes up against the barriers of the national market so its operation on the world market becomes a matter of life and death. The expansion of existing capital simply cannot continue within the confines of national boundaries. The expansion of capital abroad requires a major reorganization of the economy. Capital becomes ever more concentrated in a smaller number of hands in the shape of monopolies and cartels. Banks and the state step in to underwrite the expansionism of the national monopolies. Lenin called the era one of finance capital (a term derived from Hilferding) or monopoly capital. Through finance capital, the fusion of banking and industrial capital, the ruling class acquires the means to invest and extract surplus value in every part of the globe.

The reorganization of capital accumulation gives world market relations a primary importance. The drive to dominate the world market is not just an episode but becomes intrinsic to the survival of the system. The establishment of world market domination presupposes the oppression of countries that serve as the source of surplus value to the imperialist nations. Thus a handful of imperialist countries survive but only by dominating the rest of the world.

The shift from free competition to the rivalry of monopolies and its transfer to the world market has important implications. It means that the form of competition which predominates in capitalism is no longer that between individual capitalists, it is between the capitalist classes of different nations. The struggle to dominate world market relations creates national rivalries. These rivalries become all the more bitter because the survival of the capitalist class is decided by its success on the world market. Imperialist rivalries tend to embrace the whole globe and result in its division into specific spheres of influence. The expansionist carve-up of the world in this era should not be confused with the international rivalries of the past. It comes about spontaneously through the drive to expand capital accumulation. As Lenin observes, the 'capitalists divide the world, not out of any particular malice, but because the degree of concentration which has been reached forces them to adopt this method in order to obtain profits.'[8]

The division of the world can be achieved in many ways. In certain periods it can be enforced through diplomatic agreement and settled relatively peacefully. At other times the struggle for spheres of influence can only be resolved through military means. However, once imperialism is established, sooner or later competition *must* take on a military dimension. The reason for this is that once the world has been partitioned through the seizure of colonies and the establishment of spheres of influence, the only way that one imperialist power can forge ahead of its competitors is through the repartition of the globe. As Lenin puts it: 'For the first time the world is completely divided up and territories can only pass from one "owner" to another, instead of passing as one "ownerless" territory to an "owner".[9]

The struggle between imperialist powers not only provokes wars but it also unleashes a drive for colonies. Colonialism existed before capitalism, but pre-capitalist colonies are qualitatively different to annexations in the imperialist epoch. Before capitalism, colonialism was arbitrary and episodic. In all events it was not necessary for the maintenance of social relations in the colonizing country. Under imperialism the drive towards colonialism is organic to the reproduction needs of the metropolitan country. The expansion of capital depends on establishing profitable spheres of investments, cheap sources of raw materials and new markets.

It is above all the need to export capital abroad that stimulates the expansionary tendencies. Through capital exports in the form of direct investments, loans and portfolio investments, new points of production are established. The imperialist powers are now faced with the problem of how to secure their long-term investments. The best guarantee is political control in either a direct or an indirect form. This has the advantage of breaking down barriers to profitable investments as well as excluding potential rivals. In Lenin's words:

> The interests pursued in exporting capital also give an impetus to the conquest of colonies, for in the colonial-market it is easier to employ monopoly methods (and sometimes they are the only methods that can be employed) to eliminate competition, to ensure supplies, to secure the necessary 'connections' etc.[10]

It is because of the striving for world market domination that Lenin characterized the 'division of nations into oppressor and oppressed' as the 'essence of imperialism'.[11] This striving for world market domination provokes tensions, brings rivalries to a head and provokes war and destruction. The more capital is forced to regulate competition the more it exacerbates tendencies towards war.

Lenin's theory of imperialism elaborates Marx's discussion of capitalist stagnation in relation to the historic period when further expansion comes up against the limitation of accumulation on a national scale. The full development of this phase of capital cannot be reduced to a simple definition. Instead, imperialism should be seen as a system of structured changes and policy measures that capitalism assumes to counter the effects of the crisis of accumulation. As the countervailing tendencies to the fall in the rate of profit become less and less effective, capitalist competition becomes increasingly a struggle for the world market. Thus stagnation and aggression run parallel embracing the whole globe.

There is much about the post-Second World War world which is very different from that portrayed by Lenin in his description of imperialism, but a remarkable amount remains the same. A world system in which a few rich and powerful countries monopolize power – sometimes in cooperation but sometimes in competition with each other – alongside many poor and dominated countries, i.e. the Third World, were features of the world which Lenin depicted and are features of the world today. Direct colonialism as a form of domination has been largely abandoned, but many other methods exist and are used (▶ aid, ▶ CIA, ▶ neo-colonialism, ▶ Reagan doctrine). As long as the Third World continues to suffer domination we will remain in the age of imperialism.

Further reading
A. Brewer, *Marxist Theories of Imperialism: a critical survey*, London 1990.
H. Magdoff, *The Age of Imperialism: the economics of US foreign policy*, New York 1966.

Notes
1. Cited in N. Etherington, *Theories of Imperialism*, London 1984, p. 17.
2. K. Marx, *Grundrisse*, Harmondsworth 1973, p. 154.
3. See L. Anell and B. Mygren, *The Developing Countries and the World Economic Order*, London 1980, p. 18.
4. See K. Hutchinson, *The Decline and Fall of British Capitalism*, New Haven, Conn. 1966, p. 70.
5. V. Lenin, *Collected Works*, Vol. 22, Moscow 1960–80, p. 302.
6. Ibid., p. 253.
7. Ibid.
8. Ibid.
9. Lenin, op. cit., p. 254.
10. Ibid., p. 262.
11. Lenin, *Collected Works*, Vol. 21, Moscow 1960–80, p. 409.

import-substituting industrialization ▶ ISI

indicators
It has been and will remain a subject of eternal debate whether it is possible to indicate the level of development of a country with quantitative indicators. The debate turns around a number of issues: the usefulness in general of quantitative indicators; the usefulness of particular indicators; the relative merit of using a single indicator versus a number of indicators combined into an index. It is certain that the choice of an indicator expresses some particular priority or outlook. The most frequently used single indicator is the ▶ GDP or income per capita (though that is itself a composite of many numbers) and critics increasingly complain that this indicator gives too much weight to commercial economic activity and assumes that imitating the West is the desirable pattern of development. The recently devised index of ▶ human development is one attempt to replace GDP per capita.

The problem with using many indicators combined into an index is that it becomes less and less clear what exactly the resulting numbers actually mean. It is easy to understand what the difference between an infant mortality rate of 10 and 100 per 1000 live births means in the real world. It is much more difficult to understand the difference between an index of human development of 0.336 and 0.678.

A further problem with all indicators is that a particular quantity does not necessarily describe very well a particular quality. For instance, two countries may have the same level of ▶ urbanization but it may mean two completely different situations – in one a situation of settled town dwellers with access to public services and in the other a chaos of shantytowns. Few quantitative indicators are completely free of this problem.

Nearly all indicators, as they are currently available, fail to take into account the distribution of the variable among the population. This is another reason why quantitative indicators may give a very incomplete and distorted picture of reality.

Finally, all statistics must be distrusted. There are massive problems in collecting accurate statistics in the best of circumstances and these are even greater in conditions of underdevelopment; and, in addition, nearly all indicators come from government sources and so are liable to have been doctored for many different reasons which the reader can be left to imagine.

In any event, the Table on pp. 156–9, gives a selection of various indicators which are readily available in the statistics published by international organizations. In the case of each one, the table indicates the country with the 'highest' or 'best' value of the indicator, the country with the 'lowest', the value of the indicator in each case with the ratio between the two, and finally the value of the indicator for the world as a whole and examples of countries with values close to the world average.

Further reading

N. Baster (ed.), *Measuring Development: the role and adequacy of development indicators*, London 1972.

indigenismo

The indigenismo movement in Latin America was one of the first attempts consciously to resist the often insidious effects of cultural imperialism. For centuries, Western colonial powers, first Spain and Portugal and later the UK and the USA, sought to assert their intellectual and cultural hegemony in Latin America. By implication, the indigenous cultural heritage was devalued and dismissed as primitive and irrational.

As in many other parts of the Third World it was the intelligentsia of Latin America that felt most provoked by the effects of cultural imperialism. The growth of new nationalism in the 1920s saw a flowering of cultural resistance. Unfortunately, the approach adopted by Latin American intellectuals was one that emphasized the rediscovery of the glories of the past. In parallel with the Afro-Caribbean intellectuals, the indigenismo movement sought refuge in a mythical past where harmony prevailed in a simple communal environment (▶ Negritude).

The pre-Spanish Indian civilization became the model for the indigenismo movement. It was argued that the survival of elements of the pre-conquest social organization of Andean Indians was proof that it constituted a viable alternative for the contemporary period. This

Table: Indicators of development

Indicator	Highest country	Value	Lowest country	Value	Ratio	World Average	Average countries
1 GDP per capita (1987 $)	Switzerland	$27,500	Mozambique	$100	275.0	$3470	South Korea, Portugal
2 GDP per capita (1987 purchasing power parity $)	USA	$17,615	Zaire	$220	80.1	$4110	Brazil, Poland
3 Human development index	Japan	0.996	Niger	0.116	8.6	0.7	Dominican Republic, Saudi Arabia
4 Life expectancy	Japan	80 yrs	Sierra Leone	42 yrs	1.9	65	Iraq, Brazil
5 Adult literacy	Japan, etc.	99%	Somalia	12%	8.3		
6 Literacy (men)	Japan, etc.	99%	Somalia	18%	5.5		
7 Literacy (women)	Japan, etc.	99%	Somalia	6%	16.5		
8 % with access to health facilities	Japan, etc.	100%	Mali	15%	6.7		
9 % with access to safe water	Japan, etc.	100%	Kampuchea	3%	33.3		
10 % with access to sanitation	Japan, etc.	100%	Nepal	2%	50.0		
11 Daily calorie consumption	United Arab Emirates	3733	Rwanda	1665	2.2	2321	Thailand, South Yemen
12 Scientists and technicians per 1000	Japan	317	Togo	0.3	1056.7	44.4	New Zealand, Egypt

13	% of births in presence of medical personnel	Japan, etc.	100%	Somalia	2%	50.0	51	Senegal, Colombia
14	% of babies with low birth weight	Spain	1%	Laos	39%	39.0	15	Zimbabwe, Nicaragua
15	Infant mortality per 1000 live births	Japan	5	Angola	172	34.0	71	South Africa, Zimbabwe
16	Under-5 mortality per 1000 live births	Sweden	7	Afghanistan	300	42.9	108	Honduras, Algeria
17	% of year-old children immunized	Bulgaria	99%	Bangladesh	18%	5.5	69	Brazil, Australia
18	% of children under 5 underweight			Nepal	70			
19	Maternal mortality per 100,000 live births	Norway	2	Bhutan	1710	855.0	250	Madagascar, Botswana
20	Population per doctor (1000)	Italy	0.2	Ethiopia	77.4	387.0	4.0	South Yemen, Myanmar
21	Population per nurse (1000)	France, etc.	0.1	Bangladesh	9.0	90.0	1.6	China, Iraq
22	Public health spending as % of GDP	Sweden	8.0%	Niger	0.2%	40.0	4.2	Czechoslovakia, Saudi Arabia
23	% of age-group in primary school (boys)	Japan, etc.	100%	Somalia	19%	5.3	89	Bolivia, Jordan
24	% of age-group in primary school (girls)	Japan, etc.	100%	Somalia	10%	10.0	82	Algeria, Iraq

Table: *continued*

Indicator	Highest country	Value	Lowest country	Value	Ratio	World	Average countries
25 % of age-group in secondary school (boys)	Netherlands, etc.	100%	Malawi	5%	20.0	51	China, Saudi Arabia
26 % of age-group in secondary school (girls)	Netherlands, etc.	100%	Chad	2%	50.0	40	Iran, Brazil
27 % of age-group in higher education (men)	USA	53.5%	Mozambique	0.3%	185.0	15.1	Poland, Saudi Arabia
28 % of age-group in higher education (women)	USA	63.7%	Mozambique	0.1%	637.0	12.7	Mexico, Syria
29 Radios per 1000 population	USA	2119	Bhutan	15	141.3	369	Bulgaria, Brazil
30 Televisions per 1000 population	USA	811	Mali	0.4	2027.0	134	Malaysia, Venezuela
31 Public education spending as % of GDP	Saudi Arabia	10.6%	Zaïre	0.2%	50.3	5.0	Liberia, Japan
32 % of labour force in agriculture	UK	3.0	Bhutan	95.0	31.7	47.9	Greece, Tanzania
33 % of labour force in industry	East Germany	50.0	Mali	2.0	25.0	16.4	Netherlands, Honduras

34 Population growth rate	West Germany	−0.1%	United Arab Emirates	10.5	Infinity	1.8	Chile, China
35 Manufacturing production per capita ($)	West Germany	$5869	Tanzania	$6	978.2	$750	Argentina, Greece
36 Energy consumption per capita (kg coal equivalent)	Canada	9683 kg	Chad	18 kg	537.9	1289	Portugal, Mexico
37 % of primary products in exports	Japan	2%	Uganda	100%	50.0	25	Spain, USA

Notes: A blank means information not available. 'etc.' means other developed countries have the same value. '$' means US dollars except in item 2 (▶ purchasing power parity).

Sources: World Bank, *World Development Report 1990*, Washington, DC 1990; United Nations Development Programme, *Human Development Report 1990*, New York 1990.

orientation lacked a firm grasp of the condition of the Indian population. Under the brutal impact of colonialism, very little was left of pre-Spanish forms of social organization. The celebration of an idealized version of Indian communities by indigenismo in fact represented an evasion of realities.

What began as a positive challenge to cultural imperialism soon degenerated into a romantic fantasy. The indigenous population was held up as a community that was not corrupted by Western colonial culture. Indigenismo suggested that these communities could purge Latin America of European cultural domination.

Leading supporters of the indigenismo movement saw the answer in a sort of back-to-the-land movement related to the approach suggested by Tolstoy in relation to Russia. One of the most reactionary themes in their writing was the need for the rural highlands of Latin America to destroy the decadent cities.

The indigenismo movement was particularly influential in Mexico, Peru and Bolivia. In practical terms the movement achieved very little. There was no basis in twentieth-century Latin America for a back-to-the-land movement. Certainly, the comfortably settled intelligentsia had no intention of establishing rural Tolstoyan communities. However, despite the non-practicability of their project, the indigenismo movement achieved considerable intellectual influence. This was most manifest in the literary sphere. Novels like Ciro Alegria's *Broad and Alien is the World* or Argueda's *Yawar Fiesta* had a major impact on the Latin American intellectual milieu at the time.

The simple populism of the movement continues to exercise a degree of appeal. It offers a radical rejection of the degrading conditions of neo-colonial Latin America without realistically challenging the status quo. It appeals to those who want to limit their radicalism to the realm of ideas rather than practical action.

In Peru the ▶ Sendero Luminoso guerrilla movement has taken on board broad elements of the indigenismo literature. Their rural romanticism is expressed through counterposing the potential of rural communities to the decadent cities.

Infitah (Arabic = opening)

Infitah was the economic policy adopted by Anwar al-Sadat, then president of Egypt, in late 1973. Infitah meant that the Egyptian economy would open itself to foreign capital to increase its rate of growth. Sadat argued that foreign capital and technology could provide a boost to Egypt and help its economy take off. The introduction of Infitah gave new emphasis to market forces and competition. A corollary of this economic policy was the introduction of Western values into social and economic life. The consequences of these policies was an unbalanced society. Social inequality intensified and the separate worlds of the rich and the poor became more compartmentalized. The ostentatious Western lifestyle of the élite became the object of popular hatred.

The reaction against Infitah led to the assertion of indigenous Islamic values. Today, the popular rejection of Western lifestyle and resentment against the rich provide a potent mixture which can explode at any time. Infitah has become an object of popular hatred. In its reaction against Infitah, the Egyptian masses converge with the broad anti-Western currents that flourish in the Middle East.

inflation

Inflation is a sustained rise in prices. Many Third World countries suffer from chronic high levels of inflation. The average annual rate of price increase in the 1980s was 47 per cent, three times as high as in the previous two decades. Inflation generally reflects competition for resources between different groups in society. Faster inflation reflects more intense competition. Excess demand for goods, demands for higher wages or attempts to obtain greater profits can all help to fuel inflationary processes, but an essential element in most inflations is that the government prints sufficient money for it to continue. Very often one of the root causes of the inflation is the government's attempt to attract resources to itself by spending more than it is able to raise in taxation. The inflation, therefore, must partly be judged as good or bad according to the purpose for which the government intends to use the resources it attracts, and whose consumption suffers in the process. Inflation is thus a powerful force for the redistribution of income between those who cannot and those who can ensure that their income rises faster than prices.

Inflation tends, however, to have one generally bad consequence, namely that it makes speculative activity progressively more profitable than productive activity. This becomes almost completely true if inflation develops into hyperinflation – an inflation which is so fast that it becomes its own cause since society loses faith in money altogether. A number of Third World countries have suffered crippling hyperinflations in recent years, including Bolivia, Lebanon, Nicaragua, Brazil and Argentina. Hyperinflation can usually only be eliminated by the introduction of a completely new currency. ▶▶ monetarism.

influx control

Influx control means the series of measures to control the movement of blacks into white areas in South Africa and has been one of the pillars of ▶ apartheid.

informal sector

Since the report by the International Labour Organization (ILO) on Kenya, *Employment, Incomes and Equality* (1972), the term 'informal sector' has acquired widespread usage in development studies literature. The term encompasses economic activities which involve those not in formal employment or not in legitimate self-employment on the land or in commerce or business. Formal in this sense tends to mean a combination of legal, stable, regulated and registered in official statistics; informal tends to mean the opposite.

The main impetus behind the invention of the term was the rather belated recognition of the existence of a large group of unemployed, underemployed and landless migrants who none the less engaged in some activity in order to survive.

The ILO report suggested that those involved on the margins of the capitalist economy in trading and other enterprises ought to be recognized for their positive contribution. The report implied that such activities ought to be encouraged since they had the potential for absorbing large pools of labour. Since 1972 a large number of studies sponsored by the World Employment Programme have promoted the informal sector as a positive factor in employment.

The invention of the term 'informal sector' was a cynical exercise in making a virtue out of necessity. Poverty and landlessness have forced upon millions of people in the Third World a continuous struggle for survival. Millions live in shantytowns, eking out a day-to-day existence. Many of these impoverished people are forced to hustle, others sell their services for a day or two. Often forced into a life of illegality, these marginalized people make a bare living in constant fear of the police and corrupt officials.

There is nothing positive about these marginal activities which constitute the so-called informal sector. The very existence of these activities is symptomatic of the all-pervasive impoverishment of many Third World societies. The enthusiasm of the ILO for the informal sector is at first sight curious. In fact the promotion of the sector represents the practical abandonment of a strategy for creating real employment through development as traditionally conceived.

It was the recognition of the slow tempo of development in many Third World countries that led the ILO to redefine its objectives. It gave up on the development of the economy. Instead of growth it now placed an emphasis on redistribution. Its calls for expenditure on the informal sector may appear well-intentioned, but in fact it accepts that millions will be doomed to a life of perpetual degradation and poverty. It shows that the ILO is primarily concerned with stability and order rather than with social change.

Most of the writing on this subject refers to the *urban* informal sector (largely petty commerce and other services) and suggests that it is a relatively new phenomenon. There is, however, nothing new in the Third World about the existence of a vast number of people unable to make a proper living in the developed activities of capitalism and forced, therefore, to secure their subsistence in marginal activities. The urban informal sector is just one more example of the failure of Third World development to reach maturity. It has clear parallels, therefore, with marginal agrarian activities – they, too, are hidden from statistics; they, too, are a response to the absence of adequate employment; and they, too, are marginal and degrading.

A significant feature of Third World nations is the striking coexistence of an advanced industrial sector alongside traditional, usually agrarian, producers. The latter account for a large slice of the total economic activity of such countries. This raises problems of how precisely to assess and quantify economic activity.

Estimates of economic output rely upon indicators such as marketed production, waged employment, capital investment, etc. It is the monetary aspect of these economic phenomena that make them accessible to quantification and comparison, yet in more traditional sectors the process of production, distribution and consumption of goods is often far removed from the process of commodity exchange that is the overriding norm for advanced capitalist countries. For instance, a peasant farming family may produce all its subsistence needs together with a surplus product for the local landowner. In such a situation market exchange, money and account books are of little relevance to any measurement of economic activity.

The worldwide expansion of capitalist production means that traditional forms of economic activity have been successively incorporated into its orbit. Nevertheless, the outcome in countless instances has been to maintain rather than transform traditional sectors in a way that benefits capitalist interests. This is where the parallel with the urban informal sector is significant.

The formation of a wage-labouring class does not always mean breaking such workers completely away from their rural roots. They may still gain part of their subsistence from family landholdings. Such a situation provides capitalist industry with the opportunity to depress wages to an absolute minimum. In effect, workers are forced into doing extra work on the land in order to bring their consumption levels up to subsistence.

In one notorious case, namely the homelands system of ▶ apartheid in South Africa, the balance between the capitalist industrial sector and the informal rural sector is sustained by state edict. The homelands are too barren and impoverished to sustain the millions of black South Africans forced to live in them. So thousands are forced to migrate for work. Yet, the very fact that the homelands go some way to providing subsistence enables the wages of migrant workers to be kept to minimal levels.

In effect, the informal sector is a notion which describes the continuation of unequal economic arrangements, be they traditional or new, but within the overall context of capitalist development.

The South African example is one extreme. There are instances at the other extreme where capitalist industry leads to the development of a fully urbanized working class which gradually loses its direct economic relation to the rural areas. At the same time, rural areas themselves may become regions of capitalist enterprise. Instead of agricultural production for direct consumption, output becomes that of cash crops sold on either the domestic urban or the world market.

Nevertheless, a full transformation of this kind is rare; the subordinate position of Third World countries in the world capitalist economy is a fundamental obstacle to sustained and complete capitalization of economic activity. The contrast between 'formal' modern industrial sectors and 'informal' backward sectors tends to be reproduced in different forms. For instance, even a capitalist agrarian sector may still sustain a large-scale informal sector from which rural workers are forced to eke out a living after labouring for the capitalist farmer. The persistence of urban wages below levels of subsistence provides an impetus for the 'ruralization' of towns where workers are forced to take to keeping livestock and growing food. They are often forced to build and sustain their own accommodation – shantytowns.

This aspect of the informal sector is not the same as the ▶ black economy in industrial countries. The black economy is the counterpart of the petty commercial activities of the urban informal sector; but it is not the same as those activities of the informal sector which directly produce subsistence because wages are insufficient.

Something similar to this concept of an informal sector exists in all advanced capitalist economies – in the form of the unpaid domestic drudgery borne primarily by women in the household. This type of labour assumes an exaggerated significance for numerous workers subject to capitalism in the Third World.

Further reading

R. Bromley and C. Gerry (eds), *Casual Work and Poverty in Third World Cities*, New York 1979.

infrastructure

This term describes facilities and activities which in some sense may be seen as necessary conditions of industrial development within a nation. Infrastructure includes roads, railways (and other transport), communications systems, buildings, power supplies (water, gas, electricity) and sewerage. The notion of 'social overhead capital' includes this physical infrastructure but also embodies factors which relate to the quality of human capital (health, education, skills).

The development of an industrial infrastructure is essential to economic development. All industries need effective transport, communications and power supply systems. They reduce costs and enlarge markets for all other productive activities.

Because infrastructure projects are often very expensive and can be expected to have excess capacity in the early part of their lives, they are often too costly and insufficiently profitable to attract private investors. They tend, therefore, to be financed by the state. Rational though this may be, it often affords a perfect opportunity for graft in the offering of construction contracts.

Both states and aid providers often like to build highly visible infrastructure projects when these may not be the best way of spending the same sum of money. More, smaller and less centralized projects are often more efficient and more democratic than large prestige ones but the power structure often militates against them.

integration

In the post-independence Third World, economic (and to a lesser extent political) integration between countries has been a constant theme of debate, proposal, initiative and, for the most part, failure. The impulse towards economic integration comes from the simple fact that the majority of Third World countries have very small populations and very little development of industry. Integration is seen as stimulating development through:

(1) increasing the size of the home market and so improving efficiency and the incentive to invest;
(2) reducing duplication in administration and so economizing resources;
(3) increasing bargaining power vis-à-vis foreign firms and governments;
(4) taking advantage of complementarity between countries.

These arguments seem to be irrefutable and, not surprisingly, there have been many attempts to form free trade areas, common markets and economic communities. Yet hardly any of these have advanced rapidly and decisively and a number have failed. In Africa the Central African Federation of Rhodesia and Nyasaland failed in large part because it was imposed by the colonial power; the East African Community between Kenya, Tanzania and Uganda collapsed after a few difficult years; and the West Africa Common Market (ECOWAS) remains long behind its original schedules for integration. The Caribbean Common Market (▶ CARICOM) survives but has had to cut back its aims on a number of occasions. The Central American Common Market crash-landed during the 1980s partly as a result of the region's political instability. In South America the ▶ Andean Pact has also spent some years of stagnation, despite very advanced aims. In Asia the Association of South-East Asian Nations (▶ ASEAN) has only taken very minor steps towards integration.

Why does the obvious logic of integration not produce more results in practice? In part it is because in circumstances of very slow economic growth or even decline, the member states argue more intensely over the distribution of the gains and costs of the scheme. Periods of rapid growth might make for easier decisions, but, more basically, integration movements have encountered problems common to all efforts at South–South cooperation: in a world economy so dominated by the North, it is the relationship with the developed countries (through trade, aid, loans and so on) which is usually the most important immediate question. The North exploits this fact to counter the threat of more South–South solidarity of any kind. That has been particularly true in the period since the ▶ debt crisis with the imposition on each country separately of structural adjustment programmes (▶ IMF) and a new more liberal relationship with the world market. In 1991 Mexico went so far as to agree to economic integration with the North in the form of a free trade area with the USA and Canada. Once this neo-liberal phase concludes, it can be expected that the logic towards South–South cooperation will once again reassert itself, new plans for integration will emerge and old ones may be resurrected. There were even small signs in

1991 that the major capitalist powers were ready to encourage new integration projects. ►► LAIA, ►► Mercosur.

Further reading

P. Robson, *Economic Integration in Africa*, London 1968.

intermediate technology ► appropriate technology

International Bank for Reconstruction and Development ► World Bank

International Development Association ► World Bank

International Finance Corporation ► World Bank

International Monetary Fund ► IMF

intifada (Arabic = uprising)

The popular uprising of Palestinians against Israeli repression began on 7 December 1987 in the ► Gaza Strip and rapidly spread to the occupied territories and within Israel. The first protagonists were young people, including schoolchildren, but the uprising rapidly gained the support of the whole population. It has consisted of demonstrations, strikes, boycotts and attempts to force Arab officials (especially policemen) to leave their posts.

The Israeli government has responded with more repression. Many hundreds of Palestinians have been killed and thousands arrested and held without trial. The Israeli authorities have tried to quell the revolt by identifying and detaining leaders but have found that the uprising has such strong roots that the arrests have the perverse effect of feeding the revolt.

ISI, import-substituting industrialization

This term is used in Third World development studies as a description of the strategy by which particular Third World countries seek to achieve industrial development. It involves a Third World nation prioritizing industries which replace manufactured goods previously imported from the advanced nations.

The ISI approach has been regarded as a radical solution to economic backwardness in the Third World for a number of reasons. First, the development of specifically 'import-substituting' industries requires a high level of state control over the economic resources of a nation. Freely operating market forces provide no assurance that resources will be distributed in accordance with the aims of an ISI strategy. The state, therefore, attempts to control market forces and direct the course of economic development.

Second, ISI economic policies have often been justified by some form of anti-West political ideology. Western economic influence – through investment and control of world markets – is presented as the main obstacle to economic development. As such, the pursuit of import-substitution is seen as an attempt to reduce links with the world market and the West.

Third, ISI has also been associated with opposition to ruling classes and élites within Third World countries. This is made necessary by the need to confine the use of scarce foreign currency to importing goods that make a contribution to industrial development – machinery and raw materials – and so reduce consumption of Western-manufactured consumer goods by local élites. For this reason ISI strategies invariably involve strict import and foreign exchange controls.

Recent opinion has been extremely critical of the practice of ISI. Nowhere did it really produce the results originally expected, and typically it produced an industrial sector of tiny foreign-owned plants operating at extremely inefficient levels of output, duplicating each other's activities and selling their products to a very reduced market of the rich and privileged at astronomical prices made possible by protection. In the end hardly anybody benefited from this state of affairs, except possibly the bureaucrats who were bribed to allow the establishment of industrial plants behind the tariff walls. In many cases, it was found that ISI not only failed to save on foreign exchange, which was part of its justification, but even involved the spending of more foreign exchange (on imported parts and machinery) than would have been necessary to import the final products which were produced.

As a critique of the practice these points are valid, but it has to be remembered that ISI, like every other policy which may have a reasonable theoretical rationale, is not introduced in a vacuum but in a real social set-up. It was that set-up – extreme income inequality, corruption, multinational corporations and so on – which distorted ISI and produced many disastrous results. Import substitution will certainly form part of a more healthy process of industrialization. It is worth noting, however, that, in the countries where ISI was most popular in the 1960s, the scope for import substitution had been much reduced by the early 1990s because the ▶ debt crisis had led to a drastic decline in imports. Until these countries are able to stop payng back their debt they will continue to have very few imports to substitute.

Islam (from Arabic *salima* = submission, i.e. to the will of Allah)

Islam is the religion initiated by Mohammed in the seventh century and encapsulated in the Koran. It spread through the Middle East, Africa and Asia and now has an estimated 700 million adherents. There are two main branches: Sunni Islam and Shi'ite Islam.

Sunni Islam. The word Sunni is from sunna, a body of legal and moral principles that predates the Islamic era and comes from the tribal traditions that existed before Mohammed. It stresses the authority of the temporal chief. Unlike Shi'ites, Sunni Muslims have no clergy and the ummah, or Muslim community, are guided by a code of behaviour, the Sharia. Sunni Muslims are the vast majority within Islam. Sunnis trace the succession from Mohammed through his father, Abu Bakr. Mohammed's successors are called caliphs, but, unlike the Shi'ites' ▶ Imam, they were temporal leaders of the ummah rather than religious leaders. The line of caliphs was destroyed by the Mongol invasions of the thirteenth century but the title caliph was taken over by the Ottoman Turks, who installed themselves in Istanbul. The last sultan of Turkey also held court as caliph of Islam until he was removed by Kemal Atatürk in 1924. Various attempts have been made since to claim the title caliph, the most recent being associated with the Saudi Arabian royal family.

Shi'ite Islam. The Shi'ites number around 77 million in total. They are mainly based in Iran where the Shi'ite clergy, the mullahs, have exercised state power since the overthrow of the Shah of Iran in 1979. The Shi'ites are also the majority in Iraq and form substantial minorities in most Middle Eastern countries (▶ AMAL).

An important split from the Shi'ite sect are the Isma'ili Muslims. Sometimes called the 'seveners' (as opposed to the 'twelvers'), they believe that, though the sixth Imam, Jaafar al-Sadiq (d. 765), was succeeded by his elder brother, Ismail, the son, Musa al-Kazim, was the rightful successor. The Isma'ilis, a community with many wealthy members, today live mainly in India, Pakistan, Soviet Central Asia, Syria, Iraq and East Africa. They are led by the Aga Khan. The Lebanese ▶ Druze are a split from the Isma'ili Muslims.

Further reading

N. Ayubi, *Political Islam: religion and politics in the Arab world*, London 1991.
E. Burke III and I. M. Lapidus, *Islam: politics and social movements*, Berkeley, Calif. 1988.

Islamic Brotherhood ▶ Muslim Brotherhood

Islamic Revolutionary Guards (Farsi: *Pasdaran-e Enqelab-e Islami*)

The Guards were formed by Ayatullah Khomeini on 6 May 1979, shortly after he assumed power in Iran. They were to be his own anti-left militia 'to protect the Islamic Revolution'. Armed with machine-guns, they guarded offices and leaders, broke up demonstrations and strikes, monitored the activities of liberals and the left as well as those of soldiers and police. They formed anti-sabotage squads and patrolled Iran's borders. Their hard-core leaders received their initial training from the Palestine Liberation Organization (▶ PLO) in southern Lebanon. Members were recruited from demonstrators against the shah, usually from the ranks of the lower middle class or urban poor. During the Iran–Iraq War, the Guards expanded and acquired their own air and naval detachments, forming shock battalions to lead Iranian forces in the land war. By 1983 they were 170,000 strong. Since the death of Ayatullah Khomeini and the election of President Rafsanjani in 1989, the Guards have lost some of their power.

J

Jagan, Cheddi (1918–)

The Guyanese political leader was born in 1918 in Port Mourant, British Guiana (now Guyana). His parents were Indian immigrants. Jagan was raised as a Hindu, and was sent to the USA to obtain a university education in 1936. He attended Northwestern College, Illinois, where he received a degree in dentistry, and also studied at Chicago YMCA College, where he came under the influence of teachers involved in the struggle for Indian independence. After he married, Jagan returned to Guyana in 1943 to start a dentistry practice. In 1946 he formed the Political Affairs Committee to discuss the problems of independence and social reform. In 1950, together with his wife Janet and L.F.S. Burnham, he formed the People's Progressive Party (PPP), after Henry Wallace's Progressive Party in the USA and the People's National Party in Jamaica.

Jagan's party claimed to be influenced by ▶ Nehru's brand of socialism rather than Gandhism (▶ Gandhi and Gandhism). He also identified with Charles Beard, Matthew Josephson and Trinidad's Eric Williams. However, the PPP admitted to being influenced by Marxism as well.

In the first-ever national election victory of an openly Marxist party in the Americas, Jagan's PPP won control of the colonial administration in 1953. This lasted for 133 days, when London decided to eject him from power. By 1955, however, the PPP had split along ethnic lines and Burnham formed the rival People's National Congress, which solely targeted the Afro-Caribbean section of Guyana's population. Jagan won power again between 1957 and 1964, but the British imposed a new constitution which effectively excluded the PPP from power. Consigned to permanent opposition after independence in 1966, Jagan became increasingly pro-Soviet.

jihad (Arabic = holy war)

According to the Koran, Muslims are obliged to defend the faith against infidels (unbelievers). Sometimes referred to as the sixth pillar of Islam, jihad is the only political obligation. In recent times, the Ottoman sultan/caliph proclaimed a jihad against the Allies in the First World War. Colonel Gadhafi also proclaimed a jihad against Saudi Arabia in 1981, and Saddam Hussein (▶ Ba'th) against the USA and its allies in 1990–1.

junta (Spanish = board or council)

Initially, junta meant government established by military conspiracy. It was first used in the Peninsular Wars, but popularized in the struggle of the Latin Americans against Spanish rule in the early nineteenth century. In the twentieth century the term came to be used in English to describe dictatorial rule by a clique of military officers though it has a much wider usage in Spanish-speaking countries.

K

Kenyatta, Jomo (c. 1889–1978)

The first leader of independent Kenya, Jomo Kenyatta was born about 1889 and educated at a Scottish mission school. In 1922 he joined the Kikuyu Central Association and became its president. From 1931 to 1944 he studied in the UK, taking classes from the anthropologist Bronislaw Malinowski at London University; under the latter's influence he wrote his book *Facing Mount Kenya* (1938). Returning to Kenya in 1946 he founded the nationalist Kenya African Union (KAU). In 1952 he was sentenced to hard labour as a leader of ▶ Mau Mau; in 1958 he was released but subject to internal exile. In 1961 he was elected to parliament as member of the Kenya African National Union (KANU) and became prime minister in 1963 and president after full independence in 1964. He died in 1978. Kenyatta played a leading role in the development of African resistance to British colonialism but on reaching power he adopted largely conservative pro-Western policies.

kibbutz

Kibbutzim were originally agricultural settlements established in Palestine by Jewish immigrants from Europe between 1905 and 1914. A socialist gloss was added by the requirement that all property be held in common within the community. Kibbutz members were in the vanguard of ▶ Zionism and formed a large proportion of the membership of the armed forces of Israel and the Israeli state. Formerly exclusively agrarian, some kibbutzim are now engaged in manufacturing. In 1984 they numbered 250 and had 105,000 members or 3 per cent of the population of Israel.

Moshav villages, also based on the family farm, grew in popularity after the Second World War, especially among the Holocaust survivors who came to Israel and among Oriental Jews.

Kurdistan

The land of the Kurds is currently divided between Turkey, Iraq, Iran, Syria and Soviet Armenia. It contained 25 million Kurds in 1990. The struggle for an independent Kurdistan has been going on since the seventeenth century – without success. A Kurdish state was envisaged in the Treaty of Sèvres in 1920, part of the post-First World War settlement, but this was prevented by the policies of the Kemal Atatürk regime in Turkey after 1922.

Today Kurdish nationalist forces exist in Turkey, Iraq and Iran, in all of which they have experienced repression. A Kurdish uprising in Iraq in 1988 was put down with particular brutality, including the use of poison gas, by the regime of Saddam Hussein. In the aftermath of the US-led war against Iraq in 1991, a widespread and sudden revolt in the Kurdish areas of Iraq gained control of a considerable amount of territory. It was again bloodily suppressed by the Iraqi army with no intervention from the USA and its allies, provoking millions of Kurds to flee as refugees into Iran and Turkey. An international relief campaign was not sufficient to avert a gigantic human tragedy for the Kurdish people.

Further reading

G. Chaliand (ed.), *People without a Country: the Kurds and Kurdistan*, London 1980.

L

LAFTA ▶ LAIA

Lagos Plan

The plan for the achievement of self-reliance of black Africa – primarily by industrialization – was agreed by the heads of state of the Organization of African Unity (▶ OAU) in Lagos, the capital of Nigeria, in April 1980. They undertook to reach 1 per cent of world industrial output by 1985, 1.4 per cent by 1990 and 2 per cent by 2000. In 1988 the figure remained at less than 0.5 per cent. The OAU dropped the Lagos Plan at the 1985 conference.

LAIA, Latin American Integration Association

This organization is dedicated to fostering initiatives for integration in Latin America. LAIA is a successor organization to the Latin American Free Trade Area (LAFTA) which was set up by the Treaty of Montevideo in 1960 with the declared aim of instituting a free trade area from Mexico to Argentina in a space of 12 years. It was roughly modelled on the European Free Trade Area. The signatories were Argentina, Brazil, Chile, Mexico, Paraguay, Peru and Uruguay, later joined by Colombia and Ecuador (1961), Venezuela (1966) and Bolivia (1967).

Though the share of inter-regional trade in total trade grew during the 1960s and 1970s, LAFTA signally failed in its aim of eliminating tariffs. In its place the same nations agreed in 1980 to substitute LAFTA with a new organization, LAIA, with much less specific aims. LAIA supports any partial initiative towards Latin American integration between two or more countries, insisting only that it not be exclusive but is open to the membership of other countries in the future. The achievements of LAIA remain limited since its life has coincided with the period of the ▶ debt crisis which has been a bleak one for ▶ integration (▶ Amazon Pact, ▶ Andean Pact, ▶ Mercosur).

laissez-faire

Laissez-faire is the fundamental principle of classical economics. Originally put forward by eighteenth-century physiocrats, it was given coherent exposition in Adam Smith's famous *An Enquiry into the Nature and Causes of the Wealth of Nations* (1776).

It involves the notion that economic welfare is best ensured by allowing the free play of individual private enterprise. On this basis state interference in the economy is considered self-defeating.

In reality the laissez-faire doctrine was and still is used to justify society based upon the freedom to exploit the labour of others through the private ownership of capital. Though capitalist production does not correspond to Smith's notion of a nation of independent, industrious individuals, its suitability as an apologia for capitalist exploitation ensured its hallowed status as the core principle of modern economics.

In relation to the Third World, neo-classical economists have always used the laissez-faire notion as a stick with which to beat various state-led development projects, protection, development planning and subsidies to the poor. During the 1980s the doctrine has swept the world anew. It is much beloved by aid donors, by the ▶ World Bank and most of all by the International Monetary Fund (▶ IMF), which makes it the principle of economic adjustment and stabilization schemes. Many governments – especially in Eastern Europe and the Third World – have undergone sudden conversions to the doctrine, but nowhere has it rectified the problems which, to be sure, were produced by its opposite, economic ▶ dirigisme. The causes of the problems must have been more basic than errors of government policy. ▶▶ neo-liberalism.

land reform

The continued stagnation of agriculture in many regions of the Third World represents the gravest indictment of the prevailing strategies of development. Without an agrarian system capable of producing food for subsistence and a surplus, the possibilities for economic development are seriously restricted. Agricultural stagnation is not just a sectoral economic problem. Impoverishment, landlessness and even famines are widespread throughout the rural sector of the Third World.

Agrarian stagnation and peasant resistance have forced governments to take steps to ameliorate the situation by introducing land reform measures. In Latin America land reforms were attempted even before the Second World War. However, it was in the 1960s that land reform emerged as a fashionable policy for Third World development.

The main impetus behind the popularization of land reform was the recognition that rural poverty was not merely an economic problem but also a threat to political stability. In Latin America it was the Cuban revolution and the fear of its repetition elsewhere that forced land reform onto the political agenda. In the years following the Cuban revolution, a series of land reform laws were passed throughout the continent. New land reform institutions were established and projects were drawn up to provide land to the peasantry.

The main pressure for the land reform legislation came from the USA. President Kennedy recognized that, unless something was done to ameliorate the position of the Latin American peasant, the whole continent would explode. Kennedy devised a programme of aid, the Alliance for Progress, to assist the implementation of land reform. The aim of Washington's policy was to counter communism through securing the adherence of Latin American governments to the principle of integrated reform. In 1961 a special meeting of heads of Latin American governments was convened in Punta del Este, Uruguay, to launch the new era of land reform. The declaration of Latin American governments at Punta del Este promised major changes for the campesino. The declaration promised:

> To encourage in accordance with the characteristic of each country, programmes of integral agrarian reform, leading to the effective transformation, where required, of unjust structures and systems of land tenure use, with a view to replacing [▶]latifundia and dwarf holdings by an equitable system of property, so that, supplemented by timely and adequate credit, technical assistance and improved marketing arrangements, the land will become for the man who works it the basis of his economic stability, the foundation of his increasing welfare, the guarantee of his freedom and dignity.

The declaration promised a new future for the peasant, and yet it came to nothing. Why did this initiative prove to be such an unmitigated failure?

The main opponents of land reform in Latin America were the powerful landlord class. Large landowners dominated the countryside and held the peasantry in check through their economic power and monopoly over the means of coercion. Since they profited from the existing land tenure system they had little incentive to change. Through their ownership of land they could control its resources. While the mass of peasants were impoverished, landlords could enjoy an affluent and privileged life.

Washington and many politicians in Latin America recognized that the landlords represented a barrier to progress. They also understood that the intransigence of the landlords could provoke unrest thereby destabilizing whole countries. Land reform was designed to put pressure on them to change their ways. However, there were limits to this. The landlord class was the main guarantor of stability in the rural areas. The power structure of Latin American nations depended on their ability to maintain law and order. It was feared that if the landlords were pushed too far the whole structure would collapse and the ruling class as a whole would lose its power.

Such fears were well-founded. In the years following Punta del Este, peasant unrest, land invasions and revolts became widespread in Peru, Brazil, Colombia, Ecuador, Chile and Venezuela. Finally, Latin American rulers opted for repression and supported the landlords against the peasantry.

In the context of the perpetuation of landlord power, there can be no genuine land reform, but if landlordism is destroyed the power relations in society as a whole are put into question. This was the dilemma that faced the reformers. In the end land reforms proved to be token measures that could be implemented without undermining landlord power.

The conservative character of land reform is evident throughout the

Third World. In most cases landlords are asked to make a few concessions so that peasant revolts can be pre-empted. It is often presented as a political necessity – a form of counter-insurgency measure. As the President of the World Bank stated: 'But the real issue is not whether land reform is politically easy. The real issue is whether indefinite procrastination is politically prudent. An increasingly unequitable situation will pose a growing threat to political stability.'[1]

Even after the negative experience of the Alliance for Progress, land reform continues to be argued for on the grounds of promoting political stability and thus preserving the existing social system. The authors of the World Bank-sponsored report *Redistribution and Growth* explain that:

> Most importantly, there is the general thesis that once the peasantry's immediate demands for land are met, it becomes a conservative force, a bulwark of the *status quo*. Provided the process is controlled, therefore, a land reform in a setting where land ownership is initially highly concentrated can do much to alleviate the lot of the poor without tearing apart the fabric of society.[2]

With such a political focus it is not surprising that land reform has been so irrelevant to the real needs of Third World rural society.

Experience has shown that there can be no real land reform without a fundamental transformation of the power structure of rural society. Landlords will not tolerate any threat to their property rights. The rural rich can use their wealth to control rural society and perpetuate the poverty of the peasantry. This happened even in Mexico, where land reform has gone further than in most cases. As far back as 1917, land reform legislation was introduced and, during the years 1934–40, significant amounts of land were distributed to the peasants. It was the peasant revolts of 1910–17 that forced the Mexican ruling class to make such far-reaching concessions. Yet, by the mid-1970s, the situation had reverted to that of the pre-land reform era. The London *Financial Times* reported in 1975: 'The crude reality is that the "winners" of the 1910–17 revolution are almost as badly off today as they were before the bloody conflict which cost more than 1 million lives.'

Real land reform is not merely a question of government legislation. Too often governments in the Third World have intimate links with vested interests in rural areas. The failure of the Aquino government in the Philippines to implement any real reforms is a recent instance of this.

Real land reform is a question of overthrowing the prevailing property relations on the land. It presupposes taking away the land of the landlords and distributing it in order to give that land to those who cultivate it. Even this is only a first step. Peasants must have access to credit, finance and agricultural inputs so that they can raise output. Without such assistance peasants can easily fall into debt, become prey to middlemen and lose the land they have gained. Investment in agriculture and the redistribution of the land are the necessary elements for an effective programme of land reform. ▶ agrarian question.

Further reading

D. Christodoulou, *The Unpromised Land: agrarian reform and conflict worldwide*, London 1990.

D. Lehmann (ed.), *Agrarian Reform and Agrarian Reformism: studies of Peru, Chile, China and India*, London 1974.

Notes

1. Cited in M.L. Gakou, *The Crisis in African Agriculture*, London 1987, p. 59.
2. Ibid., p. 60.

latifundia (Plural of *latifundium* [*latus* = broad + *fundus* = estate] = large estate)

Latifundia (Spanish = *latifundios*) are the large rural estates or plantations which are the basis of the landholding system in most South American countries (in imitation of the pattern of holdings in much of the Iberian peninsula). These estates are often known in South America as haciendas (but not in Argentina and Uruguay where they are known as estancias, nor Brazil where they are called fazendas). The latifundia are owned by local gentry, absentee landlords (better known in Spanish as latifundistas) or foreign corporations. Despite recent efforts at land reforms, latifundismo remains the dominant mode of land ownership and accounts for 65 per cent of Latin American farm acreage. Alongside the few latifundia exist thousands of minifundia (Spanish = *minifundios*), tiny holdings often insufficient to provide a living for a peasant family. ▶ agrarian question, ▶ land reform.

Latin America

This term was coined by French writers in the nineteenth century to promote French leadership of the Roman Catholic world. Now in common usage, the term is generally take to comprise all of the Western hemisphere south of the US–Mexican border, especially those countries in which Spanish, Portuguese and French are spoken. The Brazilians were responsible for rejecting the alternative 'Hispanic America'.

Latin American Free Trade Area ▶ LAIA

Latin American Integration Association ▶ LAIA

least developed countries

Sometimes referred to as the Fourth World, these countries are those designated by the UN Secretary-General, as recommended by the General Assembly in 1968, that fulfil the following criteria:

(1) gross domestic product (GDP) per capita of not more than a certain figure (US$100 per annum in 1968, US$300 in 1989);

(2) manufacturing represents not more than 10 per cent of GDP;
(3) a literacy rate of not more than 20 per cent for people over 15 years old.

There were 25 countries placed in this category in 1968. By 1991 the list had grown to 41, 27 of which were in Africa. The World Bank denotes a similar group of countries the 'low-income' countries.

Further reading

M. van Wallenburg, *Least Developed Countries: a game of appearances?*, Amsterdam 1987.

liberation

One of the most misused terms in Third World politics, liberation is often used as a synonym for freedom or independence. In our usage, it has both a *social* and a *political* connotation.

Liberation in its political sense refers to the attainment of national independence. In this sense the liberation struggles in Palestine and South Africa have as their objective the achievement of national independence, the achievement of the right to self-determination, which itself represents a major gain. However, national independence alone does not mean liberation. Many nations have discovered that the independence they have won is a restricted one. Political independence on its own is not sufficient to give people the freedom to determine their future.

Nations have found that their lack of economic power and the cultural influence of imperialism can deprive independence of any real content. Sometimes, the ex-colonial powers can continue to dictate to the independent government. Lack of economic independence calls into question the meaning of national independence. It is for this reason that many radical writers in Africa have called for a 'second independence'.

The experience of national independence shows that real liberation must mean something more than a change in the political regime. Real freedom means that the members of a society control the use of their own resources and thereby make real choices and exercise their rights. Thus the nation has to be not only *politically* but also *economically* independent, and its citizens have to enjoy democratic rights.

Liberation therefore implies not just political but also social change. In practice, the separation of the political from the social aspect of winning freedom must have negative consequences. Political independence without social change permits the continuation of exploitation and imperialist domination. Once political independence has been won under such circumstances, it becomes an instrument for the denial of real freedom. Independence thus becomes not a first step towards liberation but a manoeuvre to avoid it.

To win real liberation it is necessary to fight for both political and social change. Indeed, the two mutually reinforce each other. The fight against imperialist rule requires mass mobilization and the surest form of mobilization is that which aims to change society. It is only through changing society that political independence becomes real; and the more

179

society changes the more it consolidates the freedom to govern its own destiny.

Liberation represents a succession of stages through which the members of a society become free of constraints. The first stage is the winning of freedom from the external political and economic dictates of imperialist nations. Such a freedom is always qualified since no single nation can be entirely free of the power of the world market, but if society has been mobilized to transform itself internally it at least has the means to defend itself from the worst manifestations of foreign domination. The next stage in winning liberation is the elimination of poverty and the restricted availability of resources. This stage implies a protracted struggle to eliminate internal exploitation through establishing a society that can begin to produce for social need. This requires the cooperation of other nations that are jointly determined to build a new world. Liberation can begin in one country but can only go forward through Third World cooperation. At every stage the fight for liberation demands the intensification and extension of the struggle for social change.

Further reading

J.N. Pieterse, *Empire and Emancipation*, London 1989.

liberation theology

It was the English publication in 1973 of *A Theology of Liberation* by the Peruvian theologian Gustavo Gutiérrez that gave the name to a new movement. The emergence of the liberation theology movement was a direct response to the dislocation caused by the expansion of capitalist social relations in Latin America during the previous two decades. Industrial growth on one side and impoverishment on the other disrupted the existing patterns of social life. Rapid urbanization, the growth of landlessness and state repression created a powerful undercurrent of dissatisfaction and resistance. In many Latin American societies, all forms of political protest were met with state repression. Often the only area free from direct state coercion was the Church. Consequently the 'free' sanctuary offered by the Church became a focus for dissidents and Roman Catholicism became an important influence on the emerging popular movement. The Medellín conference of Latin American bishops in 1968 was very much a response to this development and opened the door to a more radical interpretation of Roman Catholic practice.

Since the 1960s, the theology of liberation has become one of the most important and novel expressions of popular resistance in the Third World. The growth of the people's church in Latin America has been impressive. Grassroots Christian community groups – *communidades eclesiaticas de base* or 'base Christian communities' – have mushroomed throughout Central and South America. Liberation theology has also spread to other parts of the Third World. It is very influential in South Africa, the Philippines and South Korea.

The association of liberation theology with popular resistance in places like El Salvador, South Africa and the Philippines has forced reaction to go on the offensive. The murder of the popular Archbishop Oscar Romero in El Salvador in 1980 illustrates the fear which liberation theology arouses among the repressive rulers of Latin America. The Vatican has also been concerned with what it considers to be the dangerous deviations of liberation theology. Pope John Paul II has fiercely opposed liberation theology and has silenced some of its leading advocates. During his visit to Latin America in 1983, he affirmed the traditional reactionary stand of the Church hierarchy with a denunciation of liberation theology's association with a radical social outlook.

Discussions of liberation theology often focus on doctrinal matters. To be sure, it is possible to isolate certain strands of thought specific to liberation theology. Unlike the Vatican, liberation theology places great emphasis on the prophetic elements of the Scriptures. At the same time, liberation theology concerns itself with the analysis of contemporary society. It propounds a powerful moral critique of capitalism and often uses some of Marx's concepts to put the case for liberation. Liberation theology stresses the communal rather than the hierarchical framework of Church organization. According to this outlook, the Church is a community in which the clergy serves. The role of the clergy is to serve the community in communal worship and service to God.

While doctrinal matters may fascinate scholars and theologians, they are only of secondary importance for understanding liberation theology. The growth of the influence of this movement has little to do with the power and eloquence of its ideas. It is the growing yearning for freedom and dignity throughout the Third World which provides the foundation for the rise of liberation theology. The power of liberation theology resides in its ability to give articulation to the aspirations of the masses. In many cases (e.g. in South Africa) the Church has been one of the few institutions through which these aspirations can be expressed. Consequently the masses incorporate the Church into their struggles and in turn become influenced by the outlook of liberation theology.

It can be argued that liberation theology as such has nothing to do with the Catholic Church. A number of Protestant theologians have also identified with popular sentiments and the ideas of liberation are coherently articulated in the writings of the Methodist Argentinian, José Bonino. Indeed, all religions in the Third World need to develop a popular strand if they are to appear relevant to the needs of the people. Despite major differences in culture, there are some important parallels between the evolution of liberation theology and the revival of ▶ Islam.

Studies of anti-imperialist movements show that the desire for freedom often expresses itself in religious form. Many anti-imperialist leaders such as James Connolly, Amilcar ▶ Cabral and José Carlos Mariátegui have drawn attention to the importance of ideas of liberation in the language of religion. In many parts of Asia, Africa, Latin America and the West Indies, anti-Western resistance movements, often labelled messianic or rivivalist, have organized or participated in rebellions against foreign oppression.

Liberation theology is in every sense the product of the experience of oppression. It is this experience that has forced sections of the Roman Catholic Church to reformulate their practice. The close proximity of the People's Church to the everyday life of the poor of Latin America is the product of this rethinking. The vitality of liberation theology stems from the close relationship of radical Christians with the struggles of the masses. Through this relationship, liberation theologians have succeeded in inspiring popular support.

To survive, liberation theology has had to become more than doctrine. Its supporters have become organizers and activists in the social and political struggle. As a result, liberation theology has developed an active practical side which links it to radical politics. The writings of leading liberation theologians like Gutiérrez, the Brazilian Leonardo Boff and Ignacio Ellacuría (murdered by death squads in El Salvador) often represent a social and politial critique of their societies.

Popular religions always run the risk of institutionalization. In such circumstances, whatever the original intent, the influence of religion becomes a force for consolidating the power of the ruling classes. It is too early to say whether liberation theology will follow this path, but there are clear danger signs. In the Philippines, the Church played a key role in the movement which overthrew President Marcos and installed Mrs Aquino. This experiment in people's power has turned out to be a cosmetic exercise. Mrs Aquino has continued the basic policies of the Marcos regime but, unlike Marcos, Aquino is able to enjoy a measure of popular support partly because of her close links with the Church. Many radical advocates of liberation theology have been taken aback by this development and are critical of the Aquino regime. However, damage has already been done. The anger of the masses has been manipulated by the Church hierarchy so as to preserve the status quo.

The experience of the Philippines shows that, though liberation theology can have a positive role, it is not a substitute for an anti-imperialist movement. We have no intention of questioning the motives of the supporters of the People's Church, but there is a strong danger that all the good work of the radical clergy may end up by strengthening the credibility of a Church which remains dominated by reactionaries. For liberation theology to become unambiguously anti-imperialist it would have to break with the Roman Catholic or any Western-controlled Church. Without such complete independence, liberation theology risks playing into the hands of the oppressors.

Liberation Tigers of Tamil Eelam ▶ Tamil Tigers

Lomé Convention

This name is applied to the periodic talks between the European Community (EC) and the African, Caribbean and Pacific (▶ ACP) countries over trade and economic cooperation. It is the successor to and extension of previous agreements arrived at in the wake of decolonization in Africa.

On 15 December 1960 the African and Malagasy Organization for Economic Cooperation was established at a summit meeting of ten French-speaking African states in Brazzaville, Congo; it was subsequently renamed the African and Malagasy Union of Economic Cooperation (1961) and the Common Afro-Malagasy Organization (1965).

The associated states of the Common Afro-Malagasy Organization signed a convention with the EC at Yaoundé, the capital of Cameroon (hence the Yaoundé Convention). This was a trade and economic cooperation agreement which ran from 1 January 1965 to 31 December 1969. The convention was renewed for a further five years from 1 January 1970 to 31 December 1974 and involved 18 former French, Belgian and Italian colonies.

In addition, the Arusha Convention (named after the city in north-eastern Tanzania) was signed on 26 July 1968. There was a similar economic agreement between the EC and three African states: Kenya, Tanzania and Uganda. The convention expired in 1975.

Both these agreements were succeeded by the various Lomé agreements. The Lomé Convention was signed in Lomé, the capital of Togo, on 28 February 1975. It was to last for five years and its signatories included the then nine EC countries and 49 ACP countries. An agreement for its renewal was concluded on 20 November 1979 in Brussels and again on 8 December 1984 in Lomé, the latter coming into operation on 1 March 1985 for a period of five years. The latest agreement (Lomé IV) was signed in December 1989 after long and acrimonious negotiations between the now 12 EC nations and 68 ACP countries, joined by Namibia to make 69 in 1990. Lomé IV is to last for 10 years, though the aid package will be renegotiated after 5 years.

The convention covers a wide range of trade and economic cooperation issues. All ACP manufactured goods and 96 per cent of the agricultural exports of the ACP countries are allowed to enter the EC free of import tariffs or quotas. This arrangement requires no similar reciprocal action on the part of the ACP countries.

An export earnings stabilization scheme (▶ stabex) provides ACP countries with protection against price and production fluctuations of certain goods (bananas, cocoa, coconuts, coffee, cotton, hides and skins, iron ore, palm nuts, tea, timber products and raw sisal). An Export Stabilization Fund provides compensation for large earnings losses from export price falls. In the case of the poorest countries, these funds do not have to be prepaid.

The EC provides finance for development projects in the form of both grants and loans. Special 'soft loans' are also made available.

Other commitments by the EC involve action to promote private investment, the transfer of technology, industrial and managerial training programmes, the provision of trade and market information, help in marketing ACP products and the provision of various infrastructural requirements of trade.

The Lomé IV agreement represented a series of marginal changes to the previous agreements: the addition of a new trade development service, designed to assist the ACP countries market their products, a small increase in aid and in the finance of stabex (but by much less than that sought by the ACP negotiators) and an improvement in the Sysmin facility to aid mineral imports, plus a small amount of aid designed to assist structural adjustment.

If we are to judge the Lomé agreements by the performance of the ACP economies, they must be declared a failure. For most of the period of their operation, the ACP countries in general have not developed but have become even more impoverished. Despite the apparent trade benefits of Lomé, imports from the ACP countries have declined as a share of EC trade, and even more as a share of world trade. The amount of aid given by the EC under Lomé is very small; and many member countries (especially the UK) are strongly against increasing it since they prefer the tighter neo-colonial control afforded by bilateral aid.

low income countries ▶ euphemisms, ▶ least developed countries

LTTE ▶ Tamil Tigers

Lumumba, Patrice (1925–61)

Holding power for less than a year and brutally murdered at the age of 35, Patrice Lumumba has become a powerful symbol of the national liberation movement – particularly for the youth of Africa. A complex character with wide intellectual interests and abilities, Lumumba led the Congolese people to independence only to become the victim of a vicious civil war financed and manipulated by external powers.

Born in the village of Onalua, Kasai Province of the then Belgian Congo (now Zaïre) on 2 July 1925, Lumumba was the son of a poor Batetela peasant. He started work at six, helping his father in the fields in order to pay for his education at a local mission school. Rejecting the priesthood and the military, Lumumba started training as a medical orderly after school.

Taking jobs in several different regions of the country and reading avidly, Lumumba built up a comprehensive working knowledge of the colonial system and was able to develop his own political philosophy piecemeal. During his stay in Stanleyville (now Kisangani), Lumumba became actively involved in politics and headed six organizations, including a section of the Belgian Liberal Party.

Lumumba's political development was somewhat uneven – in 1952 he spoke of a dynamic theory of political organization which, he argued, derived from the 'collective creativity of its members'. Yet he spoke of the possibility of a 'Belgian–Congolese community' as a means of decolonization and was personally acquainted with the Belgian King Baudouin, and argued for gradual consistent action towards the emancipation of the Congolese.

At the same time, many of his compatriots were arguing for total war on colonial rule and the achievement of independence within the shortest space of time. A number of trips to other African states and meetings with radicals in Europe and North America quickly persuaded Lumumba to change his mind. In October 1958 he founded the Mouvement National Congolais (MNC, Congolese National Movement) which rapidly became the most broadly based and authoritative political movement in the country.

The MNC manifesto, authored mainly by Lumumba, indicated his changed thinking: it stated that the party would 'use every means to liberate the Congo from imperialist colonialism'. Lumumba attended conferences in Ghana and Nigeria where he argued for a united Africa to take a strong stand against imperialism – his views at this time coalescing with many of ► Nkrumah's views.

Lumumba was particularly sensitive to the problem of tribalism – he referred to it as a 'most dangerous internal enemy' in the Congo where there were more than two hundred different tribes and ethnic groups at varying levels of social and economic development. He strongly opposed the Belgian plan to divide the Congo into small tribally divided provinces which would be quasi-independent from their former colonial rulers.

The Belgian pattern of colonialism had exacerbated these ethnic differences as there were only rudimentary communication links between regions and even between town and country. The most serious secessionist problems were in the Lower Congo, Kasai and Katanga whose people were led by Moïse Tshombe, a political activist acknowledged to have been working for the Central Intelligence Agency (► CIA).

Lumumba led the MNC in an increasingly radical direction, but continually stressed the need for national unity. However, he clashed with the Congo's conservative political élite on several occasions. Mass support for the MNC helped to hasten independence for the Congo with Lumumba declared head of the first national government after the Republic of the Congo was declared on 30 June 1960.

Immediately, Lumumba embarked on radical domestic economic measures such as restricting capital flows, implementing price controls and wage rises, as well as a militant foreign policy which included the expulsion of all foreign troops from Congolese soil and the shutting down of the Kamina military base.

Their countries' economic and strategic interests under threat, Belgian and US agents started to destabilize the Lumumba government by waging propaganda campaigns against him and financing some of the secessionist movements. Just three months after the declaration of independence, a group of opposition leaders removed Lumumba from office and jailed him. In January 1961 he was flown to Elisabethville (now Lubumbashi) with two of his colleagues and brutally beaten and then shot.

lusophone (= Portuguese-speaking)

The term derives from Lusitania, an ancient name for Portugal. Lusophone Africa comprises Angola, Mozambique, Guinea-Bisseau, Cape Verde, and São Tomé and Principe. Luso-American is a way of referring to Brazilians that stresses the old colonial link. ►► francophone.

M

M-19, Movimiento 19 de Abril (19 April Movement)

This Colombian guerrilla group was formed in 1974 (taking its name from 19 April 1970 when the former Colombian dictator Gustavo Rojas Pinilla was defeated in presidential elections) as the armed wing of Pinilla's Alianza Nacional Popular (ANAPO, Popular National Alliance), a populist, Christian-influenced movement with radical economic and conservative social policies. In 1970 ANAPO was the biggest opposition party but had disappeared by the mid-1970s. The M-19, however, continued to function and converted itself into a movement claiming to be Marxist and fighting for a socialist state. It was and is, however, ideologically diffuse.

It launched its first guerrilla operations in 1974 and in 1976 kidnapped the President of the Colombian Federation of Workers, and, when its demands were not met, killed him. In 1980 it occupied the embassy of the Dominican Republic and secured a ransom of US$2.5 million. In 1981 it attacked the presidential palace in Bogotá. By 1982 it was estimated to be 800-strong. In 1983 it formed an alliance with the Ejército de Liberación Nacional (▶ ELN, National Liberation Army) and the Fuerzas Armadas Revolucionarias de Colombia (FARC, Revolutionary Armed Forces of Colombia), the armed wing of the Colombian Communist Party. In 1984 M-19 members attacked a prison and freed 158 political prisoners, but the leader of the movement condemned the raid, seeing it as a setback to his efforts to deal with the government, which led to the M-19 and FARC agreeing to a ceasefire in return for the right to campaign openly. However right-wing death squads did not respect the ceasefire, nor did many rank-and-file guerrillas. The insurgency was renewed in late 1984 and, under pressure from death-squad activities, the M-19 ended the ceasefire in June 1985. The army declared total war on the M-19 and the struggle continued.

Finally, in 1990, the M-19 negotiated a ceasefire with the government and agreed to enter legal political activity. In 1991, while the other guerrilla groups ELN and FARC continued the armed struggle, the M-19 won a surprising plurality in the national elections for a constituent assembly to redraw the constitution. This success may have influenced the other guerrilla groups to follow in M-19's footsteps.

Maghreb

The name refers to the western section of the Islamic world, comprising the North African states of Morocco, Tunisia, Algeria and Libya. Initially the subject of confrontations between the Berbers (hence Barbary Coast) and Arabs, it was invaded by the French and Spanish in the nineteenth century and the Italians in the twentieth century. It was the scene of the desert war in the Second World War.

Mahdi

The Mahdi is a Messiah figure and is a popular feature of the Shi'ite, Sufi and Dervish sects of Islam. In 1885 Mohammed Ahmed al-Mahdi (1848–85) drove the British out of Sudan where they were unable to return until 1898.

Further reading

P.M. Holt, *The Mahdist State in the Sudan*, Oxford 1958.

Malayan Races' Liberation Army ▶ MRLA

Malthusianism

Malthusianism is the doctrine advanced by T.R. Malthus (1766–1834) in his *Essay on the Principle of Population* (1798). Malthus maintained that while population tends to grow geometrically (at a constant rate), the means of subsistence only increase arithmetically (by a constant amount). Hence poverty and want are virtually inevitable and, according to Malthus, in large measure are due to the fast breeding of the lower classes. Neo-Malthusianism represents the application of this theory to the study of contemporary social problems. The neo-Malthusian outlook has had a major influence on Western studies of the Third World. According to the neo-Malthusian outlook, poverty and underdevelopment are to a considerable extent the consequence of the fast increase in population. If population growth causes poverty it follows that the solution to underdevelopment is a strategy based on birth control. Throughout the post-war period, but especially from the 1960s onwards, international aid agencies have exhorted Third World countries to adopt birth control as a key policy of development.

The theme of 'population explosion' is a recurrent one in the literature of the development industry. Indeed, studies on developmental questions often contain an obligatory chapter on population. A recent illustration is the report of the UN Food and Agriculture Organization published in September 1986 entitled *African Agriculture: the next 25 years*. This otherwise sober and detailed report on the problems of agriculture suddenly ends up warning that it is the doubling of Africa's population every 25 years which threatens the continent with major disaster. The authors of the report feel the need to back up their arguments about agricultural production with logical argument and evidence; but the major conclusion about population is thrown in without any such careful, detailed argument.

In general the prevalence of neo-Malthusianism derives from its apparent commonsensical logic: the more people, the less food must be available per person. It is logic like this which has led many Third World countries to initiate birth control programmes.

In fact, there is no such simple correlation between numbers and poverty, and while there are connections between the two they are

187

profoundly complex and take place through the mediation of many other elements of social and economic reality. Neo-Malthusianism – the assertion of the simple correlation – is false.

Population cannot be isolated from the question of how people are used – whether they are employed productively or pushed out of economic life. In many poor countries there exist considerable resources but they are not made available to the population. Many countries in Africa have a low density of population, yet they remain impoverished while Belgium, with a high level of population density, is affluent. It is the way that production and consumption are organized more than the size of population that determines living standards. Thus widespread poverty in Brazil, especially in the north-east, coexists with fabulous wealth and an impressive base of national resources. The potential for generalized increases in living standards is thwarted not by numbers but by the prevailing form of social organization.

Neo-Malthusian arguments thus deflect attention from social and economic causes of poverty and 'discover' a natural cause – human reproduction. They shift the blame from the structure of underdevelopment to the reproductive customs of Third World people.

This approach is also ethnocentric. When economic difficulties in the Western world are under consideration, the growth of slump and unemployment are treated as economically related issues. It is only when the obstacles to economic growth in the Third World are under discussion that population growth is treated as a problem in its own right. Nobody ever argues that, because there are 'too many' people in the world, the developed countries should *reduce* their (often overfed) population. Quite the contrary: in Europe declining population is now a fashionable 'problem'.

Many experts and political figures now argue that the Western concern with Third World population is motivated by the desire to obscure the role of international forces in the reproduction of underdevelopment. This point was stressed by representatives of Third World countries at the August 1975 World Population Conference in Bucharest. A report on this conference noted:

> The stress laid on economic power relations in the world which thereby came to colour not least the plan of action of the conference may at the same time be seen as expressing the desire of many developing countries to emphasise that population growth does not constitute the principal cause of the poverty of developing countries.

Another way of stating this point of view is that it is only when poverty is already widespread that the growth of population becomes a problem. From this perspective, that simply means that if society has difficulties in providing for itself today it will not be able to look after future generations.

The invalidity of neo-Malthusian arguments does not end the relevance of the question of the control of births. For millions of women this is a real question. What they need, and increasingly demand, is the access to healthy and safe means of controlling their fertility. This is, of course, an argument for the free availability of high-quality birth control facilities and information, but it is in no way an argument for many of the population control programmes in the Third World which force or bribe women into birth control measures which have sometimes turned out to be a danger to their health and an infringement of their right to free choice.

Further reading

B. Hartmann, *Reproductive Rights and Wrongs: the global politics of population control and contraceptive choice*, New York 1987.

Malvinas/Falklands ▶ Falklands/Malvinas

Mandela, Nelson (1918–)

Born in 1918 in Transkei, South Africa, Nelson Mandela became prominent in South African politics when, along with Walter Sisulu, Oliver Tambo and others, he formed the youth wing of the African National Congress (▶ ANC) in 1944. Between then and the banning of the ANC in 1960, he was one of its principal organizers. After the banning he commanded the military wing of the ANC and was captured by the South African authorities in 1962. He was sentenced to life imprisonment at the end of the Rivonia trial in 1964. He was finally released in February 1990 and was immediately named Vice-President of the ANC (Oliver Tambo, the titular President, was still in exile and recovering from a stroke). Since then he has been the effective leader of the ANC during the disintegration of ▶ apartheid. During his 25 years in jail, Mandela became the focus of an extraordinary worldwide campaign of solidarity. He became a unique symbol of resistance and liberation.

Mandela, Winnie (1934–)

Winnie Mandela was born in 1934 at Bizana Pandoland (South Africa) and became the first African medical social worker in South Africa at Baraguwanath Hospital.

Since her separation from her husband Nelson, it has become fashionable to attack and criticize Winnie Mandela. And yet, despite this personal tragedy, Winnie Mandela remains in every respect the mother of the South African nationalist movement.

During the imprisonment of her husband Winnie Mandela emerged in her own right as a major political leader. She was closely associated with the militant youth in her township of Soweto. Her expressions of support for direct action earned her a reputation as a hardliner. She was an obvious high-profile target on which the state could focus its campaign to crush and criminalize black militancy. In the past Winnie Mandela was banned and prevented from influencing political life.

In recent years the focus of the government attack shifted towards the courts. Through a series of judicial prosecutions Winnie Mandela's personal reputation became the issue. Since 1991 the courts have been mobilized to destroy her credibility.

That the strategy of criminalizing Winnie Mandela has succeeded to some extent is shown by her growing isolation within the ANC. But the blow to her personal standing is not an individual matter. It expresses the weakening of the militant wing of the ANC and the growth of conservative trends within African nationalism.

Mao Zedong (1893–1976) and Maoism

Maoism is a version of Stalinism propounded by Mao Zedong, leader of China from 1949 until his death in 1976. It stresses reliance on peasant support in transforming society. It also rejects Soviet support for peaceful coexistence with imperialism and regarded the USSR after Stalin as an example of 'social imperialism'.

Mao Zedong (former transcription Mao Tse-tung) was born in 1893 to a rich peasant family in Hunan province. Introduced to Marxism in 1919, he was one of the 13 founding members of the Chinese Communist Party (CCP) in July 1921. In June 1923 he was elected to the Central Committee and was appointed director of the organization department. He became a leading advocate of a 'united front' with the Kuomintang (KMT), the Chinese Nationalist Party led by Sun Zhong Shan (Sun Yat-sen) and later Jiang Jie Shi (Chiang Kai-shek). In November 1925 he became head of the CCP's propaganda department. From March 1926 the KMT and CCP began to split as landlords in the KMT-backed nationalist army put down peasant unrest. Mao had begun to emphasize the revolutionary role of the peasantry in his Hunan report 'On social classes in China' in 1926. In 1927 Mao helped found the Chinese Red Army to fight the landlords. The CCP was beaten and had to retreat to the border provinces, from where, in 1934, the Long March began. It lasted over a year and during it Mao became the recognized leader of the CCP. In 1937, when the Japanese war began, Mao initiated a turn towards the KMT again and they briefly worked together against the foreign invaders. During the Second World War, the communist–nationalist alliance fell apart and civil war broke out in the summer of 1946. In October 1949 Mao proclaimed the People's Republic of China.

From 1956 the CCP became increasingly critical of the USSR and failed to recognize Khrushchev as Stalin's successor as head of the world communist movement. Three months after Khrushchev's secret speech, Mao declared 'Let a hundred flowers bloom'. The Chinese intelligentsia were encouraged to express diverse ideas, but their criticisms of the regime were interpreted as threatening stability and they were repressed. In autumn 1957 the ▶ Great Leap Forward was inaugurated as a 'turn to the masses'. Communes were established in the countryside.

This campaign was wrong as well, as industrial production fell. As the bureaucracy strove to recentralize control of the economy, Mao was dropped from his post as chairman of the republic and replaced by Liu

Shaoqi (Liu Shao-chi). It was some time before he recovered his power. This he did – through his control of the party and influence over the People's Liberation Army (PLA) – in the ▶ Cultural Revolution which lasted from 1966 to 1969. He defeated the 'conservative' Liu who was ousted as head of state in autumn 1968 and replaced by Lin Biao (Lin Piao). Mao and Lin soon split as well, and the latter died in mysterious circumstances after an aircrash in September 1971. Mao died in 1976.

It was during the period 1936–40 that Mao produced his major works. His own version of dialectical materialism was outlined in *On Contradiction* (1937) and *On Practice*. He also produced several military studies. In *On Contradiction*, Mao postulated that of Engels' three fundamental laws of dialectics only 'the law of unity of opposites' was a 'fundamental law of thought'. Of the others, the negation of the negation was repudiated and transformation of quantity into quality was only a special form of the 'law of unity of opposites' or, as Mao called it, 'the law of contradiction in things'. From this, Mao deduced his concepts of primary and secondary contradictions. Any social process had its fundamental or primary contradictions, which can change and so change the form of the process. So the Chinese revolution had primary contradictions, and relatively unimportant secondary contradictions which it was important not to mix up with the more fundamental ones. At one time the principal contradiction could be feudalism – the struggle between landlords and peasants – and then – 'maybe tomorrow' – it could all change, and the principal contradiction could become imperialism – the struggle between the Japanese and the Chinese.

Translated into practice, this theory justified sudden reversals of political line: in 1937 the class war against the landlords was stopped as the formation of a bloc with the KMT was justified on the grounds that the primary contradiction in China was between the Chinese people and the foreign Japanese usurper. The contradiction between the KMT-backed landlords and the peasantry was relegated to being only of 'secondary' significance. Later on, other Maoists were to develop the concept of 'proletarian nations' to describe the contradiction between the West (and the USSR) and the former colonial countries. ▶▶ Introduction.

Further reading

J. Ch'en, *Mao and the Chinese Revolution*. London 1987.
S. Schram, *The Political Thought of Mao Tse-tung*, Harmondsworth 1969.

Mariátegui, José Carlos (1894–1930)

Born in 1894 in Moquegua, Peru to impoverished parents, José Carlos Mariátegui left school at 14 to help supplement the family income. He became a noted journalist in Lima. He was exiled to France and Italy between 1919 and 1923 where he joined the revolutionary movement and studied Marxist classics. He returned to Lima in 1923 but was confined to a wheelchair from 1924. He addressed workers' and students' meetings and wrote articles for his magazine *Amauta*. In very poor health, in 1928, he finished his *Seven Interpretative Essays on Peruvian Reality* which attempted to reconcile Marxism with the Peruvian indigenist movement.

The following year, he helped found the General Confederation of Peruvian Workers and became secretary-general of the communist Peruvian Socialist Party. Physically worn out by continual harassment by the authorities, he died in April 1930. Mariátegui was all but forgotten until the 1960s when his collected works were published in a 20-volume edition, and he became the major political influence on the ▶ Sendero Luminoso.

Mariátegui represents the current known as 'national left' – in other words, Marxism adapted to the reality of Latin America, especially its cultural traditions. ▶ indigenismo.

Marxism

The Third World was still being formed as Karl Marx (1818–83) was writing in the mid-nineteenth century. Marx, however, showed remarkable awareness of it even though the opinions of later Marxists were to diverge considerably from his own. As a product of the enlightenment, Marx held a universalist conception of humanity and its history and saw it as progress towards a common future. In this history capitalism, for him, played a major progressive role, establishing the material conditions on which socialism (a society of abundance and free choice) would be based. Though he recognized the way in which early European capitalism had (through slavery and pillage) exploited what is now the Third World as part of the process he called 'primary accumulation', Marx none the less expected when he wrote *Capital* that capitalism would industrialize the colonies as well as Europe, and while he emphasized the brutality of colonialism he also saw that it would have historically progressive results. In both his economic and political analysis, however, he provided analytical ideas which would later have a fruitful specific application to the Third World (e.g. ▶ Bonapartism, ▶ unequal exchange).

Before Marx died, however, his followers began to question how his analysis of history was to be applied to the less-industrialized areas of the world economy. There raged a major debate among Russian Marxists as to whether Russia should expect to pass through the same stages as Western Europe on its way to socialism via capitalist industrialization or whether it could bypass the process by building a more rural, communal form of socialism. The debate put Marx in a serious quandary in the last years of his life and he came to question if not to reject his earlier views.[1]

Marx's orthodox followers, Lenin in particular, overcame the problem by arguing that capitalism in Russia produced development but of a very uneven kind. This might accelerate the development of the social conditions for revolution but meant that socialism could not be built unless that revolution became international and incorporated the most economically advanced parts of capitalism, in particular Germany.

When, after Lenin's death in 1924 that failed to happen, the idea arose in Marxism that capitalism would not industrialize the world but that from now on it must be the task of socialism. One version of this new idea was Stalin's strategy of 'socialism in one country' – a kind of forced industrialization in conditions of intense oppression of the working class – later followed by ▶ Mao Zedong. Though this was very different from anything which Marx had thought, it became orthodox Marxism within the communist movement.

Similar ideas, however, appeared from less orthodox sources. One of the main ones was ▶ dependency theory, which argued that capitalist development in the Third World was excluded in the modern epoch and so development could be generated only after social revolution under a social regime. Ideas of this kind coalesced with the orthodox Marxist tradition, especially the theory of ▶ imperialism.

While Marxist ideas continue to produce rich insights into the social reality of the Third World, there remains no agreement among those who regard themselves as Marxist on the central question of what is the role of capitalism in the Third World today. The experience of the newly industrializing countries (▶ NICs), the revival of ▶ neo-liberalism and the temporary setbacks for many socialistically oriented experiments in the Third World has resurrected the debate.

Further reading

H. Carrère d'Encausse and S. Schram (eds), *Marxism and Asia*, London 1969.
S. Clarkson, *The Soviet Theory of Development: India and the Third World in Marxist-Leninist scholarship*, London 1979.
U. Melotti, *Marx and the Third World*, London 1977.
M. Rodinson, *Marxism and the Muslim World*, London 1979.
T. Shanin (ed.), *Late Marx and the Russian Road*, Basingstoke 1985.
E. Terray, *Marxism and 'Primitive' Societies*, New York 1972.

Note

1. See T. Shanin (ed.), *Late Marx and the Russian Road*, Basingstoke 1985.

Mau Mau

This is the usual name given to the armed revolt of Kenyan peasants and workers which broke out in October 1952 against British colonialism. This bitter struggle which was eventually crushed by the British military at the cost of tens of thousands of African lives represented one of the most important experiences of African liberation.

The term 'Mau Mau' is a subject of controversy. According to the colonialist ideologues Mau Mau is a Kikuyu word meaning an oath. In fact the term has no literal meaning in Kikuyu or Swahili. It is clear that the term was invented by colonialists to evoke an image of 'primitivism' and 'atavism' about a liberation movement which they sought to discredit. The term was used as part of an especially violent ideological offensive to criminalize African protest in Kenya even before the outbreak of the revolt.

Mau Mau was portrayed in the most lurid and sensational manner imaginable. Blood lust, orgiastic oath taking ceremonies, brutal and hideous slaughter of people and animals provided the main themes of the anti-Mau Mau campaign. In the Western media, the Mau Mau became portrayed as the forces of darkness attacking civilization and Christianity. To this day the impressions conveyed through this campaign retain their influence.

The anti-Mau Mau media offensive aimed to portray the movement as driven by base and irrational passions. In this way the forces of colonialism attempted to present their cause as one that was upholding freedom and democratic values.

It is ironic that the term 'Mau Mau' is now used proudly by many participants in the liberation struggle. It has been redefined by them to mean a struggle for land and freedom.

For students of cultural imperialism the Mau Mau experience provides an important case study. Since Mau Mau, many other liberation movements have received the same treatment from the Western media. Any anti-imperialist fighter can expect to be labelled as a terrorist, psychopath or fanatic by the Western media. The contemporary treatment of the people of the Middle East has strong parallels with the Mau Mau episode. As in Kenya, it is the irrational and fanatical forces beyond human comprehension that are assigned responsibility for the upheavals. In contrast, Western gunboat diplomacy is usually portrayed as legitimate force to keep the peace. It seems that when struggles in the Third World break out the Western media possess only one script. ▶▶ Kenyatta, Jomo.

Further reading

D.L. Barnett and K, Njama, *Mau Mau From Within: autobiography and analysis of Kenya's peasant revolt*, New York 1966.

F. Furedi, *The Mau Mau Revolt in Perspective: the betrayal of a dream*, London 1989.

Mercosur

Mercosur refers to the treaty signed in March 1991 between Argentina, Brazil, Paraguay and Uruguay to establish a full common market of the four countries by the end of 1994 (▶ integration, ▶ LAIA).

migration

In the period since decolonization, migration has become one of the most important elements in North–South relations. There have been three main migrations from Third World countries, two to parts of the North and the third to a richer part of the Third World, the oil-producing states of the Middle East (see Table).

The situation of the migrant in the three cases is very different. In general the oil-producing states have attempted to restrict the rights of the migrant to the right to work under very controlled conditions, often in a form of indentured labour. When the work ends the migrant is expected to return to his or her place of origin, and he or she acquires no rights in the host country. In the USA, in 1964 a change in the law eliminated the old pro-European quotas and allowed immigration from

Table: Migration from the Third World

Source	Destination	Years
West Indies, North Africa, Turkey, South Asia	Western Europe	1950–73
South Asia, East Asia, Egypt	Middle Eastern oil-producing countries	1973–86
West Indies, Latin America, East Asia, South Asia	USA	1964–

other countries. Though they suffer discrimination, many of the migrants settle and acquire political and civil rights, becoming full members of US society. In Europe the situation is between the two extremes. Though some migrants were obliged to leave during the 1970s and 1980s when unemployment rose, European countries do now contain quite large numbers of residents and citizens whose origin is in the Third World.

The decline in the oil price followed by the Gulf War have considerably reduced migration to the Middle East; and, as the European Community at the start of the 1990s prepares for a single internal labour market with free movement of workers, it is attempting to stem the flow of migration from the Third World with new legal controls. Only the USA remains open to large-scale immigration from the Third World; at present at least 500,000 new migrants enter the country each year legally and possibly the same number illegally. Asian countries have replaced Latin American ones as the main source of this immigration; but there is immigration from virtually all parts of the Third World. This migration is helping quite rapidly to change the structure of the US population; it is estimated that by the year 2030 its white population will be in the minority as it is already in many of the country's major cities. It is interesting to speculate on the changes which might occur in the political complexion of the leading imperialist power when the majority of its population has its origin in the Third World.

Migration has major effects on the economies of the Third World countries from which the migrants come. Migration is often used as a solution to the problems of poverty at home and many migrants send remittances to their families. These reach major proportions in some countries. As a proportion of exports, migrants' remittances in 1988 were over 50 per cent in Jordan, Burkina Faso, Egypt, Sudan, Bangladesh and South Yemen. As a proportion of the national income, they reached over 20 per cent in the case of Jordan and South Yemen. Countries in this situation could not at present manage economically without the contribution made by migrants. The curtailing of migrants' employment in Saudi Arabia and Kuwait in 1991 was a bitter economic blow to Jordan, Yemen and particularly to the Palestinians (▶ PLO).

While migrants often suffer discrimination and low wages in the countries to which they migrate, they none the less often succeed in ameliorating their own, their family's and even their country's economic situation. For all the problems of the life of the migrant, migration probably makes a positive contribution to the redistribution of world income.

While in many countries measures are being taken to exclude migrants, the failures of development in the Third World mean that the demand to migrate is almost infinite. Inevitably that means that the issue of illegal migration will become an ever more important one in the developed countries, probably with severe consequences for the level of democratic rights in them, especially for people who are not white.

Further reading

S. Castles and G. Kosack, *Immigrant Workers and Class Structures in Western Europe*, London 1973.

R.H. Sabot (ed.), *Migration and the Labour Market in Developing Countries*, Boulder, Col. 1981.

military government

About half of all Third World countries are ruled by military regimes and in many Latin American and African countries in particular the military coup has become the most common means of changing government. The physical power and social weight of the military have resulted from many factors: the poverty and lack of resources of other social strata; the active cultivation of the military by the governments of the West; a high level of social conflict which can only be suppressed by military force. Military government, therefore, can be seen in part as an example of Marx's notion of ▶ Bonapartism in the current context.

It has often been argued, most especially within the context of ▶ dependency theory, that it is the weakness of the dependent bourgeoisie in Third World countries which makes the military alternative almost inevitable. This thesis was easy enough to sustain in Latin America during the 1970s when virtually the whole continent came under military rule, but the military rulers failed to gain legitimacy and everywhere provoked popular resistance. Hence in the 1980s even the Latin American bourgeoisie, despite a worsening economic situation which if anything reduced their options, turned everywhere to parliamentary democracy. By the beginning of the 1990s scarcely a military regime remained in South America. It seems that there is no inevitability that Third World ruling classes will always turn to the military option. This is also illustrated by cases such as India. The Indian bourgeoisie can hardly be said to have more options, or to be less dependent, than the Latin American, and yet India has avoided military rule up to now.

In addition, the policy-makers of the West seem to have less enthusiasm for military rule than hitherto. This must be partly because military rule in Third World countries tends to be extremely brutal and repressive and thus to create internal political problems in the West for neo-colonial alliances with Third World rulers. While military rule may be at times the only option, it is sometimes an uncomfortable one from the point of view of the imperialist ruling class whose internal rule depends on espousing an ideology of democracy, even though that in practice means little more than periodic elections.

Further reading

R. First, *The Barrel of a Gun: political power in Africa and the coup d'état*, London 1970.
W.F. Gutteridge, *Military Regimes in Africa*, London 1976.

military spending

The governments of the world spend about US$1000 billion a year on armaments and the armed forces. The majority of this is spent by the superpowers (the USA and the USSR) which until recently confronted each other in the Cold War. The total amount of military spending is equal to the annual income of the poorest half of the world's population. Yet ironically military spending in recent years has been rising most rapidly in Third World countries. Between 1960 and 1987 the share of the gross domestic product of the developed countries going to military use fell from 6.9 per cent to 5.5 per cent; in the same years in the Third World it rose from 3.9 per cent to 5.2 per cent. This is more than three times what Third World governments spend on public health and 60 per cent more than they spend on education.

This rise in spending is closely associated with the growth in the number of wars within the Third World. The period since 1945 is often known as 'peacetime', a definition only possible from a totally Western-oriented perspective. Of the 149 wars which have taken place during this period of 'peace', 147 have taken place in the Third World. Some of these are wars of intervention by the great powers; others are wars between Third World countries which almost invariably have an element of 'war by proxy', since each side is supported by one or other of the superpowers.

As a result of these facts the Third World, in general a poor market for industrial goods, is a thriving market for arms. US$47.2 billion of arms were sold in world trade in 1987. The first five exporters were the five permanent members of the Security Council of the United Nations. Of these exports, 76 per cent were destined for the Third World and took up 7 per cent of its total exports. Or, to put it another way, the purchase of arms imports was equal to about three times the total amount of development aid received.

Some 25 million people are estimated to have been killed in the various wars taking place in the Third World since 1945. More than three-quarters of these have been civilians. Modern warfare, despite the myth that it is between machines, involves more civilian casualties than ever before, mainly due to the widespread use of mass bombing.

Thus the period since decolonization has been for the Third World one of widespread war (officially known as peace); and the vast military expenditures of the period, officially directed at neutralizing the

197

sophisticated machines of potential superpower enemies, have in fact been used to kill and wound civilians in the Third World.

Further reading

R. Leger Sivard, *World Military and Social Expenditures*, Washington, DC (annual).

MIR, Movimiento de Izquierda Revolucionaria (Revolutionary Left Movement)

This is the name of various political organizations in several Latin American countries (including Bolivia and Peru). The best-known is the Chilean group formed in 1965 to fight the reactionary Chilean authorities. It combined armed struggle with more orthodox political activities. It suspended its armed struggle during the government of Salvador ▶ Allende and provided an armed guard for the president. It suffered much repression during and after General Pinochet's coup of 1973 and resumed clandestine activities and armed struggle. During Pinochet's regime it claimed responsibility for a number of bomb attacks and assassinations of officials of the dictatorship.

In 1981 the MIR joined exiled Unidad Popular (Popular Unity) leaders in a declaration of unity for a joint struggle against Pinochet. It then backed the formation of the Movimiento Democrático Popular (MDP, Popular Democratic Movement) in 1983 with other left-wing groups including the Chilean Communist Party. The MDP split in 1985 when conservative Chilean democrats announced a national accord calling for the restoration of civil liberties. The MDP was renamed Izquierda Unida (United Left). In March 1984 the Communist Party launched its own guerrilla movement, which the MIR countered by relaunching its armed wing as the Fuerzadas Armadas de la Resistencia Popular (FARP, Armed Forces of the People's Resistance) in November 1984.

The MIR did not join the large front of opposition parties which supported the 'no' vote in the 1989 referendum on Pinochet's rule. The return of a more democratic regime after Pinochet failed to win the referendum has divided the MIR between those who continue the armed struggle and others who wish to concentrate on open, legal political activity.

MLN ▶ Tupamaros

MNCs, multinational corporations

In the main, multinational or transnational corporations or firms are private concerns whose operations cover more than one country. MNCs invest in Third World countries for four separate reasons, which in some instances are combined: to gain assured access to raw materials; to gain access to local markets; to gain access to cheap labour; and to escape environmental and other controls on their activities.

The oldest motive, and one which continues to be important, is the first – to gain access to raw materials and primary products. MNC investments are common in such activities as banana or pineapple plantations, or in copper, tin or bauxite mines. The largest volume of this kind of investment in recent decades has been in petroleum. Most of these primary production investments represent the desire of the MNC for vertical integration, i.e. to own and control all stages of the production of its product. The raw materials or other primary products which these companies produce in the Third World are usually processed and marketed in the developed countries. These operations have a number of drawbacks for the Third World country: they may create islands of development which do not spread to the rest of the economy; they have little or no interest in developing the internal market and so they keep wages low; they do not train local workers for skilled posts; they ship out (repatriate) their profits rather than investing them locally.

During the 1960s and 1970s there was something of a boom in investments by MNCs in parts of the Third World with the objective of taking advantage of their growing internal markets or of jumping protective tariffs. The criticisms levelled at such investments are different from those levelled at primary production MNCs: it is sometimes said that foreign investment for the local market excludes local manufacturers; that the production is for a small élite market; and that it allows the entry of undesirable Western patterns of consumption.

The third motive, the search for cheap labour, is probably of increasing importance as the world market for manufactured goods becomes more competitive. Here the criticisms of foreign investment by MNCs largely focus on its failure to spread its effects into the economy as a whole and on its interest in maintaining very low wages. Such investments often take place in border areas (such as the maquiladoras (assembly plants) on the Mexican–US border) or in special economic zones. Virtually all the production of such investments are exported.

The growing consciousness of environmental problems in developed countries has probably encouraged some firms to try to locate 'dirty' activities in Third World countries, where it is less easy to enforce environmental controls or where governments may be so desperate to get foreign exchange that they deliberately impose no environmental controls. The disaster at the Union Carbide plant in Bhopal, India in 1984 is often quoted as an illustration. Some of the worst examples of this type of investment (the dumping of toxic wastes in Africa) have in recent years received considerable adverse publicity and have been banned by many countries. ▶ environment.

Against the above criticisms of these various forms of MNC activities, their defenders argue that MNCs bring both capital and technology to the Third World and their utility is proved by the fact that Third World countries compete for MNC investments in their country. This last point has been especially true in the epoch of the ▶ debt crisis which has obliged Third World countries to institute neo-liberal economic policies which open them to the world market, and to search for any means possible to obtain foreign exchange.

199

From the development point of view, MNCs may bring benefits and drawbacks in varying combinations, depending on the circumstances. It is difficult to argue that many of either their benefits or their costs result from the fact that they are *multinational*. Many of the criticisms directed against MNCs could equally be directed against domestic investors, and where MNCs can be shown to have negative effects this is always in combination with domestic economic and social structures which exist alongside the MNCs. The attempt to portray the MNC as the grand and special villain of underdevelopment is usually the expression more of a nationalist than a socialist outlook, one which assigns a positive role to domestic private or state capitalism as opposed to foreign capitalism.

This nationalist perspective often exaggerates the quantitative importance of the MNCs. It is instructive, therefore, to quote a few figures. The total value of foreign-owned capital in the Third World is about 8.5 per cent of annual income. This means it must be a very small percentage indeed of the total capital stock of the Third World (probably no more than 3 or 4 per cent). In general the percentage will be higher in the less poor countries, since in recent years the MNCs have invested very little in the poorest Third World countries. In a number of countries the importance of foreign investment in employment, production and exports in the manufacturing sector is much greater than the aggregate capital stock figures would suggest (see Table).

Table: Foreign affiliates as a percentage of employment, production and exports in the manufacturing sector of 12 Third World countries

Country	Employment (%)	Production (%)	Exports (%)
Brazil	23	32	32
Costa Rica			70
Fiji	29	32	
Hong Kong	10	14	16
India	13	7	
Mexico	21	27	42
Singapore	55	63	90
South Korea	10	19	25
Taiwan	17		26
Trinidad	44		
Zaïre	30		
Zimbabwe		70	

Note: A blank means information not available.
Source: United Nations Centre on Transnational Corporations, *Transnational Corporations in the World Economy: trends and prospects*, New York 1988.

The figures in the table show that in the manufacturing sector MNCs play a major or dominant role in some economies. In these cases the decisions made by individual companies may very well have a large influence on what happens to the economy as a whole, and MNCs in such countries often possess undue leverage on the policies of governments. A notable feature of the data in the table is that in the most successful newly industrializing countries (▶ NICs), with the exception of Singapore, the MNCs are not so important.

In the Third World as a whole the relative quantitative importance of foreign investment in recent years has declined in relation to other possibly detrimental forms of involvement with the world economy, in particular debt. If foreign investment is equivalent to 8.5 per cent of the annual income of the Third World, the total volume of debt is equivalent to 44.7 per cent. The debt, therefore, is a much larger 'liability' than the accumulated total of foreign-owned capital, and much more money flows out of the Third World as payments to service the debt than in the repatriation of profits by MNCs. It can also be argued that the deleterious economic effects of adjusting Third World economies in order to pay the debt are much more damaging than the distortions produced by the investments of the MNCs. ▶ IMF.

If the traditional industrial and agricultural MNCs reduce the sovereignty of Third World countries, it is the creditor institutions in recent years which have reduced that sovereignty still further. For Latin American countries the creditors are generally the foreign banks (which are, of course, financial MNCs); and for Africa they are the governments of Western Europe and the international lending agencies. ▶ debt crisis, ▶ Club of Paris.

The directly investing MNCs, along with banks and governments, are part of an international structure which clearly reduces the economic sovereignty of Third World countries, but there is no good reason to single them out as the dominant instruments of this system.

Further reading

T.J. Biersteker, *Distortion or Development? Contending perspectives on the multinational corporation*, Cambridge, Mass. 1978.

R. Jenkins, *Transnational Corporations and Uneven Development: the internationalization of capital and the Third World*, London 1987.

S. Lall and P. Streeten, *Foreign Investment, Transnationals and Developing Countries*, Boulder, Col. 1977.

H. Radice (ed.), *International Firms and Modern Imperialism*, Harmondsworth 1975.

United Nations Centre on Transnational Corporations, *Transnational Corporations in World Development*, New York 1988.

modernization

Modern and modernization are highly subjective terms. The term 'modern' implies that which pertains to the contemporary period. It suggests a counter-position to that which went on in the past. To modernize is to adopt the customs, habits and culture of present times. In its applications to the Third World, modernization implies the adoption of the institutions and values of the West. Behind this view is the assumption that progress in the Third World means the discarding of traditional institutions in favour of those that exist in the West. Western society is posited as a model to which modernizing nations ought to aspire. Modernization theory posits that 'old' societies should or do become increasingly more differentiated and complex until they approximate the Western model.

The main influences on modernization theory are the sociological theories of Max Weber and Emile Durkheim. Weber's thesis explains the development of capitalism as the product of cultural and psychological changes which predispose the individual to modernization. With the rise of the pursuit of individual self-interest, the old traditional institutions with their pre-determined social rules break down and, according to Durkheim, change is expressed through a process of social differentiation through which society becomes more complex.

From the application of Weber and Durkheim to the Third World it is argued that the slow rate of progress is the product of the persistence of traditional institutions, values and attitudes. These are portrayed as obstacles to progress and to the achievement of a modern society.

Modernization is generally presented as the product of changing attitudes. Issues like economic exploitation or imperialist domination are ignored, or it is argued, following Weber, that economic development has as its prerequisite cultural change and a disposition towards new values. Slow progress is the result of attitudes which obstinately refuse to adapt.

According to one influential proponent of modernization theory, David Lerner,

> Modernity is primarily a state of mind – expectation of progress, propensity to growth, readiness to adapt oneself to change. The nations of the North Atlantic area first developed the social processes – secularisation, urbanisation, industrialisation, popular participation – by which this state of mind came to prevail.[1]

In a sense, a circular argument is put forward whereby one symptom of change, e.g. urbanization, is explained by another, a new state of mind.

Lerner's focus on the state of mind leads him to draw a sharp counterposition between the modern and traditional psyche. A modern psyche is mobile and adaptive and able to perform new roles. In contrast, the traditional psyche is rigid and inflexible. The tradition-oriented mind itself becomes the obstacle to change. Thus individual psychology is the key determinant of development.

In another influential work, Everett Hagen argues that modernization requires people with creativity and problem-solving ability. The slow pace of change in the Third World is therefore explained through the absence of these characteristics. Hagen states that the 'traditional society is associated with a rather low level of creativity among the members of society'.[2] Hagen's explanation is devastatingly simple: it is the lack of creativity (intelligence) of Third World people that accounts for its slow rate of economic growth.

Modernization theory thus places the blame for the stagnation of the Third World on the backward mental outlook and attitude of Third World people. It insults the victims of imperialist domination by holding them responsible for their circumstances. Even in its less insulting and less ethnocentric form, the modernization perspective contains a number of methodological flaws.

Individual attitudes are not the motor of change. It was not the Protestant ethic that made Europe industrialize. On the contrary, many of the values associated with the Protestant ethic were symptomatic of the social changes which Europe was experiencing. With overseas expansion, European trade, commerce and industry could flourish. The changes brought about through the growth of market forces transformed the outlook of European society. As people began to adapt to the transformation of society, new views and attitudes came to prevail. The new spirit of industrialization was born of the opportunities created through commerce and trade.

Individuals are products of society. To say that individual mental change produces social change is to eliminate social explanations in favour of psychological ones. In the Third World, the obstacles to change are social ones. Indeed, it is ironic that people in the Third World yearn for change. The numerous rebellions and revolutions in the Third World are a testimony to the popular desire for change. The absence of steady progress is the result of the historic forces which have impoverished the Third World and placed it in a position of subservience to the West.

Nor can it be said that the Third World is unmodern. Modernization cannot be equated simply with Western progress and prosperity. Even the most modern societies contain large pockets of impoverishment, illiteracy and hopelessness. The inner city ghettos of the USA are just as modern as the glittering lights of its cities which convey the impression of affluence. Inner city ghettos have no roots in tradition. The same historic process which created the wealth of the USA's rich is also the one which forced people into living in the most squalid of circumstances.

The corollary of Western affluence in the Third World is impoverishment. This relationship is strikingly illustrated by the case of South Africa where the polarization acquires extreme proportions. Are the ▶ Bantustans created in the twentieth century any less modern than the white suburbs of Cape Town? The Bantustans may be poor; their peoples may lack skills and education; but they are very modern.

Many of the unpleasant features of the Third World such as the civil war in Lebanon or communal strife in Sri Lanka or the explosion of ethnicity in Africa tend to be dismissed as the products of traditional society. Yet most of these problems have no roots in tradition or even in the historical past. Pre-colonial societies have disintegrated under the impact of Western domination. There is no traditional society. Millions of people have been uprooted and dispersed throughout the Third World. Third World societies are the creation of the vast historic changes that have transformed the globe during the past century. The Chinese plantation worker producing rubber in Malaysia for car tyres made in Japan and the USA appears to live in a different world from the owner of a new car in New York; yet these different worlds are closely interlinked and are entirely part of the same process of historic change, but that change has very different consequences for different parts of the globe.

The modernization perspective is a confusing one. It equates modernity with only a limited sphere of social experience. It assumes that the modern West has become prosperous through its own internal efforts and it studiously evades discussing the relationship between Western prosperity and Third World exploitation. By obscuring the international dimension of change, modernization theory attributes Third World stagnation to the lack of will or creativity of its own people. Development is reduced to individual psychological time travel and the meaning of 'modern' is transformed to mean 'Western'.

Modernization is meaningless for the Third World. Third World societies are no less modern than those of the North. What the Third World lacks is not modernity but the resources necessary for the creation of a stable and prosperous society. In so far as the Third World is behind the West, it is not so much in terms of culture, values, creativity or problem-solving abilities. The superiority of the West in the field of culture is questionable. The superiority of the West resides entirely in its economic power and resulting access to material resources.

It is the high levels of productivity and economic output that place the West ahead of the Third World. The difference between the two parts of the globe cannot be understood merely in terms of comparing statistics. More important is the relationship between the two worlds. The economic power of one implies the powerlessness of the other. Despite its economic inferiority, the Third World continues to transfer its resources to the West.

In the prevailing conditions of international subordination there can be no generalized steady progress in the Third World. Instead of catching up, the gap widens. For every example of progress in the Third World, e.g. South Korea, there are several examples of actual regression, e.g. Lebanon and the Sahel. Of course, progress is never steady and unilinear but in the case of the Third World change is often deprived of its progressive connotation.

For the Third World the issue is how to gain control over its economic life so that it can establish the foundation for steady social progress. It is through acquiring economic control that the gap which divides the two worlds may be closed.

As far as the Third World people are concerned, there is no problem about creativity, intelligence or the desire to be experimental. The problem is to create an environment within which their creativity could flourish. What is the use of intelligence and creativity in an environment of economic insecurity and impoverishment? In the squatter settlements and shantytowns that surround the great cities of the Third World the struggle for survival absorbs all of the human capacity for conscious action. In most situations in the Third World the potential of the population is wasted. People who are forced to live hand-to-mouth do not have the luxury of reflection. Nor can they exercise their capacity for experimentation or intellectual exploration. Once the economic constraints which doom life to an everyday struggle for survival are removed, the creative impulse of the Third World people will flourish. Human history will take a major leap forward as the creative potential of billions of people will be harnessed to the cause of progress.

The modernization perspective reduces Third World development to imitation, but imitating the West has no benefits for the Third World; on the contrary it leads to a perpetuation of economic exploitation. Modernization obscures the fact that it is a revolution in the structure of economic power which the Third World requires if it is to enjoy real progress.

Further reading

S.C. Dube, *Modernization and Development: the search for alternative paradigms*, London 1989.

J.G. Taylor, *From Modernization to Modes of Production: a critique of the sociologies of development and underdevelopment*, London 1979.

Notes

1. D. Lerner, *The Passing of Traditional Society*, New York 1965, p. viii.
2. E.E. Hagen, 'How economic growth begins: the theory of social change', in G.D. Ness, *The Sociology of Economic Development: a reader*, New York 1970, p. 165.

monetarism

This economic theory, much debated in Latin America in the 1960s, attributed the continent's high level of ▶ inflation to excessive creation of money by national governments to finance deficits in the state budgets. It was contrasted with structuralism, a rival explanation which attributed inflation to rigidities in supply (especially of food) resulting from the social and economic structure of Latin American societies (especially the unequal structure of land holding which held back marketed food production).

Monetarism suggests an appropriate policy to control inflation – namely to reduce the government's fiscal deficit and the printing of money. In the guise of policy rather than theory, monetarism made another appearance, from a different quarter, in Chile after the military coup in 1973. The Pinochet dictatorship instituted a policy of ruthless cuts in government spending and real wages, implemented with the advice of 'monetarist' economists from the USA, the most prominent of whom was Milton Friedman.

Friedman had long propounded a simplistic monetarist theory of inflation and economic control in the industrialized countries. He argued that the main economic function of the government should be to maintain the growth of the money supply in line with the growth of the economy. In that way, the economy would proceed on its 'natural' growth path without inflation and with its 'natural' level of unemployment. The application of these ideas to a case such as Chile involved more than the application of an economic policy, right or wrong; the imposition of controls on government spending was tied up with the brutality of the dictatorship in cutting back all the gains made by the people under the ▶ Allende government.

This specific and sinister reappearance of monetarism in the Third World was followed by a much more general form of monetarism. During the 1980s the monetarist ideas of Friedman and other economists gained a new prestige with the arrival in power of governments such as those of President Reagan in the USA and Prime Minister Thatcher in the UK. 'Monetarism' came to be the phrase used to describe a set of economic policies which involved much more than the control of the money supply (monetarism in the strict sense). These policies centred on an attempt to 'roll back' the economic functions of the state. It included the privatization of state-owned enterprises, the implementation of free markets everywhere possible and the cutting of state spending, especially on social welfare and subsidies.

These were the policies of ▶ neo-liberalism rather than monetarism in the strict sense. But the 'monetarism' label often stuck to them, both in the developed countries, and when they were also introduced on a grand scale throughout the Third World during the 1980s, often as a result of structural adjustment programmes of the International Monetary Fund (▶ IMF). ▶▶ inflation.

Montoneros ▶ Peronism

Movimiento 19 de Abril ▶ M-19

Movimiento de Izquierda Revolucionaria ▶ MIR

Movimiento de Liberación Nacional ▶ Tupamaros

MRLA, Malayan Races' Liberation Army
This Communist-backed guerrilla movement in Malaya (now part of Malaysia) was originally called the Malayan Peoples' Anti-British Army. It was set up by the Central Committee of the Malayan Communist Party (MCP) in 1948 as part of a strategy of armed insurrection under the new leader of the MCP, Chin Peng. This followed what was seen as the failure of the campaign of strikes to secure the departure of the British and establish a people's republic. The movement recruited mainly among former members of the predominantly Chinese Malayan Peoples' Anti-Japanese Army (MPAJA) founded during the Second World War to fight the Japanese. It soon had 4000 members and its legal front organization, the Mip Yuen, 40,000. In the face of armed action, the British declared a

state of emergency and brought in troops and the air force to put down the revolt using air strikes on jungle targets. Chinese squatter communities were resettled in closely guarded 'New Villages', a tactic which gradually cut off supplies to the guerrillas, called by the British 'CTs' for 'communist terrorists', who were forced back into the jungle.

In 1951 the new British Conservative government sent General Templer to take charge. He introduced covert military operations and a 'hearts and minds' operation among the Chinese supporters of the MRLA, paying MRLA members to spy on their comrades. By May 1954, when Templer left, the British had full military control. In 1957 the British handed independence to a Malay-dominated government; the chief minister, Tunku Abdul Rahman, offered MRLA members who had committed no 'crimes' an amnesty but negotiations with Ching Peng soon broke down, as the government refused to grant legal recogition to the MCP. The emergency was officially ended in 1960. Remnants of the MRLA fought on out of bases in Thailand for the next thirty years. In the late 1980s it was estimated that there were still 700 members of the MCP in the Thai–Malaysian border area.

Further reading

A. Josey, *Lee Kuan Yew: the struggle for Singapore*, London 1974.
E. O'Balance, *Malaya: the Communist Insurgent War 1948–60*, London 1966.

Mujahedin, Sazman-e Mujahedin-e Khalq-e Iran (Organization of People's Combatants of Iran)

This left-wing Islamic organization was formed in 1965 by radical urban students with the aim of creating an egalitarian Islamic society through the fusion of Islam with Marxism by fighting against imperialism, capitalism, dictatorship and clericalism. It received military training from the Palestine Liberation Organization and launched its first guerrilla operations in 1971. In 1975 it split, with left-wingers endorsing Marxism and rejecting Islam; these left to found Paykar (Combat). Masoud Rajavi became leader of the Mujahedin. By 1979 the Mujahedin had become the 100,000-strong organization of young merchants, shopkeepers, clerics and artisans seeking a modern egalitarian Iran to replace the shah's dictatorship. They participated in the February 1979 uprising against the shah but differences with Ayatullah Khomeini soon emerged over democracy, secret courts, the rights of national minorities and the role of the ▶ Islamic Revolutionary Guards.

After Rajavi was disqualified from standing in the 1980 presidential elections, they supported Bani-Sadr, Khomeini's candidate. There were increasing conflicts with the Guards who killed several Mujahedin supporters; nevertheless, many Mujahedin joined the army to fight Iraq. The regime blamed the Mujahedin for a number of bomb outrages and launched an all-out attack on them. By May 1982 Khomeini had won, with thousands of Mujahedin killed or imprisoned. The Mujahedin leadership moved abroad, eventually settling in Baghdad, losing credibility within Iran by talking to Iraqi officials on ending the war. Rajavi broke with Bani-Sadr in 1984 and the Mujahedin have continued to fight the Iranian regime from Kurdistan and to wage a propaganda war against it in other countries. Mujahedin supporters were reported to have fought alongside Saddam Hussein's forces against the Iraqi Shi'ite rebels in the aftermath of the Gulf War.

multinational corporations ▶ MNCs

Muslim Brotherhood (Ikhwan al-Muslimin)

This Sunni Muslim secret society was formed in Egypt in 1930 with the aim of pressing Arab political parties and states to observe Muslim doctrine in full, for example by Islamizing the courts so that they follow the strict Sharia code set out in the Koran.

The Brotherhood was founded by Hasan al-Banna, a schoolteacher. It began as a religious movement but soon developed an anti-Western political focus. In 1947 the Egyptian premier banned the 40,000-strong Brotherhood. He was assassinated. Brotherhood members were prominent in fighting alongside the Grand Mufti of Jerusalem's forces in the 1948 war against Israel. In 1949 Banna himself was assassinated, and thousands of Brotherhood members were imprisoned in Egypt.

The Brotherhood at first welcomed Nasser's 1952 coup against King Farouk, but the new regime soon sought to suppress the organization again. This led to the Brotherhood spreading across the Middle East. Members dispersed to Syria, Iraq, Jordan and Saudi Arabia. Since then, they have periodically been made the targets of state repression. In 1980 President Asad of Syria made membership of the Brotherhood a capital offence. The Syrian army slaughtered thousands of members in Hama two years later.

Elsewhere, however, the Brotherhood has experienced a revival in the wake of Shi'ite fundamentalists' success in Iran. In Egypt a tamed Brotherhood is still officially banned; but, led by Maamoun al-Hodeibi, it has used front organizations to form the biggest opposition bloc in parliament, has renounced violence and has backed President Hosni Mubarek's promotion of official Islamization. The Brotherhood was widely blamed for assassinating Egypt's President Sadat in November 1981, in retribution for his peace pact with Israel. It seems likely, however, that the extreme splinter group Jihad (Holy War), led by Dr Ahmed Salim, was responsible. During the 1980s the Brotherhood gained support among the hitherto hostile Palestinian population in the Occupied Territories, and in Jordan it gained important parliamentary representation in the elections of 1990. Though still banned in Egypt, there too – in an improbable alliance with the Socialist Party – it posed an unexpectedly strong challenge to the peace of mind, if not the heavily rigged majority, of President Mubarak.

N

Nasser, Gamal Abdel (1918–70) and Nasserism

Gamal Abdel Nasser, Egyptian leader and key figure in the Arab liberation movement, was born in 1918, the son of a postmaster. He graduated from the military academy in 1938 and fought in the 1948 war against Israel. In 1949, he formed an illegal Free Officers Movement with other officers dismayed by Egypt's performance and hostile to British tutelage. He led the 1952 coup which overthrew the monarchy, becoming deputy prime minister to General Naguib and secretary-general of the new party, the Liberation Rally, while the Free Officers Movement became the Revolutionary Command Council (RCC). In 1954 he ousted Naguib and became both prime minister and chairman of the RCC. He negotiated the withdrawal of British troops in 1954 and then moved to crush the fundamentalist ▶ Muslim Brotherhood. In 1955 the West refused him arms and he turned to the East which supplied him. In July 1956 the USA and the UK decided not to finance the Aswan Dam and Nasser nationalized the Suez Canal. The UK, France and Israel conspired to invade Egypt, but were compelled to withdraw after a brief occupation of part of the Canal Zone. Nasser was the hero of the Arab world and embarked on plans for Arab unity, forming the United Arab Republic with Syria in 1958, which broke down in 1961 (▶ Ba'th). Nasser's decline began with defeat in the June 1967 war with Israel. He died in 1970.

His ideas were set out in his *Philosophy of Revolution*, asserting that Egypt was at the centre of the Arab world and calling for a united Arab nation as a focus to attract the wider Muslim community. His ideas caught the imagination of the Arab world. In 1962 Nasser set up the Arab Socialist Union to mobilize popular support, with a programme of eliminating capitalism and foreign influences, state control of the economy, increasing health and education spending and liquidating landlordism; but the 1967 military defeat eclipsed the man and his ideas. The foremost advocate of Nasserism today is Colonel ▶ Gadhafi.

Further reading

P.J. Vatikiotis, *Nasser and His Generation*, London 1978.

national question

The national question is one of the most pervasive problems facing the Third World. The desire of a nationality to control its future through the creation of a nation-state which looks after its interest can be a straightforward issue or can involve numerous difficulties.

In relation to the struggle against imperialism the national question is straightforward. For example, in Palestine and South Africa the majority of the population are denied the right to constitute themselves into an independent nation. In these cases the situation is fairly clear – the issue is the right of Palestinians and Africans to determine their future. The rights of the privileged minority in South Africa cannot be equated with the rights of the oppressed majority. As in all cases of self-determination it is for the majority to decide how they exercise their rights.

The national question becomes more complicated when one considers the situation in the post-colonial societies. The independent nations of the Third World that emerged in the post-war period were generally the artificial creations of colonialism. National consciousness in these nations was relatively weak since most people never conceived themselves as part of the artificial unit which colonialism created. In many of the states of Africa and Asia there are a large number of nationalities with a distinct language and culture. In some societies, such as Guyana and Malaysia, there are distinct communities with profoundly different identities.

Forging a national identity in a multi-cultural society is always difficult. It is particularly difficult in a multi-cultural society where communal divisions were manipulated and institutionalized during the colonial era. In such circumstances the transfer of power often coincides with the ascendancy of one nationality at the expense of another. Conflicts between nationalities are inevitable. To retain power the representatives of ruling nationalities are often tempted to discriminate against those nationalities that are excluded from influence.

As a result, a number of nationalities are not only excluded from influence over the institutions of the state but they also experience discrimination and oppression. In some cases physical force is deployed to sustain national oppression. For example, the Kurds in Iraq, the Tamils in Sri Lanka, the Chinese and Indians in Malaysia all experience national oppression.

Even when national oppression is not systematically practised the national question emerges on the political agenda. Sometimes sections of the ruling élites seek influence through mobilizing their regional base. This is done through the assertion of regional identity which is directed against the national government. Often this parochial approach is adopted by the capitalists of the most prosperous regions of a country. The aim is to reserve their privileges and wealth at the expense of the other regions. National movements among the Asante in Ghana, the Baganda in Uganda, the Kikuyu in Kenya and the Punjabi in India have this regressive parochial orientation.

With such conflicting motives, the national question is a complex one. It requires determining whether the issue at stake is national oppression, as is the case with the Ethiopian domination of Eritrea, or regional chauvinism, as is the case with the Punjabi movement for an independent Khalistan.

In analysing this question the issue is not one that can be approached by a ready-made schema. Some writers have attempted to define a nationality by indicating that it must fulfil a number of different criteria such as a common language, culture, historic homeland, etc. It is not possible to adopt an objective set of criteria since the very process through which a national identity is formed is a subjective one. Those who fervently identify themselves with a national outlook will not be impressed by being told that according to objective criteria they are not a distinct nationality.

The solution to the national question is the consistent extension of democratic rights. There is little point in artificially fabricating a national identity for those who identify themselves differently. A lesson of colonialism is that it is not possible to overcome the attachment of people to their specific culture and language. It is far better to provide a framework where every nationality can pursue its life in the way it chooses. Once respect for national identity is institutionalized then expressions of regional chauvinism and discrimination can legitimately be opposed. To make this possible the institutions of the state must include all national groups. Preferably the smaller and more insecure minorities should be allocated positions of influence so that they develop a stake in the new system.

The above approach does not provide a solution to a situation where a particular region or nationality is determined to separate. In such circumstances it is preferable to allow the nationality to gain autonomy rather than risk permanent conflict. Of course, when a separatist movement aims to dominate other nationalities, as in Punjab, no such concessions can be made without creating new problems of oppression.

In some situations, the very artificiality of the independent nation precludes any lasting solution within the boundaries of the nation-state. The best course to follow in these cases is one that seeks to establish a wider form of regional cooperation. For example, in Africa the creation of a political system which covers the whole continent is the appropriate strategy to follow. It is much easier to forge a pan-African identity than a Nigerian or Kenyan one. Through an all-African approach the artificial boundaries which promote suspicion between nationalities would be eliminated, opening the way to a solution based on voluntary agreement.

The ultimate solution to the national question lies in the social transformation of the Third World. Through the elimination of exploitation and of the class of exploiters, society can rid itself of the main beneficiaries of national oppression and chauvinism. In such circumstances the main obstacle to unity between people of different nationalities will have been removed.

Further reading

T.L. Hodgkin, *Nationalism in Colonial Africa*, London 1956.
E. Kedourie, *Nationalism in Asia and Africa*, London 1970.
A.D. Smith, *Theories of Nationalism*, London 1971.

Negritude

Negritude developed as the outlook of the black intellectuals in the French colonies in the West Indies and Africa. Many of these nationalist intellectuals, especially those from the West Indies, placed an emphasis on cultural renewal rather than political action. One of the key influences on black intellectuals in the West Indies was the Harlem Renaissance literary movement. Under this influence West Indian intellectuals in Paris launched *La Revue du Monde Noir* in 1931. A year later a new publishing venture, *Légitime Défense*, was launched.

The writings of the proponents of Negritude represented a response to the French policy of assimilation. French colonial policy emphasized the virtues of the culture of the metropolitan country and promoted it as the high point of European civilization. By implication the culture of the colonial peoples was dismissed as inferior and of little value. This strident form of cultural imperialism inevitably provoked a response from the black intelligentsia. The defence and further development of 'Negro-African' culture became the preoccupation of this social group.

The key figures in the Negritude literary movement were Léopold Sédar Senghor of Senegal, Aimé Césaire of Martinique and the writer Léon Damas. According to Senghor, Negritude was the 'cultural heritage, the values and particularly the spirit of Negro-African civilization'. The aim of the Negritude movement was to develop a 'Negro-African culture' consistent with 'the realities of the twentieth century'.[1] The most successful popularizer of Negritude was Césaire who through his journal *Tropique*, published in Martinique, succeeded in gaining considerable influence and prestige.

The concept of Negritude is inherently ambiguous and difficult to define. It placed an emphasis on what were suggested to be some inherent characteristics of the African personality and culture. It was implied that there were certain innate features peculiar to black people and culture.[2] Writers on Negritude have tended to fall into a form of mysticism in the search for the unique spirit of the African personality. The positive element in Negritude was its assertion of African history and culture and its attack on cultural imperialism; but, unfortunately, by redirecting attention from the Afro-Caribbean realities of the times to the mythical past, it developed into a profoundly conservative doctrine. Human beings of whatever culture do not possess an inherent self. Man is the product of society and specific social circumstances. Moreover, no society produces a common spirit which motivates every section of society. Society is composed of classes which often have conflicting interests and outlooks. The discovery of Negritude in the past inevitably becomes a romantic recreation of an ideal which never existed in the first place.

The conservative orientation of Negritude was no accident. Many of the proponents of this ideal were reacting not only to cultural imperialism but also to Marxism. The nationalist intellectuals in the French colonies had a restricted political outlook. Their concern was primarily with foreign domination rather than social change. Consequently, they were hostile to any notion of the class struggle. Negritude asserts the irrelevance of the class struggle for the Afro-Caribbean condition. It asserts that what is important is Negritude, the common spirit that binds all Afro-Caribbeans together. As Sekou Touré argued, Africa is 'essentially communocratic' and African life is one of organic solidarity.

Negritude, or its attempt to develop a non-class outlook based on a romanticized version of the harmonious collectivism of the past, is but a variant of the general approach of the intelligentsia of societies where agriculture dominates and the formation of classes is still at an early stage. Its arguments mirror those of the Narodniks in nineteenth-century Russia who argued that the Russian self of the peasant negated the relevance of Marxism. In Indonesia ▶ Sukarno's philosophy of Marhoenism and in the Middle East Ba'thism (▶ Ba'th) adopt a similar approach. In all these cases a romantic recreation of the past is used to suggest the irrelevance of the class struggle.

The conservative implications of Negritude became evident in the postcolonial era. Many of its leading advocates became leaders of the newly formed independent states and used their positions to preserve the status quo. Senghor, as president of Senegal, typified this approach. Change was restricted to the Africanization of government, but life continued as before. In economic terms France continued to dominate independent Senegal as effectively as during the colonial era. ▶ African Socialism.

Notes

1. See I.L. Gendzier, *Frantz Fanon: a critical study*, New York 1973, pp. 34–71.
2. See A. Césaire, *Discourse on Colonialism*, New York 1972.

Nehru, Jawaharlal (1889–1964)

Leading anti-colonial activist and prime minister of independent India, Jawaharlal Nehru was born in Allahabad into a family of Kashmiri Brahmans on 14 November 1889. His father, Motilal Nehru, was an advocate and a leading member of the Indian National Congress (INC).

Ironically, in view of his anti-colonial activism, Nehru was educated at Harrow, one of England's most expensive private schools, and Cambridge University and followed his father into legal advocacy. Joining the INC in 1912, on his return from England, Nehru became active in the anti-colonial movement.

When Mahatma ▶ Gandhi took over the leadership of the INC in 1919, Nehru became his supporter and closest associate. First arrested in 1921 for anti-colonial agitation, he spent a total of ten years in prison for his militant anti-colonialism. A popular figure with rank-and-file activists, Nehru was elected chairman of the INC on five separate occasions.

A strong internationalist, Nehru attended the 1927 Conference of Oppressed Nations in Brussels as a representative of the INC. He was also an activist in the Anti-Imperialist League where he met representatives from the revolutionary and national liberation movements of Europe, Asia and Africa. These early experiences laid the foundations for his contribution to later internationalist initiatives such as the Pancha Sila doctrine for peaceful coexistence between Asian states as well as the historic ▶ Bandung Conference in 1955 which was a major step towards unifying the liberated and yet-to-be liberated states of Africa and Asia.

A leader of the radical socialist wing of the INC, Nehru was prepared to subordinate his ideology to Gandhi's strategy of building a united national opposition (including industrialists and landowners as well as workers and peasants) to colonial rule. Nehru was appointed deputy prime minister in the provisional government of India (the viceroy was prime minister) and then held the posts of prime minister and foreign minister from 1947 until his death in 1964.

Nehru's government reorganized the administration of India into states according to national, ethnic and language factors which ended the British administrative system based on the precepts of divide and rule. This first post-independence government also started to implement a programme of agrarian reform which redistributed land and diminished the power of the feudalistic landowners.

Economic policy under Nehru emphasized planning and national self-sufficiency in industrial and agricultural products for which the motor would be a strong state sector. Nehru played a direct personal role in the drawing up of the first five-year plan after independence. Like Gandhi, Nehru was an avowed democrat and a strong opponent of the caste system and the other forms of economic and political oppression that were the legacy of traditional and colonial India.

While a key supporter of the Gandhian satyagraha campaign, Nehru took a more combative view on the resolution of class and other social contradictions. Nehru was the undoubted leader of the radical wing of the anti-colonial movement in India, but the warmth of his personal relationship with Gandhi transcended political disagreements.

The prophecy that after Gandhi's death Nehru would speak with the voice of Gandhi was to some extent borne out by developments in the 1950s when the ideas of revolutionary socialism gave place to ideas of liberation and social reformism in Nehru's political vocabulary. However, Nehru cogently argued that he had to take a more moderate stand to ward off the powerful forces of political conservatism in India at the time if his government was to succeed in forwarding modest social reforms. Despite the INC's frequent references to socialist policies, Nehru merely described India as a capitalist economy with a substantial public sector.

It was in foreign policy that Nehru proved most radical with his strong support for peaceful coexistence, ending the arms race and universal disarmament. Most notably he was one of the founders of the ▶ non-aligned movement, which for him did not signify passive neutrality but an international commitment to freedom and justice (▶▶ Nasser and Nasserism, ▶▶ Nkrumah and Nkrumahism). The Afro-Asian bloc and the non-aligned movement played a crucial supportive role in the anti-colonial struggles of the 1950s and 1960s.

Numerous members of Nehru's family held high office in India even during his lifetime. After his death, however, the family established a kind of dynastic rule in the Congress Party and in the country. The longest serving prime ministers since Nehru's death have been his daughter Indira Gandhi (assassinated by Sikh guards in 1984) and his grandson Rajiv whose assassination in 1991 threatened to mark not only the end of the Nehru–Gandhi dynasty but perhaps also of the secular, social democratic tradition which Nehru established.

Further reading

Tariq Ali, *The Nehrus and the Gandhis: an Indian dynasty*, London 1985.

neo-colonialism

Since the end of the Second World War, the Third World has experienced a profound shift in its relations with the West. The most dramatic symptom of this shift has been the decline of *colonialism* and the establishment of a system of *neo-colonialism*.

Colonialism in its imperialist form implied a relationship of direct political domination. During the era of imperialist colonialism (1870–1914), a small number of powerful Western nations divided large parts of the Third World to hold as their own private fiefdoms. These colonies which were under the direct control of their imperialist masters provided important resources for the expansion of the North (▶ colonialism). By 1945 the colonial system had come under major pressure. The intensity of imperialist oppression had provoked resistance and revolts throughout the world. The Chinese revolution was a warning sign of the impending collapse of the colonial system as a whole. At the same time, the USA had emerged as the leader of the imperialist world. The USA looked upon the existing colonial system as a barrier to its own expansionist aims and therefore encouraged its breakup. Three factors – the threat of revolt, the high cost of perpetuating colonial rule, and the opposition of Washington to the prevailing form of colonization – compelled the colonialists to retreat. Over the next two decades most of the colonized world obtained its national independence (▶ decolonization).

The demise of colonialism did not mean the end of foreign domination. What had changed was the form through which this domination was exercised. The direct political control of the colonies was replaced by a more complex mechanism of indirect domination. The Western-dominated world economy incorporated the Third World as a subordinate part. Former colonies could exercise their independence only to a limited extent; in economic terms they remained enslaved to their former masters. During the 1950s and 1960s the major capitalist powers strengthened their grip over the economies of the formerly colonized countries, forcing them into long-term economic subservience. This new form of foreign domination is characterized as neo-colonialism. Kwame ▶ Nkrumah, the former president of Ghana who coined the term, defined it in the following way: 'The essence of neo-colonialism is that the State which is subject to it is, in theory, independent and has all the outward trappings of international sovereignty. In reality its economic system and thus its political policy is directed from outside'.[1]

The success of neo-colonialism was founded on the strategy of transferring power to an indigenous capitalist class and a well-groomed civil service and political élite. This new indigenous ruling class looked to the old colonial powers for its survival and more often than not was prepared to follow the dictates of foreign interests.

This partnership between the neo-colonial ruling class and foreign capital provides the lynchpin of the system. To maintain such a system the West has interfered systematically in the policital life of the Third

World. Radical governments have been overthrown while those Third World regimes which set out on the path to economic independence have faced economic war and campaigns of destabilization. Only those countries which have succeeded in eradicating the colonial political structures, such as Cuba and Vietnam, have managed to give real meaning to their independence.

The neo-colonial system is policed by pro-Western client states through a network of military alliances. Such alliances have allowed the establishment of numerous Western military and intelligence bases in the Third World. In the former French colonies of Africa, for example, more French military personnel are stationed at present than during the pre-independence era. In cases where direct Western intervention is problematic, client states such as Israel and South Africa can always be counted on to intervene.

In many respects neo-colonialism is a more formidable foe than the old-style colonialism. As Pham Van Dong, Prime Minister of Vietnam, argued at a summit meeting of the non-aligned movement:

> We have in the main recovered our political independence. The historical mission assigned to our movement now consists in perfecting our undertaking, consolidating what has been obtained, and promoting the struggle for economic independence without which political independence will be but an edifice with no foundations . . . . Forced to back down, old colonialism with its brutal methods has given way to neo-colonialism, which is more subtle and better camouflaged, but more enterprising, more destructive of our material and spiritual riches, and therefore more dangerous and more difficult to expose, to combat and to defeat.[2]

Pham Van Dong's emphasis on the subtlety of neo-colonialism is very much to the point. Neo-colonialism perpetuates not just economic but also cultural domination. Through its control of the institutions of education, the media and communication systems, the West is in a position to subvert whole spheres of Third World social life.

In recent literature there has been considerable discussion about the importance of political independence in the context of neo-colonialism. Nkrumah's denunciation of 'sham independence' has been criticized by Soviet writers for going too far and underestimating the significance of political independence.[3] Ben Turok adopts a similar perspective and argues that 'independence was both victory and handover'.[4] Bill Warren has argued that the concept of neo-colonialism is highly 'misleading' for it underestimates the significance of formal independence,[5] but identifies independence as such with the potential to act independently, without considering how this potential can be realized. All these ways of posing the problem miss the essential truth which the concept of neo-colonialism is designed to reveal.

The collapse of colonialism is symptomatic of the weakness of the imperialist order. However independence is achieved – whether through a revolt or a handover – it is, of course, always a step in the right direction.

Independence, the right of a people to determine its future, represents the most elementary of democratic rights. However, neo-colonialism – a system of economic domination – acts so as to prevent Third World nations from *exercising* that right. It is the obstacles to the exercise of Third World independence that constitute the core of the problem. Critics of the concept of neo-colonialism fail to distinguish between independence and its exercise, between a formal right and a real right.

By emphasizing the purely formal character of independence, the concept of neo-colonialism suggests a potential way out. The exercise of independence necessitates the destruction of neo-colonialism. As it is destroyed, the field for independent action constantly widens. Every blow against the neo-colonial system makes independence less formal and gives it greater real content. Through this approach the importance of the fact of independence is not denied but an all-important distinction is made between actual gains and potential gains, between results and preconditions.

Further reading

K. Nkrumah, *Neo-colonialism: the highest stage of capitalism*, London 1974.

Notes

1. K. Nkrumah, *Neo-colonialism: the highest stage of capitalism*, London 1974, p. ix.
2. Cited in Anon., *Colombo Summit*, New Delhi 1976, pp. 14–15.
3. See R.A. Ulyanovsky and others, *Fighters for National Liberation*, Moscow 1983, pp. 147–58.
4. See B. Turok, *Africa: what can be done?*, London 1987.
5. Bill Warren, *Imperialism: pioneer of capitalism*, London 1980, p. 184.

neo-liberalism

Neo-liberalism is the name given to the recent revival of support by governments, international organizations and intellectuals for policies of ▶ laissez-faire. 'Liberalism' in this context refers to hostility to state interference and control in economic activity. It was above all the governments of President Reagan in the USA and Prime Minister Thatcher in the UK which broke with a long interventionist ideology and advocated 'rolling back' the state. Their ideas, supported by a change in the prevailing views inside the economics profession, spread to most of the governments in the world and this was helped by the crisis of the command economies of the East.

Neo-liberalism advocates lower state spending, decontrol and deregulation, free trade, free capital movements and low taxes and extols the almost magical virtues of the free market and free enterprise. It does not, however, advocate free movement of labour, and neo-liberals can turn rapidly into nationalists, protectionists and interventionists if their national interest seems to be threatened. The recent wave of neo-liberalism, therefore, contains a large amount of hypocrisy, but power relations in the world mean that the obligation to implement its policies are felt more strongly in the Third World than in the developed countries of the West. ▶▶ GATT, ▶▶ monetarism.

Further reading

Tariq Banuri (ed.), *Economic Liberalization – No Panacea: the experiences of Latin America and Asia*, Oxford 1991.

Neto, Antonio Agostinho (1922–79)

Leading the Movimiento Popular de Libertação de Angola (MPLA, Popular Movement for the Liberation of Angola) to victory in what is generally acknowledged as one of the toughest anti-colonial struggles in Africa, Antonio Agostinho Neto made his mark as one of the major intellectual and organizational figures in the African national liberation movement.

Neto was born in the village of Ikolu-i-Bengu just outside Luanda on 17 September 1922; his father was a Methodist minister and the young Neto was educated at a Protestant school in Luanda. From an early age Neto showed a keen interest in political and social affairs and a natural aptitude for literary expression.

Between 1944 and 1947, Neto worked in health service organizations in Luanda, and in 1947 left for Portugal to study at the medical department of Lisbon University and the University of Coimbra. While studying in Portugal Neto played an active role in agitation for independence for Portugal's colonies and made contact with some of the proscribed radical socialist movements in the country.

At the same time, Neto's poetry earned him early recognition on the Portuguese literary scene. Disconcerted by his strident political activism, the Portuguese authorities frequently arrested him both in Portugal and on his return to Luanda. In December 1956, while in prison, Neto founded the MPLA; he was later released and the following year he graduated as a surgeon from Lisbon University.

Continually harassed by the colonial authorities, Neto tried to practise as a doctor and at the same time to build a national anti-colonial alliance. When he was exiled to Cape Verde in 1961 and then taken to a Portuguese military prison, such international figures as Jean-Paul Sartre and Diego Rivera protested at his treatment. In July 1962 Neto was sprung from house arrest in Lisbon by his MPLA colleagues who informed him that his imprisonment had become a cause célèbre in Angola.

The MPLA was then operating out of Léopoldville (now Kinshasa) in the Belgian Congo and was reconsidering its tactics after an attempted uprising had been brutally repressed by the colonial authorities in Angola. It ruled out taking power by putsch or military coup and made preparations for a protracted guerrilla war developing into an all-out patriotic war.

At the first national conference of the MPLA, Neto and his colleagues argued that armed resistance should not be considered as a specifically military act, but as a form of political struggle, requiring the mobilization and unification of all patriotic forces and the raising of their political consciousness. This strategy entailed forming an alliance and seeking cooperation with all opponents of colonialism not just in Angola but beyond its boundaries.

The former general secretary of the MPLA, Viriato da Crus, argued for a much narrower movement, spurning cooperation with progressive Portuguese or mixed race elements, and giving a greater role in the struggle to the country's tribal associations. It was the divisive role of the tribal connections that was later exploited by externally funded movements such as Holden Roberto's Frente Nacional de Libertação de Angola (FNLA, National Front for the Liberation of Angola) and Jonas Savimbi's União Nacional para a Independência Total de Angola (UNITA, National Union for the Total Independence of Angola).

In the early 1970s, these rival organizations gathered momentum as their foreign backers boosted supplies but, in large part due to Neto's adopted strategy, the MPLA remained the only organization with a solid military and political base in the country. Anti-fascist agitation in Portugal increased and in 1974 the Salazar–Caetano regime fell after a junior officers' coup; the new government wanted to hand over power in Portugal's African colonies as soon as possible.

Sensing their opportunity, the FNLA forces from the north and the UNITA forces from the south marched towards the MPLA's stronghold in Luanda as the Portuguese were scheduled to hand over power in November 1975. With assistance from Cuba and the USSR, the MPLA was able to hold the capital against the US- and South African-backed aggression. After the crisis was defused, the FNLA and UNITA forces, because of their relative lack of popular support within the country, were driven back to their foreign bases.

These were undoubtedly Neto's greatest moments and they marked a signal triumph for his broad-based military and political strategy. The remaining four years of his life (he died in September 1979) were devoted to formulating an economic and political reform programme. A Marxist, Neto wanted more popular accountability and responsiveness from government, but he was not willing to push clichéd slogans onto people, nor to risk national unity for the sale of political dogmas.

Neto consistently defended the idea of the unity of all tribes, races and nationalities living together in Angola, and his greatest legacy to his people was the development of the MPLA into a truly nationwide organization devoid of tribal or racial tendencies (▶ Angolan liberation movement).

New International Economic Order ▶ NIEO

New International Information Order
In recent decades the spheres of culture, communications and the media have become major concerns for Third World activists. A growing awareness of the need to control the instruments of communications has led to calls for a New International Information Order.

Since its inception, the movement of the non-aligned countries has addressed the issue of cultural imperialism. From the 1950s onwards, there has been a growing recognition that Western domination of the Third World has had an important cultural consequence. The denial of the historical past of the Third World and the celebration of Western values have contributed to a negative image of the role of Third World people. Since colonial rule, the Western monopoly over the technology of communications has been an important source of power for sustaining domination over the Third World.

The principle of cultural equality has been one of the central demands of the movement of the non-aligned. Since 1974 Third World countries have discussed ways of cooperating in the field of culture and communications. At a symposium on information of non-aligned countries in March 1976, emphasis was placed on promoting mass media in their countries and they undertook to fight their dependence on Western systems of communication. Three months later, a special ministerial conference was held in New Delhi to establish a pool of news agencies. The ministers adopted a declaration calling for the 'decolonization of information' and stated that 'the establishment of a New International Order for Information is as necessary as the New International Economic Order [▶ NIEO]'.

The New Delhi declaration justified its call for the New International Information Order in the following terms:

> The means of communicating information are concentrated in a few countries. The great majority of countries are reduced to being passive recipients of information which is disseminated from a few centres.
>
> The situation perpetuates the colonial situation of dependence and domination . . . .
>
> In a situation where the means of information are dominated and monopolised by a few, freedom of information really comes to mean the freedom of the few to propagate information in the manner of their choosing and the virtual denial to the rest of the right to inform and be informed objectively and accurately.
>
> Non-aligned countries have, in particular, been the victims of this phenomenon. Their endeavours, individual or collective, for world peace, justice and for the establishment of an equitable international economic order, have been underplayed or misrepresented by international news media . . . . Their efforts to safeguard their political and economic independence and stability have been denigrated.[1]

The declaration calling for a New International Information Order touches on a subject which provokes much hostility in the West. Attempts by Third World countries to use the United Nations Educational, Scientific and Cultural Organization (UNESCO) to challenge the system have met with hysterical attacks from Washington. The withdrawal of funding from UNESCO by the UK and the USA shows the importance that they attach to the perpetuation of the existing system of cultural domination.

The battle over UNESCO has helped underline the significance of culture and the media in the battle for the future direction of the world order. In all the flashpoints of the Third World – the Middle East, Central America and Africa – the world media have succeeded in monopolizing the communication of information. Those who oppose imperialism are generally portrayed as 'terrorists' or 'fanatics'. Often, news is fabricated or cynically manipulated to legitimize Western intervention. For example, during the weeks leading up to the invasion of Grenada in 1983, the media were full of stories about the danger facing US medical students on the island. After the invasion, it became clear that these scare stories merely served as a pretext for the invasion.

Unfortunately, the dominant system of information also influences the people of the Third World. The Western viewpoint influences opinion, lifestyle and even patterns of consumption. Through the media the West is able to exercise a domination over the mind. Mental domination, precisely because it is less tangible than physical coercion, is difficult to combat. It is for this reason that the struggle in the cultural domain acquires exceptional importance in the Third World.

There is little point in just asking for cultural equality. Those who control the system of communication will not voluntarily relinquish their power. It is necessary to create an alternative mass media from the bottom upwards. The technology of mass communication needs to be modified so that it becomes cheap enough for mass distribution in the Third World. Experimentation in the field of culture and the media is the prerequisite for eroding the existing Western monopoly over the system of international communication.

Note

1. Cited in A.W. Singham and S. Hune, *Non-Alignment in an Age of Alignments*, London 1986, p. 142.

New Jewel Movement ▶ NJM

New People's Army ▶ NPA

newly industrializing countries ▶ NICs

Ngouabi, Marien (1939–77)

As founder of the Parti Congolais du Travail (PCT, Congolese Labour Party) in the Congo on 31 December 1969, Marien Ngouabi made history, since the PCT was the first ruling party in Africa to declare scientific socialism and Marxism-Leninism as its ideological basis. The announcement that the PCT was going to take an unequivocally socialist line in the Congo, a small, economically weak state of some million and a half people, took observers by surprise.

The Congo's social composition is, however, atypical for Africa: some 40 per cent of its population is urbanized and, as the administrative centre of French Equatorial Africa, a more sophisticated infrastructure of health and education facilities was built up during colonial rule. However, Ngouabi was born in the village of Ombele in the heart of the country. Both his father and his mother belonged to the families of tribal chiefs, but led ordinary traditional patriarchal peasant lives.

Ngouabi was born in 1939 and went to primary school at Ovando in 1953, entering the Leclerc Military School in Brazzaville from where he graduated in 1957. After the four-month probationary period, he was promoted sergeant in the colonial army, serving in Cameroon from 1959 to 1960. Serving in Cameroon at that time, when the French were brutally suppressing the guerrillas led by the underground Union des Populations du Cameroun (UPC), did much to shape Ngouabi's political outlook.

Politicized by these experiences, Ngouabi was arrested for participating in demonstrations demanding independence for the Belgian and French Congos. He completed his studies in Strasburg and then at the military school at Saint-Cyr, where he again made contact with militant African nationalists and was inspired to read some of the classic works on national liberation.

The Congo won its independence from French rule in 1960, but on Ngouabi's return to his country in July 1962 he became convinced that the post-colonial government under Fulbert Youlou was staying in power through repression rather than popular support. Commissioned as an officer and posted to the coastal city of Pointe-Noire, he frequently defended the rights of the ranks against the arbitrary rule of the commanding officers.

A three-day national strike involving industrial and white-collar workers in August 1963 proved to be a turning-point and Ngouabi played an active role. A broad social front developed to overthrow the Youlou government, and in June the following year a new political party, the Mouvement Revolutionnaire Nationale (MRN, National Revolutionary Movement), held its constituent congress and announced it would follow socialist policies.

Towards the end of the 1960s, serious divisions developed in the MNR between centrist groupings around President Massamba-Débat and more radical groupings who were demanding a faster pace of economic and political reform. Ngouabi was transferred to Brazzaville in 1965 where he became commander of an infantry battalion. His apartment in Brazzaville became a meeting-place for military personnel opposed to Massamba-Débat's rule.

Ngouabi and his supporters then tried to broaden the opposition movement to include the working class and students, as well as dissident military personnel. Seeing these developments, the military authorities ordered Ngouabi to return to Pointe-Noire. He refused to go. Eventually the authorities rescinded their order and Ngouabi was assigned to research duties at general headquarters in Brazzaville.

By mid-1968 a powerful opposition had formed threatening the Massamba-Débat government which dissolved the national assembly, banned the opposition groupings and arrested their leaders. Ngouabi was arrested on 28 July 1968, but was released by a small group of officers on 31 July. This began the 31 July movement which mobilized enough general support to precipitate the collapse of the Massamba-Débat government.

The National Council of the Revolution was set up in Brazzaville with Ngouabi as chairman and head of state. A year later, the PCT was set up, but its initial programme stressed that the main task of government was to build a national, democratic and popular revolution to fight foreign economic and political influences in the country. Ngouabi defined the battle against foreign economic domination of the Congo as the primary task. He was particularly critical of the 'development aid' industry, arguing that the Congo, like many African countries, was experiencing 'growth without development'.

At the same time, Ngouabi was equally critical of domestic developments, such as inefficiency and corruption in the state-run enterprises, and the widening gap between the party and the masses, shown by the 'revolutionary posturing' of some party members.

Ngouabi's forthright style of leadership made him enemies on both the right and left wing of the party and in turn they attempted coups against him in 1970 and 1971. After an extensive reorganization of the party, culminating in a purge in the mid-1970s, opposition to Ngouabi sharpened from those who saw their position threatened. In the midst of preparations for the PCT congress that year, Ngouabi was assassinated by conspirators on 18 March 1977.

NICs, newly industrializing countries

NICs are those Third World countries which experienced a rapid growth of manufacturing output during the 1970s. As a result of this process of industrialization they have emerged as significant exporters of manufactured goods in the world market. According to the Organization for Economic Cooperation and Development (OECD), the following NICs achieved rapid rates of industrial growth up to the end of the 1970s: Brazil, Hong Kong, Mexico, Singapore, South Korea and Taiwan. The OECD also classifies four southern European countries as NICs: Greece, Portugal, Spain and Yugoslavia.[1] It was almost exclusively the Asian NICs which maintained their success through the 1980s.

In economic terms the growth of the NICs has been remarkable. During the 1970s, while the industrial nations were in a slump, the annual real growth in gross domestic product (▶ GDP) of the NICs averaged 7.5 per cent. During the same period, the growth of manufactured exports of the NICs averaged over 13 per cent a year – and three of these countries exceeded 20 per cent. It was the ability of the NICs to compete effectively in the world market that has drawn attention to their achievements. By 1979 the NICs, especially those of East Asia, were supplying 38 per cent of the OECD's imports of clothing and 30 per cent of its leather goods.

The dramatic development of the NICs was highlighted by their ability to compete against advanced capitalist countries even in sectors like automobile and aircraft production and shipbuilding.

In the 1980s the experience was different. The Latin American NICs were left behind, owing to the effects of the ▶ debt crisis, while the Asian NICs continued to surge ahead. South Korea maintained a growth rate of manufacturing production of nearly 9 per cent a year during the 1980s, while its exports grew by nearly 10 per cent a year. Taiwan, Hong Kong and Singapore had similar success and some other Asian countries, such as Malaysia and Thailand, began to join in the manufactured exports boom.

By 1987 the manufactured exports of South Korea, Taiwan, Hong Kong and Singapore combined amounted to about half of those of the Third World as a whole (compared with 6 per cent for Mexico and Brazil combined); at the same time they were equal to two-thirds of the manufactured exports of the USA and more than half of those of Japan or West Germany.

The success of the NICs throws up a number of interesting questions for economic and development theory. It is worth noting that until recently outside the Western nations the only market-based economies that have managed to build an advanced industry were Japan and South Africa. The obstacles to Third World industrialization have been much discussed and yet in the 1970s and 1980s important strides were made by the NICs.[2]

The large labour force for the new industries has largely been recruited among young women; in the four East Asian NICs of Hong Kong, Singapore, South Korea and Taiwan women form more than half the paid labour force. Employers have preferred to employ women, as did their predecessors in the early years of the English Industrial Revolution, because their oppressed social situation makes them easier to exploit in the factory. This exploitation takes the form of long hours, relatively low wages and a form of work which tends to create severe health problems within a few years. As a result, there is a fairly high level of labour turnover, though as the reserve of labour is reduced this may be changing.

Nevertheless, the initial success of the NICs was based on their ability to rely on low wage rates to compete in what were essentially labour-intensive industries. This advantage was used to good effect against Western competitors. The NICs were also fortunate in that in the 1970s there was plenty of credit available due to the surfeit of ▶ petrodollars. In some cases credit and foreign investment provided the resources for the foreign technology necessary for the new industries. South Korea and Taiwan, however, generated most of their own capital and have moved increasingly into capital-intensive industries.

Can the experience of the NICs be seen as constituting a viable model for other Third World countries? (▶ development). Many, especially those who have clung to ▶ dependency theory, have argued that the growth of the NICs does not constitute real industrialization. It has been suggested that the NICs merely service the economies of the West and

Japan and carry out labour-intensive activities which the advanced countries are no longer interested in pursuing.[3]

That the NICs have benefited from some special favourable circumstances cannot be denied, but that does not constitute an argument against the durability of their achievement. In so far as industrialization in the NICs is dependent on external capital, technology and markets, its viability must be seriously qualified. However, during the 1980s, it has become evident that at least the Asian NICs have acquired a strong internal base for their industrialization. South Korea, copying many of the experiences of Japanese development, has gone a long way towards becoming a powerful industrial nation.

The achievements of the NICs require a balanced assessment. The gains made have to be weighed against the partial character of their transformation. It can be argued that the heavy emphasis on export-led growth has led to the neglect of the domestic sector. In the Latin American NICs new industries in a few sectors coexist with a stagnant hinterland and agriculture remains unreformed. Brazil portrays the most striking paradox: new industries in Saõ Paolo and Rio de Janeiro survive in a sea of poverty and underdevelopment. Life in the north-east of the country has barely been affected by industrialization.

These legitimate reservations notwithstanding, the emergence of the NICs has diminished the dominance of the West over the world economy.

Further reading

L. Turner and N. Macmullen (eds), *The Newly Industrializing Countries: trade and adjustment*, London 1982.

Notes

1. See Organization for Economic Cooperation and Development, *The Impact of the Newly Industrialized Countries on Production and Trade in Manufactures*, Paris 1979.
2. For a discussion of the obstacles to industrialization see B. Sutcliffe, 'Imperialism and industrialization in the Third World' in R. Owen and B. Sutcliffe (eds), *Studies in the Theory of Imperialism*, London 1972.
3. For an influential discussion of the subject see F. Frobel and others, *The New International Division of Labour*, Cambridge 1980.

NIEO, New International Economic Order

The term originates from the Algiers action programme of 1973 which was incorporated in a Declaration and Programme of Action for the Establishment of a New Economic Order by the Sixth Special Session of the UN General Assembly in April 1974. As an objective, the NIEO represented the demand for a thoroughgoing restructuring of the world economy in favour of the South. It was the conclusion drawn by numerous Third World countries that the world capitalist economy discriminates against the poorer countries of the world which motivated the demand for the NIEO.

The main impetus behind the elaboration of the NIEO came from the ▶ non-aligned movement, which made its appearance at the Asian–African conference in Bandung, Indonesia in 1955. This conference of 29 independent nations is traditionally seen as calling into question the world's political order by launching the non-aligned movement. However, there was also a discussion of economic affairs at Bandung and this anticipated the Programme of Action adopted almost twenty years later. The Bandung Conference discussed proposals for economic cooperation between countries of the South. It demanded the stabilization of prices for raw materials and greater control by producer countries over the processing of raw materials. Since the main concern of the non-aligned movement was to win freedom from colonial rule, the discussion of economic equality was not followed up in the succeeding years. Nevertheless, pressure for economic equality on an international scale was evident in the 1950s and 1960s in institutions such as the United Nations (UN).

In 1961 the UN adopted a programme for economic development and the 1960s were designated the First Development Decade. There were other major UN-sponsored initiatives. A United Nations Conference on Trade and Development (▶ UNCTAD) was organized in Geneva in 1964. This conference was important in that for the first time the international debate took the form of a conflict between 'South' and 'North'. During the months leading up to the conference, Third World countries coordinated their policies and acted as a unified bloc. It was through this coordination that the ▶ Group of 77 emerged as a force in international relations; henceforth a measure of unity among the nations of the South was evident at nearly all international forums concerned with development.

Though the Group of 77 acquired prominence and other conferences were organized (e.g. UNCTAD II in New Delhi in 1968), the discussion had few practical consequences. The UN's Development Decade and other initiatives were flops as the demands of the Third World for a new deal were systematically ignored by the West. In the 1970s the focus shifted from the UN to the non-aligned movement. At its meeting in Lusaka, Zambia in 1970 the movement adopted a resolution demanding a fundamental change in the relationship between the Third World and the industrial nations. The final resolution of the Lusaka conference also emphasized the need for cooperation and self-sufficiency among member-states. During the next two years these ideas were further developed and formed the basis of the Programme of Action accepted at the conference of the non-aligned movement in Algiers in 1973.

The following are a sample of the principal proposals put through various resolutions in the NIEO:

(1) the attainment of the UN global development aid targets (0.7 per cent of the gross national product of the donor countries);
(2) linking aid to the creation of special drawing rights (SDRs) at the International Monetary Fund (▶ IMF), which should become the world reserve currency in place of the US dollar;

(3)   the negotiated redeployment of productive capacity in certain industries from developed to underdeveloped countries;

(4)   lower tariffs and non-tariff barriers on manufactured exports from the Third World;

(5)   the transfer of technology from developed to underdeveloped countries by means other than direct foreign investment;

(6)   measures to oblige multinational corporations to contribute to development in the Third World;

(7)   elimination of restrictive practices in international trade which restrict the market share of Third World countries;

(8)   reform of the procedures and structures of the IMF, the World Bank and the International Development Association in order to facilitate financial transfers to the Third World;

(9)   measures to improve the competitiveness of natural resource exports vis-à-vis synthetics;

(10) the renegotiation and reduction of Third World debts;

(11) creation of buffer stocks and price stabilization and compensation schemes for exports of primary products;

(12) freedom of choice of economic, social and political system and of international economic relations;

(13) the right of countries to sovereignty over their natural resources;

(14) compensation for damage done to natural and other resources during colonialism;

(15) the use of funds from disarmament to finance Third World development;

(16) restructuring of the UN to meet development needs of the Third World.

It is hardly necessary to say that in most respects the structure and functioning of the world economy has gone, sometimes quite a long way, in the opposite direction since these demands were formulated in the 1960s and 1970s. There is more debt, less aid, less support for primary products and more protectionism. To be sure, there is a new international economic order but it is a travesty of what was envisaged by the formulators of the NIEO.

To this day, therefore, the NIEO remains merely an idea. Nevertheless, it is an idea that cannot be ignored. It is clear that the distribution of the world's wealth and economic equality are issues that are here to stay. In the meantime any progress towards the realization of the NIEO will come from united initiatives by the countries of the South rather than international negotiation.

Further reading
J. Williamson, *The Open Economy and the World Economy*, New York 1983.

NJM, New Jewel Movement

Founded in 1973 by Maurice Bishop (1944–83), the NJM established a revolutionary regime in Grenada in 1979 and remained in power until its overthrow by US military forces in October 1983. The NJM represents a unique experiment in the application of ▶ black power politics to the conditions of the Caribbean. The main influences on the development of Bishop were: the writings of Fidel ▶ Castro, Frantz ▶ Fanon, Ernesto 'Che' ▶ Guevara, Malcolm X and Kwame ▶ Nkrumah; the black revolt in the USA in the late 1960s; and black power uprisings in Trinidad and Tobago in 1970. The NJM adapted many of the themes current in the discussions of the black power movement. State repression of the previous Gairy regime in Grenada had a radicalizing effect on the NJM, and during the mid-1970s the movement assimilated many aspects of the Marxist viewpoint. On 13 March 1979, in alliance with a group of senior army and police officers, the NJM carried out an insurrection and assumed power.

The policy adopted by the NJM was one of gradual reforms designed to improve the quality of life of the 100,000 inhabitants of this tiny island. Though the scope for reforms was modest, they represented a major improvement in the life of the population. This was in sharp contrast with conditions in the neighbouring Caribbean states. The main reforms were free secondary education, free milk and school lunches, maternity leave for women, land reform and the establishment of cooperatives in agriculture and fishing. These policies and the efficient deployment of resources and foreign assistance led to steady economic growth and the reduction of unemployment from 50 per cent to 12 per cent. However, it was in the sphere of foreign affairs that the NJM acquired an international reputation and in the process provoked the wrath of the USA. The People's Revolutionary Government (PRG) became an articulate advocate of national liberation movements. Bishop became known as a leading Third World statesman and Grenada became a leading force in the ▶ non-aligned movement. The PRG was effective in its opposition to US intervention in the Caribbean and successfully pre-empted several attempts by Washington to isolate Grenada.

That the NJM could not prevent its overthrow by superior US forces can in no way detract from its achievements. Nevertheless, the PRG left a number of critical issues unresolved which may have contributed to its ultimate demise. In the economic sphere the PRG attempted to establish a mixed economy based on a thriving state sector and private capital. The relative prosperity of the local capitalist class ensured that private enterprise retained considerable appeal among the masses – limiting support for socialist measures. Growing social inequality between rich and poor created the inevitable tensions undermining the case for further reforms.

It was in the sphere of politics that the NJM made its most serious mistakes. Throughout its four years' existence the NJM failed to address the questions of political participation and mobilization. Though it retained popular support the NJM did little to establish popular institutions of political debate and discussion and, despite its intentions, excluded the masses from political life.

In the absence of the need to be accountable to its supporters the NJM acquired many of the bad habits associated with élite politics. Intolerant of criticism and aloof from everyday life, political discussion in the NJM became inward-looking. Debates acquired the character of personality clashes and eventually got out of hand. In October 1983 the deputy prime minister, Bernard Coard, overthrew Bishop on the grounds that the founder of the NJM was counter-revolutionary. The lack of popular involvement in the NJM was a material factor in making the coup possible. In the fighting that ensued, forces loyal to Coard killed Bishop, three cabinet ministers and more than a hundred of Bishop's supporters. These atrocities not only implied the destruction of the NJM experiment but also helped prepare the way for the US invasion.

It is clear that no matter what happened Washington would have invaded Grenada, but the coup carried out by Coard provided Washington with a semblance of an excuse. Worse still, it helped undermine the moral authority which the NJM achieved in such a short period of time. The ultimate destruction of the NJM experiment can in no way negate the contribution that it made to the politics of Third World liberation. Under massive US pressure, this tiny island inspired millions in the Third World. The defiance of the NJM gave confidence to people throughout the Caribbean, and Maurice Bishop remains one of the most original contributors and practitioners of the politics of non-alignment. In passing it should be noted that the US invasion of Grenada constitutes one of the most sordid episodes of gunboat displomacy in the post-war period.

Nkomati Accord

The River Nkomati is the border between Mozambique and South Africa and a non-aggression pact between the two countries was signed at the Komatiport resort on the river in March 1984. Mozambique agreed to refrain from harbouring African National Congress guerrillas who were launching attacks on South Africa, while South Africa agreed to stop backing the RENAMO rebel movement operating in Mozambique. South Africa has since admitted that it breached the agreement. ▶ FRELIMO.

Nkrumah, Kwame (1909–72) and Nkrumahism

For many African intellectuals, the ideas of Kwame Nkrumah provide the most coherent expression of the perspective of ▶ Pan-Africanism and ▶ liberation. For example, according to Kwame Touré (formerly Stokely Carmichael), 'the highest political expression of Black Power is Pan-Africanism and the highest expression of Pan-Africanism is Nkrumahism.'

Nkrumah was born at Ankroful on 18 September 1909 and educated at Achimota College in what was then known as the Gold Coast, and then at Lincoln University, Pennsylvania and the London School of Economics. Returning to Africa in 1949 he formed the Convention People's Party. He was sent to prison by the British authorities but while there he was elected to parliament under a new constitution. In 1951 the British were obliged to release him and he became Leader of Government Business in the Assembly. He was confirmed in power by the election of 1956 and became prime minister of the independent state of Ghana in 1957 and president of the republic in 1960. He was overthrown by a Western-inspired military coup in 1966 while on a visit to China. He returned to Guinea where he was declared joint head of state. He died in 1972.

Nkrumah's outstanding intellectual achievement was not as a politician or as a philosopher. In both of these domains he made important contributions, but it can be argued that his philosophical writings are of limited relevance to Africa and that as leader of Ghana his political experiment failed to realize its objectives. Nkrumah's main achievement was his ability to synthesize the experience of Africa in the crucial decades of the 1950s and 1960s. Nkrumah's own struggle against British colonialism, and afterwards against the forces of neo-colonialism, provided him with the necessary experiences for developing African political thought.

After his overthrow Nkrumah set about working out the problems facing African liberation. Previously, Nkrumah showed an appreciation of the limited significance of political independence for ex-colonies. He constantly argued that independence was not the end but a means to real freedom. However, during the period of the transfer of power he tended to underestimate the difficulties that stood in his way.

In particular, he was not yet aware of the strength of the local forces of imperialism, which, in collaboration with the old colonial powers, sabotaged attempts at progress. Nkrumah's attempt to use the institutions left behind by the colonial powers ended in his own political destruction. From the experience of defeat, Nkrumah drew the conclusion that there was an urgent need for a major rethink of the strategy for African liberation.[1]

It was this process of assessment that pushed Nkrumah to reanalyse the situation and develop his concept of neo-colonialism. In line with this reassessment came a reorientation of tactics and strategy. Hitherto, Nkrumah had emphasized non-violence as the main method of anti-imperialist struggle. However, with the experience of the previous decade it became manifest that non-violent forms of struggle could not seriously challenge the armed might of the puppet regimes backed by the Central Intelligence Agency. In his book *Class Struggle in Africa*, a major reorientation in tactics is evident. He writes:

> Under neo-colonialism a new form of violence is being used against the people of Africa. It takes the form of indirect political domination through the indigenous bourgeoisie and puppet governments tele-guided and marionetted by neo-colonialists; direct economic exploitation through an extension of the operations of giant inter-locking corporations; and through all manner of other insidious ways such as the control of the mass communication media and ideological penetration.
>
> In these circumstances, the need for armed struggle has arisen once more. For the liberation and unification of Africa cannot be achieved by consent, by moral precept or moral conquest. It is only through

resort to arms that Africa can rid herself of the remaining vestiges of colonialism, and of imperialism and neo-colonialism; and a socialist society can be established in a free and united continent.[2]

This emphasis on armed struggle is not the product of some morbid fascination with violence. It represents a recognition of a trend towards the armed suppression of the anti-imperialist struggle in Africa. The armed struggle is not a choice but a necessity under these conditions. This lesson has been learned by the liberation movements in southern Africa. Today, after the numerous military invasions and interventions in Africa, Nkrumah's message has grown in relevance.

In his reassessment of tactics and strategy, Nkrumah developed his perspective on the achievement of pan-African unity. He warned that the Organization of African Unity (▶ OAU) was fast becoming an obstacle to African unity instead of a force for change:

An examination of recent weeks exposes serious weaknesses within the OAU. The organisation failed to solve the crisis in the Congo and Rhodesia: both of them test cases . . . . In fact the OAU is in danger of developing into a useful river for the confused sterile action of conflicting interests, the only difference being that in the context of one big brotherly organization, reactionary tactics are camouflaged and applied through negotiations.[3]

According to Nkrumah, the OAU had become a face-saving device for many African governments which were hostile to the objectives of Pan-Africanism. Such governments could then use the inaction of the OAU as an excuse for their own lack of action on issues like apartheid.

From his review of the OAU, Nkrumah drew the conclusion that the struggle for African unity would not get very far through reliance on diplomacy and government-to-government negotiations. He proposed that in future the struggle should be conducted through a unified command, coordinating progressive forces. In other words, Nkrumah saw the unity of like-minded forces as the point of departure for the liberation of Africa. In 1968 he argued for the establishment of the All-African People's Revolutionary Party (AAPRP) and the creation of an All-African People's Revolutionary Army:

The formation of a political party linking all liberated territories and struggling parties under a common ideology will smooth the way for eventual unity, and will at the same time greatly assist the prosecution of the All-African people's war. To assist the process of its formation, an All-African Committee for Political Co-ordination (AACPC) should be established to act as a liaison between all parties which recognise the urgent necessity of conducting an organised and unified struggle against colonisation and neo-colonialism. This committee would be created at the level of the central committee of the ruling parties, and would consolidate their integrated political consciousness.[4]

With this shift in forces, Nkrumah attempted to revitalize Pan-Africanism by basing it firmly on the mass movements. Nkrumah believed that, through the unification of like-minded progressive forces drawn from across the continent, an effective liberation movement could emerge.

Finally, Nkrumah had a keen perception of the common destiny of the peoples of the Third World. Though he was a pan-Africanist his vision was internationalist. In many respects it was his understanding of the international character of the class struggle that turned him into such a forceful advocate of Pan-Africanism. His message of liberation, though drawn from the experience of Africa, is profoundly universal. C.L.R. James, a leading black theoretician, considered Nkrumah to be one of the four great statesmen of the twentieth century alongside such giants as Gandhi, Lenin and Mao Zedong.[5] His role in history is not yet decided and it will only be resolved through the outcome of Africa's contemporary crisis.

Notes

1. See K.B. Hadjor, *Nkrumah and Ghana*, London 1988, pp. 88–95 from which this analysis is drawn.
2. K. Nkrumah, *Class Struggle in Africa*, London 1970.
3. K. Nkrumah, *Revolutionary Path*, London 1971, p. 472.
4. Ibid., p. 486.
5. See C.L.R. James, *Nkrumah and the Ghana Revolution*, London 1977, p. 189.

non-aligned movement

After the conference of Afro-Asian nations in ▶ Bandung in 1955 a somewhat more ambitious and permanent proposal for cooperation among the newly independent Third World countries was launched. The non-aligned movement established itself in 1961 in a conscious effort to increase the weight of the Third World in an increasingly bipolar world dominated by the ▶ Cold War. Politically, therefore, the non-aligned movement was the most important effort to give an organizational form to the concept of a Third World with different priorities.

There have been eight non-aligned summit conferences: 1961, Belgrade; 1964, Cairo; 1970, Lusaka; 1973, Algiers; 1976, Colombo; 1979, Havana; 1983, New Delhi; 1986, Harare. The three-year periodicity has now been broken and no new summit seems imminent.

The non-aligned movement has disappeared, and long ago ceased to be important for many reasons. First, most of its members were deeply aligned, being client states of one or other of the superpowers. Second, despite many pious resolutions, the movement was not able to solve any of the major conflicts between its own members. Third, the movement had no resources or ongoing existence aside from the summits, and so the resolutions were little more than showpieces. It did, however, pass a vast number of resolutions, most of them supporting elements of the proposed New International Economic Order (▶ NIEO) or demanding a peaceful settlement of all international disputes. Meanwhile its members prepared for or waged war (▶ military spending). Its failure to develop a truly independent Third World presence in world affairs was the international expression of the fact that its member states had formally, but not fully, gained their independence (▶ liberation, ▶ neo-colonialism, post-colonial state). In 1991, Indonesia assumed the chairmanship of the moribund institution.

Further reading

G.H. Jansen, *Afro-Asia and Non-Alignment*, London 1966.

G. Willetts, *The Non-Aligned Movement: the origins of the Third World Alliance*, London 1978.

North–South dialogue

This concept refers to the opening up of communications between the rich industrialized countries of the North and the poor underdeveloped countries of the South with the aim of considering the poverty of the latter and possible ways of alleviating it. The first North–South conference took place in Paris in December 1975.

If the idea of a North–South dialogue remains implicit in much of international relations, the possibility of improving the situation of the South through some collective negotiation is very far indeed from the present realm of the possible. Even in the case of the problems of debt – faced by so many countries of the South – each country is treated as a separate case by the creditors; and the debtors have been loath to show too much of a common front. In the trade negotiations within ▶ GATT, some Third World countries have grouped together but usually as supporters of one country of the North against others; but in the long run the North–South dialogue may reappear as the only alternative to growing confrontation between the North and the South.

NPA, New People's Army

This Filipino guerrilla movement was formed in 1969 and originated in the Hukbalahap (Huks, People's Anti-Japanese Army), a guerrilla movement formed by the Filipino Communist Party (PKP) in 1942 to fight the Japanese occupation in central southern Luzon. In 1945, led by Luis Taruk, it joined the Democratic Alliance formed by the newly installed President Sergio Osmeña to campaign for immediate independence from the USA; in this the Huks were the largest component. The Alliance was defeated in the post-war elections by the pro-collaborationist party led by Manuel Roxas. The PKP split over how to deal with the reactionary offensive: some, led by José Lava, the PKP's secretary of organization, favoured reviving the armed struggle, while others, led by Pedro Castro, the party leader, backed a parliamentary campaign. Lava won out and the Huks renewed the guerrilla campaign against landlords, renaming their movement the People's Liberation Army, which was banned.

In October 1950 Lava and other leaders were arrested and eventually bought off, while the US Central Intelligence Agency counter-insurgency expert Edward Lansdale, later to be one of the first CIA agents in South Vietnam, effectively took over the Filipino armed forces. Taruk was captured in 1954. Jesus Lava became leader of the PKP and it became a pro-establishment force, accepting the parliamentary road in 1955 after the collapse of the armed struggle. By the time President Marcos declared an emergency in 1972, Lava was urging his members to support it and join the constabulary.

With the PKP inactive in the 1960s, students at the University of the Philippines began to campaign against the government. They were organized by José Maria Sison, a poet, who set up youth, labour and peasant organizations, and in 1968 established his breakaway Communist Party of the Philippines, based on 'Marxism-Leninism-Mao Zedong Thought' (though the link with Beijing did not last long). It advocated armed struggle combined with political struggle ('protracted people's war') among the rural masses, seeking to avoid what it saw as the urban-centred 'putschism' and stress on conventional warfare waged by the Huks.

It soon fused with surviving Huk factions and in 1969 they established the New People's Army which aimed at carrying out an agrarian revolution, building rural bases, advancing the armed struggle and helping construct a united national front. Initially their stress was on practical help to the peasants to improve their everyday lot.

Following the emergency in 1972 Sison adapted the NPA's strategy to take account of the fact that the Philippines is an archipelago, seeing the solution in the creation of a number of separate guerrilla fronts on different islands, each of them having a considerable degree of autonomy from the party centre. The NPA dropped the armed struggle in 1975. Sison was captured in 1977 and was replaced as leader by Rafael Baylosis, a University of the Philippines graduate.

Meanwhile the Muslim-based Moro National Liberation Front (MNLF), formed in 1972 in western Mindanao, was actively waging armed struggle against the government with funds from both radical and conservative Muslim states. The MNLF itself has come to be dominated by a conservative interpretation of Islam, though there are several factions.

By 1980 the NPA had revived its own armed struggle, claiming 26 fronts in Luzon, the Visaya Islands and the eastern, Christian, half of Mindanao. In 1983 the Communist Party of the Philippines claimed membership of 30,000 and the NPA claimed to have over 20,000 members on 45 fronts. It acquired most of its weapons from the security forces and got little outside help. Where it was best entrenched, in north-east Luzon, it set up an alternative administration.

To extend its influence in the urban areas, it set up the National Democratic Front (NDF) in 1978, with a strongly socialist and anti-US 10-point programme. It received much support from the Roman Catholic Church through the Christian Left movement set up in 1972 which has cooperated with the NPA in passing messages, transporting the wounded and so on.

In June 1981 the NDF was able to mobilize rural supporters to boycott the elections, and it joined with the forces led by Corazón Aquino to boycott the 1984 elections. By that year the NDF was claiming 50,000 full-time organizers in two-thirds of the country and 1 million members in its constituent mass organizations. The success of the NDF led the NPA to restrict its activities to the more remote rural areas.[1]

In 1986 Cory Aquino and 'People Power' swept Marcos out of office. The NDF took a position of guarded support on condition freedoms were restored and human rights violators punished. Aquino's subsequent success led many middle class supporters of the NPA and NDF to leave and they began to reassess the policy of boycotting elections.

In the countryside the NPA's struggle has continued. Over objections from within the military, Aquino tried to get it to negotiate, but a truce arranged in December 1986 was short-lived. The military has increasingly resorted to organizing death-squads to work with landlords to kill land reform. Such moves have won new support for the NPA. In 1987 it began to shift resources to the cities to try and gain control of the urban movement that had supported Aquino.

Further reading

E.G. and J.M. Maring, *Historical and Cultural Dictionary of the Philippines*, New Jersey 1973.

Note

1. See D.A. Rosenberg, 'Communism in the Philippines', *Problems of Communism*, Sept.–Oct. 1984; and Z. Grossman, 'Inside the Philippine resistance', *Race and Class*, 23 (2), Autumn 1986.

O

OAU, Organization of African Unity

The OAU was founded by 30 African states in Addis Ababa on 25 May 1963, but subsequently crippled by divisions among the member countries over their relations with the Western powers and liberation movements.

By the start of the 1960s, the independent black African states were beginning to form two distinct blocs. At a conference in Casablanca, Morocco in January 1961, Ghana's Kwame Nkrumah sponsored a radical bloc comprising his own country, Egypt, Guinea, Mali and Morocco plus representatives from the Algerian provisional government and from Libya. The Casablanca bloc favoured the political unity of Africa.

A second bloc of 19 states met in Monrovia, Liberia in May 1961, under the sponsorship of President Tubman of Liberia, Emperor Haile Selassie of Ethiopia and Prime Minister Tafawa Balewa of Nigeria. This more conservative bloc favoured economic cooperation rather than political unity, and strongly backed the principle of non-intervention in the internal affairs of sovereign states.

When the OAU was formed, its charter mainly reflected the interests of the Monrovia bloc, but as a concession to the Casablanca delegates, the OAU established the Coordinating Committee for the Liberation Movements of Africa (or African Liberation Committee, ALC). This aimed at removing the colonial presence from the rest of Africa, in particular the Portuguese and the South African state. The ALC began by making a major error, however, when it backed the Central Intelligence Agency-sponsored FNLA in the Angolan war against Portugal (▶ Angolan liberation movement). Only in 1974 did it rectify its position by backing the popular MPLA. It has always refused any support to the fronts in the ▶ Eritrean liberation movement.

The OAU has been seriously weakened by divisions between the member-states, mainly along black/Arab lines. These were most sharply exposed in differences over the wars in the Western Sahara (▶ POLISARIO), Chad (▶ Gadhafi), Ethiopia and Uganda. In 1982 a majority of members voted to recognize POLISARIO as the government of Western Sahara. Morocco and 19 other states walked out of the summit and Morocco has never returned, resigning its membership in 1985. After protracted negotiations the other countries returned in 1983 and remain members even though POLISARIO continues to be recognized, though not as a full member.

The split led the OAU increasingly to avoid difficult political questions and the meetings now confine themselves largely to passing resolutions with little force on economic questions, such as one condemning the dumping of toxic wastes in Africa and another calling for measures to alleviate the debt burden of African countries. The attendance of heads of state at the summits has declined and the organization has become increasingly marginal to the affairs of the continent. With the accession of Namibia in 1990 the OAU has 51 member states.

Further reading

E. M'buyinga, *Panafricanism or neo-colonialism? The bankruptcy of the OAU*, London 1982.

ODA ▶ aid

OECD, Organization for Economic Cooperation and Development

The 24-member international body was established in Paris in September 1961 with the aim of achieving the highest sustainable economic growth and employment on a rising standard of living among members, while maintaining financial stability and contributing to the expansion of world trade. Its members are (except for Greece, Portugal and Turkey) the rich, industrialized, capitalist countries of North America, Western Europe and Japan. Its Development Assistance Committee (▶ DAC) coordinates Western aid policies through conferences and the centralization of information.

official development assistance ▶ aid

OPEC, Organization of Petroleum Exporting Countries

Founded in September 1960 by Iraq, Saudi Arabia, Iran, Kuwait and Venezuela, OPEC tried to organize a price cartel against the oil majors but did not succeed until the 1973 Arab–Israeli war. The Arab members of OPEC organized a boycott of those countries which backed Israel. The price of oil rocketed and the oil sheikhs were blamed by many in the West for the onset of major economic recession. In fact, however, the fourfold increase in the crude oil price which OPEC imposed during the crisis was also tacitly accepted by the oil companies and by the government of the USA, which hoped that it might do more damage to its oil-importing competitors, West Germany and Japan, than to itself.

The OPEC price rise produced a major redistribution of wealth and liquidity in the world economy, especially towards the Gulf States which had high oil production and low population. Their income increased dramatically and they accumulated huge overseas assets which became the ▶ petrodollars which when recycled became the debt of Latin America.

OPEC was able to maintain enough internal unity during the 1970s to control the world market and keep oil prices high, imposing another major increase in 1979–80. During the 1980s, however, the power of OPEC collapsed. This was in part because of the coming onstream of major new oilfields in non-OPEC countries, but also because of major conflicts of interest between OPEC members, including the Iran–Iraq war and later the invasion of Kuwait by Iraq in 1990.

In 1989 OPEC countries produced only 36.5 per cent of current world petroleum output and its efforts to raise the price in the aftermath of the 1991 Gulf War were in vain. None the less, OPEC cannot yet be written out of history. If it produces only a little more than a third of current output, its member states possess more than three-quarters of the world's known reserves and account for an even higher share of recent discoveries. If OPEC holds together, it can therefore expect within a decade or two to wield tremendous market power once again.

Many Third World primary product producers in the 1970s looked enviously towards OPEC in the hope of setting up a cartel of similar power for their own raw material export. Despite many attempts, none have really been successful. The reasons are many, the main ones being conflicts between producing countries and the fact that most Third World primary exports are not as economically indispensable as oil.

The current membership of OPEC includes its founder members with the addition of Algeria, Bahrain, Brunei, Educador, Gabon, Indonesia, Libya, Nigeria, Oman, Qatar, Trinidad and Tobago, and the United Arab Emirates.

Further reading

F.J. Al-Chalabi, *OPEC at the Crossroads*, Oxford 1989.

R. Mabro (ed.), *OPEC and the World Oil Market: the genesis of the 1986 price crisis*, Oxford 1986.

Organization for Economic Cooperation and Development ▶ OECD

Organization of African Unity ▶ OAU

Organization of Petroleum Exporting Countries ▶ OPEC

Ortega Saevedra, Daniel (1945–)

Daniel Ortega Saevedra was born in 1945 in south-west Nicaragua and was educated at the Universidad Centroamericana in Managua. Politically active from 1959, he edited *El Estudiante*, the official organ of the Frente Estudiantil Revolucionaria, and in 1966 became a member of the National Directorate of the FSLN (▶ Sandinistas); he was imprisoned between 1967 and 1974, being freed in a hostage exchange organized by the Sandinistas. He was flown to Cuba, returning secretly in 1976 to take a commanding role in the guerrilla war.

This was a moment of considerable weakness and strategic disunity among the Sandinistas, whose leaders were divided into two tendencies: the Proletarian tendency and the Prolonged People's War tendency. Daniel Ortega, his brother Humberto, and Victor Tirado formed a third tendency, the Terceristas, which advocated bold military initiatives in the cities as a means to provoke a revolutionary insurrection. The circumstances proved propitious for such an initiative and, when later the tendencies reunified, Daniel Ortega was well placed to play a leading political role.

In 1979 Daniel Ortega was prominent in the overthrow of President Somoza and became a member of the ruling junta. In the 1984 elections he was the Sandinista candidate for the presidency and was elected with 66.9 per cent of the votes. He led the country through its confrontation with the USA, the US-backed ▶ Contras and an ever-graver economic crisis. Under pressure from his Central American neighbours and the country's main supplier, the USSR, he was obliged, in 1988, to engage in direct negotiations with the Contras. The decline in the level of the Contra war was not enough to stem a tide of disillusion with the Sandinistas and he lost the 1990 presidential election to Violetta Barrios de Chamorro who was heading a coalition of right-wing parties.

Daniel Ortega retains considerable prestige and has continued to play a leading role in Nicaraguan politics since Chamorro's government has been obliged, by the disunity of the electoral coalition which brought it to power, to seek Sandinista support.

239

P

PAC, Pan-Africanist Congress

This South African black nationalist movement was formed in 1959 by Africans in the African National Congress (▶ ANC) unhappy with the policy of cooperation with whites. The leading theoretician of the group, Robert Sobukwe, was elected president. The PAC won support among black workers in southern Transvaal and among migrant workers in the Cape with a campaign against the pass laws.

In March 1960 it organized a rally at Sharpeville; the police shot dead 67 black protestors. The PAC was banned in the ensuing wave of repression, and Sobukwe was arrested, dying in 1978. PAC members fled to Lesotho and Botswana and prepared to launch an armed struggle. Potlako Leballo led the military wing Poqo (Xhosa = pure). It turned to Beijing for support and was recognized by the Organization of African Unity (▶ OAU) and the United Nations but it was riven by factionalism and South African police raids smashed it in 1965. Some members joined the ▶ black consciousness movement in the 1970s. In 1979 Leballo was ousted and replaced by John Pokela.

Its leaders began to be released from jail in the thaw of 1990 and the organization retains some support. In 1991 it negotiated with the ANC a united front against apartheid, though this agreement has still to be put to the test.

pacification

This controversial term means either (1) peace-keeping or (2) the use of armed force to terrorize into submission the population of a region or to put down any demonstration against authority.

PAIGC, Partido Africano da Independência da Guiné e Cabo Verde
(African Party for the Independence of Guinea and Cape Verde)

Founded in 1956 by Amilcar Lopes ▶ Cabral as the African Party for the Independence and Union of the Peoples of Guinea and Cape Verde (PAI), it was renamed in 1960. The PAIGC was the liberation movement which ended Portuguese rule in Guinea-Bissau and the Cape Verde islands. Initially the party was predominantly made up of clerks and civil servants, but soon won working class support, especially after the brutal repression of the dock strike in 1959 when 50 strikers were killed. In 1960–1 it organized a mass agitation campaign to secure an end to colonial rule and then moved to armed struggle on the mainland. By 1970 it had won control of two-thirds of the countryside. While the countries of the North Atlantic Treaty Organization armed Portugal, the USSR began to sell arms to the PAIGC in the early 1970s. In 1973 the United Nations recognized the PAIGC which in September of the same year declared independence. In 1974, within a month of the military coup in Portugal, a Portuguese delegation arrived to negotiate independence. Luis Cabral, Amilcar's brother, was the first president of Guinea-Bissau. He was overthrown in 1980 by the prime minister and former commander-in-chief, João Bernardo Vieira, in a coup which was widely seen as a Guinean attack on Cape Verdeans, many of whom were now removed from the government. Cape Verde broke with the PAIGC, and diplomatic relations were only restored two years later. Under Vieira, initially a military ruler but elected president in 1984, Guinea-Bissau has moved towards reconciliation with Portugal and closer ties with the West.

Further reading

Basil Davidson, *The Liberation of Guiné*, Harmondsworth 1969.
L. Rudebeck, *Guiné-Bissau: a study in political mobilization*, Uppsala 1974.

Palestine Liberation Organization ▶ PLO

Pan-Africanism

This ideology is based on the view that African unity is the only practical foundation for the liberation and development of the continent.

From the late nineteenth century, the development of Pan-Africanism is clearly in evidence. The colonial partition of Africa divided up the continent into a number of artificially created territorial units. The people of Africa were uprooted according to the convenience of the colonial administrators, with little regard for their history and culture.

Indeed, the establishment of colonial rule was explicitly oriented towards the destruction of Africa's history. According to the European colonialists, Africa was a tabula rasa, it had no history or cultural identity. From the beginning of colonial rule, the people of Africa struggled to assert their identity. Increasingly, the intellectuals of the continent searched out the common elements in Africa's experience. In the late nineteenth century, Ethiopia emerged as a symbol of black emancipation. Ethiopia's independence and successful resistance to colonial domination provided an important focus for the development of a new African identity. New Churches and religions sprang up in the late nineteenth century in Africa which called themselves Ethiopian Churches.

The emergence of the Ethiopian Churches was the first manifestation of the growing aspiration for a liberated Africa. That this inspiration first took on a religious form is entirely understandable since African politics were severely restricted in colonial Africa. Nevertheless, the spread of the idea of African liberation in its religious form was to have important political consequences. It meant that chronologically the idea of African liberation preceded the emergence of more specific nationalist identities based on the particular territorial units.

The growth of the African identity was reinforced by the very nature of colonial partition. African societies became fragmented and mixed

241

together in units which made little sense. The Somalis were distributed in four territorial units: in British, French and Italian Somaliland as well as in Ethiopia. The Ewes were divided up between the Gold Coast and British and French Togoland. Similarly, the Bacongo were fragmented by the colonial boundary that separated the French Middle Congo, the Belgian Congo and Portuguese-held Angola. Under these circumstances it became increasingly clear that freedom from colonialism required a unity that transcended the prevailing territorial frontiers.

The original impetus behind Pan-Africanism came from the USA. Black Americans looked upon African unity as an important weapon in their fight against oppression. During the 1920s, the objective of liberating Africa won widespread support among black Americans. The militant black nationalist movement of Marcus Garvey (▶ Garveyism) promoted Africa as the home of all African blacks. Garvey's movement, the Universal Negro Improvement Association (UNIA), had as its goal the establishment of Liberia as the home for the mass emigration of US and West Indian blacks. Though this project failed in its intent, the millions of US blacks who joined the UNIA indicated growing support for the African identity.

The formation of the pan-African movement as a coherent political force is closely linked to the work of the US black leader, W.E.B. Du Bois (1868–1963). From the turn of the century onwards, Du Bois launched a series of initiatives designed to bring together representatives from all parts of the black diaspora. Under the influence of Du Bois, a series of conferences between Africans, Afro-Americans and West Indians were held in 1900, 1919, 1921, 1923, 1927 and 1945. The 1945 conference, held in Manchester, England, brought together many of the future leaders of the anti-colonial movement in Africa such as Nnamdi Azikiwe, Jomo ▶ Kenyatta and Kwame ▶ Nkrumah.

In the aftermath of the 1945 pan-Africanist conference, the initiative for the advance of the movement passed into the hands of radical African politicians. As a result, the pan-Africanist perspective became an important influence on the anti-colonial movement. During the anti-colonial struggle, Ghana emerged as the centre of Pan-Africanism. There the Convention People's Party was explicitly committed to the pan-Africanist ideal. Its constitution affirmed its determination 'to support the demand for a West African Federation and . . . Pan-Africanism by promoting unity of action among peoples of Africa and African descent'.[1]

During the 1950s, Pan-Africanism began to experience a major crisis. Most anti-colonial leaders still gave rhetorical support to the pan-Africanist ideal but, by the latter part of the decade, it became clear that their concern was with winning political power within the confines of their territorial units. After independence, their rhetorical support for Pan-Africanism was revealed as a meaningless gesture.

The separation of Pan-Africanism from the perspective of the newly formed governments of independent Africa coincided with the mounting influence of conservatism on the movement. In its origins Pan-Africanism represented a radical affirmation of human liberation. In the 1940s Marxism and socialism were important influences on Pan-Africanism. At the 1945 pan-African congress, the resolutions adopted were phrased in explicitly radical language.

During the process of decolonization, radical African leaders became less and less inclined to fight for fundamental social change. The colonial authorities fought hard to transform the nationalist movement into moderate parties that could be relied on to perpetuate the existing socio-economic structures. Either radicals had to conform or they were victimized. Increasingly, Pan-Africanism was presented in conservative terms, as an alternative to radical change. George Padmore, a sometime communist writer and organizer of Trinidadian origin, was an important advocate of a moderate pro-capitalist Pan-Africanism. His book *Pan-Africanism or Communism: the coming struggle for Africa* (1956) summed up the approach.

During the post-colonial era, Pan-Africanism has become a meaning-less doctrine. Clearly, without a radical perspective Pan-Africanism can have no practical consequences. Pan-Africanism can only acquire meaning through a struggle to overcome the legacy of colonialism – its boundaries and socio-economic structures. The Organization of African Unity (▶ OAU) represents the very antithesis of the pan-Africanist approach. The OAU is formally committed to African unity – yet the energies of most of its members are entirely absorbed in safeguarding the integrity of the post-colonial institutions. Even the challenge posed by the apartheid system of Pretoria to the integrity of Africa has not been sufficient to force the OAU to take practical measures to unify the continent.

The most serious alternative to the talking-shop approach of the OAU was the attempt of Ghana under Nkrumah to give some real meaning to Pan-Africanism. Under Nkrumah, Ghana became the first practitioner of a pan-Africanist foreign policy. In the period 1958–61, Nkrumah initiated a number of pan-Africanist projects. The All-African People's Con-ference held in December 1958 in Ghana brought together repre-sentatives from all over the continent. This was the first genuine all-African assembly. In Ghana, agencies like the African Affairs Secretariat and the All-African Trade Union Federation were established.

The focus of Nkrumah's foreign policy was the establishment of a unitary African state. Nkrumah's call for a 'Union Government of Africa' received widespread popular support, and even those African leaders who opposed it did not dare to take a stand against it in public. For a while it appeared that Nkrumah's policies were on the verge of a breakthrough. In November 1958 the formation of the Ghana–Guinea Union represented the first tentative step towards African unification. This union attracted the support of Mali in 1961. However, this is as far as Nkrumah was able to go. By 1961 it had become clear that the leaders of most of the newly independent African states were not prepared to unite. To preempt the constitution of a mass pan-Africanist movement, the conservative leaders founded the OAU. The OAU, nominally established to promote African unity, was really set up to prevent it.

Through the establishment of the OAU, Pan-Africanism was turned into an intellectual gesture. The pleas of Nkrumah for practical action

243

met with a stony silence. At the second conference of the OAU in 1964, Nkrumah warned: 'Every day we delay the establishment of a Union Government of Africa, we subject ourselves to outside economic domination. And our political independence as separate states becomes more and more meaningless'.[2]

Nkrumah's warning was prophetic. An Africa divided along the old colonial boundaries cannot sustain its people. It is unviable economically and too fragmented to resist outside political pressure. Africa has become an economic disaster area easily manipulated by the old colonial powers.

The setback to Pan-Africanism during the post-independence period does not mean that as a worldview it has become irrelevant. Indeed, Pan-Africanism is more relevant to the needs of the continent than at any time previously. There are indications that a new generation of African thinkers is giving the subject the attention that it deserves. One of the most powerful advocates of Pan-Africanism is Elenga M'buyinga, a leader of the Union des Populations du Cameroun. He argues that the only alternative to a pan-African solution is the continuation of imperialist domination. For M'buyinga, independence as it is now constituted is bogus and only a pan-Africanist orientation can bring about the liberation of the continent.[3]

With the tragic experience of neo-colonialism as its background, Pan-Africanism is set for a new stage in its development.

Further reading
R.H. Green and A. Seldman, *Unity or Poverty? The economics of pan-Africanism*, Baltimore, Md. 1968.

Notes
1. Cited in T. Hodgkin, *Nationalism in Colonial Africa*, New York 1957, p. 161.
2. K. Nkrumah, *Revolutionary Path*, London 1971, p. 288.
3. See E. M'buyinga, *Pan-Africanism or Neo-Colonialism: the bankruptcy of the OAU*, London 1982.

Pan-Africanist Congress ▶ PAC

Partido Africano da Independência da Guiné e Cabo Verde ▶ PAIGC

Partido Comunista de Perú ▶ Sendero Luminoso

Partido Revolucionario de los Trabajadores ▶ PRT

Partido Revolucionario Institucional ▶ PRI

Peace Corps
This US volunteer youth organization was established on 21 September 1916 by Act of Congress with the task of rendering economic, technical and cultural assistance to developing countries. In 1966 Senator Robert

Kennedy proposed the formation of a multinational peace corps, but it failed to win the necessary backing after press reports that the US Peace Corps was being used for espionage activities.

per capita income ▶ GDP, ▶ purchasing power parity

Peronism

Peronism is the political tradition of General Juan Domingo Perón Sosa (1895–1974) of Argentina and his followers, and a political movement also known as Justicialismo.

Perón participated in the 1943 military coup and built up a powerful base in the trade unions as head of the secretariat for labour and social welfare. His popularity grew so much that in 1945 an attempt was made to arrest him, but the labour movement's show of strength forced the government to back down. In 1946 Perón was elected president, defeating a coalition which included socialists and communists.

Peronism stood for the redistribution of wealth to wage earners, industrialization, nationalization of foreign-owned assets and support for the Church and the army. His wife, known as Evita, was also enormously popular, leading a campaign for women's suffrage, which was introduced in 1947. However, she died in 1952. From 1953 economic pressure pushed Perón rightwards and he became so isolated from his mass base that he was deposed in a military coup in 1955. He went into exile in Franco's Spain, and his Peronist Party was banned.

In the early 1970s Peronism's fortunes revived and in 1973 Perón's nominee, Dr Héctor Cámpora, was elected president as the candidate of the Frente Justicialista de Liberación (FJL, 'Justicialista' Liberation Front). He invited Perón back and resigned, thereby enabling Perón to be elected president.

By this time guerrilla groups were already active in Argentina, notably the Movimiento Peronista Montonero (MPM, known as the Montoneros) which suspended operations when Perón was elected. When it became clear that there would be little change, the Montoneros resumed their attacks on military and industrial leaders, each side claiming the Peronist mantle.

When Perón died in 1974, he was succeeded by his third wife, Maria Estela Martinez de Perón (known as Isabelita). The violent struggle between left and right escalated and she was deposed in a military coup in 1976. The army cracked down on the guerrillas; thousands of radicals and dissidents were killed or simply disappeared in the following years, the latter becoming known as the ▶ desaparecidos, the disappeared ones, their fate unknown. The Montoneros suffered badly and in 1977 merged with the banned Partido Peronista Auténtico (PPA, True Peronist Party), established in 1975 by dissident Peronists to go back to the original worker-based Peronist programme, to form the Consejo Supremo de Montoneros Peronistas (SMP, Supreme Council of the Peronist Montoneros).

Another guerrilla group was formed in 1970, the Ejército Revolucionario del Pueblo (ERP, People's Revolutionary Army) with a Trotskyist orientation linked to the Partido Revolucionario de los Trabajadores (PRT, Workers' Revolutionary Party). Its policy of kidnapping industrialists and military commanders earned it rapid notoriety. It was banned in 1973 and expelled by the Fourth International in the same year, but it continued attacks on police and army targets. The armed forces used all their resources to crush it and by 1977 its rural bases were destroyed, though the PRT continued to be active. The Peronist Montoneros split in 1980 and soon after were effectively moribund.

In 1980 the military allowed representatives of the Peronist 'Justicialista' party (i.e. the FJL) to take part in discussions on the return to democracy, but they lost the 1983 elections to Raúl Alfonsín's Unión Civica Radical (UCR, Radical Civic Union) and lost again in 1985. The Peronists split, only to reunite uneasily and regain control of congress after Alfonsin's mid-term setbacks in 1987 following austerity measures.

After a bitter struggle with Antonio Cafiero (leader of the 'renovador' or modernizing wing of Peronism) for the presidential nomination in 1989, Carlos Menem, governor of Rioja province and an inheritor of the populist tradition of Peronism, became president in succession to Alfonsín. Taking office in a moment of extreme economic crisis, he has attempted to stabilize the economy by pursuing policies which are completely at variance with the Peronist tradition. In place of Peronist corporatism, he has systematically privatized the state-owned industries and tried to reduce state expenditure. His policies have created a very severe decline in production and employment which has considerably weakened the once powerful Peronist trade unions. He has gone out of his way to maintain good relations with the international banks and with the USA (sending token military support to the Gulf War in 1991); and he has given very few jobs to senior Peronists in his administration, other than to those from his own province. Ironically, a movement which was never particularly coherent appears threatened with disappearance under a Peronist president. The sort of class collaboration which Peronism represented cannot confront the problems of Argentina during the debt crisis. The only available solutions are to conform to the dictates of capitalism or to mobilize a popular struggle against them. Menem, with difficulty, has attempted the former.

petrodollars

Petrodollars refer to the deposits in US dollars of oil-producing countries largely held in Western banks. The term was coined (to parallel 'Eurodollars') when these deposits suddenly increased after the 1973–4 oil price increase (▶ OPEC). Petrodollars were recycled by the banks and permitted the huge increase in loans to Third World countries which took place between 1973 and 1982 (▶ debt crisis).

PLO, Palestine Liberation Organization

This umbrella organization was formed in 1964 to bring together the major groups fighting for the liberation of Palestine from Israeli rule. It has endured repression in some Arab states, been manipulated by various Arab regimes and been subject to splits over whether armed struggle or diplomacy is the better path. It was set up by the Arab states with a view to controlling Palestinian exiles, but after 1967 more militant Palestinians took it over and in 1969 the Palestine National Council, its highest body, adopted the Palestine National Covenant setting out the programme for the liberation of Palestine and condemning ▶ Zionism. Members include: Fatah (which grew largely in the refugee camps in Lebanon and Jordan, but has a middle class leadership); the Popular Front for the Liberation of Palestine (PFLP, a Marxist-Leninist organization, with a membership largely of students and professionals, led by Georges Habash); the Democratic Front for the Liberation of Palestine (DFLP, led by Naif Hawatmeh); Al Saiqa (Thunderbolt); the PFLP-General Command; the Arab Liberation Front; the Palestine Popular Front; and the Palestine Communist Party.

Since 1969 the PLO has been dominated by the Fatah group and its leader Yassir Arafat (1929–). Fatah is the biggest section of the PLO with 18,000 fedayin in 1984. It stresses an appeal to Palestinians alone.

In 'Black' September 1970, King Hossein of Jordan tried to eliminate the Palestine guerrilla movements in Jordan, and most groups moved their headquarters to Lebanon. Differences arose, with the PFLP resorting to hijacking airliners and the DFLP moving towards political concessions and the idea of 'intermediate stages' towards the liberation of Palestine. After the 1973 defeat of Egypt and Syria, Arafat opted for more diplomacy, which won the PLO mass support on the West Bank for the first time, and in 1974 the Arab League recognized it as the 'sole legitimate representative' of the Palestinian people.

Israel and the Arab states felt the PLO was growing too strong and launched fresh offensives against it. In 1975 Syria crushed the PLO's bases in southern Lebanon. It was driven into the Beirut ghettoes and pounded by repeated Israeli air-raids. Israel invaded Lebanon when the PLO began to fire missiles into northern Israel. In 1982 Israel moved again into Lebanon in an effort finally to remove the PLO, laying siege to Beirut and obliging Lebanon to eject the PLO after fierce resistance and the massacre of thousands. The PLO was scattered all over the Middle East.

Arafat moderated his stance further but his concessions to King Hossein caused much dissent within Fatah and Syria took advantage to promote a radical breakaway group led by Abu Musa in an attempt to get the PLO under Syrian control. Meanwhile, Israel continued to strike at the PLO, bombing Arafat's Tunis headquarters in 1985.

The factions reunited at Algiers in 1987, in view of the failure of Arafat's diplomatic strategy to yield results and the need for unity to face both Syria's campaign of extermination against the refugee camps in Lebanon, and Israeli air-raids.

During the war of 1990–1 between the USA and its allies, and Iraq, Arafat publicly identified himself with the Iraqi cause, reflecting much popular opinion among Palestinians and in the rest of the Arab world. The defeat of Saddam Hussein, however, left the PLO more friendless than ever. Relations with the Syrian and Egyptian governments (members of the US coalition) worsened, making it more likely than ever that they might participate in an international 'solution' to the Palestinian question which scupper the PLO. In the aftermath of the war the PLO was thrown into financial crisis by the loss of its traditional funding from Kuwait, Saudi Arabia and other Gulf States (also members of the US alliance). At the same time many Palestinians lost their means of livelihood as anti-Iraq states expelled Palestinian workers in revenge for the PLO's role in the war. The PLO was obliged to make a drastic cutback in its international representation.

Whether there will be compensations for these blows was not clear at the time of writing. Yet it remains clear that the PLO continues to be the recognized leadership of the national struggle and that it will be hard for other states to arrive at a negotiated settlement of the Palestine question without the explicit participation of the PLO.

Further reading

H. Cobban, *The Palestinian Liberation Organization: people, power and politics*, Cambridge 1984.

POLISARIO, Frente Popular para la Liberación de Sakiet el Hamra y Rio de Oro (Popular Front for the Liberation of Sakiet el Hamra and Rio de Oro)

The liberation movement in the Western Sahara, a former Spanish colony now annexed by Morocco, was founded in 1973 by a group of Saharawi students educated in Morocco (where their parents had fled to escape Spanish repression in the 1950s) and led by El Ouadi Mustafa Sayed, a former law student. It called for armed struggle to free the 'Saharan Arab African People' from Spanish colonialism. In its first two years it received no outside support. Morocco claimed Western Sahara and Spain abandoned plans for internal autonomy. In 1975 outside interest in the area increased and Algeria began to supply POLISARIO with arms, predominantly from the USSR. In September 1975 POLISARIO and Spain struck a deal for the handover of power to the former in return for the latter being allowed to exploit the country's phosphates and fishing for 15 years. In October King Hasan of Morocco countered by launching a 'Green March' of Moroccans to occupy the Western Sahara. Moroccan troops moved in to attack POLISARIO. Spain, in the final weeks of the Franco regime, backed down and made an agreement with Morocco and Mauritania to share the Western Sahara between them. POLISARIO at once turned its efforts against Mauritania, the weak link, and declared the Saharawi People's Democratic Republic in February 1976. Ouadi was killed in action and replaced by Mohammed Abdelaziz.

POLISARIO pressure on Mauritania precipitated the July 1978 coup there and the country's subsequent abandonment of all claims to the Western Sahara. POLISARIO then turned against Morocco. It adopted socialism as its goal and Islam as its religion and advocated the unity of the ▶ Maghreb as a step to total Arab unity. In 1984 it was accepted as a member of the Organization of African Unity (▶ OAU). To take on US-backed Morocco, POLISARIO had 25,000 fighters and some 190,000 people in Algerian refugee camps plus aid from the USSR via Algeria. To prevent POLISARIO attacks, Morocco built a 1700-mile sand wall completed in 1985, manned by half the Moroccan army and equipped with modern sensoring devices. The war is stalemated. It has forced most Saharawis into Algerian refugee camps. POLISARIO wants direct negotiations with Morocco and a referendum with no Moroccan troops or administration present. Closer ties between Morocco and Algeria (and Libya) have led to speculation that Algeria might end its support. The issue has produced splits in the OAU, but the organization still recognizes POLISARIO, as do 70 countries.

POLISARIO's international support finally began to bear fruit when in 1991 the United Nations voted to organize a referendum in which Saharawis could decide between independence and legal incorporation into Morocco. Despite imposing many obstacles, the Moroccan government seems unable to prevent the referendum which is due to take place in 1992.

Further reading

T. Hodges, *Historical Dictionary of Western Sahara*, Metuchen, NJ 1982.

population control

The question of population control is one of the most hotly debated issues in Third World politics, and it is one which makes for strange bedfellows. Both the Pope and Mao Zedong have been strong opponents of government-sponsored population control measures. The ▶ Malthusianism which predominates in development circles, and in organizations like the World Bank, argues that population increase threatens growth, and therefore birth control programmes should receive a very high priority in development policy. Material bribes or legal obligation are often regarded as legitimate means to this end. It reached extremes in China after the death of Mao with the introduction of the policy which limits all families to one child, backed by severe economic and social penalties for violation of the rule. Indira Gandhi in India lost an election partly as a result of popular reaction against a coercive vasectomy campaign.

The opposition to birth control policies has traditionally come from one of two positions: that of Mao Zedong and others that socialism does not have a population problem and is capable of providing for all; and that of the Pope and others that birth control violates morality. What is too often missing from the debate is the interests of the women who are by and large the subjects of the campaigns and on whom any number of dubious forms of contraception have been tested in the interests of development. There is every reason, as part of development policy, to provide free, easy and healthy access to birth control information and methods to women in order that they can control their own fertility and in many instances escape from a life of successive pregnancies. There is usually all the difference in the world between a policy of this kind which is part of expanding the rights of women, and the state-sponsored birth control programmes which aid agencies love to finance.

Further reading

B. Hartmann, *Reproductive Rights and Wrongs: the global politics of population control and contraceptive choice*, New York 1987.

population explosion

This emotive phrase is used to describe the high population growth rate in Third World countries. Since explosions have a bad reputation, the phrase tends to have a strong flavour of ▶ Malthusianism, suggesting that population growth is a problem. Its use is thus part of a popular ideology which blames the poor for their own poverty.

Europe's development also produced a population 'explosion' in the nineteenth century, though annual growth rates never reached the levels of parts of the Third World today. At present, population growth in Africa is about 3.2 per cent a year, in Latin America 2.2 per cent and in Asia 1.8 per cent.

The increase in population results from a rapid decline in death rates after 1950 and the maintenance of relatively high birth rates. Everywhere in the Third World, however, birth rates have also begun to decline suggesting that, as in the developed countries, a 'demographic transition' is taking place between a regime of high birth and death rates to one of low birth and death rates.

post-colonial state

The experience of the Third World since decolonization has provoked a theoretical debate about whether or not there has emerged a new form of state, the post-colonial state. Unfortunately, this singularly unresolved debate has been a confused and imprecise attempt to offer an alternative to Marx's theory of the state. The excessively scholastic character of the discussion has ensured that it remains abstract and inconclusive. The main object of the upholders of the post-colonial state thesis is to suggest that this institution is to some extent independent of foreign interests and can therefore be used in the interests of the nation concerned.

In reality, those who have tried to use the post-colonial state for progressive ends have quickly realized that it was not a realistic option.

For example, ▶Nkrumah realized after the failure of his experiment that, rather than his controlling the post-colonial state in Ghana, it controlled him. According to Nkrumah, the state only appears independent – in reality it is controlled by outside forces.[1]

An examination of the structures of the post-colonial state shows that its institutions – the army and the civil service – as well as its traditions have been carefully shaped by the colonial power. That is why any attempt at a radical experiment, such as those by Nkrumah, ▶Sukarno or ▶Lumumba, faces sabotage and ultimately military opposition from the colonial state machine.

Those who argue that the post-colonial state is a neutral institution that may be used for progressive ends fail to carry out a structural analysis of the subject. Thus, for example, Ben Turok confuses the subjective desires of the individual nationalist politicians with the state machine when he asks:

> Are there not cases where the group that came to power at independence, albeit weak and perhaps filled with illusions, nevertheless, tried to gain real and not token independence? Can Nkrumah really be said to have been a 'selected heir' or puppet? And what of Tanzania and Zambia? Can it be argued that Kaunda and Nyerere were the 'selected heirs' chosen by Britain or did they emerge in the political struggle for independence? That both were manipulated is not in doubt but that is not the same as saying that they were essentially compradorist from the start.[2]

Turok entirely misses the issue at stake. The individual motives of a nationalist politician are a matter for the psychologists. Whatever these motives are is neither here nor there. However, what is significant is that Nyerere, Kaunda and Nkrumah all ended up being controlled by the post-colonial state. This shows that there is an objective pattern at work – one that is decisive whatever the intentions of the leaders of post-colonial governments.

The post-colonial state thesis is theoretically justified through the notion of the 'relatively autonomous' state. The first and also the most coherent advocate of this position was Hamza Alavi, who initiated the debate in 1972. His main point was summarized as follows: 'The role of the bureaucratic–military oligarchy is relatively autonomous because, once the controlling hand of the metropolitan bourgeoisie is lifted at the moment of independence, no single class has exclusive control over it.'[3]

Since Alavi's contribution dozens of articles have been written on the subject. These articles are derivative from Alavi's relative autonomy thesis which is repeated with monotonous regularity. Thus an article by Craig Chaney which reviews the discussions suggests that:

> The place of the petit bourgeoisie in the state apparatus gives it a certain relative autonomy with respect to foreign capital. This autonomy is that of the capitalist state itself, a formerly autonomous instance within the capitalist mode of production. While it does not

251

permit the local dominant classes to break the yoke of foreign capital, this autonomy can enable them to set limits to its power or bargain with it.[4]

Chaney follows a recent fashion of identifying the alleged relatively autonomous role of the state with the role of the petty bourgeoisie. John Saul attempts to substantiate this ostensibly progressive role of the petty bourgeoisie through his references to Tanzania:

> The Arusha Declaration package of policies – the opting for collective solutions to the Tanzanian development problem – represented, first and foremost, an initial victory for a progressive wing of the petty bourgeoisie . . . rather than some cold-blooded fulfilment of the class interests of that stratum's bureaucratic core.[5]

A more cynical interpretation would suggest that the Arusha Declaration was fine rhetoric but of little practical consequence. It is certainly difficult to discern any of the 'collective solutions' in contemporary Tanzania that Saul finds so encouraging.

The notion of the relatively autonomous post-colonial state is contradicted by experience. It is also theoretically implausible. As Marx argued, every state has a class basis. The state acts to reproduce the general conditions necessary for the perpetuation of the ruling class. In most post-colonial societies the ruling class is made up of capitalists. What gives the post-colonial state its appearance of independence is that the capitalist class is very weak and therefore cannot overtly rule as a class. To compensate for its economic weakness the capitalist class often relies on the military or on an individual dictator to run the state machine. Marx called this underdeveloped capitalist rule ▶ Bonapartism.

The real nature of the Third World state becomes apparent whenever individual leaders adopt a radical course of action. They soon discover that state autonomy is a myth and that the legacy of colonialism is very much alive. Yet the inescapable consequence of the relative autonomy thesis is that Third World governments must be responsible for failing to make better use of their state. This is the conclusion drawn by Turok and those who think like him. Their obsession with making better use of the state grossly underestimates the fundamental structural obstacles to reform. A more rational analysis based on bitter experience would suggest that the precondition for any meaningful change is the liquidation of the post-colonial state.

Notes

1. See K. Nkrumah, *Neo-Colonialism*, London 1965.
2. B. Turok, *Africa: what can be done?*, London 1987, p. 97.
3. H. Alavi, 'The state in post-colonial societies: Pakistan and Bangladesh', *New Left Review*, 74, July 1972, p. 62.
4. C. Chaney, 'Political power and social classes in the neo-colonial state', *Review of African Political Economy*, 38, Apr. 1987, pp. 48–65.
5. J. Saul, *The State and Revolution in Eastern Africa*, London 1979, p. 184.

252

post-imperialism

According to a number of academic writers in the past fifteen years, post-imperialism is a new historical epoch in which imperialism is no longer in operation and for which the theory of imperialism is inappropriate for providing insight into the relation between North and South. As a theory, post-imperialism developed as a reaction to the failures of ▶ dependency theory, especially its inability to account for the high economic growth experienced by a handful of newly industrializing countries (▶ NICs). More broadly, post-imperialism can be seen as a pessimistic reaction to the slow progress of radical forces in the Third World.[1]

To be sure, dependency theory is in need of criticism. However, post-imperialist theory provides no alternative to the advocates of the dependency thesis. Indeed, in attacking the dependency thesis, the advocates of post-imperialism go so far as to deny the relevance of imperialist domination for understanding the Third World. There is an underlying assumption which tends to regard all the regimes of the world as qualitatively equal and therefore obscures the relation of exploitation between North and South.

Most opinions which suggest that imperialism has no significance tend to be held by the apologists of the right. In contrast post-imperialism, it is claimed, is in a radical tradition. Its supporters often criticize inequalities and repression and sometimes speak of the desirability of socialism. What gives their view a conservative and even apologist content is that they tend to present inequalities and exploitation as accidental facts and not as fundamental consequences of the world capitalist system. Consequently, post-imperialist contributions tend to portray the relation between North and South as essentially harmonious.

According to the two most prolific supporters of the post-imperialism thesis, Becker and Sklar, the *dependentitas'* views are based on 'the erroneous premise that internationalist capitalist expansion is necessarily and ineluctably imperialist'.[2] Becker and Sklar argue that transnational corporations (TNCs) seek to promote the integration of national economies on the basis of the new international economy. Though there may be conflict over the distribution of resources, 'there lies a mutuality of interest between politically autonomous countries at different levels of economic development'.[3] From this perspective, the economies of the Third World and those of the West stand in mutually beneficial relation to each other. TNCs provide capital, dependable markets, essential technology and other services for Third World countries.

Sklar in particular argues that the mutually beneficial relation between North and South has led to close cooperation between Third World élites and Western capitalists. The coalescence of these two groups leads to a transnational class formation which transcends national boundaries. Post-imperialism sees TNCs as the instrument through which an international oligarchy is gradually being forged.

The post-imperialist thesis is often presented in the language of class analysis. It suggests that imperialism – the domination of one nation over another – is being 'superseded by transnational domination of the world as a whole'.[4] Post-imperialist writers argue that those seeking social change should direct their fire at the international oligarchy rather than concentrate on national solutions. It is, therefore, one more version of a 'one world' thesis (▶ Introduction).

In its outlines, post-imperialism is deeply indebted to Karl Kautsky's theory of ultra-imperialism. Like Kautsky, the post-imperialists analyse capitalism from a technical rather than a social point of view. Sklar draws heavily on organizational theory to substantiate his claims. From a technical point of view it is possible to argue that capitalism can overcome its national restrictions and operate as one conglomerate, but in social reality, such a development is unlikely. The capitalist class cannot operate in the world market without the support of nation-states to enforce its interests on the rest of society.

The enduring importance of the national foundation of capitalism can be seen in the perpetual conflict that exists in the international arena. The relation of competition is not just between individual capitalists but also between the capitalist classes of specific nations. Throughout this process the capitalist class of one nation attempts to resolve its problems at the expense of that of another.

The idea of post-imperialist theory that the world has a single ruling class appears at least superficially to be very radical. In fact, the perspective is profoundly apologetic. To treat the relations of nations as unproblematic is to portray all countries as qualitatively more or less the same. Post-imperialist theorists frequently argue that national domination has become a historic relic.

In fact, national domination remains all too prevalent in the contemporary international system. To deny the inferior status of the Third World in this system is to ignore one of its essential features. The inferior position of the Third World is not merely the product of its economic weakness. Despite decolonization, many parts of the Third World continue to experience political or military national domination. From the Persian Gulf to Central America Western armadas patrol continually, and when necessary they attack and invade as in Angola, Grenada, Iraq, Panama, Nicaragua and Vietnam, to name only a few. The gunboat diplomacy of the nineteenth century was tame compared with the West's military interventions during the 'post-imperialist' epoch.

Post-imperialist theory ignores these inconvenient facts regarding national domination. Its basic argument that capitalism is one and the same the world over is fundamentally flawed. It may well be the case that capitalism is a problem throughout the world. However, in the Third World, the colonial legacy and the contemporary forms of foreign domination create problems of an entirely different order than those of imperialist countries. Imperialism may have changed its spots – but it is alive and kicking throughout the Third World.

Notes

1. For an introduction to this viewpoint see D.G. Becker and others (eds), *Postimperialism: international capitalism and development in the late twentieth century*, Boulder, Col. 1987.
2. Ibid., p. 6.
3. Ibid.
4. Ibid., p. 14.

PRI, Partido Revolucionario Institucional (Institutional Revolutionary Party)

The dominant force in Mexican politics, the PRI was originally the Partido Nacional Revolucionario (PNR, Revolutionary National Party) founded on 4 March 1929 by Mexican leader Plutarco Elías Calles. He had taken power after President Obregón was assassinated in 1924 and ruled directly until 1928, when he resigned the presidency only to set himself up as Jefe Máximo (Big Boss) to rule from behind the scenes – via the PNR from March 1929. The PNR was a coalition of interest groups which had emerged out of the Mexican revolution of 1910–20. It was later divided into 'popular', labour and peasant sections. Today the labour section still organizes workers in the trade union federation, the Confederación de Trabajadores de Mexico (CTM, Mexican Workers' Confederation). Small farmers are organized in the National Peasants' Confederation. A military section also existed until it was abolished in 1940. Since 1946 all Mexican presidents have been civilians.

In 1934 Calles appointed Lázaro Cárdenas as his next stooge 'president' but, unlike his predecessors, Cárdenas fought Calles for political control. By 1936 he had won and Calles was exiled from Mexico.

Cárdenas was born in Jiquilpan, Michoacán province, in 1895. He served under Obregón in the Mexican revolution and rose to the rank of general. After the revolution he became governor of Michoacán, minister of the interior and minister of war and the navy before he was appointed president by Calles. Cárdenas introduced an agrarian reform which expropriated 40 million acres of land for the peasantry. In 1935 he granted workers a minimum wage, and organized their unions into the CTM in 1936. In 1937 he nationalized the railways. In March 1938 he nationalized the oil industry – a move which almost provoked US intervention – and established the state oil company Permex. Cárdenas changed the name of the PNR to the Partido de la Revolucionario Mexicana (PRN, Party of the Mexican Revolution) in 1938.

To consolidate popular support, Cárdenas revived the ▶ indigenismo movement that had blossomed under Obregón (▶▶ Aprismo). Under pressure from the influential painter Diego Rivera, Cárdenas agreed in 1936 to permit the exiled Bolshevik Leon Trotsky to reside in Mexico, on condition that he refrain from participating in internal politics. Trotsky lived in Mexico City until he was murdered in 1940, the same year Cárdenas ended his presidency. Cárdenas eventually resigned from the PRI in 1961 in order to fight for ▶ Castro's Cuba, then being intimidated by the USA. He was refused permission to leave Mexico, however, and died in 1970.

The PRI adopted its present name in 1946. It has maintained its monopoly on power in Mexico through its flexibility, which has allowed the party leadership to switch to the left or the right according to changing circumstances. The party usually manages to win between 80 per cent and 90 per cent of the popular vote by pulling off a delicate political balancing-act and rigging the vote. On the one hand, it has often imposed harsh policies at home. In 1968, for example, a PRI government used great brutality to put down riots in Mexico City during the Olympic Games. In 1986 the current PRI regime used the same methods against homeless squatters when the World Cup was held in the city. Yet at the same time, the PRI has preserved its popular credentials by adopting radical postures in foreign relations. Mexico's overbearing northern neighbour, the USA, has provided a particularly useful target against which the PRI leadership can strike independent postures, while often bowing to Washington's will behind the scenes. The last PRI incumbent, Miguel de la Madrid Hurtado, publicly refused to cooperate with Mexico's US creditors, while imposing austerity measures on the Mexican people to meet the country's massive foreign debt obligations.

In March 1987 Lazaro Cárdenas's son, Cuauhtemoc Cárdenas, leader of the left-wing Democratic Current faction in the PRI, initiated a rare public challenge to the official PRI candidate for the 1988 presidential elections. After an unwise alliance with disgruntled right-wing elements he failed to gain control of the party. Mounting an electoral challenge from outside, he managed to win a significant percentage of the vote; his supporters claimed that he had been robbed of victory by PRI vote rigging. This challenge certainly dealt a blow to the serenity of the PRI leadership and the successful PRI presidential candidate, Carlos Salinas de Gortari, has campaigned vocally for a profound democratic renewal of the PRI. There is every sign, however, that the bureaucratic structure is too arthritic to move fast enough. The PRI can expect more outside challenge but remains an overbearing presence in Mexican politics.

Further reading

V. Randall (ed.), *Political Parties in the Third World*, London 1988.

Progressive Socialist Party

This Lebanese political party was founded in 1949 and operates as the political movement of the Lebanese ▶ Druze community, a Muslim sect with a strong military reputation traditionally excluded from mainstream Muslim life. Through ever-shifting alliances it has sought to improve the position of the traditionally disadvantaged Druze. Its founder was Kamal Jumblatt, the leader of the Druze community in the Chouf mountains above Beirut and a member of the family that has dominated Druze politics since the seventeenth century, now wealthy industrialists and landowners. Jumblatt was anxious to ally his feudal base with European socialist thought to modernize the Druze community. Backing Arab nationalism and the USSR did not prevent him making deals with the pro-Western Lebanese groups.

From 1967 Jumblatt backed the Palestine Liberation Organization (▶ PLO) to increase his leverage within Lebanon and in 1969 organized the PLO and the Lebanese left into the broad-based Lebanese National Movement (LNM), with the aim of overthrowing the quota system in the 1944 constitution which discriminated in favour of Maronite Christians.

This led to the civil war in 1975. Syria intervened decisively on the side of the Maronites. Jumblatt was killed in 1977 and was succeeded by his son Walid Jumblatt, but the LNM disintegrated in 1981. In 1983 Jumblatt sided with ▶ AMAL when the Maronites and Israelis attacked them. When the Israelis withdrew, all-out war broke out between the Druze and the Maronites, with US warships and French jets helping the Christians. When the US military finally withdrew in 1984, the Druze succeeded in pushing the Lebanese army out of the Chouf mountains.

protectionism

All nations maintain various restrictions over imports and exports. Barriers to the movement of goods may involve the imposition of tariffs on imports, prohibitions on the import or export of certain items, restriction of imports to defined quota levels and controls over access to foreign exchange. In addition, legal rules and patents and quality controls act to restrict the movement of goods between nations. Also, bilateral trade agreements between nations constitute a restriction as they effectively exclude other nations from particular markets.

Protectionism denotes the existence of a comprehensive programme of trade restrictions on the part of a particular nation. Many undeveloped nations exhibit a high propensity to utilize restrictions in the pursuit of industrial development. Protectionist policies are used in an attempt to minimize the debilitating influence that stronger economies in the world can have on development strategies.

These same stronger, or more developed, economies also use protectionism to prevent newcomers breaking into their markets, and all countries use protectionism to try to insulate themselves from adverse external economic events like a world crisis. This latter form of protectionism tends (as in the 1930s) to have a perverse effect and to exacerbate the depression; an attempt by all countries to protect themselves individually means that all suffer more.

For Third World countries the systematic use of protectionism as part of an industrialization strategy has become more difficult in recent years. One reason for this is disillusion with the protectionist experiments of the 1960s and 1970s such as the attempts at import-substituting industrialization (▶ ISI) in Latin America. Protectionism often did not work because what was being protected was a very small élite market and so protectionism encouraged small-scale, inefficient plants; and in other ways, too, protectionism can protect inefficiency rather than dynamism. None the less, there are in principle answers to these problems: redistribution of income so as to create a broader-based internal market and economic ▶ integration so as to industrialize on the basis of the internal market of more than one country.

In the 1980s both income redistribution and economic integration have been prevented in many countries because of the concentration in economic policy on stabilization and creating the conditions to repay debts (▶ debt crisis). Third World countries have been obliged in recent years to go in the direction of free trade rather than protectionism

(▶ GATT, ▶ IMF, ▶ neo-liberalism). Yet at the same time developed countries have maintained and in some ways intensified protectionist policies which damage the economic interests of the Third World. The world campaign against protectionism and in favour of free trade has been in many ways a hypocritical one.

Further reading

J. Bhagwati, *Protectionism*, Cambridge, Mass. 1989.

PRT, Partido Revolucionario de los Trabajadores (Workers' Revolutionary Party)

This name is used by many left-wing, especially Trotskyist, parties in Latin America. One of the best known is a Peruvian Trotskyist organization and local section of the Fourth International formed in 1978, under the leadership of Hugo Blanco, a well-known guerrilla leader. It developed partly from the Frente Obrero, Campesino, Estudiantil y Popular (FOCEP, Worker, Peasant and Student Popular Front) which had been formed in 1962 and came third in the 1978 Constituent Assembly elections. In the 1980 election FOCEP won only one seat, and then entered the Izquierda Unida (IU, United Left), a coalition dominated by the Peruvian Communist Party (not to be confused with the Communist Party of Peru, ▶ Sendero Luminoso), which had broken from Moscow and emphasized Third Worldism. The PRT won only 1 per cent of the vote in the 1983 elections and itself applied for IU membership. IU's withdrawal from the 1985 presidential election helped APRA to win (▶ Aprismo). For the Argentinian PRT ▶ Peronism.

purchasing power parity

This concept refers to a method of comparing the income or product of different countries. Normally, national estimates of income are converted into a standard currency (usually the US dollar) at the going exchange rate (▶ GDP) but, as economists have long been aware (and as tourists know very well), the exchange rate is often not a good indicator of the comparative purchasing power of money. The United Nations has therefore sponsored a long-term study of the comparative purchasing power of different currencies (the International Comparison Project) so as to produce rates of conversion which give a better guide to real differences in income between countries.

The results began to be available at the end of the 1980s and they produce estimates of income per capita which are sometimes startlingly different from the customary income per capita figures. The comparisons are shown in the table (see pp. 260–2). In general the pattern is that purchasing power parity conversions raise the lowest incomes and lower the highest ones. The ratio of the richest to the poorest country is cut from 275 to 80 (▶ indicators). The purchasing power parity estimates suggest that, while the world distribution of income is extremely unequal, it is not quite as unequal as the customary estimates indicate.

The most striking differences are for large Asian countries, presumably because their size means that international economic relations (which are reflected in the exchange rate) are relatively less important compared with the internal market. The ratio of per capita income converted by purchasing power parity to income converted by exchange rates is as follows: India 3.4 to 1; Pakistan 4.5 to 1; China 7.3 to 1. The extraordinary difference in the case of China means that the total size of the Chinese gross domestic product converted by purchasing power parity is almost as great as that of the USA.

While almost all economists agree that the purchasing power parity method is the best in theory, there is still controversy over the adequacy of these new estimates. Many people, of very different shades of opinion, have a vested interest in using the traditional figures using exchange rate conversion.

Further reading

United Nations Development Programme, *Human Development Report 1990*, London 1990.

Table: Income per capita and index of human development (HDI), 1987

Country	GDP per capita US$ 1987	GDP per capita ppp$ 1987	HDI
Afghanistan			0.212
Albania			0.790
Algeria	2680	2633	0.609
Angola	470		0.304
Argentina	2390	4647	0.910
Australia	11,100	11,782	0.978
Austria	11,980	12,386	0.961
Bangladesh	160	883	0.318
Belgium	11,480	13,140	0.966
Benin	310	665	0.224
Bhutan	150		0.236
Bolivia	580	1380	0.548
Botswana	1050	2496	0.646
Brazil	2020	4307	0.784
Bulgaria	4150		0.918
Burkina Faso	190		0.150
Burundi	250	450	0.235
Cameroon	970	1381	0.474
Canada	15,160	16,375	0.983
Central African Republic	330	591	0.258
Chad	150		0.157
Chile	1310	4862	0.931
China	290	2124	0.716
Colombia	1240	3524	0.801
Congo	870	756	0.395
Costa Rica	1610	3760	0.916
Cuba			0.877
Czechoslovakia	5820		0.931
Denmark	14,930	15,119	0.971
Dominican Republic	730		0.699
Ecuador	1040	2687	0.758
Egypt	680	1357	0.501
El Salvador	860	1733	0.651
Ethiopia	139	454	0.282
Finland	14,470	12,795	0.967
France	12,790	13,961	0.974
Gabon	2700	2068	0.525
Germany, East	7180		0.953
Germany, West	14,400	14,730	0.967
Ghana	390	481	0.360
Greece	4020		0.949
Guatemala	950	1957	0.592
Guinea			0.162
Haiti	360	775	0.356
Honduras	810	1119	0.563

Table: *continued*

Country	GDP per capita US$ 1987	GDP per capita ppp$ 1987	HDI
Hong Kong	8070	13,906	0.936
Hungary	2240		0.915
India	399	1053	0.439
Indonesia	450	1660	0.591
Iran			0.660
Iraq	3020		0.759
Ireland, Republic of	6120	8566	0.961
Israel	6800	9182	0.957
Italy	10,350	10,682	0.966
Ivory Coast	740	1123	0.393
Jamaica	940	2506	0.824
Japan	15,760	13,135	0.996
Jordan	1560	3161	0.752
Kampuchea			0.471
Kenya	330	794	0.481
Korea, North			0.789
Korea, South	2690	4832	0.903
Kuwait	14,610	13,843	0.839
Laos	170		0.506
Lebanon			0.735
Lesotho	370	1585	0.580
Liberia	450	696	0.333
Libya	5460		0.719
Madagascar	210	634	0.440
Malawi	160	176	0.250
Malaysia	1810	3849	0.800
Mali	210	543	0.143
Mauritania	440	840	0.208
Mauritius	1490	2617	0.788
Mexico	1830	4624	0.876
Mongolia			0.737
Morocco	610	1761	0.489
Mozambique	170		0.239
Myanmar	200	752	0.561
Namibia			0.404
Nepal	160	722	0.273
Netherlands	11,860	12,661	0.984
New Zealand	7750	10,541	0.966
Nicaragua	830	2209	0.743
Niger	260	452	0.116
Nigeria	370	668	0.322
Norway	17,190	15,940	0.983
Oman	5810		0.535
Pakistan	350	1585	0.423
Panama	2240	4009	0.883

Table: *continued*

Country	GDP per capita US$ 1987	GDP per capita ppp$ 1987	HDI
Papua New Guinea	700	1843	0.471
Paraguay	990	2603	0.784
Peru	1470	3129	0.753
Philippines	590	1878	0.714
Poland	2070		0.910
Portugal	2830	5597	0.899
Romania	2560		0.863
Rwanda	300	571	0.304
Saudi Arabia	6200	8320	0.702
Senegal	520	1068	0.274
Sierra Leone	300	480	0.150
Singapore	7940	12,790	0.899
Somalia	290		0.200
South Africa	1890	4981	0.731
Spain	6010	8989	0.965
Sri Lanka	400	2053	0.789
Sudan	330	750	0.255
Sweden	15,550	13,780	0.987
Switzerland	21,330	15,403	0.986
Syria	1640		0.691
Tanzania	180	405	0.413
Thailand	850	2576	0.783
Togo	290	670	0.337
Trinidad and Tobago	4210	3664	0.885
Tunisia	1180	2741	0.657
Turkey	1210	3781	0.751
Uganda	260	511	0.354
UK	10,420	12,270	0.970
United Arab Emirates	15,830	12,191	0.782
Uruguay	2190	5063	0.916
USA	18,530	17,615	0.961
USSR	4550		0.920
Venezuela	3230	4306	0.861
Vietnam			0.608
Yemen, North	590		0.328
Yemen, South	420		0.369
Yugoslavia	2480		0.913
Zaïre	150	220	0.294
Zambia	250	717	0.481
Zimbabwe	580	1184	0.576

Note: A blank means information not available.
Source: United Nations Development Programme, *Report on Human Development 1990*, New York 1990.

R

Rapid Deployment Force ▶ RDF

Rastafarianism (from Amharic *Ras Tafari* = chief)
A Rastafarian is a follower of a West Indian (especially Jamaican) Christian sect that believes all blacks are in exile in the West (Babylon) from Africa. It emerged in the 1930s out of Marcus Garvey's Universal Negro Improvement Assocation (▶ Garveyism). The Rastafarians grafted on to Garvey's 'Africa for Africans' slogan an apocalyptic vision in which white political control would be loosened, allowing all black people to be 'returned' to Africa – in the mind, if not in reality. The faith interprets the coronation of Haile Selassie as emperor of Ethiopia in 1930 as heralding an imminent end to the black diaspora. His name before he was crowned was Ras Tafari. Haile Selassie is viewed as a divinity and so his death in 1975 is not considered important by the cult's followers. Ethiopia symbolizes Africa before its invasion by the European colonialists.

Rastafarianism has experienced rapid growth since the 1960s, first in Jamaica and later in England among West Indian migrants; its spread was aided by the fame of the Rastafarian reggae musician, Bob Marley (1945–81). The faith has spread even more widely: Rastafarians participated in the New Jewel Movement (▶ NJM) in Grenada; they are to be found in black ghettos in the USA and Canada and have been reported even among aboriginal people in Australia and Maoris in New Zealand.

Further reading
L. Barrett, *The Rastafarians*, London 1977.
E.E. Cashmore, *The Rastafarians*, London 1984.

RDF, Rapid Deployment Force
This airmobile US military force, 400,000-strong, was formed in 1982. It is based in the USA but designed to intervene in the Third World at a moment's notice, and is seen as a back-up force in the event of the collapse or decline of US client states in the Middle East. A series of 'staging posts' and 'rear bases' to back up the RDF encircles the Gulf Zone – in Egypt, Turkey, Greece, Cyprus, Oman, Sudan, Kenya, Pakistan, and Diego Garcia in the Indian Ocean. Other Western powers, such as the UK and France, have developed similar forces on a smaller scale.

Reagan Doctrine
President Reagan in his 1985 State of the Union address enunciated the doctrine associated with his name. The aim of this doctrine is to provide the aggressive interventionist policy of the USA in the Third World with

an ideological justification in the form of the threat of Soviet expansionism and the danger that it poses for freedom.

On 6 February 1985 Reagan declared that the USA would support the fight for freedom everywhere in the Third World. A year later in his studied Hollywood style he stated:

> To those imprisoned in regimes held captive, to those beaten for daring to fight for freedom and democracy – for their right to worship, to speak, to live and prosper in the family of free nations – we say to you tonight: You are not alone, Freedom Fighters. America will support you with moral and material assistance; your right not just to fight and die for freedom, but to fight and win freedom in Afghanistan, Angola, Cambodia and Nicaragua.[1]

The right of Washington to intervene in the affairs of Third World countries has been upheld by successive US presidents for more than a century; and Reagan was not the first president to rationalize gunboat diplomacy as a response to the Soviet threat. Ever since the Truman Doctrine of 1947, every US president has reserved the right to intervene in Third World countries to contain the USSR. The novelty in the Reagan Doctrine is the tactics to be employed in the Third World.

The first motivation behind the Reagan Doctrine was the desire to shift public opinion in the USA away from the so-called Vietnam syndrome to a more interventionist stance. The US defeat in Vietnam led to a major crisis of confidence. Public opinion turned hostile towards Third World adventures in the 1970s. However, continued instability in the Third World threatened US interests, forcing Washington to adopt a more interventionist strategy. The question was how to sell an interventionist strategy to the US people. The answer was a highly professional public relations campaign which fabricated an escalating Soviet threat throughout the Third World. The keynote phrase was Reagan's description of the USSR as the 'Evil Empire'.

One of the most striking features of the Reagan Doctrine was the gap between rhetoric and reality. Despite its crusading rhetoric, Washington has learned the lessons of ignominious defeat in Vietnam. It was reluctant to involve itself in major military engagements in the Third World. Instead, Washington has sought military glories through attacking soft targets. Its invasion of the small island of Grenada and then Panama summed up the nature of the Reagan crusade.

One of the main features of the Reagan Doctrine was its emphasis on *low-intensity conflict*. This implies the deployment of military forces on short and limited engagements. The rationale behind such operations is to prevent long-term military entanglements with unpredictable results. Low-intensity conflict allows for the use of military resources without paying the penalty of significant loss of life of US troops. The ideal form of such operations was the US bombing of Libya in 1986.

The most innovative feature of the Reagan Doctrine was its promotion of so-called freedom fighters against radical Third World regimes. Washington encourages the creation of groups of guerrilla fighters to maintain the facade of non-intervention. Local mercenaries, financed and armed by the USA, are used to destabilize radical Third World regimes. Politically, this option makes good sense for Washington since it does not have to use its own troops directly. Groups like the ▶ Contras in Nicaragua and UNITA in Angola (▶ Angolan liberation movement) are utilized as instruments of US foreign policy.

The basic idea behind the Reagan Doctrine is to pursue a high-profile, interventionist policy but at a low cost. It represents a first step in the escalation of gunboat diplomacy. The occupation of the Persian Gulf by the US navy during the Iran–Iraq war illustrated this policy. The justification for this naval presence was to guarantee the freedom of shipping. Its objectives in the short term were limited to intimidation and the selective use of military sanctions.

However, it was predictable that gunboat diplomacy could not be restricted to that level. In such inherently volatile situations matters can get out of hand, forcing the USA to up the stakes. The crisis provoked by Iraq's occupation of Kuwait in 1990 showed that once the limitations of the Reagan Doctrine were reached – low-intensity conflict and the deployment of necessary units would prove insufficient – Washington, under Reagan's successor George Bush, was forced to adopt more traditional forms of foreign aggression. The Reagan Doctrine thus served as a form of political preparation for later attacks on the Third World.

Further reading

S. Landau, *The Dangerous Doctrine: national security and US foreign policy*, Boulder, Col. 1988.

Notes

1. *New York Times*, 5 February 1986.

refugees (from French *réfugié* = someone seeking a shelter)

The term was originally applied to French Protestants (Huguenots) who came to England after the revocation of the Edict of Nantes in 1685. Today, the term applies to all those who are forced to leave their countries by war or oppression. The United Nations set up an Office of the UN High Commissioner for Refugees (UNHCR) in January 1951 to deal with the 'international protection' of refugees. In the middle of 1991 there were between 15 and 20 million refugees in the world. When the UNHCR was established most of the world's refugees were in Europe; now nearly 90 per cent of them are in or from the Third World.

The largest concentrations of refugees in the world at present have fled from Palestine, Iraq, Afghanistan, Kampuchea, Vietnam, Ethiopia, Mozambique, Angola and Central America, and the countries which have received the largest number of refugees are Iran, Pakistan, Turkey, Sudan, Somalia, Zaïre, Tanzania and the USA.

The number of refugees mounts alarmingly with the rise of wars, civil upheavals and famines in the Third World (▶ famine, ▶ military spending). The existence of refugees, who are usually obliged to live in extreme poverty in overcrowded camps, is a manifestation of a major political injustice or economic disaster. The receiving countries usually take in refugees very reluctantly, refuse to allow them to integrate themselves in the country of exile and often force them to return to the conditions from which they have fled. One such case is that of the Vietnamese 'boat people' in Hong Kong. The Hong Kong (and therefore British) authorities have attempted forcible repatriation which has been opposed even by the USA. In relation to the Vietnamese in particular an attempt has been made to deny rights to the majority of refugees by calling them 'economic' as opposed to 'political' migrants. Those who flee repression, it is argued, may have some rights to asylum, but not those who flee material deprivation. As the demand of inhabitants to migrate to the rich countries increases (▶ migration), we can expect to hear more of this relatively spurious and opportunistic distinction.

Further reading

A. Bramwell (ed.), *Refugees in the Age of Total War*, London 1988.
I. Cimade and K. Min, *Africa's Refugee Crisis: what's to be done?*, London 1986.

religion

All of the world's major religions today have their origins in parts of the world which now form the Third World. However, one – Christianity – spread to Europe and became in its many forms part of the ideological baggage of capitalism and imperialism. The crusades, the conquest of America, the indoctrination of Africa were all justified in the name of Christianity. Christianity, therefore, today the nominal religion of almost the whole of Latin America, is very widespread in Africa south of the Sahara and has strong implantation in a few Asian countries, but came to the Third World as something external, often imposed and identified with the foreign rulers. In the name of Christianity, Third World religions were denounced as pagan idolatry and many religious customs labelled barbaric. Yet Christianity has always had a problem reconciling the identification of many of its church leaders with riches and oppression and the doctrines of peace and poverty preached by its founder. The tension has shown up throughout the history of Christianity in the Third World, from the eloquent denunciation of the practices of the early Spanish colonists in America by the priest Bartolomé de las Casas to the many radical Christian movements which flourish in the Third World today. These include many churches which have played a leading role in the struggle against apartheid in South Africa and ▶ liberation theology in Latin America. In many places in the Third World indigenous Christian or partly Christian religions reject the doctrinal and organizational authority of Western churches (▶ Rastafarianism). The question of the Third World is producing a crisis for the Western Christian churches.

Christianity also faces a growing challenge in parts of the Third World from a new rise of ▶ Islam which, unlike Christianity, is in its main centres a religion currently in a state of upsurge rather than decline.

Some of the rise of Islam in recent years also marks a conscious challenge to the influence of imperialism and to the Third World rulers who compromise with it.

Thus, while in modern times the movement against the established order has been by and large associated with growing secularism, this is much less the case in the Third World. The major exception to that is in countries which have been ruled by communist governments where measures to repress religion have been taken. It remains to be seen whether these effects are permanent.

While religion in the Third World is often associated today with challenging Western imperialism, it also forms the nominal basis of many destructive communal conflicts (▶ communalism) in countries like India, though in some cases the real causes may be more social than is admitted.

The relationship between religion and development has been frequently debated with very inconclusive results. Reflecting the relationship postulated by the sociologist Max Weber between Protestantism in Europe and the development of capitalism, writers often search for the new equivalents of Protestantism in the Third World. Thus Islam and Hinduism are often condemned as fatalistic or socially conservative and so not very conducive to development and, as one economist has recently claimed to discover, Japanese Confucianism has been very conducive to development because of its stress on loyalty, while Chinese Confucianism is not because of its stress on solidarity.[1] All such hypotheses suffer from a definition of development as merely imitating the West and an excess of inspired speculation rather than scientific rigour.

Note

1. M. Morishima, *Why Has Japan Succeeded? Western technology and the Japanese ethos*, Cambridge 1982.

Rio Summit

Held in June 1992 in Rio de Janeiro, the United Nations Conference on Environment and Development was the largest and most complex international conference ever staged. It brought together more than one hundred heads of state (including President George Bush of America, Chancellor Helmut Kohl of Germany, Prime Minister Kiichi Miyazawa of Japan and Prime Minister John Major of Britain), and 30,000 people in total, to discuss issues raised in 24 million pages of preparatory documents.

The 'Earth Summit', as it became known, was supposed to confront both the world's most pressing environmental problems and issues of poverty and underdevelopment. The hope of the organizers was that the relaxation of Cold War tensions, combined with the new awareness of ecological matters, would create a climate conducive to truly global cooperation in tackling these great problems.

The reality revealed by the conference, however, was that the old

East–West tensions had simply been superseded by conflicts between the industrialized North and the underdeveloped South and by competition among the rich nations themselves. The Earth Summit turned out to be something of a diplomatic fiasco, where the leaders of the Western world espoused some fine principles but refused to grant the third world anything worthwhile in practice.

The agenda for Rio contained a number of important issues with a North–South dimension: global warming, forest conservation, biological diversity and technology transfers. Both before and during the conference, every one of these issues became a source of conflict, especially between the representatives of the West and the third world. Global warming and deforestation were stark examples.

The debate about the problems which might be caused by global warming centred on the issue of how to reduce emissions of carbon dioxide (CO_2). The Western governments wanted to focus attention on the need to restrict the production of CO_2 and other 'greenhouse gases' in the third world. This was despite the fact that the industrial nations of the North produce, on a per capita basis, 10 times as much CO_2 as the countries of the South: the USA alone accounts for 22 per cent of all CO_2 produced. In effect, the West was saying that it wanted to combat global warming by restricting economic development in the third world, whilst refusing to make any meaningful concession itself.

The question of what to do with the world's remaining areas of forest probably divided North and South more bitterly than any other issue at Rio. The Western representatives wanted the tropical rainforests to be treated as global treasures and environmental assets which must be preserved. To impoverished developing nations, however, the rainforests are assets of a more tangible kind; clearing them can create profitable export goods and clear farmland at the same time.

When the Bush administration tried to highlight the rainforests issue in the run-up at Rio, with a proposal for an outright ban on logging in tropical forests, the developing countries retaliated with a call for the ban to cover northern-style forests as well. The USA has always resisted any attempt to investigate what it does in the publicly owned forests of Pacific Northwest. The result of this row at Rio was that the noble 'statement of principles' about forestation had no real practical consequences.

Western leaders not only obstructed any attempt at constructive discussion in Rio. They also sought every opportunity to scapegoat the impoverished Southern countries for global problems (like global warming) and to shift responsibility for the crisis in the third world on to the peoples of those societies themselves. Perhaps the clearest case was the way that the Western spokesmen sought to blame overpopulation for all of the suffering in Africa and Asia, thus distracting attention from the poverty and degradation created by the austerity policies of international financiers.

The disputes which dogged proceedings in Rio centred on the Western governments' determination to subordinate both the future of the environment and the welfare of the third world to their own strategic and commercial interests. The pressures of economic slump in the advanced capitalist nations ensured that they were less willing than ever to make humanitarian or environmental concessions. George Bush said, 'We cannot shut down the lives of many Americans by going to the extreme on the environment.' His actions showed that what he meant was 'American business comes first, and your concerns come last.'

S

SADCC, Southern African Development Coordinating Conference

This association of ▶ front line states was founded in 1980 in an attempt to reduce economic independence on South Africa. SADCC comprises Angola, Botswana, Lesotho, Malawi, Mozambique, Swaziland, Tanzania, Zambia and Zimbabwe.

Further reading

S. Amin, D. Chitala and I. Mandaza (eds), *SADCC: problems and prospects for disengagement and development in Southern Africa*, London 1989.

Sahel (Arabic = edge, border, coast)

Sahel is used to describe the swathe of land 120–80 miles wide between the Sahara and Sudan. It stretches from Mauritania in the west to Ethiopia in the east. An area of low rainfall, it is mainly pastoral. It is claimed to be the area most threatened by ▶ desertification.

Further reading

N. Cross, *The Sahel: the people's right to development*, London 1990.

sanctions

The term was first introduced by the Treaty of Versailles of 1919, when setting up the League of Nations. Article 16 of the league's constitution provided – in the case of one member making war on another – for

> the severance of all trade and financial relations, the prohibition of all intercourse between their nationals and the nationals of the covenant-breaking state, and the prevention of all financial, commercial or personal intercourse between the nationals of the covenant-breaking state and the nationals of any other state, whether a member of the League or not.

It is striking that of the many attempts to introduce sanctions the most assiduously carried out and damaging have been those directed against radical and Third World governments, or more generally against enemies of the leading capitalist powers in the Third World, e.g. Cuba from 1960, Nicaragua from 1984 and Iraq from 1990. Those directed against Western or pro-Western regimes (e.g. Italy from 1936, Southern Rhodesia after 1965 or South Africa in the 1980s) have been less thoroughly implemented and have had less impact. Since it is the major industrialized countries of the West which possess economic power, it is not surprising that sanctions work when they are in the interests of those major countries. A typically cynical case was that of the sanctions imposed against China after the Tiananmen Square massacre in 1989. Most of these were lifted when, in 1990, the Western powers wanted China's support in the United Nations Security Council for their war against Iraq.

Further reading

D.C. Hufbauer and J.J. Schott, *Economic Sanctions in Support of Foreign Policy Goals*, Washington, DC 1987.

Sandinistas, Frente Sandinista de Liberación Nacional (FSLN, Sandinista National Liberation Front)

The Sandinistas are the Nicaraguan guerrilla front formed in 1962 which led the revolution of 1979. They are named after the Nicaraguan guerrilla leader Augusto César Sandino, who fought the US marines occupying Nicaragua from 1927 to 1932 and was murdered in 1934 by members of the newly formed National Guard commanded by General Anastasio Somoza. The latter became president of Nicaragua 1936–56 and was later succeeded by his sons, Luis and then Anastasio.

The FSLN was formed in 1962 by young former members of the Stalinist Partido Socialista Nicaragüense (PSN, Nicaraguan Socialist Party) inspired by ▶ Castro's Cuba and disillusioned by the PSN's conciliatory policy towards the Somoza dictatorship. It suffered heavily in the bush at the hands of the National Guard. It split into three in 1975: the Prolonged People's War tendency, led by Tomás Borge Martinez, following the ▶ focismo line; the Proletarian tendency, led by Jaime Wheelock Roman, advocating 'mass work'; and the Terceristas, led by Daniel ▶ Ortega and his brother Humberto, advocating bold insurrectionary initiatives in the cities but also looking for temporary alliances with the Unión Democrática Liberal (UDEL, Democratic Liberal Union), an anti-Somoza alliance of the Nicaraguan establishment.

In 1978 the war was stepped up and following bombing of cities by the government, Los Doce (the Group of 12 prominent public figures) broke away from the UDEL to join the Terceristas to overthrow Somoza. All factions of the Sandinistas came together in March 1979, and in June the Catholic Church backed them. In July the Group of 12 and the FSLN agreed to share power in a 'Government of National Reconstruction' after Samoza had been overthrown, and this took power on 19 July. It was replaced by a five-man junta in December dominated by FSLN members. In September 1980 there were the first of recurrent clashes between the Miskito Indians of the Atlantic coast and the Sandinistas.

The USA initially backed the new regime but in 1981 the new President

271

Reagan reversed that policy, cutting off loans. In July 1981 Edén Pastora, one of the best-known Sandinista commanders, suddenly resigned and left the country, to re-emerge in 1982 calling for the overthrow of the regime. In September 1981 the Sandinistas declared a state of emergency. Claiming that the Sandinistas were supplying arms to guerrillas in neighbouring El Salvador, the Central Intelligence Agency (▶ CIA) stepped up support for the ▶ Contras fighting the Sandinistas. After efforts by other Latin American states Nicaragua agreed to cease aiding them (▶ FDR–FMLN). By late 1983 the CIA was directly conducting operations against Nicaragua. In November 1984 general elections endorsed the Sandinista regime and Daniel Ortega became president. In 1985 Reagan ordered a total economic blockade of Nicaragua and stepped up military aid to the Contras. In August 1987, faced with the economic squeeze, the Sandinistas agreed to a plan put forward by the Costa Rican President Oscar Arias to end the emergency, allow a free press and permit freedom of association. Ortega agreed to hold indirect talks with the Contras for a ceasefire, but the Contras stepped up their demands.

No definitive ceasefire had been reached by the time of presidential elections in February 1990 when the Sandinista candidate, Daniel Ortega, lost to US-backed Violetta Barrios de Chamorro, heading the Unión Nicaragüense de la Oposición (UNO, Nicaraguan Opposition Union) alliance of anti-Sandinista parties. The surprise defeat was a bitter blow to the morale of the Sandinistas who entered a period of profound internal debate and self-criticism. None the less, they remain the single party with the largest following and they have the largest bloc of votes in the National Assembly.

Chamorro has tried to pursue policies of national reconciliation which have led to a major split in her electoral alliance and to her increasing reliance on a form of undeclared political coalition with the Sandinistas. Humberto Ortega has been retained by Chamorro in his post as minister of defence and so the army continues in part to be a Sandinista institution.

During their period of rule in Nicaragua the Sandinistas attempted to introduce a number of radical, egalitarian policies including land reform, literacy campaigns and the extension of basic schooling, the introduction of a national health service, and rationing of basic foods. Many of these measures had some success but increasingly the government was dominated by problems associated with US economic and military sabotage and the war with the Contras. These problems reduced to such an extent the resources available for other activities that many of the reforms had to be abandoned. Production collapsed, hyperinflation developed and the country became dangerously dependent on outside aid for mere survival. The Sandinistas showed that they had genuinely revolutionary intentions and Nicaragua came to represent a new model for a Third World socialism which was not clearly aligned with the Soviet bloc. Yet the Sandinista experience in the end revealed that, for all its originality, it could not escape from the existence of ▶ neo-colonialism, though the US government had to dedicate a phenomenal amount of resources of every kind to inflict the damage which they did on the Nicaraguan experiment.

Further reading

G. Black, *Triumph of the People: the Sandinista revolution in Nicaragua*, London 1981.

R.R. Fagan, C.C. Deere and J.L. Coraggio (eds), *Transition and Development*, New York 1986.

Carlos Vilas, *The Sandinista Revolution: national liberation and social transformation*, New York 1986.

Sazman-e Cherika-ye Fedayin-e Khalq-e Iran ▶ Fedai Khalq

Sendero Luminoso (Spanish = shining path)

Sendero Luminoso is the popular name for the Partido Comunista de Perú (Communist Party of Peru), a Peruvian guerrilla group formed in 1970 by Dr Abimael Guzman Renoso and a group of Maoists who left the Peruvian Communist Party, and remained committed to Maoism after Mao's death, but were also influenced by José Carlos ▶ Mariátegui and ▶ indigenismo. Guzman is known as 'President Gonzalo' and the party is officially guided by 'Marxism-Leninism-Maoism-Gonzalo thought'.

In the 1970s Sendero Luminoso did political work among the peasantry in the Ayacucho region; it went underground in 1977 and took up arms in 1980 as Peru's first civilian president in 12 years – Fernando Belaúnde Terry – took over. Its strategy was to form liberated zones wherein it could operate freely, setting up people's courts and executing mayors and other representatives of the old order, but in July 1982 it moved out of its rural bases and proclaimed itself a new type of Marxist-Leninist-Maoist party waging a people's war from the countryside with the aim of carrying it into the cities.

In response to its attacks in cities Belaúnde declared martial law in eight provinces in 1983, but Sendero Luminoso again launched bomb attacks in Lima and in 1984 attacked a military base. Martial law was extended to 13 provinces. Attacks continued into 1985. Thousands of alleged 'Senderistas' were arrested but the bombing continued as Alan García Pérez was inaugurated as the first APRA president of Peru (▶ Aprismo, ▶ PRT). In 1986, 300 Senderistas were machine-gunned to death in a prison, and the number of deaths due to insurgency under President García surpassed 10,000.

Sendero Luminoso has carried out numerous attacks against economic, military and civilian targets, attempting to set up highly authoritarian new communities among the peasantry, and conducting trials in 'people's courts' of local officials who in many cases have been executed. It is also involved in a war with another guerrilla group, the Movimiento Revolucionario Tupac Amaru (MRTA, Tupac Amaru Revolutionary Movement), which has links with parties in the Izquierda Unida (IU, United Left). The surprise election of Alberto Fujimori as president of

273

Peru in 1990 has so far not affected the armed struggle and Sendero Luminoso continues to attempt to extend its influence from its original centre in Ayacucho to new areas of the country.

Shantytown (from Irish *sean tig* = old horse)

A shantytown is a settlement, lacking services, which consists of a collection of small crude shacks made of discarded materials serving as habitations for poor people on the outskirts of cities, especially in South America and Africa. A shantytown is also called favela or rancho (South America), barrio (Central America), Busti or Kampong (Asia) and bidonville or shanty (Africa). The inhabitants of shantytowns generally lack adequate access to any of the supposed benefits of urban life: safe water, sanitation, electric power and health services.

In cities such as Mexico City, Alexandria, Ouagadougou, Bombay, Karachi, Dar es Salaam and many others between one-third and three-quarters of the urban population are estimated to be living in shantytowns. Demographers estimate that the population living in Third World shantytowns is growing much faster than the rural poor population and so poverty is being rapidly urbanized.

Further reading

P. Lloyd, *Slums of Hope? Shanty towns of the Third World*, London 1979.

Sharia (Arabic = the correct law)

Sharia is the moral code to be followed by believers in ▶ Islam as recorded in the Koran. Though originally a purely personal religious code, Islamic states now incorporate its provisions: for example, laws against drinking alcohol in Saudi Arabia and elsewhere, a law for the chopping off of the hands of thieves in Sudan under Numeiri, and the public flogging of adulterers in Pakistan.

Shawras ▶ workers' control

Shia, Shi'ite ▶ Islam

South Commission

This commission of 28 prominent Third World politicians and intellectuals, chaired by former President Julius Nyerere of Tanzania, aims at redefining development priorities from the collective point of view of the South. Its report, *The Challenge to the South* (1990), repeats many of the same ideas which appeared in the ▶ Brandt Report or formed part of the proposed New International Economic Order (▶ NIEO). The report

274

concludes that it is necessary for the South to speak for its interests more loudly and with one voice, but offers no breakthrough on how the existing opposite tendencies are to be reversed.

Further reading

South Commission, *The Challenge to the South: the report of the South Commission*, London 1990.

South Pacific Forum

The international conference of the Pacific islands of Fiji, Nauru, Tonga, Western Samoa and the Cook Islands plus Australia and New Zealand first met at Wellington, New Zealand in August 1971. Subsequently other islands have joined. In 1983 the forum called for the independence of New Caledonia from France, and has since been in the forefront of the campaign to stop French nuclear testing in the Pacific.

South West Africa People's Organization ▶ SWAPO

South West Township ▶ Soweto

Southern African Development Coordinating Conference ▶ SADCC

Soweto

Soweto, which is an acronym for South West Township, was originally a squatters' camp just outside Johannesburg, South Africa and is now the largest black city in the Southern hemisphere. In 1976 and 1977 it was the centre of an enormous popular uprising against the ▶ apartheid regime. Though it was defeated through bloody repression by the regime, it brought a new generation of Africans into the political fight against apartheid and fundamentally changed the dynamic of politics in South Africa. In retrospect it can be seen to have inflicted a wound on the apartheid system from which the latter was unable to recover. ▶ ANC, ▶ black consciousness.

spheres of influence

This term was introduced at the end of the nineteenth century to describe the division of Africa by the European powers. It was a concept much used in the division of world power between the victorious allies after the Second World War. Nowadays the USA regards the whole of the Third World as its sphere of influence.

275

stabex

This export earnings stabilization scheme was introduced in 1975 as a consequence of the ▶ Lomé Convention to provide aid by way of loans to member countries suffering losses on export earnings from basic commodities. Over forty commodities qualify for claims. The object of the scheme is to stabilize incomes in the face of fluctuating commodity markets. Stabex only applies to the exports of the African, Caribbean and Pacific (ACP) countries to the European Community, and its funding is insufficient to compensate for major declines in raw material prices.

stages of economic growth

W.W. Rostow's influential book, *The Stages of Economic Growth* (1960), is generally seen as the most developed exposition of the Western theory of modernization as applied to the problem of economic growth.

The central argument of economic growth theory is straightforward. It is suggested that the free enterprise system that made Western industrialization possible is absent in Third World societies. Furthermore, the values and institutions of traditional societies discourage individual initiative, thus preventing the take-off of their economies. Lecturing the Third World about the virtues of private enterprise is the main message of economic growth theory. As Dean Acheson, a leading figure in the US State Department, told Latin America:

> This country has been built by private initiative . . . . The preponderance of our economic strength depends today as in the past upon the technical and financial resources and, even more, upon the abilities and morale of private citizens. I venture to say that the same thing is true of the other American nations.[1]

Acheson's lecture is based on the assumption that the pattern of historical development that characterized the West provides the model for change in the Third World. Western experience is seen as providing the solution to the economic problems of Third World societies. It was Rostow's achievement to transform this ethnocentric prejudice into an elaborate economic theory.

According to Rostow, it is possible to identify five stages in the economic growth of all societies: traditional society, preconditions for take-off, take-off, the drive to maturity and the age of high mass consumption. The first three stages are described in the following terms:

> First, the traditional society. A traditional society is one whose structure is developed within limited production functions, based on pre-Newtonian science and technology, and on pre-Newtonian attitudes towards the physical world . . . . The second stage of growth embraces societies in the process of transition: that is, the period when the preconditions for take-off are developed: for it takes time to transform traditional society in the ways necessary for it to exploit the fruits of modern science . . . the stage of precondition

arises not indigenously but from some external intrusion by more advanced societies . . . the third stage . . . the take-off . . . is the interval when the old blocks and resistance to steady growth are finally overcome . . . . Growth becomes the normal condition.[2]

Rostow's schema suggests that at one time Europe and North America were at stage one. In other words, at some point in the past traditional Western societies were in a position comparable to that of the Third World today. In equating the present position of the Third World with that of Europe hundreds of years ago, Rostow ignores the reality of underdevelopment. The development of Western capitalism was a global process through which the Third World was transformed.

Rostow's equation of the first stage of economic growth – traditional society – with the Third World ignores this process of history. The Third World itself is the creation of world capitalism just as much as is the West. The only difference between the two regions of the world is that in one case capitalism stimulated economic growth, in the other the end result was stagnation.

The neglect of history by Rostow is entirely understandable. Had he really inspected the past, it would have been evident that there is a clear connection between Western development and Third World underdevelopment. The deindustrialization of India in the nineteenth century is only the most striking example of a pattern of exploitation through which the transfer of resources from the Third World assisted the development of Western capitalism. Whatever were the stages of economic growth in the West they can throw little light on the problems facing the Third World.

Even if one ignores this central deficiency, it is still difficult to find any redeeming features in Rostow's theory. A close examination reveals, for example, that his analysis has very little economic content. He explains the shift from the traditional to the take-off stage by placing emphasis on values and attitudes. The procedure is breathtakingly simplistic. He asks why it was that the take-off first occurred in the UK. He then lists the significant features of British society in transition and suggests that the UK developed because it possessed all these features. Tautology is put forward as a substitute for explanation. Rostow concludes that the UK modernized first because it had a strong sense of nationalist purpose. He states that 'a society modernizing itself in a nationalist reaction to intrusion or the threat of intrusion from more advanced powers' provides the main impulse for taking-off.[3] Why did not other societies, including those from the Third World which also reacted to foreign intrusion, take off? Rostow remains silent on this subject.

In emphasizing British nationalism as the major force behind take-off, Rostow shifts the focus of his work onto cultural and social values. From this perspective the main obstacle to economic growth is the attitudes that prevail in society. He explains that the 'achievement of preconditions for take-off required major changes in political and social structure and even in effective social values'.[4] Since the take-off has not occurred in many parts of the Third World it follows that it is its social structure and values that are at fault.

277

Rostow's work provides the economic corollary of modernization theory. It follows the same procedure and designates the attitudes and values of Third World societies as constituting the main obstacle to economic development. From this perspective it follows that the Third World can only blame itself for putting up with such old-fashioned views and institutions. The West as such bears no responsibility for the state of affairs in the Third World. On the contrary, the West is a model for what the Third World ought to aspire to achieve.

The Stages of Economic Growth is an invitation to the Third World to imitate the West. Those Third World countries that have accepted this invitation have generally found that it is easier to imitate than to experience real economic growth.

Rostow's important work is subtitled 'a non-communist manifesto' and he claims that his theory discredits Marxism and communism. What he means is that it offers the perspective of all countries' reaching the stage of high mass consumption under capitalism without the need for any social revolution; the whole world can, with the right policies, become like the USA.

None the less, it might be wondered what is the difference between Rostow and Marx since the latter also believed through the greater part of his life that capitalism would industrialize the world on the model of Europe (▶ Marxism). The difference is that while Rostow sees the development of each country as a separate historical event without any real association with the development of any other country, Marx sees development in terms of the accumulation of capital on a world scale. The development of one country may be at the expense of others, as was the case with the primitive accumulation of capital through which Europe entered into the phase of modern economic growth by pillaging the wealth of Asian, African and American countries.

It was later Marxists, rather than Marx, who extended that analysis to argue that capital accumulation does not homogenize the world, it polarizes it. In fact, ▶ dependency theory was in part born out of an attack on Rostow's perspective that countries develop independently of each other and can all follow the same path to development regardless of history.

To Rostow, all countries start from the same point. To Marxists, however, ▶ underdevelopment is a state which is not equivalent to that of the European countries or the USA in the nineteenth century; it is the result of centuries of capital accumulation in the world which has had the effect of impoverishing and disrupting the economies of the Third World. In other words, Rostow implicitly denies that world capitalism has entered an imperialist phase in which growth in the Third World is possible, but at best has a restricted and distorted character which prevents it from following the path of the developed countries.

Notes

1. Cited in D.A. Baldwin, *Economic Development and American Foreign Policy 1943–62*, Chicago 1966, p. 193.
2. W.W. Rostow, *The Stages of Economic Growth*, Cambridge 1960, pp. 4–9.

3. Ibid., p. 34.
4. Ibid., p. 36.

Sudan (from Arabic *Bilad al-Sudan* = the country of the black people)

The name covers an area of moderate rainfall between the Sahel and the African tropics, stretching from Senegal on the west coast to Ethiopia in the east. It is rich farming and pastoral land with a high population. In the past it was the home of the old African empires of SongHai, Ghana and Mali. It is the main centre of Islam in Africa.

Sudan is also the name of the largest country in Africa, located around the upper reaches of the river Nile.

Sukarno, Ahmed (1901–70)

Prominent in Indonesia's struggle for independence from Dutch colonial rule, Ahmed Sukarno was active in his country's political life from the 1920s until his death. Born in Surabaya, Java in 1901, the son of a schoolteacher, he received his political education at an early age. In 1926 he graduated as a civil engineer from the Bandung Technical Institute and in the same year joined the Bandung Study Club, whose members called for rejection of cooperation with the Dutch colonial authorities.

Out of the activities of the Study Club, the Nationalist Party of Indonesia was established in July 1927 with Sukarno as its first chairman. During the early debates and discussions about anti-colonialism, Sukarno was able to develop his philosophy of Marhaenism, an Indonesian variant of socialist thought.

His arrest in 1929 by the Dutch colonial authorities, and his subsequent trial, popularized his name and cause in the country. Sukarno made a brilliant anti-colonial speech from the dock, after which he was sentenced to three years' imprisonment. On his release, he continued his political activity and was arrested again. After subsequent terms of imprisonment, he went into exile until the Japanese army occupied Indonesia in 1942.

Sukarno was able to forge a coalition of convenience with the Japanese authorities against the former Dutch colonizers; when the Japanese saw the prospect of defeat in 1945 they allowed Sukarno to head the Committee for the Preparation of Indonesian Independence. On 17 August 1945 Sukarno formally announced Indonesia's independence and became its first president.

This did not deter the Dutch who tried to re-establish their colonial authority following the formal cessation of hostilities in the Second World War. They managed to destabilize Indonesia and took Sukarno prisoner in December 1948, but pressure from Indonesia's effective guerrilla liberation movement as well as widespread support from international opinion forced the Dutch to recognize independent Indonesia's sovereignty.

Sukarno's Marhaenism (named after the Indonesian peasant who inspired him) looks, like Gandhism, to an idealized rural past and is at once both a nationalistic and a 'socialistic' philosophy. Communist ideas had gained wide currency in Indonesia during the Communist Party's activism in the 1920s, but Sukarno argued that support for communist or socialist ideas would have to be combined with religious and nationalist currents of thought. He synthesized these into NASAKOM – from the Indonesian words nasionalis (nationalist), agama (religion) and komunis (communist) – a doctrine which he saw as the basis for a popular front.

Reality progressively diverged from the ideals of these philosophies. The government's bold reform programme, including land reform, was implemented with declining vigour. The Communist Party (the PKI), aligned with Beijing, grew and Sukarno both depended on it and was unable to offer an alternative to it. During the 1950s and 1960s Indonesia was plagued with secessionist disputes and economic problems about which Sukarno admitted to having little interest or knowledge.

Seeing growing instability in the country, the conservative landowning classes in alliance with the Indonesian military put pressure on Sukarno to halt his reform programme. Sukarno's response was to restrict political activity and concentrate more power with the executive, and the country's political forces polarized. Sukarno explained his decision to increase his personal power as a means to reassure the PKI that the military right would not seize the state, and at the same time reassure Muslim groups that the radical left would not gain ascendancy. Sukarno conferred upon himself the title of president-for-life in 1963 through the Provisional People's Consultative Assembly.

This failed to mollify the opposing factions, with the military – supported by the USA and (more tacitly) by the USSR – becoming ever more strident. In 1965 an attempted pre-emptive coup by a group of left-wing officers was supported by the PKI. This offered the right-wing military officers, under the commander-in-chief of the ground forces, General Suharto, the opportunity to seize power in all but name and declare war on the PKI. There followed a massacre of hundreds of thousands of PKI members and supporters. Sukarno, robbed of a base, was obliged to surrender effective power to Suharto in 1966 and titular power in 1967. He died in 1970.

Sukarno's failure to overcome Indonesia's domestic problems did not prevent him taking several important effective initiatives on the international scene, the most notable of which was the ▶ Bandung Conference of Asian and African countries in 1955 and his joint founding of the ▶ non-aligned movement.

Sunni ▶ Islam

sustainable development

Sustainable development is development which maintains an appropriate balance with the material environment. This idea, which has emerged from recent debate on the ▶ environment, is based on the assumption that there is a limit to the amount of pollution which can be produced and the quantity of resources which can be used up without human life destroying its own physical environmental base. It stresses recycling, the uses of renewable resources, the reduction of waste, the design of new technologies and changes in consumption habits. By its nature it is a global concept and thus for rational implementation requires a global decision-making process which at present shows little sign of emerging. ▶ development.

Further reading

M. Redclift, *Sustainable Development: exploring the contradictions*, London 1987.

SWAPO, South West Africa People's Organization of Namibia

The liberation movement which led the fight to free Namibia from South African occupation, SWAPO was formed in 1957 and led by Sam Nujoma and Andimba Toivo Ja Toivo. In 1966 it adopted armed struggle and formed the People's Liberation Army of Namibia (PLAN). The United Nations (UN) terminated South Africa's mandate over Namibia in that year, but South Africa ignored it. SWAPO was badly squeezed when South Africa invaded newly independent Angola (▶ Angolan liberation movement). South Africa repeatedly tried to impose an internal settlement first via the Turnhalle Conference in 1975, and then with the Multi-Party Conference in 1985.

In September 1978 the UN adopted the Western-sponsored Resolution 435 to end the war through UN-supervised elections. South Africa rejected it but agreed to attend a conference in Geneva in 1981 with SWAPO, the Western powers and the ▶ front line states. It withdrew with the advent of the more sympathetic Reagan administration, which proposed that South Africa hold on to Namibia until Angola agreed to expel Cuban troops, thereby launching a policy known as 'constructive engagement with South Africa'. The USA implicitly backed repeated South African attacks on SWAPO and incursions into Angola. In 1984 the USA made a breakthrough with the Lusaka agreement for a joint South Africa–Angola commission to supervise withdrawal of South African forces from Angola in return for the establishment of a demilitarized zone on the Angolan–Namibian border. SWAPO agreed but refused to stop PLAN activities until South Africa accepted Resolution 435. South Africa continued to raid Angola.

After many further attempts at a settlement, breakthrough finally come in 1988 when, partly as a result of the Reagan–Gorbachev summit, South Africa, Angola and Cuba reached an agreement to implement the UN's independence plan for Namibia in 1989. This was part of the settlement which was to lead also to the withdrawal of South African and Cuban troops from Angola. Elections in November 1989 produced a SWAPO parliamentary majority and the new assembly elected Sam Nujoma as president of the new republic in February 1990. Namibia became independent under a SWAPO government on 21 March 1990. It has pursued cautious, conservative policies and has attempted to reconcile the white population, to the point of maintaining in office the pre-independence head of the police force.

281

T

Tamil Tigers, Liberation Tigers of Tamil Eelam (LTTE)

This guerrilla group was formed in 1976 to seek the creation of a separate Tamil state, Tamil Eelam, in the north and east of Sri Lanka in the face of discrimination against the Tamils by the Sinhalese majority.

In 1972 three Tamil organizations, representing the indigenous Sri Lankan Tamils (cultivated by the British as administrators) and Indian Tamils (brought over during the colonial period to work in the tea plantations) came together to form the Tamil United Front in order to fight for official recognition of the Tamil language, ethnic minority rights, administrative decentralization and the abolition of the caste system. Having made no progress, in 1976 it became the Tamil United Liberation Front (TULF) pledging itself to 'restore' the state of Tamil Eelam as a separate state.

In 1977 the right-wing Sinhalese United National Party (UNP) came to power under Junius Jayawardene. The TULF becoming the largest opposition grouping under its new leader Appapillai Amirthalingam. S. Thondaman of the Ceylon Workers' Congress, however, representing the Indian Tamils, accepted a place in the government. An anti-Tamil pogrom broke out after the election, with 30,000 forced to flee their homes and 100 killed. In 1978 Jayawardene brought in a new constitution making Buddhism the state religion (Tamils are predominantly Hindus, Catholics or Muslims).

As violence against Tamils continued unchecked, younger Tamils became disillusioned with the TULF and turned to the Tamil Intelligence Group for Eelam Research (TIGER), founded by Velupillai Prabhakaran to produce a Tamil nation as the only solution. They opted for armed struggle and renamed themselves the Tamil New Tigers (TNT), later taking the name Liberation Tigers of Tamil Eelam (LTTE). The movement was banned in 1978 and repression against it was stepped up. The LTTE really took off in 1979 with the declaration of a state of emergency and military occupation of the northern Tamil city of Jaffna. By the time of the 1981 elections, the LTTE had overtaken the TULF and won 75 per cent of the vote in Jaffna. The TULF held talks with the government, which accepted many of its demands, and agreed to end campaigning for Tamil Eelam and stop its boycott of parliament. By 1982 Amirthalingam was publicly condemning the LTTE as 'criminals'. Militants in the TULF split in 1982 to form the Tamil Eelam Liberation Front (TELF) to support the Tigers' military campaign.

In 1983 the LTTE published its policy for a social and political revolution. This, along with Sri Lankan military outrages, rallied support to the LTTE who organized a boycott of the 1983 local elections in Jaffna, and the TULF disintegrated. A mass pogrom of Tamils instigated by the government ensued, in which thousands died and thousands were driven out of Colombo and other non-Tamil-majority areas. Jayawardene blamed the killings on Sinhalese left groups and the Janatta Vimukti Peremuna (JVP, People's Liberation Front). The JVP was a rural Sinhalese organization formed among lower Buddhist castes in central and southern Sri Lanka in the late 1960s to challenge upper caste control of the country. It had engaged in terrorist attacks against the government and led a widespread uprising in 1971 which was only put down with British and Indian aid leaving 5000 dead.

After the 1983 crackdown, rivalry among Tamil groups became intense. The Tigers' main rival was the Maoist People's Liberation Organization of Tamil Eelam (PLOTE), which was heavily dependent on connections with Indian Maoists, and open fighting broke out between the two groups in 1986. The Tigers also fought with the Eelam People's Revolutionary Front and the Tamil Eelam Liberation Organization in 1986–7.

Seeing the confusion, the Colombo government ordered an all-out onslaught on the Tigers in February 1987, aiming to take the Tigers' main base in Jaffna. It failed but caused a vast slaughter. Indian Prime Minister Rajiv Gandhi put pressure on Colombo to achieve a settlement and ordered an airdrop of supplies to Tamils in Jaffna. In July Gandhi and Jayawardene signed an agreement for autonomy for Jaffna province and a referendum on it in the Eastern province, in return for the Tamil fighters laying down their arms. Only the Tigers refused to accept the plan, though their leader was induced to issue a statement in New Delhi interpreted as accepting the agreement. India sent in 9000 troops to police the ceasefire and replace the Sri Lankan army. In October 1987 they launched an attack on Jaffna to drive out the Tigers. It took them three weeks. Prabhakaran escaped to lead the resistance to the joint Indian–Sri Lankan attack on the Tamils. After increasing to 45,000 and inflicting immense damage on the Tigers, the Indian army finally withdrew in 1989 and the situation reverted to one of intense armed conflict between the Tigers and the Sri Lankan forces, simultaneously involved in a war with the JVP.

Tamils

The Tamils are an ancient Indian people concentrated in the southern tip of the subcontinent but also scattered throughout the region. In particular, they form a substantial minority in Sri Lanka, from which they have been claiming secession for their own state – Eelam – since the mid-1970s. ▶ Tamil Tigers.

Further reading

S. Ponnambalam, *Sri Lanka: the national question and the Tamil Liberation Struggle*, London 1982.

technology transfer

This term refers to the spread of technological knowhow between nations. Part of development is generally regarded as involving the increasing use by Third World countries of technologies now in use only in the developed countries. There are many ways in which such transfer is restricted, including patents and copyright (intellectual property), business secrecy and legal bans on the transfer of strategic technologies. One of the demands of the New International Economic Order (▶ NIEO) is that the Third World should have freer access to restricted technology which it might need. In fact, however, in the negotiations in ▶ GATT known as the Uruguay Round, the USA insisted that Third World countries which 'pirate' computer software and other copyrighted products should be made to pay royalties. Freedom of access may as a result be reduced.

Freedom of access, however, would not solve all the problems of technology transfer. Technology is normally embodied in machines and production methods and so its transfer may require also a transfer of productive capacity. That means investment either by the Third World country or by multinational corporations. On what terms can or will domestic or foreign firms use transferred technology? One problem may be the price which has to be paid (the price of the machine, or the royalty for the right to use the technology); another may be that multinational corporations may transfer technology only if they can dictate certain conditions such as the insistence on management teams from the home country, limitations on exporting the products or on the future course of product development, or controls on the conditions of labour. The transfer of technology, in other words, is the simultaneous transfer of other conditions and obligations which may have their drawbacks.

While there is no doubt that the transfer of much technology is a key aspect of development, it would be wrong to overestimate its importance. Not all technological development in the Third World should be simply the result of transfers from the developed countries. Technology assumes a pattern of production and consumption and a certain kind of social relations. For many reasons, therefore, the technology of the West may not always be appropriate to development in the Third World. That means that some technology transfer may be bad, regardless of its conditions. It also means that at least as important as technology transfer is research and development in the Third World in order to produce more appropriate technologies. ▶ appropriate technology.

Further reading

D.S. Thomas, *Importing Technology into Africa: foreign investment and the supply of technological innovations*, New York 1976.

terms of trade

Terms of trade are a numerical measure of changes in the conditions under which a country's exports exchange for its imports. The aim of measuring the terms of trade is to indicate changes in the effective purchasing power of a country's exports or in the effective cost of imports in terms of the domestic resources which are required to purchase them.

The most commonly encountered measure of the terms of trade is a simple ratio of an index (a form of average) of export prices to an index of import prices. (This is known technically as the barter terms of trade.) If from one year to another the price of exports rises by 10 per cent and the price of imports remains the same then the purchasing power of a given amount of exports has increased or, in other words, the terms of trade have improved.

An improvement in the terms of trade is not necessarily desirable for a country. A rise in the price of its exports may mean that there is a more than proportional drop in the amount sold (in technical terms the product is 'price elastic') and so the purchasing power of a unit of exports may rise but the purchasing power of exports as a whole may fall. When countries devalue their currency their terms of trade worsen; but they expect that their balance of trade will improve. The World Bank estimates that the terms of trade for the Third World as a whole declined by 11 per cent between 1980 and 1988. The terms of trade of the newly industrializing countries (▶ NICs), however, declined by even more (16 per cent) and yet in their case the decline was compensated by a large rise in the demand for their products.

In another sense, too, a worsening of the terms of trade may not be damaging; when export prices fall, the productivity of labour may rise in order to compensate. In this case a given amount of imports costs more in terms of the amount of exports exchanged for it but may cost less in terms of the amount of labour used. There is another measure of the terms ('the factorial terms of trade') which takes this into account, but it is so difficult to calculate that it is seldom encountered in practice.

These points suggest that it is difficult to draw simple conclusions about movements of the terms of trade and their consequences. None the less, a particular hypothesis about the terms of trade has played a major role in the history of the analysis of the economic situation of the Third World. There is a long-term tendency for the terms of trade of the Third World to decline, mainly because its exports are concentrated in primary products for which world demand expands very slowly, while its imports tend to be manufactured goods for which world demand expands more rapidly.

This hypothesis, associated with the name of Raul Prebisch, the first director of the United Nations Economic Commission for Latin America (ECLA), became one of the pillars of most radical analyses of the Third World. It appears as part of most versions of ▶ dependency theory and in a different form as the theory of ▶ unequal exchange. Some radical analysts, however, such as the US Marxist Paul Baran, rejected it out of hand on the grounds that the export prices of raw materials did not mean anything because they were simply the internal accounting prices used by vertically integrated multinational corporations (▶▶ underdevelopment).

For this reason, as well as some of the above-mentioned complications of the concept of the terms of trade, the long-term hypothesis is very difficult to prove or disprove for certain and it is a matter of constant debate.

What is clear is that there is a group of primary products which form a high percentage of the ▶ exports of many Third World countries for which demand is growing slowly, if at all, and whose prices, since the brief boom around 1973, have tended to fall steadily. This has been one of the reasons (among several others) why, in a number of especially poor countries, total exports have fallen or risen very slowly during recent years. These price falls have not only reduced the purchasing power of exports in terms of imports but they have also led to an increase in the real burden of debt (▶ debt crisis).

Third World ▶ Introduction

Tupamaros, Movimiento de Liberación Nacional (MLN, National Liberation Movement)

This Uruguayan guerrilla organization was formed in 1963. The Tupamaros were named after Tupac Amaru, an eighteenth-century Peruvian Indian rebel. Organizing among sugar workers, they launched guerrilla operations in 1963.

The Tupamaros emerged as a prominent political force in the wave of unrest which followed right-wing President Jorge Pacheco Areco's programme of economic austerity in 1968. By mid-1972 they had reached their peak with 6000 members, mainly recruited from among students and teachers. The military, however, used the danger represented by the Tupamaros as one of its pretexts for seizing power and instituting a dictatorship in 1973. The Tupamaros were crushed under the repression; a large proportion of them were either killed or jailed.

In 1985, with the return of constitutional rule, the Uruguayan Supreme Court reviewed cases of imprisoned Tupamaros and ordered many of them to be released. In September 1985 Raúl Sendio Antonaccio, the Tupamaros leader, announced that they had abandoned armed struggle and the MLN became a political party campaigning for the nationalization of banks, land reform and the abrogation of all foreign debts as part of the Frente Amplio (Broad Front).

U

UDF, United Democratic Front

This umbrella organization was the public face of most anti-apartheid protests within South Africa in the 1980s (► apartheid).

The UDF was conceived at a Johannesburg conference in January 1983 by Dr Allan Boesak, President of the World Alliance of Reformed Churches. It was launched in August of that year in Mitchells Plain, Cape Town and successfully campaigned for a boycott of the new South African constitution setting up a mock parliament for Indians and Coloureds. The UDF had the sponsorship of the African National Congress (► ANC) but also obtained the affiliation of 700 opposition groups with 2 million members, though not ► black consciousness organizations like ► AZAPO. Its charter called for an end to forced removals, the release of Nelson ► Mandela and all political prisoners, the lifting of the bans on persons and political organizations, the ending of police harassment, the building of more homes, a stop to rent increases, the lifting of the freeze on township development and the building of more schools and crèches. It ended with a call for a democratic, united and non-racial South Africa.

Violent confrontations broke out between UDF supporters and AZAPO during US Senator Edward Kennedy's visit to South Africa in January 1985. The South African authorities also targeted the UDF as an 'ANC front'. The biggest threat to the UDF, however, was the apartheid regime's ability to manipulate ethnic tensions. Vigilantes loyal to Zulu Chief Gatsha Buthulezi's conservative Inkatha organization were prominent in helping the state's attempt to smash the UDF.

The UDF was banned in 1987, and in 1991 it dissolved itself arguing that the legalization of other organizations (in particular the ANC) meant that its transitional role was complete.

Ujamaa (Kiswahili = communityhood)

This word, which is used to denote community or national familyhood, was chosen by Julius Nyerere, former prime minister and later president of Tanzania, to express the content of a socialism deeply rooted in African tradition or more specifically ► African Socialism. The meaning of Ujamaa is outlined in Nyerere's *Ujamaa: the basis of African Socialism*.[1] The political strategy of Ujamaa is elaborated in the government of Tanzania's definitive statement, the Arusha Declaration.[2]

Ujamaa as a philosophy is based on an alleged organic relationship between the African tradition of the past and African Socialism of the future. According to Nyerere, the main defining features of socialism were already evident in embryo in traditional African society. For Nyerere, socialism is primarily about egalitarianism and the absence of exploitation. According to the Arusha Declaration, it is based on the assumptions of human equality, on the belief that it is wrong for one man to dominate or to exploit another and in the knowledge that every individual hopes to live in society as a free man able to lead a decent life in conditions of peace with his neighbours.

Nyerere argues that egalitarianism and the absence of exploitation were prevalent in pre-colonial Africa. The institution of the extended family, the communal ownership of land and the sense of community this instills are seen as traditions and values which can provide the foundations for African Socialism.

Nyerere recognizes that egalitarian traditions and institutions do not prevail in post-colonial Africa and therefore Ujamaa is promoted as an objective of development, and the declaration warns: 'Tanzania is a nation of peasants and workers but it is not yet a socialist society. It still contains elements of feudalism and capitalism – with their temptations. These feudalistic and capitalistic features of our society could spread and entrench themselves.' To minimize the risks of non-socialist conventions gaining strength, Nyerere sought to introduce policies which narrow the gap between rich and poor.

The strategy of building Ujamaa was based on discouraging exploitation and the accumulation of private wealth. It relied on nationalization, the rejection of money as a basis for development and the policy of self-reliance. In 1969 Nyerere attempted to implement Ujamaa Vijijini (socialism in the rural areas) through the establishment of Ujamaa villages based on cooperation, self-reliance and socialist practices which were envisaged as the cornerstone of Ujamaa.

As is widely known, the strategy of Ujamaa and its policies such as the establishment of the Ujamaa villages have not been particularly successful. The Tanzanian government has managed to avoid many of the excesses and mistakes of most post-colonial African governments, but it has not been able to evolve an effective development strategy. The policy of self-reliance has not worked and Tanzania has become seriously reliant on foreign assistance. In 1985 Nyerere himself declared that Tanzania was no closer to self-reliance than it was in the 1960s.

The main weakness of the philosophy of Ujamaa is that its objectives are ethical ones rather than ones based on the conditions prevailing in Tanzania. The attempt to resurrect past traditions as the foundations for Ujamaa itself shows its irrelevance in the present. Without any foundations in material reality, Ujamaa becomes merely an ethical norm – more a form of wishful thinking than a guide to action. The gap between the reality and the objectives of Ujamaa could not be overcome through education or exhortation. The implementation of Ujamaa through reliance on highly motivated selfless individuals flies in the face of reality. Any strategy based on motivation is essentially voluntaristic and an act of will is no match for the mundane obstacles posed by everyday life. Socialism in Africa, as elsewhere, requires the transformation of existing institutions and social relations for its realization. As an objective, it must be based on *what is possible* and not simply on *what ought to be*. Although a practical failure, the experience of attempting to implement Ujamaa provides valuable lessons for those interested in evolving an enlightened development strategy for the Third World.

Further reading

J. Boesen, T. Moody and B.S. Madsen, *Ujamaa: socialism from above*, Uppsala 1978.

G. Hyden, *Beyond Ujamaa in Tanzania: underdevelopment and an uncaptured peasantry*, London 1980.

B.U. Mwansasu and C. Pratt (eds), *Towards Socialism in Tanzania*, Toronto 1979.

Notes

1. Reprinted in J. Nyerere, *Freedom and Unity/Uhuru na Umoja*, Dar es Salaam 1964.
2. *The Arusha Declaration/Azimio na Arusha: Ujamaa na Kujitegemea*, Dar es Salaam 1967.

UNCTAD, United Nations Conference on Trade and Development

Founded in Geneva in June 1964, its aims are to promote international trade with a view to accelerating development, initiate multilateral trade agreements and harmonize the trade and development policies of governments and regional economic groups.

UNCTAD has held seven major international conferences (Geneva 1964, New Delhi 1968, Santiago de Chile 1972, Nairobi 1974, Manila 1979, Belgrade 1983 and Geneva 1987). The resolutions of the conferences, and the work of the agency in general, have conformed closely to the policies advocated by the ▶ Group of 77 Third World Countries. Many of its policies are consistent with the demands of the New International Economic Order (▶ NIEO). Since it is often seen in the West as an economic pressure group for the Third World, UNCTAD has consequently found it increasingly difficult to obtain financing from the major contributors to the United Nations. For this reason, among others, UNCTAD has lost some of its impact in the recent epoch of the ▶ debt crisis and the fashion for ▶ neo-liberalism in economic policies.

underdevelopment

This is a concept first formulated in the 1950s by the US Marxist Paul Baran in his book *The Political Economy of Growth* (1957). For Baran, underdevelopment does not consist in the absence of development but the undermining of the potential for development of a country through the removal to the industrialized countries of the surplus which could generate growth. In a slightly different form the concept acquired even greater importance for writers in the school of ▶ dependency theory, especially André Gunder Frank. Underdevelopment is seen not as a condition of a country at a particular moment but as a process which is the necessary counterpart of the process of development in the developed

289

countries. Thus the process of underdevelopment acquires a verb – to underdevelop, as in the title of a book by the Guyanan follower of dependency theory, Walter Rodney, *How Europe Underdeveloped Africa* (1988).

Further reading

S. Amin, *Accumulation on a World Scale: a critique of the theory of underdevelopment*, New York 1974.

I. Roxborough, *Theories of Underdevelopment*, London 1979.

unequal exchange

Unequal exchange is a concept which appears in Marx's *Grundrisse* but which in relation to the Third World was developed by Arghiri Emmanuel in his book *Unequal Exchange*[1] and by Samir Amin in his *Unequal Development*.[2] It holds that surplus value is extracted from the Third World and transferred to the advanced capitalist countries through exchange as well as through direct exploitation in production. The price ratios established in the world market mean that the Third World is obliged to exchange more of its labour for less of the labour of advanced countries. Emmanuel drew the controversial conclusion from this theory that the working class in the advanced countries also benefited from imperialism and so participated in the exploitation of the workers of the Third World. As a result, international solidarity of the working class was not possible. He drew much fire for this conclusion and in particular waged a polemical debate with the Marxist economist Charles Bettleheim.[3]

Notes

1. A. Emmanuel, *Unequal Exchange: a study in the imperialism of trade*, New York 1972.
2. S. Amin, *Unequal Development*, Brighton 1973.
3. C. Bettleheim, 'Theoretical comments', Appendix I of Emmanuel, op. cit.

UNESCO, United Nations Educational, Scientific and Cultural Organization

UNESCO was founded in London in November 1945, with present headquarters in Paris. Its purpose is to promote collaboration among nations through education, science, culture and communications in order to further universal respect for justice and the rule of law and fundamental freedoms for all, as affirmed in the United Nations Charter.

In recent years the work of UNESCO has suffered from an acute shortage of funds brought on by the withdrawal of support by the USA, the UK and other major contributors. The withdrawal was in part a protest against policies which were considered too favourable to the demands of the Third World and opposed to the interests of the industrialized West. ►► New International Information Order.

UNHCR ▶ refugees

United Democratic Front ▶ UDF

United Nations Conference on Trade and Development ▶ UNCTAD

United Nations Educational, Scientific and Cultural Organization ▶ UNESCO

United Nations High Commission for Refugees, Office of the ▶ refugees

urbanization

Throughout the Third World, urbanization is going on at a very rapid pace. The urban population of the Third World as a whole is growing at 4 per cent a year, compared with total population growth of 2 per cent. East Asia and Latin America are now almost as urbanized as the developed countries with almost 50 per cent of the population living in cities of more than 500,000 inhabitants. In 1960, 7 out of 10 of the world's largest cities were in developed countries; in the year 2000, 8 out of 10 will be in the Third World, with the prediction that Mexico City will have 25 million inhabitants by that time.

Third World cities are, however, very different from cities in the West in that an enormous (and growing) proportion of their populations live in ▶ shantytowns which are, in some ways, the negation of the traditional concept of the city as a place with stable dwellings and developed domestic and public services.

In relation to its level of development, therefore, the Third World is experiencing a precocious urbanization. In Europe and North America urbanization was a product of agricultural revolution, rising productivity and development; in the Third World it is a symptom of agrarian crisis and underdevelopment. Urbanization involves the translation of the problems of underdevelopment in the countryside into new kinds of poverty and social and economic problems in the cities. ▶▶ agrarian question.

Further reading

B. Roberts, *Cities of Peasants: the political economy of urbanization in the Third World*, London 1978.
R.E. Stren and R.R. White (eds), *African Cities in Crisis*, Boulder, Col. 1989.

V

Vietcong (Vietnamese = Vietnamese communists)

Vietcong was originally a derogatory name for the People's Liberation Armed Forces (PLAF), the guerrilla movement based in South Vietnam from the 1950s to the 1970s, inspired by Ho Chi Minh, the founding father of the Vietnamese liberation movement. Vietcong was also abbreviated derogatorily by the Americans to VCs.

Ho Chi Minh (1890–1969), the son of a bureaucrat in the French colonial administration, travelled widely, working at sea; in London and Paris he came into contact with Marxist groups. In the 1920s he became a convinced Leninist and later worked for the Comintern in Moscow and, in 1930, was the key founder of the Vietnamese Communist Party (later renamed the Indochinese Communist paty (ICP)). In 1926 he wrote *The Road to Revolution*, adopting the Stalinist two-stage theory and arguing that national independence for Vietnam must precede the abolition of capitalism there, and that the proletarian revolution could not succeed without peasant support. The ICP was harshly persecuted in the 1930s after supporting a peasant uprising in 1930, but in 1936 was legalized by the National Front government, only to be banned again in 1939, by which time it claimed 2000 members and 40,000 followers. It was forced to retreat to its rural bases and many members were arrested.

In 1940 Ho joined up with another long-standing ICP member Vo Nguyen Giap, who had been in southern China since 1930, and together in 1941 they set up both the Vietnamese Liberation League – a front organization with the ICP's role concealed which attracted many of the youth – and the League for the Independence of Vietnam (Vietminh). The latter was a combat organization to fight inside Vietnam, subordinating the class struggle to the national struggle for the independence of Vietnam and trying to maximize support by concealing the role of the ICP. It made rural guerrilla warfare its prime tactic, being inspired by ▶ Mao's successes in China. It formed its initial base in the Viet Bac mountains on the Vietnamese–Chinese border, which by 1943 had become a full-fledged liberated zone from which the Vietminh began to spread south.

On 28 August 1945, after the defeat of the Japanese and before the return of the French colonialists, the Democratic Republic of Vietnam (DRV) was proclaimed, with Ho as president, Giap as interior minister and several non-communists in the government. The government preached moderation, but Chinese Nationalist troops entering the north of the country on behalf of the Allies took the side of anti-Vietminh nationalists. British troops arriving in the south demanded that all Vietnamese groups surrender their arms and moved against the Vietminh. Ho endeavoured to conciliate the Chinese and Vietnamese nationalists, formally dissolving the ICP in November. There were serious clashes between the Vietminh and Allied troops, especially in Saigon.

Ho's appeals to the USA and USSR went unanswered and eventually he signed an agreement with the French in March 1946. Under the agreement, Vietnamese independence would be given up in return for autonomy for the DRV and a small French presence in the north while a plebiscite would be held to decide the future of southern Vietnam (Cochin). Vietnamese nationalists and French settlers bitterly opposed this agreement.

The Vietminh continued to extend its support in both the north and the south and clashes with French troops grew more frequent. On 22–3 November 1945 there was a major clash in which many were killed. The Vietminh appealed in vain to the socialist government in Paris for restraint, and the USA and USSR refused to help them. They retreated back to the Viet Bac mountains and resumed the guerrilla war in the north as well as in the Mekong delta in the south. The French responded by setting up a government under the former emperor Bao Dai, but it won little support, and they continued to rule out independence for Vietnam.

The communist victory in China in 1949 provided the DRV with a new base of support and China began providing military supplies. The DRV began to move more openly away from its neutral stance of 1945 towards the so-called socialist camp, and the Communist Party was re-established; in 1951 separate parties were set up for Cambodia (Khmer Rouge), Laos (Pathet Lao) and Vietnam (Vietnam Workers' Party (VWP)). In France, meanwhile, resentment began to increase against conscription for the war.

As the French troops proved increasingly unable to hold off the Vietminh and the French-created 'associated state' of Vietnam under Bao Dai won little enthusiasm, the USA stepped up supplies to the Army of the Republic of Vietnam (ARVN). Guerrilla war began to merge into conventional war. By 1952 the war in the north was stalemated. The VWP therefore altered its agrarian policy to mobilize wider support, reducing land rents and seizing and redistributing the land of landlords not involved in the struggle. By 1953 there were 350,000 armed insurgents against 500,000 French troops and 100,000 ARVN, and there was pressure for compromise in Paris. In November 1953 French troops occupied Dien Bien Phu, a town at the head of the Red River deemed to be impregnable. In March 1954 the PLA laid siege to it largely to impress the participants in the upcoming peace conference in Geneva that the USA, the USSR, the UK and France had agreed to hold to resolve the Indochinese question. After a massive feat of ingenuity by the Vietminh, Dien Bien Phu fell on 7 May, the day the conference opened, delivering a shattering psychological blow to the French.

France agreed to the independence of all Vietnam and the opposing forces were to regroup in two zones either side of the 17th parallel, the communists to the north and the French and Bao Dai supporters to the south: there were to be national elections in 1956. In the south the effective leader was now the premier, Ngo Dinh Diem, an anti-communist Vietnamese nationalist opposed, like the USA, to the Geneva accord. Diem soon removed Bao Dai and became president of South

Vietnam, with US backing. Diem's forces began to harass supporters of the peace agreement in the south, including the 15,000 Vietminh who had remained when the other 90,000 moved north, and he refused to implement the settlement. In response the VWP stepped up attacks on government agents in the south and, thanks to Diem's persecution and his policy of allowing landlords to return to land from which they had been evicted and collect back rent, it rebuilt its strength in the south. The USSR pressured the DRV to hold off its attacks, but casualties still rose – in 1957 over 2000 communist suspects were killed and 65,000 arrested. Some party sections began to disobey the party line and form guerrilla units north of Saigon: they were called Vietcong by their opponents. They began to build support too among the minorities in the Central Highlands.

In 1959 the VWP decided to resort to armed struggle, though this decision was kept secret and the breakdown of the Geneva process was blamed wholly on the work of 'revolutionaries' in the south, not the DRV. The 90,000 who had gone north in 1954 were infiltrated back and fresh volunteers were taken north for training; and armed attacks increased in the Central Highlands and the Mekong delta. In January 1960 the Vietcong organized risings in many provinces and, in December, the National Front for the Liberation of South Vietnam (NLF) was set up, with representatives of all classes and religious sects in its central committee to fight for a national democratic coalition government that would negotiate reunification with the North. VWP members kept a low profile – which greatly helped it establish itself as a genuinely independent force with no obvious support from the DRV. In 1961 the militia units fighting in the South were grouped together as the People's Liberation Armed Forces (PLAF), which by late 1963 had 300,000 members (from 3000 in 1959). US military aid to Saigon was increased and the USA endeavoured to turn the ARVN into a counter-insurgency force. It launched a 'strategic hamlets' programme of fortified villages to win over the masses. The US military began to press for more American military advisers and troops to be sent.

Diem's repression made him enemies. In May 1963 a riot broke out in Hué which was brutally broken up by ARVN troops. The disturbances spread to Saigon and, in November, Diem was overthrown in a military coup not opposed by Washington. The PLAF sought to take advantage of the situation. By the end of 1964 the NLF controlled half the population of South Vietnam, and was regularly supplied along the Ho Chi Minh trail from the north, down which also began to come regular DRV army units. With South Vietnam crumbling, the USA decided to step up its support. In 1965 it began direct air raids on both North and South Vietnam. The first US marines arrived in March 1965 and, by the end of 1965, there were 200,000 American troops there. The PLAF concentrated on wearing down ARVN forces and avoiding the US troops. The US troops launched 'search and destroy' operations in the South and massive air raids, ostensibly on 'military targets' in both North and South Vietnam; both these activities caught up many civilians. Many fled to the cities, increasing the government's problems.

In January 1968 the PLAF launched a well-prepared and well-coordinated large-scale series of attacks, known as the Tet Offensive, in 36 provincial capitals and 64 district capitals throughout South Vietnam, taking Saigon by surprise. US–South Vietnamese forces eventually threw them back but the psychological blow was enormous. Washington refused the army's request for more troops and began to reduce direct US involvement and, in 1969, Richard Nixon was elected American president promising 'peace with honour', i.e. withdrawing his country's ground forces and 'Vietnamizing' the war. Talks in Paris between the USA and Hanoi dragged on. To prepare their withdrawal, the USA stepped up attacks on the PLAF, setting June 1972 as the deadline for the withdrawal of US troops. They also installed Lon Nol as leader in Cambodia who demanded that all Vietcong leave Cambodia: Hanoi stepped up its support for the Khmer Rouge led by Pol Pot. In response, the USA sent troops into Cambodia, provoking an uproar of protest back home. By early 1972 US troops were reduced to 100,000 and the ARVN was bearing the brunt of the war. The DRV launched another major offensive across the 17th parallel. Nixon ordered the resumption of full-scale bombing of the North. The ARVN began to disintegrate and many pacification programmes were destroyed. This gave the DRV increased leverage in the negotiations and, in October 1972, agreement was reached for a ceasefire: US forces were to be withdrawn within 60 days; Hanoi was to stop infiltration; the US was to help in post-war reconstruction and continue limited military assistance.

Fighting broke out all over the South over demarcation lines before the ceasefire and the USA resumed bombing the North to ensure DRV compliance. In January 1973 a peace treaty was signed in Paris with both sides claiming victory: the USA because Hanoi had accepted the pro-American regime in the South, Hanoi because it had not been forced to withdraw its forces. In the South Hanoi had large liberated areas, an administrative structure, its own troops and PLAF guerrillas, the NLF and much international support. Gambling that the USA would not re-enter if it broke the treaty, the DRV decided to destabilize the Saigon government. As the Americans departed, economic crisis followed, refugees flocked into the overburdened cities, but the Saigon government refused to compromise. Between late 1974 and early 1975, the DRV launched attacks first over the Cambodian border, then in the Central Highlands. Saigon decided to withdraw its forces and the retreat became a rout. The army disintegrated. In April 1975 the Vietcong entered Saigon victorious.

For the rulers of the USA, the Vietcong victory was to prove a heavy and long-lasting blow. The war had aroused major political differences in the USA and the anti-war coalition mobilized a vast number of people outside the normal political arena. US foreign policy was to be weakened for many years, especially in Indochina. Normal relations had still not been restored with Vietnam by 1991. The militarily successful war against Iraq in 1991 was quite explicitly seen by the US government as an opportunity to wipe out the 'Vietnam syndrome' and re-establish unchallenged US hegemony.

Further reading

J. Lacouture, *Ho Chi Minh*, London 1968.
R.B. Smith, *An International History of the Vietnam War*, London 1983.

W

West Bank

Part of Palestine on the west bank of the River Jordan, it has been occupied by Israel since 1967.

WFP, World Food Programme

This programme of the United Nations concentrates on food aid for emergencies and on the financing of development projects. It receives pledges from donors and uses them to aid on a multilateral basis countries of the Third World, especially those in the category of ▶ least developed countries. Its annual expenditure at the end of the 1980s was about US$700 million a year, which was equivalent to about 23 per cent of all food aid. After a rapid increase in the scale of activities in the first two decades after the programme's establishment in 1963, pledges from the donors tended to stagnate during the 1980s.

Further reading

C.A. Stevens, *Food Aid and the Developing World*, London 1979.

women

The worldwide rise of the women's movement in the last three decades has changed perspectives on many Third World debates in which, previously, questions of gender had been completely ignored. Many indicators of development and underdevelopment tell a very different story if we look at gender differences rather than at aggregated statistics.

Discrimination against women begins from the moment of birth. One of the indices with most difference between South and North is that for maternal mortality (▶ indicators). While no estimates exist of the extent of infanticide, it is reported from some countries (in particular China since its introduction of a single child policy) that female children face the danger of death. There are statistics for child mortality which show almost universally in the Third World that girls up to the age of five are more likely to die than boys, reflecting the fact that boys may be more valued and given more access to scarce food and so on. Again, almost universally, school enrolment rates for girls are markedly lower than for boys. It appears that discrimination rises at each level of the educational hierarchy, with the greatest difference at the tertiary level. For the Third World as a whole female enrolment as a percentage of men's is 83 per cent for primary, 71 per cent for secondary and 51 per cent for tertiary education. The greater difficulty of access to education for women is also illustrated by the fact that women's literacy is on average 67 per cent of that of men. These educational differences are most accentuated in Middle Eastern, Islamic countries.

Discrimination continues at the level of employment in most parts of the Third World. The level of women's participation in the paid labour force is lower than that of men and the difference is relatively greater than in most developed countries. At the same time women in Africa and many Asian countries do a disproportionate amount of the unpaid labour not only, as everywhere, in the home but also in traditional, unpaid forms of family and communal agriculture. Since men in most countries migrate more easily from the countryside than women, this often leads in times of crisis to rural areas being abandoned by the adult male population. The ▶ Bantustans of South Africa tend to be in this state, and in the recent famines in Africa more women than men have perished.

There are instances in which women's employment has risen rapidly, though this is by no means always an unambiguous benefit. In the newly industrializing countries (▶ NICs), for instance, rapid industrial growth has coincided with a marked increase in the proportion of women in the paid labour force. Employers take advantage of the availability of very low paid workers who are supposed to display the 'feminine virtues' of docility, dexterity and obedience. They are also not supposed to complain when long hours and very intricate repetitive work cause major health problems, such as the deterioration of the sight, and force them out of the labour force within a few years.

There are other forms of women's labour which have also grown rapidly in recent years. One is domestic service done in rich countries by women migrants from poor countries. Often this form of labour amounts to slavery in all but name. Another is prostitution.

A number of writers have analysed the differential impact of the extreme economic crisis which countries in Africa and Latin America have experienced in the last few years. They have remarked on the rising role of the ▶ informal sector as a source of survival by means of low level, unproductive and undignified labour. Within the informal sector women in many countries have been the predominant participants. In this way, in times of crisis women sometimes become the breadwinners of the family as well as doing the great majority of the domestic labour. In fact, there is a tendency in countries of Central America and the Caribbean for men to disappear from the family altogether and live an unsettled, unemployed urban life, while women increasingly become heads of households, and yet have little access to stable paid employment.

There are two dangers in listing the various ways in which women in the Third World face discrimination. One is that the impression will be given that men are not also badly off. While men have different social and economic roles and may have power over women, they also experience the problems of material deprivation; but these problems often take a different form. The burden of the woman's role as mother and domestic worker for instance may increase with economic crisis; yet the role of the man, as breadwinner in the wage labour market, may disappear altogether, thereby causing severe mental and social dislocation as well as expressing itself in alcoholism and many other problems.

The second danger is that women will appear merely as victims, whereas increasing awareness of the discrimination faced by women is a symptom of the fact that women are continuously becoming more active in defining and fighting for their interests.

Further reading

E. Boserup, *Women's Role in Economic Development*, London 1970.
I. Dankelman and J. Davidson, *Women and the Environment in the Third World: alliance for the future*, London 1988.
K. Jayawardena, *Feminism and Nationalism in the Third World*, London 1986.
M. Mies, *Patriarchy and Accumulation on a World Scale: women in the international division of labour*, London 1986.
G. Sen and C. Grown, *Development, Crises and Alternative Visions*, New York 1987.

workers' control

The struggle for workers' control in the Third World stems from the exclusion of wage labourers from any position of influence. In the Third World, employers often tolerate unrepresentative moderate unions. In such a situation, workers have no choice but to form their own councils and committees if they are to advance their cause. Workers' struggles often assume the form of a fight for control and the establishment of new institutions. This is what happened after the defeat of French imperialism in Algeria when workers and peasants took over control of production. During the radical upheaval in Chile under the ▶ Allende regime, workers established cordones industriales, committees designed to coordinate the activities of industrial enterprises. Such workers' institutions have always proved to be in the forefront of the fight for radical change.

Among the most important (and little-known) workers' control experiences in recent times were the shawras in Iran. Shawras were factory councils created by workers during the revolution which led to the overthrow of the shah in 1979. The emergence of Shawras during the Iranian revolution showed that for at least a section of society change meant acquiring control over the organization of production. According to a study of this subject, shawras 'were shop-floor organizations whose elected executive committee represented all the employees of a factory (blue- and white-collar) and/or an industrial group, irrespective of their trade, skill or sex. Their major concern was to achieve workers' control'.[1]

Though the shawras had many original features specific to the experience of Iran, their development appears to be part of a wider pattern of struggle throughout the Third World. The struggle of workers for control of the economy is one of the key elements in the anti-imperialist movement. Yet these struggles tend to remain obscured from public attention. A year after the establishment of the shawras, for example, Argentina saw the emergence of comisiones de lucha. These 'struggle committees' established in 1980 had as their aim the creation of workers' committees throughout industry.

The destruction of the shawras by the Khomeini regime indicates that such committees are by their nature temporary. Third World experience has shown that the first objective of post-revolutionary regimes is to dismantle institutions of workers' control. In so doing they indicate their fear of radical change. Yet the emergence of workers' councils throughout the Third World suggests that sooner or later such institutions may well become strong enough to take control of society itself.

Note

1. See A. Bayat, *Workers and Revolution in Iran*, London 1987, p. 100.

World Bank

The World Bank is the popular name for the International Bank for Reconstruction and Development (IBRD) which was set up in July 1944 at the United Nations monetary and financial conference in Bretton Woods, USA with 38 member countries. It began operations in 1946 from Washington, DC. The IBRD was originally sponsored by the USA to regulate the post-war economy under its direction, but is now mainly confined to issuing loans to Third World countries, mainly for specific development projects, for which it is the largest source. In 1982 it had 152 members.

It has three sub-agencies, the International Finance Corporation (IFC), the International Development Association (IDA) and the Multilateral Investment Guarantee Agency (MIGA). The IFC was formed in 1956 to help finance the private sector in Third World countries. The IDA was formed in 1960 to extend concessionary loans to the ▶ least developed countries. The highly subsidized terms of IDA loans are a grace period of 10 years, 30–40 years' maturity and no interest; loans of this kind are made only to governments.

In 1990 the IBRD had total outstanding loans of US$89 billion (about 6 per cent of the total debt of the Third World). In that year the net flow of funds from the World Bank to the Third World was US$5.7 billion of ordinary loans and US$3.6 billion in IDA loans. In recent years the IBRD has lent money to assist the implementation of structural adjustment proposed by its sister institution, the International Monetary Fund (▶ IMF). The IBRD has been closely associated with the philosophy behind these schemes. At the beginning of the 1990s the World Bank came under strong pressure from the USA to lend more to the private sector and less to governments.

Further reading

R. Ayres, *Banking on the Poor: the World Bank and world poverty*, Cambridge, Mass. 1983.

C. Payer, *The World Bank: a critical analysis*, New York 1982.

World Bank third window

This is a financing facility under which poorer developing countries can receive loans on terms intermediate between the standard terms of the ▶ World Bank and the highly concessional terms of its affiliate, the

International Development Association (IDA). The third window has been subsidized since 1975 by the Interest Subsidy Fund, which supplements payments due to the World Bank from borrowers by governments on a voluntary basis.

World Food Programme ▶ WFP

Y

Yaoundé Convention ▶ Lomé Convention

Z

Zimbabwean liberation movement

This liberation movement comprised the Zimbabwean African National Union (ZANU) and the Zimbabwean African People's Union (ZAPU). In September 1957 the Southern Rhodesian African National Congress (SRANC) was formed by fusing African political groups in Salisbury (now Harare) and Bulawayo which had been working separately for two years. Its president was the trade union organizer, Joshua Nkomo. SRANC's aim was an African government working in partnership with the colonial authorities. It was banned during an outbreak of rioting in 1960, but was renamed the National Democratic Party (NDP) in June. Its objective was to win British support for majority rule. It was during this time that Robert Mugabe joined the movement.

NDP delegates in London accepted a constitution providing 15 seats for Africans and 50 for whites. This decision was later reversed under pressure and a NDP boycott of the constitution in December 1961 resulted in its banning. It was soon renamed the Zimbabwe African People's Union (ZAPU), but by August 1963 it had split over whether or not to operate in exile. While Nkomo led away the main exile faction, Ndabaningi Sithole formed the Zimbabwe African National Union (ZANU). The following year both were banned.

Frustrated at the slow progress of the politicians, spontaneous attacks began to break out in September and November 1963. To maintain credibility, ZANU launched its first military strike in the new year. In 1965 Ian Smith's white settler regime unilaterally declared Rhodesia independent (UDI). Both of the liberation movements were by then engaged in the armed struggle because the UK had 'abrogated responsibility as a colonial power' and refused to intervene militarily against Smith. Nevertheless, the armed struggle was maintained at only a very low level until late 1969, when ZANU concluded an agreement with the Mozambican liberation movement (▶ FRELIMO) to cooperate in military missions. FRELIMO trained ZANU's guerrillas – organized in the Zimbabwe African National Liberation Army (ZANLA) – to a high standard. This connection put ZANU in the best position to benefit when the Portuguese colonies of Angola and Mozambique became independent in the mid-1970s.

The 1974 successes stimulated an upsurge of anti-imperialism throughout the region. In December 1974 South Africa forced Smith to meet the ▶ front line states and the guerrilla movements in Lusaka to negotiate a compromise. Within ZANU the more radical Robert Mugabe began to challenge the conciliatory Sithole for leadership. Committed to the Lusaka Agreement, the front line states pulled out all the stops to terminate the armed struggle led by ZANU. Mozambique's Machel threatened to arrest the entire ZANU contingent of 2500. The Zambian authorities tried to provoke tribalism within ZANU, staged show trials of militants, set up the assassination of leading hardliner ZANU chairman, Herbert Chitepo, in March 1975 and arrested 1500 ZANLA members in response.

Mugabe won the leadership struggle in ZANU by condemning the Zambian regime for Chitepo's murder, distancing himself from the Lusaka Agreement and working underground with ZANLA in the Mozambican bush. By the last half of 1975, an estimated 20,000 young Africans had joined him in the newly independent Mozambique. Following South Africa's abortive intervention in Angola that October (▶ Angolan liberation movement, ▶ SWAPO), all chance for a compromise settlement disappeared and the front line states swung back to supporting the liberation struggle, releasing detained guerrillas and stepping up military supplies.

On 9 October 1976 Nkomo and Mugabe met in Dar es Salaam to form the Patriotic Front (PF) alliance. The PF formed the main political alternative to those forces, under the leadership of Bishop Abel Muzorewa, which would campaign for an internal settlement after the collapse of the Geneva conference organized by the USA and the UK at the end of that month. The basic line of the West at Geneva – a two-year transitional government before majority rule in return for the ending of sanctions, with the transitional government based on 50:50 black and white representation, with a black premier – formed the basis for the internal settlement between Smith and Muzorewa.

The Geneva plan collapsed when Mugabe insisted – under stiff pressure from the guerrillas he barely controlled – that there would be no need for elections after independence because power should pass automatically to the guerrilla organizations represented by the PF.

The front line states now moved to break those radical guerrilla leaders who opposed Mugabe in early 1977. In both Tanzania and Mozambique, ZANU guerrillas were arrested, imprisoned and murdered in an effort to impose Mugabe's leadership. By September 1977 Mugabe was in absolute control of the ZANU army. The scene was set for the Lancaster House Agreement of November 1979. The intervening period was only due to the resistance of Smith to a settlement, not to the commitment of Mugabe to the armed struggle.

Once the Lancaster House Agreement was signed, the British sent Lord Soames to be the last governor-general together with a ceasefire monitoring force. From December 1979 to the March 1980 elections, they disarmed the guerrillas and monitored the elections. Mugabe's ZANU–PF (People's Front) easily won the elections. Once in power, he began to crack down on working class unrest and peasant land seizures, and targeted Nkomo's ZAPU stronghold in Bulawayo as a scapegoat. The resulting ethnic tensions between the majority Shona and the minority Ndebele led to the isolation and ostracism of Nkomo's ZAPU.

Though one of the most highly developed black African states at independence, Zimbabwe was unable to pose an alternative to South African dominance of the region. Harare was the leading force behind the establishment of the Southern African Development Coordinating Conference (▶ SADCC) in 1980; but SADCC has been effectively undermined by South Africa's military and economic expansion through the region from the late 1970s. Only by completely shunning the African National Congress (▶ ANC) has Zimbabwe managed on the whole to avoid the full blast of South African repression that its neighbours have felt.

For most of the 1980s there was considerable hostility, often resulting in violence, between ZANU and ZAPU. The ZANU government frequently took repressive action against ZAPU supporters. In 1986 ZANU easily won new elections and ZAPU was reduced to 15 out of the 79 seats in parliament which were not reserved for whites. Mugabe, however, was unable to eliminate ZAPU and eventually in 1989 negotiated a union of the two parties, Nkomo becoming one of the two joint deputy leaders of ZANU. The united party won 116 of the 120 elected seats in the parliamentary elections (under a new constitution) in 1990. Mugabe, going against the continental trend, has argued that this result gives him a mandate to legalize a one-party state, a move which is directed mainly against Edgar Tekere's Zimbabwe Unity Movement which gained 16 per cent of the votes (but only two parliamentary seats) in the 1990 elections.

Further reading

A. Astrow, *Zimbabwe: a revolution that lost its way?*, London 1983.
T.O. Ranger, *Peasant Consciousness and Guerrilla War in Zimbabwe*, London 1984.

Zionism (from Hebrew *Zion* = Jerusalem)

Zionism is the pursuit of a Jewish nation. Theodor Herzl (1860–1904), a Hungarian journalist living in Vienna, was persuaded by the Russian pogroms and the Dreyfus trial in France to conclude in his pamphlet *Der Judenstaat* (1896) that the only way Jewish people could live was by having their own nation-state. In 1897, at the First World Zionist Congress in Basle, Switzerland, the leading Jewish intellectual and organizer, Chaim Weizmann (1874–1952), called for a Jewish homeland to be created in Palestine.

Under Weizmann's influence the British government (in the person of the Foreign Secretary Lord Balfour) declared in 1917 a national home for the Jews in Palestine. The Balfour Declaration, followed by the growth of anti-Semitism in Europe, culminating in the Nazi Holocaust and the inadequate assistance to the Jews from the Western allies, convinced millions of Jews that Weizmann was right. The Jewish state of Israel was inaugurated in 1948 by the United Nations.

This resulted in the loss of a homeland for the Palestinians, and the oppressive policies towards Palestinians were pursued by successive Israeli governments. In November 1975 the General Assembly of the United Nations passed a resolution declaring Zionism to be racist. This resolution was repealed in December 1991.

Discover more about our forthcoming books through Penguin's FREE newspaper...

Penguin Quarterly

It's packed with:

- exciting features

- author interviews

- previews & reviews

- books from your favourite films & TV series

- exclusive competitions & much, much more...

Write off for your free copy today to:
Dept JC
Penguin Books Ltd
FREEPOST
West Drayton
Middlesex
UB7 0BR
NO STAMP REQUIRED

READ MORE IN PENGUIN

In every corner of the world, on every subject under the sun, Penguin represents quality and variety – the very best in publishing today.

For complete information about books available from Penguin – including Puffins, Penguin Classics and Arkana – and how to order them, write to us at the appropriate address below. Please note that for copyright reasons the selection of books varies from country to country.

In the United Kingdom: Please write to *Dept. JC, Penguin Books Ltd, FREEPOST, West Drayton, Middlesex UB7 OBR.*

If you have any difficulty in obtaining a title, please send your order with the correct money, plus ten per cent for postage and packaging, to *PO Box No. 11, West Drayton, Middlesex UB7 OBR*

In the United States: Please write to *Consumer Sales, Penguin USA, P.O. Box 999, Dept. 17109, Bergenfield, New Jersey 07621-0120.* VISA and MasterCard holders call 1-800-253-6476 to order all Penguin titles

In Canada: Please write to *Penguin Books Canada Ltd, 10 Alcorn Avenue, Suite 300, Toronto, Ontario M4V 3B2*

In Australia: Please write to *Penguin Books Australia Ltd, P.O. Box 257, Ringwood, Victoria 3134*

In New Zealand: Please write to *Penguin Books (NZ) Ltd, Private Bag 102902, North Shore Mail Centre, Auckland 10*

In India: Please write to *Penguin Books India Pvt Ltd, 706 Eros Apartments, 56 Nehru Place, New Delhi 110 019*

In the Netherlands: Please write to *Penguin Books Netherlands bv, Postbus 3507, NL-1001 AH Amsterdam*

In Germany: Please write to *Penguin Books Deutschland GmbH, Metzlerstrasse 26, 60594 Frankfurt am Main*

In Spain: Please write to *Penguin Books S. A., Bravo Murillo 19, 1° B, 28015 Madrid*

In Italy: Please write to *Penguin Italia s.r.l., Via Felice Casati 20, I–20124 Milano*

In France: Please write to *Penguin France S. A., 17 rue Lejeune, F–31000 Toulouse*

In Japan: Please write to *Penguin Books Japan, Ishikiribashi Building, 2–5–4, Suido, Bunkyo-ku, Tokyo 112*

In Greece: Please write to *Penguin Hellas Ltd, Dimocritou 3, GR–106 71 Athens*

In South Africa: Please write to *Longman Penguin Southern Africa (Pty) Ltd, Private Bag X08, Bertsham 2013*

READ MORE IN PENGUIN

LITERARY CRITICISM

A Lover's Discourse   Roland Barthes

'*A Lover's Discourse* ... may be the most detailed, painstaking anatomy of desire we are ever likely to see or need again ... The book is an ecstatic celebration of love and language and ... readers interested in either or both ... will enjoy savouring its rich and dark delights' – *Washington Post Book World*

The New Pelican Guide to English Literature   Edited by Boris Ford

The indispensable critical guide to English and American literature in nine volumes, erudite yet accessible. From the ages of Chaucer and Shakespeare, via Georgian satirists and Victorian social critics, to the leading writers of the 1980s, all literary life is here.

The Theatre of the Absurd   Martin Esslin

This classic study of the dramatists of the Absurd examines the origins, nature and future of a movement whose significance has transcended the bounds of the stage and influenced the whole intellectual climate of our time.

The Art of Fiction   David Lodge

The articles with which David Lodge entertained and enlightened readers of the *Independent on Sunday* and the *Washington Post* are now revised, expanded and collected together in book form. 'Agreeable and highly instructive ... a real treat' – *Sunday Telegraph*

Aspects of the Novel   E. M. Forster

'I say that I have never met this kind of perspicacity in literary criticism before. I could quote scores of examples of startling excellence' – Arnold Bennett. Originating in a course of lectures given at Cambridge, *Aspects of the Novel* is full of E. M. Forster's habitual wit, wisdom and freshness of approach.

READ MORE IN PENGUIN

PHILOSOPHY

What Philosophy Is   Anthony O'Hear

'Argument after argument is represented, including most of the favourites
... its tidy and competent construction, as well as its straightforward style,
mean that it will serve well anyone with a serious interest in philosophy'
– *Journal of Applied Philosophy*

Montaigne and Melancholy   M. A. Screech

'A sensitive probe into how Montaigne resolved for himself the age-old
ambiguities of melancholia and, in doing so, spoke of what he called the
"human condition"' – *London Review of Books*

Labyrinths of Reason   William Poundstone

'The world and what is in it, even what people say to you, will not seem
the same after plunging into *Labyrinths of Reason* ... He holds up the
deepest philosophical questions for scrutiny and examines their relation to
reality in a way that irresistibly sweeps readers on' – *New Scientist*

I: The Philosophy and Psychology of Personal Identity
Jonathan Glover

From cases of split brains and multiple personalities to the importance of
memory and recognition by others, the author of *Causing Death and
Saving Lives* tackles the vexed questions of personal identity.

Philosophy and Philosophers   John Shand

'A concise and readily surveyable account of the history of Western
philosophy ... it succeeds in being both an illuminating introduction to the
history of philosophy for someone who has little prior knowledge of the
subject and a valuable source of guidance to a more experienced student'
– *The Times Literary Supplement*

Russian Thinkers   Isaiah Berlin

As one of the most outstanding liberal intellects of this century, the author
brings to his portraits of Russian thinkers a unique perception of the social
and political circumstances that produced men such as Herzen, Bakunin,
Turgenev, Belinsky and Tolstoy.

READ MORE IN PENGUIN

POLITICS AND SOCIAL SCIENCES

Conservatism Ted Honderich

'It offers a powerful critique of the major beliefs of modern conservatism, and shows how much a rigorous philosopher can contribute to understanding the fashionable but deeply ruinous absurdities of his times' – *New Statesman & Society*

The Battle for Scotland Andrew Marr

A nation without a parliament of its own, Scotland has been wrestling with its identity and status for a century. In this excellent and up-to-date account of the distinctive history of Scottish politics, Andrew Marr uses party and individual records, pamphlets, learned works, interviews and literature to tell a colourful and often surprising account.

Bricks of Shame: Britain's Prisons Vivien Stern

'Her well-researched book presents a chillingly realistic picture of the British sytstem and lucid argument for changes which could and should be made before a degrading and explosive situation deteriorates still further' – *Sunday Times*

Inside the Third World Paul Harrison

This comprehensive book brings home a wealth of facts and analysis on the often tragic realities of life for the poor people and communities of Asia, Africa and Latin America.

'Just like a Girl' Sue Sharpe
How Girls Learn to be Women

Sue Sharpe's unprecedented research and analysis of the attitudes and hopes of teenage girls from four London schools has become a classic of its kind. This new edition focuses on girls in the nineties – some of whom could even be the daughters of the teenagers she interviewed in the seventies – and represents their views and ideas on education, work, marriage, gender roles, feminism and women's rights.

READ MORE IN PENGUIN

POLITICS AND SOCIAL SCIENCES

National Identity Anthony D. Smith

In this stimulating new book, Anthony D. Smith asks why the first modern nation states developed in the West. He considers how ethnic origins, religion, language and shared symbols can provide a sense of nation and illuminates his argument with a wealth of detailed examples.

The Feminine Mystique Betty Friedan

'A brilliantly researched, passionately argued book – a time-bomb flung into the Mom-and-Apple-Pie image ... Out of the debris of that shattered ideal, the Women's Liberation Movement was born' – Ann Leslie

Faith and Credit Susan George and Fabrizio Sabelli

In its fifty years of existence, the World Bank has influenced more lives in the Third World than any other institution yet remains largely unknown, even enigmatic. This richly illuminating and lively overview examines the policies of the Bank, its internal culture and the interests it serves.

Political Ideas Edited by David Thomson

From Machiavelli to Marx – a stimulating and informative introduction to the last 500 years of European political thinkers and political thought.

Structural Anthropology Volumes 1–2 Claude Lévi-Strauss

'That the complex ensemble of Lévi-Strauss's achievement ... is one of the most original and intellectually exciting of the present age seems undeniable. No one seriously interested in language or literature, in sociology or psychology, can afford to ignore it' – George Steiner

Invitation to Sociology Peter L. Berger

Sociology is defined as 'the science of the development and nature and laws of human society'. But what is its purpose? Without belittling its scientific procedures Professor Berger stresses the humanistic affinity of sociology with history and philosophy. It is a discipline which encourages a fuller awareness of the human world ... with the purpose of bettering it.

READ MORE IN PENGUIN

DICTIONARIES

Abbreviations
Archaeology
Architecture
Art and Artists
Astronomy
Biology
Botany
Building
Business
Challenging Words
Chemistry
Civil Engineering
Classical Mythology
Computers
Curious and Interesting Numbers
Curious and Interesting Words
Design and Designers
Economics
Electronics
English and European History
English Idioms
Foreign Terms and Phrases
French
Geography
Historical Slang

Human Geography
Information Technology
Literary Terms and Literary Theory
Mathematics
Modern History 1789–1945
Modern Quotations
Music
Musical Performers
Physical Geography
Physics
Politics
Proverbs
Psychology
Quotations
Religions
Rhyming Dictionary
Saints
Science
Sociology
Spanish
Surnames
Telecommunications
Troublesome Words
Twentieth-Century History